BOOK 0
IN THE SHADOW

OUT
OF
EMBERS
AND
SHADOWS

SHELBY OVAL

Copyright © 2024 Shelby Oval

All rights reserved. No part of this book may be reproduced or used in any manner without the prior written permission of the copyright owner, except for the use of brief quotations in a book review.

To request permissions, contact the publisher at shelbyoval@sheblyoval.com

First paperback edition 2024.

Edited by Kristin Curry
Cover art by didiwahyudi.trend

ISBN: 979-8-89316-1-946 (paperback)
ISBN: 979-8-89316-1-953 (ebook)

This book is dedicated to all those who love to read and imagine, but to my mom and partner especially.

Mom - thanks for making me read the books before the movies (and reading 'faerie p*rn' with me)

Robert - thank you for listening to my head movies over, and over, and over again.

"All is fair in love and war."

- William Shakespeare

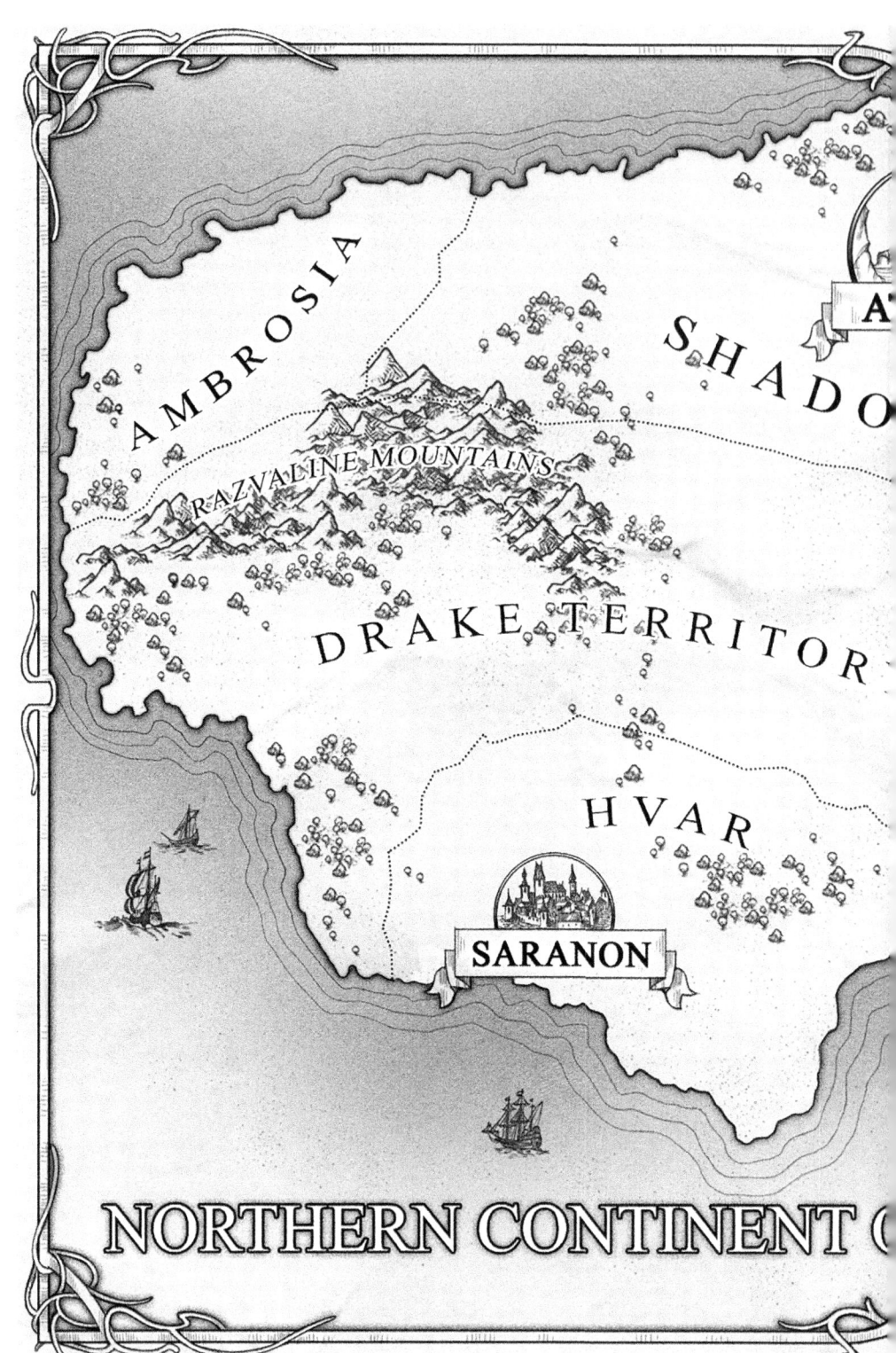

CONTENTS

Prologue xiii
Chapter 1: Not Dead 1
Chapter 2: Still Not Dead but Pissed 12
Chapter 3: Escape Attempt #1 24
Chapter 4: How is She Not Dead? 29
Chapter 5: A Potential Ally 46
Chapter 6: Saranon, Hvar 57
Chapter 7: Let's Make a Deal 69
Chapter 8: Escape Attempt #2 96
Chapter 9: Utter Confusion 108
Chapter 10: A Racing Mind 119
Chapter 11: To Fall or Fly? 126
Chapter 12: To Fly 129
Chapter 13: The Refugee Camp 134
Chapter 14: The Trade 147
Chapter 15: The Betrayal 161
Chapter 16: Dead? 177
Chapter 17: What the Fuck is Going on? 184
Chapter 18: Oh Shit 190
Chapter 19: Kacey's Story 194
Chapter 20: Decisions To Be Made 208

Chapter 21:	Escape Attempt #3	218
Chapter 22:	Thoroughly Confused	227
Chapter 23:	Let's Make *Another* Deal	235
Chapter 24:	A Sea-faring Shade	249
Chapter 25:	No More Weapons	265
Chapter 26:	A Pirate's Crime	276
Chapter 27:	Kindness Uncovered	297
Chapter 28:	A Literal Rude Awakening	308
Chapter 29:	Surprise	315
Chapter 30:	The Gora Mountains	332
Chapter 31:	The Split	340
Chapter 32:	Skipton Village	352
Chapter 33:	The Beaviers	366
Chapter 34:	On the Trace	381
Chapter 35:	Thievery with Shadows	403
Chapter 36:	Escape Attempt #4	418
Chapter 37:	Retreat to Garrison's Family Farm	426
Chapter 38:	Gamma	445
Chapter 39:	Into Town	466
Chapter 40:	Pre-festival	473
Chapter 41:	Harvest Festival	483
Chapter 42:	A Dance	498
Chapter 43:	No More Delays	518
Chapter 44:	Truth Revealed	535
About the Author		541
Acknowledgments		543

I would like to thank you for joining me on this journey by offering a free eBook copy of The Hunt for the Great Trove. *Click Here to tell me where to send it.*

PROLOGUE

Queen Regent,

The outpost at the edge of the borderlands has been evacuated. We managed to escape before the Shade army advanced, however we do believe the outpost is now gone.

My soldiers and I watched as the shadows seemed to swarm the land, and when morning came there was nothing left - not even ashes. There was literally nothing left of the outpost, or the surrounding areas. We are not even sure what has happened. The only proof that there was ever anything in the area is the scorched earth and the lingering silver glow many reported seeing the night before.

More to follow.

***

Your majesty,

Upon our further investigation it was found that the five outposts that were attacked had previously been evacuated, as we had been informed. The exact source of the attack, though assumed to be the Shades, is still unknown. Upon returning to the land where the last outpost had been located there was little evidence to be found.

Mam, let me make this clear to you when I explain – the other commanders spoke true, there are no words to describe the type of destruction that was inflicted upon the land where the outpost once stood. There was simply nothing left. As if Death herself had arrived and eviscerated everything with her cold flame.

We are asking the locals in the area if they have seen anything different within the Shade army – a new weapon perhaps. Many have mentioned that the fire was somehow made of shadows, though it could have been lost in translation as many of the people here are new to the area.

It seems you were correct in your assumption that the army marches toward the mountains. We have evacuated the area you requested in hopes to protect as many as possible.

It is unclear as to why the Shades are attacking these particular areas but we will remain vigilant and dedicated to uncovering the truth.

***

Princess Kierra,

It is with a heavy heart that I write to inform you that the small village you requested we evacuate has been destroyed. A troop of Shades was seen in the area yesterday morning, and while we evacuated all we could from the village last night, many had chosen to stay or travel into the caves.

We returned to the village upon seeing the growing shadows early yesterday evening, but there was nothing to be done. It seems that the shadows were intertwined with some type of silvery fire - they burned everything.

Nothing could survive it.

The Queen and the Prince have been informed of this loss and we pray to the gods for your aunt's guidance on how to proceed.

***

Kalon,

The influx of refugees has slowed as more villages are seeming to be simply eviscerated. I have requested all border cities to be evacuated, as well as those at the base of the mountains. Our aunt is yet to reply but I am hopeful.

These people are in terrible shape Kalon. Whatever this is – it's new. It's something we've never seen before and it's scaring the hell out of those who see it. Some have even given it a name – *Shadowfire*.

I've sent some reports – that I've included here don't worry – to Liam to see if he knows of any history regarding flaming shadows.

If it can eviscerate an entire town – what will it do to our armies? Please be careful.

I'll keep you informed. Tell Garrison and Nuva I say hello.

All my love,

Kierra

CHAPTER 1

NOT DEAD

Lora

Searing pain. Soaking tunic. Loud shouts. Strong hands at her side. Stronger hands on her shoulders. Roaring in her ears. Pain, unending pain, shooting down her arm. Then, nothing.

***

Blinding light. Whipping wind. More pain. Flailing arms, kicking legs. Muffled grunts. Sudden, jolting pain. Then, nothing.

***

Quiet. No drums. No clashing. No birds. Just quiet. Pain—sharp and searing—down her side. Eyes peeling open. Darkness to her left shifting. Warm air blowing on her cheek. Sweat. She's sweating. Cold, so cold. Fever.

"*Live.*" A command from a gruff voice in her mind. A shiver that isn't hers. A rush of cold air. Hallucinations—two men, not one. Vision blurring, eyes stinging, head throbbing.

"Veer southeast," says one.

"To the outpost," agrees the other.

Southeast? No. She could not form words - had no control over her body. Southeast was not home. No. Another shiver. Warmth against her cheek.

"*Sleep.*" A command in her very blood.

Then, nothing.

***

Lora was immediately aware of three things upon waking up.

1. She had slept through the night which was rare for her since her lullaby her whole life had been the sounds of war which lead her to:
2. It was super quiet. Like, no sounds other than breaths. *Where the hell are the birds?* Which then propelled her to become aware of:
3. The GIANT FUCKING DRAGON curled around her and the man like a gods damn cat.

No wonder she hadn't died in her sleep, the damn dragon had his big ass wing draped over her and the man to keep out the cold outside air.

It took all of three breaths to remember exactly where she was and what had happened.

She, the bastard, and subsequently adopted, daughter of King Cyrus of the Shadowlands, was currently sleeping on what seemed to be a ledge of a mountain, of which's name she did not know.

From what she could remember and piece together, five-ish days ago she was fighting a group of Drakes when all of a sudden she was swooped into the air while those fighting around her were incinerated. Not the Drakes of course, *they* are fireproof. Which she guessed comes in handy for a dragon breeding kingdom.

If you can even call them that. A *kingdom*.

They *used* to be a part of the Draco Quartam - the group of kingdoms on the Northern continent of Balaur that had been blessed by the gods with dragons. That is, until the revolution nearly thirty years ago when they killed the king of the Shadowlands and began stealing the dragons for themselves, fleeing to the northern mountain caves of Razvaline like the cowards they were.

She had been only a baby when the revolution started, but she had grown up hearing stories of the famous dragon riders and the dangers the Drakes posed to not only those in the Draco Quartam, but also to all of Balaur. She didn't know as much as others but she had experienced enough that her hatred was justified and warranted.

She took a steading breath to ease the tightness in her chest, and sat up, biting down a cry as she stopped mid motion. She had forgotten about the fourth thing she should have been aware of, the fact that when she was snatched off the battlefield before becoming barbeque the lovely black dragon curled around her had used its talons to open up her side and under her arm. The stitches had been ripping open every few days with any small movement, leaving her dizzy or unconscious most of the time. Which is why five days was a *rough* estimate for how long they had been traveling.

She silently cursed herself for ripping her sutures open again as blood began wetting her tunic, which was already caked with days' worth of blood and sweat and dirt. She tried to turn and examine the wound only to get dizzy as more stitches popped along her ribs. She swayed and would've hit her head on the way down had the dragon not caught her with its tail.

"*Must you keep doing that?*" he asked in her mind—he, because that gruff, commanding voice couldn't possibly be anything but male. His glowing amber eyes, dancing with annoyance, meeting hers in the relative dark. That was the fifth thing she should have remembered—the dragon could somehow speak IN her mind. It should freak her out but at this point, she was just trying to survive.

The thing was huge. And frankly, if she was being honest, downright terrifying, especially with the mind talking thing, but she didn't want to be honest at the moment because he was being rude.

She glared at him, trying her best to not faint as her shirt continued to dampen with blood. The beast cocked its head, as if surprised at her courage.

The dragon's eyes narrowed, detecting the unmistakable scent of blood in the air. "*Now Garrison is going to have to wake up early, and he is NOT a morning person,*" he chuffed, his voice deep and rumbling.

Garrison, the male now curled on his side against the front haunch of the dragon, looking as if he was in a plush feather bed, not the stone ledge of a cliff. She huffed a laugh of her own. *Not a morning person? They both seemed to not be an any-time-of-day pair.* From what she remembered from their journey thus far it was mostly silent, the two of them often glaring at each other before one yielded to the will of the other.

Surprisingly, Garrison seemed to win more than the dragon. Something to be said about the constitution, or stupidity, of the man—male. She kept reminding herself that the Drakes weren't fully mortal or human, and although she wasn't either, she certainly wasn't *choosing* to sleep next to a dragon.

She stared at the male but made no move to wake her captor.

"*Your funeral,*" the dragon chuffed again, "*or, at least, it will be if he doesn't wake up and seal that wound back up.*"

She only narrowed her eyes as the dragon seemed to roll his, if that was even possible. They held each other's gaze for what felt like minutes until the dragon, the bastard, moved his tail, sending pain lancing up her side and a fresh flow of blood gushed from her wound.

She swayed, muted black strands of hair coming out of her braid, but still did not make any move to wake up her captor. Another long moment of staring. The dragon's eyes narrowed further and—rolled again? She really wasn't sure how that was even possible.

"Fine, you're lucky I'm in no mood to sing today."

Sing? What did that mean? Before she could begin to process what a dragon singing would sound like she saw Garrison begin to stir. He seemed to wake up as fast as he fell asleep, only allowing himself one stretch and the rubbing of his eyes before his attention fixed on the dragon above him. He seemed to scowl as they had another silent conversation. His nostrils flared once and his eyes shifted from a sleepy daze to razor sharp focus. Focus now pinned on her. Within a flash he was on his feet, their supply bag that had acted as his pillow in the night now in hand as he bounded toward her.

She shifted a bit as to free up the space to her left for him to kneel down, the pain now nearly intolerable. As much as she hated the Drakes, and these particularly, she did not want to die on this forgotten mountain ledge in gods knew where.

Garrison knelt pulling out little glasses for his eyes and what little bit of salve he had left. He looked to her in silent permission and she gave a quick, curt nod. Taking a deep breath she fixed her gaze on the stalactites above her as he peeled back her soaked shirt and the soiled bandage beneath it.

He was gentle as he held the wound closed and withdrew a needle and thread. *This can't be sanitary*, she thought, disgust and nausea hitting her in waves. She nearly doubled over with the sudden need to throw up but the dragon was there, tail pinning her back against the stone so she couldn't move.

"*Breathe*," he instructed. She tried and failed to take a deep breath, the pain was only growing. "*Ready?*" he asked in her mind.

She glanced down again to see Garrison looking up at her, his face set in what she could only assume was resolution.

She nodded once, "Ready", her voice, though quiet, echoed in the cave and the one in her head.

The pain was sharp and searing as Garrison sewed her back up. She blacked out before he finished.

***

Lora woke to the roaring of wind. She had been strapped to Garrison with rope, to keep her upright on the dragon she assumed, and he had one arm tucked gingerly around her waist and one reached out in front of them on the ridge of the dragon's back. She had had her head rested on his shoulder and as she sat up the world seemed to slip out from under her.

"Woah there," Garrison said, as he tugged her tight against him, righting her, "that is not the direction you want to go in."

Her eyes watered with the whipping wind and the hairs that had come out of her long braid were matting in the sweat on her brow. Her vision began to swim as she swayed back against Garrison's chest.

"Shit," she heard him grunt before she passed out again.

***

Two voices drifted into her mind. One known, concerned, the other, familiar, angry:

"She is about to die. We need to get her to Liam." *Liam?* Even on the brink of apparent death her trained subconscious tucked the name away.

"We can't bring him into this, people will ask questions and he needs to be clear of this."

"*Emir.*" The name was almost pleaded and she felt attention shift to her even with her eyes closed.

"I know. I know. We'll fly fast and hard tomorrow—maybe we can get to Noor before sundown for supplies. But for now." *Noor?*

Another name to tuck away. Not like it mattered. She was falling. Slipping away from consciousness, maybe even from life.

"To hold her over," came a voice and something warm and thick slid down her throat. "We need her alive."

She wasn't sure who said it. Didn't matter. They wanted her alive and she preferred to stay that way as well. She fought to stay awake but blood loss and pain pulled her away from the two voices. Pulled her into a restless sleep filled with burning buildings, screaming people, and a bloody hand pulled from hers.

***

She woke yet again in a new place. Frankly, all this passing out was getting on her nerves and it couldn't possibly be good for her brain.

Yet here she was, again, waking up to new sites but the same two faces. They had their backs turned to her and seemed to be peering at what she could see was a tattered piece of paper. *Maybe a map?*

"Good morning boys," she said by way of greeting, startling her captors so much so that Garrison whipped around and nearly tripped, the dragon's head swinging with equal speed. Both looked at her as if they'd seen a ghost. She glanced down to see if maybe she was in fact dead and coming back as a crimea, a shadow ghost, but nope, still in her body. She felt different though, not healed but better, less feverish. Her side itched as her body tried to heal itself. She went to stand but the dragon was quicker, pinning her under his tail.

"*No sudden movements.*" His eyes danced with a mixture of annoyance and intrigue.

"We don't need your stitches ripping again until we can get you a real medic," Garrison said, clearing his throat as he walked over to where she lay propped against a rock.

Right, they needed her alive. And they were taking her to Noor? Or Liam? She opened her mouth to ask but thought better of it. Garrison knelt down in front of her offering her a now full canister of water.

So they had already been to Noor. Meaning she'd been out for nearly a day, putting their travel time at...a week? Gods, she had no idea. She hesitated and, deciding it didn't make sense to poison her now, took several greedy gulps. It was cold and clean, sloshing through her body and cooling any lingering fever and clearing her mind. Garrison, who had returned to the dragon, was now examining a certain corner of the paper, the dragon's head nearly resting on his shoulder. *Definitely a map.*

Before she could stop herself she blurted out, "Why not let me die?"

Honestly, she wasn't quite sure why they hadn't either killed her yet or let her die, other than what she heard in her fever dream the night before about "needing her alive".

"I mean, I'm not complaining, seeing as being alive sounds way better than being charred and eaten but it hasn't seemed like there was much of a plan in place when I was stolen. So unless there is a plan I don't know about, it would make sense if you did eat me. Especially since you two hadn't exactly packed to feed a fully grown human female along with the both of you."

The pair only stared at her for several long moments.

What the hell was wrong with her? Had the water been laced with something that caused her to word-vomit? It must be the blood loss—that's the only explanation for this sort of behavior. That, or magic, which feels silly. Blood loss it is!

Garrison opened his mouth as if to answer but, seeming to decide against it, closed it again. Heat crept into her cheeks as they both simply turned back around and continued looking at the map in Garrison's hand.

Can dragons even read maps? Do they need them? She let her head fall back against the rock, her mind drifting to dark corners and the stuff of nightmares. Before she knew it, she had drifted off into another fitful sleep yet again.

The buildings were all on fire. Many people were screaming. Many people lay dead or dying in the street. She had arrived midway through the cranage. She needed to find Kacey. She rushed from building to building, screaming her name. There were so many people. Soldiers, dressed in Drake red poured in from every street, burning buildings and slaughtering civilians. Why had they brought Kacey here? She heard her name shouted by a familiar voice and turned to see her friend, bloody and bruised, being pulled away by a tall figure. She screamed her name, but her friend was too far away. She was running, feet shredding on the broken glass strewn on the ground. She couldn't get to her in time. Her shadows faltered, sputtering away. Ginormous wings beat in the air, a plume of fire separating her and her friend. "Kasey!" She shouted again. A smaller set of wings, the color of moonlight darted by, smoke rising in its wake. She hurled the knife in her hand blindly. A screech in the night. "Kasey!" A roaring sound and blasting wind as wings beat straight up. She was thrown back, the image of her beaten and battered friend forever searing in her mind.

CHAPTER 2

STILL NOT DEAD BUT PISSED

Lora

Somehow she had survived yet another freezing night on a mountain ledge, though her fingers and toes had barely any feeling in them. Dawn must have been close if the glow on the horizon was any indication. The air was crisper and smelled of smoke—they must be close to another village or an outpost.

She'd never heard of Noor, so they must have been deeper in the Razvaline Mountains than she had originally thought. That did not bode well for her escape plan. After yesterday's renewed strength and last night's nightmare, she had decided to escape sooner rather than later. There was no way they were taking her on a frilly vacation, and she had no intention of being *used* by the Drakes. They, apparently, needed her alive for whatever plans they had for her, and she would rather die than assist them with anything—even if she ended up without the answers she yearned for about Kacey. About why they took her and what they did with her. Lora could handle physical torture, hell, she'd been trained to. Had the scars all over her body to prove it. But if she got there and learned that her friend had been tortured in the same way… She couldn't handle the thought. In her heart, she knew that Kacey was okay, and she knew in her fractured soul that the answers lie within the Drake kingdom, but going in as a wounded prisoner would not help either of them.

She would have to escape, lay low, heal, and then return for her. Even if running away made her a coward. *Coward*—another name to add to the growing list that ran through her head nonstop. *Murderer, Monster, Bastard, Trash, Worthless, Weak*, and now, *Coward*.

She took a shaky breath, flexing her numb fingers in an attempt to coax life into them. The dawn air filled her lungs, cooling her heating blood. Her side had stopped bleeding, which was a good sign, and she could finally take a full breath without too much of a wince, though there was a dull, constant throb in her head and under her arm. She scanned the surrounding area and realized they were lower than they usually slept. The dragon was curled around her and Garrison like usual, but this time, his head faced out toward the mouth of the damp, shallow cave. She couldn't tell if he was awake, but Garrison was definitely asleep, his breaths undulating in a steady rhythm. His head rested on their pack of renewed supplies.

She took the moment alone to really look at her captors. In all the time they'd been together, she hadn't paid much attention to them. Probably from all the blood loss and near constant loom of death.

She studied Garrison first, seeing what all she could glean about the dragon rider before he woke. Garrison, as she had noted before, was huge. He had tan skin, most likely from his time in the skies, shaggy, sandy-brown hair, and was currently sporting about a week's worth of hair on his face that made him seem older than Lora had originally thought he was. His face was not unkind. His eyes, which she was pretty sure were a hazel, had crinkles around the edges, even in sleep, that she had seen deepen when he would smile at the dragon he was currently curled against. His shoulders were broad and toned, his arms mostly covered by a dirty, cream-colored tunic. What she could see of them, though, were speckled with scars much like her own, from years of combat and training. He would be difficult to fight in physical combat without her full strength or power, but he didn't look built for speed. Perhaps she could outrun him if it became a necessity.

The dragon would be the one to contend with. He was massive, the size of six fully grown horses, at least. His black scales, slightly tinted with gold underneath, shimmered in daylight, and she presumed firelight, though they hadn't been willing to light any fires on the journey thus far. Two large, leathery wings were each tipped with razor sharp talons that matched those in its claws—the same claws that had ripped through her "borrowed" plated armor and given her the lovely wound she was now sporting down her side. He also had long-ass teeth, with the largest two being longer than her forearm. Not to mention the damn thing breathed fire. *Fuck.* She knew getting away would be difficult, but looking at the behemoth of a dragon guarding the entrance to the cave, escape felt near impossible.

No. Not impossible. Just a challenge, her biggest one yet. And if one thing was true, it was that Lora loved a challenge.

***

By mid-morning, a plan had solidified in Lora's mind as they flew. She would wait until they neared the river she'd spied through the mist that morning, then launch off the dragon's back into the water. She didn't care for swimming, but had learned in the frozen waters of Baikale as a child out of necessity. Throughout the flight, she had slowly loosened the tie that connected her to Garrison and had also pretended to be dizzy and nauseated all day.

She needed them to think she had fainted yet again when she went toppling into the water. She would then hold her breath as long as she could and hope they thought her dead. If everything went according to plan, Garrison would be still loosely tied to her as she fell, making him the dragon's first priority.

The mist grew thicker the closer they drew to the ground. *That's a problem.* If she couldn't see the water, she might end up launching herself headfirst into a pile of rocks or the forest floor.

She tilted her body a bit to one side as the dragon made a low pass through the thick mist, trying to gauge if they were above the tree line. She couldn't suppress her gasp as the mist cleared slightly. They were much closer to the ground than she had thought, descending without her realizing. If the dragon wanted, he could have touched the tops of the pine trees with his claws. They had never been this low to the ground and the air around them felt - charged, wrong.

"Something's wrong," Garrison said in a low whisper, echoing her thoughts. A rumble came from beneath her—the dragon seeming to agree. She scanned the mist for what caused both of them such alarm, but the trees only gave way to rotted limbs and charred, black rock. Stumps and heaps of stones lay strewn about. Lora couldn't make out any shapes through the mist, but the smell emanating from the earth here was rotten and charred. It was a scent she couldn't quite place, but was somehow familiar.

"What is this place?" she found herself asking no one in particular. The air was heavy, the mist thick. Something *was* wrong, she felt it in her bones. The dragon's wings stirred the mist as they made another low pass, sending the smell of charred earth and that familiar, sweet scent cramming up her nose. That smell…images flashed through her mind as she searched for what it reminded her of. She had smelled it last night, but when else?

Suddenly, the images came flying into her mind. That night. The burning buildings. Her bruised friend. Burning… flesh. As the realization crashed into her, the mist cleared enough for her to see what lay below—the charred remains of a village. And, judging by the heat still radiating from the ground, it was fresh. Lora scanned the rubble for any signs of life. She looked toward the piles of rocks she had seen through the mist moments before, only to be met with the horrible realization that they weren't rocks.

Bodies. Bodies stacked on top of each other, burned and melted together. A whole town, incinerated. But why? For what purpose?

Garrison sat so straight Lora thought his backbone may have turned to stone. She wasn't even sure he was breathing. "Emir," he said, the name snagging some memory from a fever-filled night days ago. The dragon let out a low rumble, one she felt in her very soul.

"We should go," Garrison said, breaking the silence again, "She's seen enough."

She? Wait, they came here so she could see this? This ruined village. What the fuck?

It dawned on her then. "This is Noor, isn't it?"

Neither dragon nor rider looked surprised that she knew the name.

"*It was,*" echoed in her mind before Emir banked hard, flying them away from the ruined city.

***

Lora could only think of one reason why they would show her the city. It had been circling in her mind like angry vultures for the several hours they had been flying. Noor was the city they had gotten supplies from, and then apparently incinerated, the innocent people within it as well. Showing her had to be a message—they would kill any and everything in their path.

They had the power and used it for death. A reality that didn't sit well with her, though she knew it all too well.

After another several hours of flying, Emir landed in a small clearing against a cliff face. Garrison eased her off the dragon's back, threw the pack at her, and stalked into the woods without so much as a backward glance. Emir turned from her as well, clearing an area of rocks with his claws. They had flown hard and fast for the last bit of the day, as if trying to get as far away from their destruction as they could manage, she assumed.

Anger bubbled up inside her but before she could do something truly stupid, like throw the rock she had just picked up at the dragon, Garrison emerged from the dense forest with a pile of sticks and some leaves bundled in his arms.

***

Tonight, they would risk a fire. No one would tell her why. No one spoke. Garrison pulled a small parcel from the supply bag and tossed it in her direction, the crinkles around his eyes dimmed and shadowy. If she cared to notice, she would also note that his skin was sallow, cheeks a bit sunken in. They had been traveling for a week or so, and while she was hungry, her stomach hadn't been rumbling nearly as loud as she thought it would.

She opened the parcel and took three nuts and dried fruits, sneaking another couple of each into her pocket as she refolded the parcel. She'd need her strength when she fled, and didn't feel the slightest tinge of guilt that she was taking their food. Emir was a dragon for gods' sake, couldn't he go catch them meat or something? They'd be fine. Not that she cared, and she truly didn't. Not after seeing that village. Those bodies.

She tossed the parcel back to Garrison, whose attention lingered on her a little longer than was comfortable, before he poured the rest of the contents into his mouth. No more food. They must be close to the next stop. Was it the outpost they had mentioned when they thought her sleeping? Or another village they would take from and then turn to ash?

The dried fruits turned to ash in her mouth. She felt her power surge to the surface, pushing against her skin, warming her blood in response. The fire in front of her guttered.

The dragon's head whipped in her direction, cocking slightly as if analyzing an opponent. Or a meal. Garrison was quick on his feet, a short sword she hadn't realized he had now in his hand. He stood between the two of them as if he could stop the dragon's intentions, which seemed to be incinerating her at last.

"*Something you want to say?*" seethed the dragon, venom dripping from each word. His eyes had narrowed so much, the pupils were only pin pricks. Lora merely sneered in reply.

Garrison tensed, as if he understood their silent conversation. He studied the dragon and then slowly drew his attention to her. Alarm flashed in his eyes, gone before she could fully register it as he turned back toward the dragon, locking eyes with the beast as they had their own silent conversation. His brows were furrowed in annoyance. Frankly, they both seemed annoyed. With each other? With her? She didn't care. Not after what she'd seen today.

Their *message*. What they had *done* to the people of that village. Her power thrummed through her again, begging for release. At least it was coming back to her. While she had been wounded it had all but vanished, aching in her chest like a phantom limb, like how it had when those canthite chains had been clamped…

She took a deep, steadying breath, squeezing her hands into fists. Good. Her power would help her escape. Tonight. Garrison and Emir were both staring at her now, Garrison's grip on his sword tightening.

She almost laughed. As if his sword could stop her. Sure, right now it possibly could. But when she had her full strength? He'd be dust in the wind before he could raise his arms.

The thought of that sudden violence sent a shiver down her spine. She welcomed it, welcomed the gaping hole in her chest her power was now tunneling through.

Wait, a little voice in her head told her. *Wait. You cannot beat them now. Wait.*

She hated that voice, hated that it sounded like Kacey. Hated that it was right. She took another deep breath.

Kacey.

Anger hot and fresh bubbled to the surface, spilling out as she spat in their direction, "Why would I have anything to say to you, *Emir*." The dragon's name left her tongue with as much hatred she felt in her heart, her very soul. If it or the rider was surprised by her knowing his name neither gave it away on their faces.

Garrison's lip only twitched toward—a smile?

She continued, her rage and hatred searing through her veins, "You are nothing more than a wicked, merciless beast that kills any and everything in its path."

The dragon flinched, as if Lora's words were a physical blow. Garrison merely rolled his shoulders back and settled into a fighting stance facing…the dragon. Was he going to fight Emir? The dragon drew to its full height, pulling her focus back to it.

"You have no right to call me that. No right to speak to me in such a way. When it is your people—"

Lora cut him off with a broken laugh. "No right? I am not sure I have *any* rights at the moment, seeing as I'm being held captive, taken to gods-know-where, to have gods-know-what done to me. But judging by that village today, I now have an idea."

Garrison settled into his stance a bit more, sword arm shifting higher, his attention never leaving the dragon.

"That village…" hissed Emir, his head lowering, eyes blazing with what she assumed was fresh hatred. His voice was loud in her head as he said again, *"That village—"*

She cut him off before he could spew any hateful words about the innocent people of that village, or of the "consequences of war", or any other bullshit. "That village, and so many others like it, were just collateral in your *hateful* war. I can name dozens that your *kind* has slaughtered for what you think you deserve. What you think you have a *right* to.

All you do is burn and destroy and kill. You rip families apart and murder innocents." The words crashed out of her with so much force, she couldn't stop them if she wanted to.

The dragon had gone completely still. Lora wasn't even sure if he was breathing when he said, with lethal quiet, "*If that is what you have been led to think—*"

"It is what I *know*." She cut him off again, matching his tone, his condensation with her own.

It was his turn to chuffle, a broken sound coming from deep in his throat. "*If that is what they are teaching in those commanding schools, then you are in need of a lesson.*"

It took her a moment to realize what on earth he was talking about. Commanding schools? But then she remembered that he had picked her off a battlefield, where she had been wearing a commanding officer's uniform, leading him to think that she was just that—a grunt officer.

"I did not learn in a school," she seethed, her own head cocking like Emir's had earlier. A predator assessing its prey. "I learned by watching as my friend, my *only* friend, get ripped from my arms as dragons swarmed a village of innocents."

"I *learned*," she rose from her spot on the ground as she spoke, dark power thrumming around her as she emphasized every word, "as I watched countless people murdered for nothing. I *learned* as I waded through the ashes and the bodies hoping hers was one of them, because everyone *knows* what becomes of a Shade at the hands of a Drake. What I *know* will happen to me soon enough."

Neither dragon nor rider moved, though Garrison had turned toward her. She stood at her full height now, cloaked in shadows as her power built and built, thrashing against her skin.

"The only lesson I *need*," she fumed, shadows dancing behind her, like snakes ready to strike, "is how to kill a fucking dragon like you."

And with that final statement, she exploded into shadows.

CHAPTER 3

ESCAPE ATTEMPT #1

Lora

It hadn't been the spectacular show of power Lora had wanted, but it was all she could manage. The cliffside erupted, showering the rider and his dragon with boulders and debris, giving her only a few precious minutes to launch into action.

She reigned in her thrumming power—they now officially knew she wielded shadows, but they didn't need to know to what extent. No way in hell was she giving them any insight into her people's power.

She dodged a particularly large boulder that came crashing in her direction, causing her stitches to pull a bit at her side. *Shit.* No time to worry about that now.

Emir would likely fly overhead, so she headed toward the forest—he wouldn't risk damaging his wings in the dense woods. She zigged and zagged through the trees, spreading her scent in every direction as she went. Garrison's shout rang through the air a minute or so later. *Shit, that was fast.* She headed for the thicker part of the forest, one she had seen whilst they flew overhead,. and ducked into a grove of close-fitted trees whose low-hanging branches created a curtain around the base of the trunk. She tried to steady her breathing as she listened for sounds of Garrison or the dragon.

Seconds ticked by before she heard the flapping of leathery wings overhead. *Shit, had they found her?* She didn't dare peer around to see if she could see Garrison through the dense trees.

A branch snapped to her left, and she whirled to see Garrison easing around the edge of a large pine. He couldn't see her, but he likely could scent her. She had touched that pine moments before.

She had to move.

She took another deep breath and concentrated.. Out in the distance, she could make out the gurgling of salvation—water. Nothing erased a scent like water.

With one more breath—which made her wince at the reemerging pain in her side—Lora carefully crept from her hiding spot. The beating of wings and whipping of wind stirred several dozen paces to her left, and she knew they were catching on to her pattern.

The water sounded less close and unless Emir used his fire, she would only have to outrun Garrison, which she was confident she could do. With one last deep breath, she clutched the limited supplies she had in her pocket and made a break for it.

***

As Lora drew closer to the gurgling, she prayed to the long-gone gods that she was approaching the stream she had seen yesterday, and not the raging river from days before. Sticks snapped behind her—Garrison was gaining on her. But no wing beats, a stroke of luck. No—not luck. Emir wouldn't be able to see her between the thickness of the trees and the darkness of the night, just like she'd planned. Garrison's steps became closer and closer as she weaved through another set of trees, pumping her arms to propel herself faster. The stitches in her arm stretched more, a couple pulling loose near her armpit. A wave of nausea collided with her power, her shadows banking. *Fuck. That is not good.*

The rush of water became clearer, no more than forty-five paces away, as whipping wind blasted her sideways into the trunk of a tree. Her teeth sang as she bit through her bottom lip when her face collided with the trunk. Blood pooled in her mouth, her vision dancing for several heartbeats. *Fuck!* She whirled as she heard the crashing sound of something very big and very angry land to her right, blocking her path to the water. *FuckFuckFuck.*

Emir stood, wings tucked in tight, amidst the clearing he had just *made* by landing on a patch of trees. It had to have hurt, as she noted the slight twitch of his right wing which wasn't tucked in as tightly as the other. That was where she would need to strike. *But with what?*

Garrison's steps faltered as he stumbled through the woods toward the clearing. She had minutes, maybe even seconds before he arrived and her chances for escape dwindled closer to zero. Emir angled his head, preparing to lash out.

Lora tried to pull in a breath, but it was too shallow due to her aching side. She gave herself one heartbeat then propelled forward, her remaining stitches ripping open as she dove to the ground, twisting as she picked up a large branch that had snapped off from the flattened trees. She slid across the ground, tearing her pants and twisting her ankle, a scream of pain leaving her throat as she drove the twig between the fleshy membranes of the dragon's right wing. He twisted, angling his body best he could in the small clearing, but she had been faster. The branch was deep between his wing and the joint on his back—a lucky shot.

Emir roared as Lora twisted the branch before scrambling to her feet, ducking under his now-ruined wing, and ran with all her might to the stream. But that was where her luck ran out—for as she jumped into the flowing water, she quickly realized it was no stream, but a raging, rocky river, and she had no means to cross it.

***

The water was frigid and quick and Lora had a hard time keeping her head above it. She was used to the cold from the Natron Sea, but this water, this water *hurt*. Her wounded arm was useless, and the cold water locked up the muscles as surely as the blood poured from her freshly opened wound. She couldn't hear anything over the roaring of the water and her own heartbeat in her ears as she clung to the wood. She could barely make out the shoreline on either side of her, the moonless sky still dark. That was good. She had at least a couple more hours of darkness on her side. Her shadows would be long gone by the time she needed them. Even now, she felt her power slipping from her as her energy and blood left her body.

The escape attempt had not gone as planned…but she wasn't dead yet. That's what she told herself as she clawed her way onto a piece of driftwood, clinging for dear life as it bobbed and jerked in the nearly frozen rapids. She needed to get out quickly if she was to stave off hypothermia, which was sure to set in soon. *Fuck, she really needed to get out of the water.* The log she clung to pivoted and rolled as it crashed against a large rock, causing her to lose her grip. Before she could regain it she was pulled underwater by a series of rapids.

Gasping for breath, she breached the surface looking for anything to cling to. But there wasn't anything in reach, and the roaring of the water was growing louder and louder, and—

With no small amount of horror she realized what the raging river was propelling her toward.

There was nothing she could do as she took her final breath and was propelled over the edge of a waterfall.

CHAPTER 4

HOW IS SHE NOT DEAD?

Kalon

Liam had been working on the Shade commander's various wounds, muttering curses under his breath for what felt like a small eternity. Garrison had brought her in about an hour ago, soaking wet, near dead with hypothermia, and pouring blood from the gaping wound on her side. How she wasn't dead already, Kalon had no idea. Not a single one of Garrison's stitches were still in place, and the scar was surely to be a nasty one. Long and jagged. He hoped she wasn't vain because it would ruin her self-worth if she was.

For him and his people, the scar would be worn with pride. It proved she was a fighter, a survivor. That is, if she survived this particular wound, and the several others she had sustained after launching herself into a raging river that took her over a fifteen-foot waterfall. The fact that she was even alive right now was a testament to her will, and Liam's skill.

Luckily for her, and him he supposed, Liam had been stationed at an outpost no more than fifteen miles from where they'd found her near-dead body. It had been a short, quick, and very painful flight. Also fortunately for her, Liam was the best medic in the Drake army.

But still, seriously, how is she not dead? He watched Liam pull a long, sharp knife from the worktable and began to dig something from her side.

Liam let out another curse, his dark skin beading with sweat, as his helper took another bowl of bloodied instruments away. Kalon frowned, a muscle in his jaw ticking slightly. The last week would be a waste of his time if the commander died. He needed her alive to trade for his soldiers, for Jade. Another muttered curse, and Kalon winced at the fresh bowl of bloodied items.

"I'll wait outside," he said to no one in particular, making his way out into the corridor. The outpost at Traivisa was one of their bigger training facilities, well-positioned between the Gora Mountains and the neutral territory of Hvar. It gave the Drake army access to the sea and the mountain caves. He had been stationed here when he was younger, learning all he could about the Shadowlands and their tyrant king, Cyrus.

He strode down the long hallway that connected the infirmary to the main level and the stairwell to the barracks. There were a total of five battalions stationed at Traivisa at any given time, making it an invaluable stronghold. Luckily for Kalon, today there were only two units left behind from weekly patrols. Less people to see the arrival of the commander. Less people to gossip.

He had no doubt the news would spread, though—that the Shade commander was saved by Liam, and would be used as a bargaining chip for the three high-ranking Drake commanders taken hostage nearly a month ago. Kalon had demanded to see them, and the Shade commander who held them—held *her*—had assured Kalon they were still alive. The visit hadn't gone well, but at least they were alive.

Kalon didn't trust the Shade at all. He was a squatty fellow with little power in comparison to the commander in the infirmary. She had brought down half the cliffside with less than a thought, all while very much wounded. He made a mental note to tell Garrison to have canthite chains taken to the infirmary. The chains, made of a special power-nullifying stone that hurt like hell, were something Kalon tried to avoid using - especially since he still shook thinking about how it felt to have his power snuffed out. But they couldn't be too careful.

As if conjured by the thought of him, Garrison rounded the corner at the other end of the hall. He had shaven, which made him seem younger, and the slice down his cheek was now simply a line of pink against his tan skin. It would be a kickass scar once it was fully healed. Based on the small smirk Garrison now sported, Kalon knew his friend thought the same thing.

"You've looked better," Garrison said by way of greeting. It had been several hours since the two had seen each other, and he knew Garrison wasn't just being a prick—he had seen his reflection earlier in the glass panes of the infirmary windows and had indeed not looked his best. His amber eyes had been bracketed by dark circles from lack of sleep, and his curly hair hung limp on his forehead.

Kalon chuckled, glad to see his friend in good spirits. "Yeah well, I've had a hell of a week." Which was an absolute understatement. As if in response, his right arm seemed to spring a new ache right at his shoulder blade. He rubbed at it subconsciously, and Garrison tracked the movement.

"You should get that checked out," he warned. "It could fester or inhibit your—"

"Yeah, yeah, I know," Kalon interrupted, not exactly in the mood to be mother-henned by Garrison, of all people. "Liam's been a bit occupied of late," he added, noting Garrison's narrowed gaze. At the mention of the medic though, his eyes softened slightly.

"How's it going in there?" His voice dropping to a hushed tone as soldiers hurried by. Kalon gave them a tight smile that didn't reach his eyes.

They picked up their pace, Garrison nodding in recognition to the commander at the back of the group. The commander nodded back. Kalon may be the Drake prince, but Garrison was their general. The Drakes respected each of them, but they revered Garrison.

Kalon often found himself mildly jealous of that reverent respect, the ability Garrison had to sit with any one of them and discuss their families, dreams, and lives. Kalon did not have the luxury of getting to know the soldiers in that way. Only a select few did he know, and an even smaller group did he call friends, Garrison and Liam being two of them. Jade being another.

Jade. His gaze drifted to the training ring in the courtyard where they had first met, where she'd kicked his ass in front of everyone, and he'd loved her ever since. But he couldn't think of her without feeling a gaping pit in his stomach, which opened the minute she'd been taken and only grew more and more with each passing day.

As if knowing where his mind had drifted, Garrison stepped forward, hand clasping the back of his neck and catching his gaze.

"We'll get her back, brother," Garrison said, bringing their foreheads together.

"We'll get them all back," Kalon amended, closing his eyes and taking a steadying breath. Only with Garrison could he be this open, this vulnerable. Garrison, who had the respect of the kingdom and the love of its prince. They may not be brothers by blood, but their bond was deeper than the ink of the swirling tattoos they both wore across their shoulders.

A heartbeat passed and Garrison released his neck, pulling away and standing to his full height. Kalon took a second to study his brother, oftentimes forgetting how tall he really was. The man was huge and strong, and yet that Shade bitch had managed to evade him, nearly killing him with that cliff trick. *Fuck.* She better live, if only so Kalon could kill her himself on the battlefield.

Which reminded him… "We should get some canthite chains for the commander so that when she wakes up, we don't have to worry about–"

His words died on his tongue as the infirmary door swung open and a trembling healer, covered in blood, came running in their direction. He stopped so quickly, the kid nearly tripped over himself. Kalon's eyebrows raised in amusement as Garrison coughed out what should have been a laugh.

"Your grace," said the healer, whose face was bleached of color, throwing himself into a bow. The kid needed to calm down, or he might shake so hard his bones might break.

Kalon stared at him as he rose from the bow and quickly averted his gaze, twisting his hands around what appeared to be a balled-up bandage.

"You have something to report?" asked Garrison, his voice calm and serious, so at odds with the amusement dancing in his eyes.

The healer seemed to gain a backbone as he straightened and, turning to face Kalon again, spoke in an unsurprisingly quiet, but strong voice. "The... commander," he paused, glancing around the hallway. "The person you brought into the infirmary earlier..." he paused again.

Kalon nearly rolled his eyes.

"Has she been healed enough for questioning?" Garrison asked, though Kalon knew the Shade would need at least a day or two to recover enough to be able to move, let alone talk. And, judging by the way the healer was now ringing the bandage again, the news was not that pleasant.

"Has something happened?" Kalon asked, unease creeping down his spine. The boy opened his mouth to answer, but before he could speak, the infirmary doors were blown open by a wave of darkness, followed by several soldiers being thrown from the room.

What the fuck? Garrison's face echoed Kalon's thoughts as they both charged past the now–trembling healer. The boy took one look at the shadows flaring around the entrance of the infirmary and bolted the opposite direction.

"Smart lad," noted Garrison, drawing his short sword from its sheath. "Wish I could do the same," he added, flipping it one time in his hand.

Kalon rolled his eyes in earnest this time. "No you don't," he said with a smirk as they rounded the corner. "You love this shi–"

His words were cut off by the fresh new hell unfolding in the infirmary.

What the fuck?

Garrison pulled up short beside him, "What the fuck? I was going to say, 'I really do love this shit' but, what am I even looking at?"

That was a good question, one Kalon was trying to figure out as he beheld the scene in front of him. Several soldiers were strewn about the room like used rags, all seeming unresponsive and judging by the smell of death in the air, some were no longer on this side of the veil. Scanning the darkness he saw her then, a creepy silver glow pulsing around her.

The Shade commander stood over Liam, her hair, which used to be the color of charred earth, now a bright wine red, flowing around her on a phantom wind. She was completely naked but covered in shadows and that silver fire-looking shit. Liam was on the floor, blood and some powdery shit covering his body. The same powdery shit that was now all over the walls. She wasn't moving, didn't seem to be breathing. She just stared down at the medic.

Garrison was frozen to the spot, his mouth hanging open as he, too, tried to make sense of what he was looking at. Kalon took one step forward, accidently kicking a metal pan across the floor which made a terrible screeching sound as it collided with something hard across the room. Her attention snapped to him, her eyes completely white. *What the fuck?*

Alarm bells began ringing in his head, echoed by the ones through the outpost. *Fuck.* He needed this shit handled before a flood of soldiers came rushing in, witnessing whatever the fuck was going on.

He took another step toward her, and she cocked her head in a way that resembled a predator looking at prey. *Oh shit.* Her face, though, was bracketed not with blind rage and hatred, but something else. Something far more dangerous.

Fear.

Kalon scanned the room, searching for anything he could use to detain her, but came up short. This was an infirmary—there were, at least, some sharp knives they could use to their advantage should she charge them, but they were strewn about the shadow-covered floor. Not exactly easy to access.

Garrison twirled his sword, a nervous habit that she tracked with keen, predator-like attention. Kalon took the momentary distraction as his chance and dove toward her, no real plan in mind other than getting her away from Liam. But instead of tackling the body of a twenty-something year old, he was caught by the throat, a hand solid as steel wrapping around it and squeezing.

What the fuck! He wasn't sure if Garrison shouted it or he'd thought it. The commander's attention never strayed from Garrison as her hand clenched tighter around Kalon's throat. He panicked, his mind racing with every possible outcome of this situation, and couldn't help but think that being single-handedly strangled by someone he thought was for sure dead was not one of them. Blackness danced in his vision, whether it be from her shadows or his consciousness slipping away, he wasn't sure.

Garrison shouted something, but Kason could only hear the roaring in his ears. His vision blurred in earnest as he thrashed about, trying to break her hold.

When she slid her attention to him, he felt like his very soul was being branded by her gaze. *Shit. I'm going to die.* Liam's mouth moved, saying something that Kalon couldn't hear. Still, the Shade's attention was on him.

Her glowing eyes bore into his and she cocked her head, releasing her grip a fraction.

A loud thud sounded in his ears.

As quickly as she had grabbed him, she let go, crumpling to the floor. Kalon took a deep, gasping breath as he went with her. His vision returned as the shadows in the room disappeared, sucking into the limp form beneath him. When his eyes finally focused he scanned the room, quickly jumped to his feet, and unsheathed his sword and pointed it toward the Shade commander's still-glowing body. *What the fuck?*

Liam was still on the floor, her body draped over him as if she simply fallen asleep in his lap, a dented metal tray still raised in his right hand.

Kalon choked down another breath as Garrison rushed to Liam, hauling the medic to his feet, the commander's fading body rolling limply to the side. Kalon kept his sword aimed at her, fearing she might wake and jump at him any second. *What had just happened?*

Liam, steady on his feet now, set the tray down and dusted himself off, the powder falling away in chunks, drifting to the floor. He looked only mildly afraid, and far too interested in what had just happened. He'd always been a strange kid, fascinated by the deadly and enthralled by the dangerous. More times than Kalon could count, he and Garrison had to save Liam from touching some venomous creature or pissing off some fire-breathing relative. His curiosity made him an irreplaceable scholar and an extremely gifted healer, even for his young age, but sometimes it was extremely annoying.

And now, the idiot was making his way back toward the limp commander, eyes sparkling with curiosity and wonder. Garrison caught the medic by the arm, pulling him back from the Shade's crumpled form. Liam had the gall to look angry.

"What the hell happened in here?" came the strong voice of Kalon's only other friend and commander of Winged Unit IV, Nuva. Kalon glanced over his shoulder to see her standing in the doorway, hand on her hips, assessing the area like a battlefield—which Kalon guessed it probably looked like. Flanking her solid form were about a half dozen soldiers, all wearing their flying leathers, swords drawn and aimed toward where he stood.

"A question we were hoping Liam would answer for us," said Garrison, eyeing the medic who was trying to wriggle out of his grasp. Liam opened his mouth, surely ready with a retort but Kalon interrupted him, returning his attention to the body on the floor.

"Before anything else, I say we get the commander here some—"

"Clothes," Liam finished for him indignantly, his gaze now on the naked form on the floor.

Kalon's face heated a bit. "Right. Clothes." That had not been what he was about to say, and Liam knew it.

"May I also suggest some canthite chains? Or at the very least, some rope?" called Nuva from the doorway, still not entering the destroyed space. That right there was one of the reasons Kalon liked Nuva so much—no bullshit. Just practicality.

Liam broke Kalon's train of thought as he stated frankly, "No chains."

Everyone's attention whipped to Liam, but his gaze was on the Shade commander, the final bit of glow fading from her skin. This time, when he pulled at Garrison's grip, the soldier let him go. He hurried over to the girl, being sure to block Nuva and the other soldiers' view of her as he knelt in front of her. Without looking, he ripped the curtains from the rod above him and draped them over her, wrapping her tightly in the nearly-sheer cloth.

"No chains," he repeated, scooping her up into his arms. Kalon merely gaped at the medic's lack of fear as he now cradled the lax girl. He cleared his throat and explained, "Chains are what set her off, made her…" He stopped and spun slightly to where Kalon stood, his eyes scanning over the wrecked infirmary. "Well, she woke up pretty scared, and when one of the guards tried to chain her up she…did all this." He gestured to the room.

Kalon nodded, barely understanding what was going on, what had happened, but knew now was not the time to question the medic. "She'll wake up soon enough, and then we can ask her exactly what happened." Kalon straightened and sheathed his sword. Garrison followed suit, as did the soldiers at the door.

"Commander Jensyn," Kalon said, striding toward the doorway of the infirmary, stopping short in front of Nuva. "Have your soldiers clear the infirmary of debris and the wounded moved to the east wing. The empty barracks there should be able to hold them."

Nuva straightened at the tone in her prince's voice, nodded once, and set to work doling out commands to her soldiers.

"Liam." Garrison approached him, but the medic leaned away, clutching the girl's lifeless form to his chest.

"She needs to be put somewhere she can't hurt others," he explained, taking a step toward the door, but wavering. Garrison stepped forward then, reaching out his arms toward Liam, toward the girl in his arms. Liam's gaze was hard, set in determination Kalon only saw when he worked on serious injuries.

"I've got her," Garrison said, reaching toward him again. Liam seemed to contemplate something before relinquishing the girl to Garrison's broad arms. Kalon almost didn't catch the way both of his friends glanced at the Shade—their features remained neutral, but beneath the surface, they shared a glimpse of an emotion Kalon couldn't quite place.

Kalon snapped out of it as Garrison pulled the girl in close, re-draping the curtain that had slipped from her chest. Liam took one last look at the Shade commander, merely nodded, and aimed for the hallway, not looking back.

"There are unused cells in the western portion of the outpost, from when this was a prison. She'll be away from anyone else there," he said, not even glancing at them as he strode down the corridor. He didn't seem to care or notice that he was still covered in blood.

Kalon took two long strides to meet Garrison at the door. They eyed each other warily as they followed Liam down the long corridor.

Neither of them spoke as they tracked the medic, but Kalon knew that Garrison, too, had seen the commander's exposed body. The wound on her side was now nothing more than pink scar tissue, and they were equally unnerved.

***

"Hold on a second," said Nuva later that night, as she paced in front of the fireplace in Kalon's room. "You're telling me she died, like *died*, and then what? Burst into flames and came back to life? Kalon, you know how that sounds?"

Kalon did, in fact, know how it sounded. He had been trying all day to understand what Liam had told them earlier. He had immediately shared the information with Nuva, although he had left out the part about her being wound-free. That felt like too much—which brought them to this conversation in his private rooms. Nuva paced, and Kalon drank heavily from the crystal glass in his hand, his gaze fixed absentmindedly on the fire in front of him.

"Insane," Nuva continued, taking a long pull from her glass of amber liquid. "That's how it sounds. It sounds like shit from *Fables of Flames and Flying*. Not shit you see in real life, and certainly not shit we expected to see from a low-level Shade commander." She stopped, finished the rest of her glass, and resumed her pacing.

Garrison, the bastard, was sprawled across the low-lying chaise thumbing through the story book Nuva had just referenced. Kalon couldn't remember the last time he'd read the worn book.

"To be fair," Garrison remarked from over the book, "Liam was acting super weird." An incredulous look from Nuva had him amending, "Weirder than normal, so maybe he got hit on the head and he's misremembering the ordeal."

It was a possibility, one Kalon had considered as he tried to sort through everything that had happened. "Yeah the dude's weird, but what the fuck was up with Liam calling her 'Mi Fia'? What does that shit even mean?" Nuva wasn't letting up.

"Is that what he said? I could barely hear since I was being strangled to death at the time," quipped Kalon, but it was just another question Kalon didn't have an answer to.

After Liam had put the commander in her cell and dressed her like a rag doll, he had told them what had happened in the infirmary. His gaze had never left the girl's body, not once. It had been almost as unnerving as the story he told them.

He had been trying to sew the wound on her side together, but it wouldn't stop bleeding. Her body was rejecting every medicine and magic he gave her. She started convulsing, and then she died. He felt her life leave her body. He sent the healer out to find Kalon and tell him what happened, and had just begun pulling the sheet up over her face when she just *dissolved*—it was the only word he could think of—into a pile of ashes.

Liam had just stood there, in shock, until the ashes lifted into the air on an unknown wind and hardened into the shape of a naked body. The guards in the room rushed at her, drawing their swords, and one pulled a small chain out to try and contain her. No one knew what had happened, and she had appeared afraid and confused until she saw the chain. Then she had exploded into shadows and her skin had really started to glow, and that's when she blew the doors of the infirmary off its hinges.

It all sounded crazy, every bit of it. But some piece of Kalon, deep down, knew there was truth in it. He'd sensed her fear when her gaze had shifted to him, hadn't he? But how did any of the rest make sense? What did "Mi Fia" mean? And how would this affect his plan?

Nuva asked as much. "This changes things, right? I mean, she can't just be a commander. Maybe she's more important and was just in a commander's uniform."

"She's got a point," chimed Garrison, swinging his legs onto the floor and putting the book down. He made a point to look at Kalon in a way that said, *I need to talk to you later*. Kalon only nodded.

"Point or not, it changes nothing," Kalon said, still processing everything, thinking through his options. "We go ahead with the original plan unless something big happens." Both Nuva and Garrison's eyebrows shot up. "Something *else* big," he amended. "Something that gives us insight into who she is. Without any more information, we can't barter her as anything more than a commander."

Nuva threw her hands up in annoyance, but Kalon knew he'd won. "Garrison and I will go to Hvar tomorrow to send the missive," he continued, not adding that he'd be asking his sister, Kierra, a lot of questions about the Shades. "And before you ask, no you cannot come," he added, Nuva's mouth closing after it had opened to protest. "Because you need to stay here and make sure Liam doesn't get any weirder with her."

Nuva rolled her eyes, but stopped her pacing. Before she could speak, Garrison cut in. "And yes, we'll tell Ki you said hi and send kisses." That earned him a smack across the arm from Nuva and a chuckle from Kalon.

"You two," Nuva spat half-heartedly as she made to leave the room, "are incorrigible. And I hope you get bugs in your eyes on the journey," she added as the door closed behind her. Garrison threw a pillow at the door even though it was already closed, a smile still playing on his lips. But it faded as his gaze met Kalon's.

"You're going to ask Ki about the commander." It was a statement, not a question.

Kalon nodded grimly. He hated that he'd have to bring his twin sister into any of this, especially after what she had been through. But she had been *their* prisoner for nearly fifteen years, and might have the answers he so desperately needed.

"To Hvar then," said Garrison, as he too made his way to the door. Kalon merely nodded again in his direction, thoughts swirling in his mind like oil and water. Too many questions left unanswered.

To Hvar, he thought, and downed the last sip of liquid in his glass.

CHAPTER 5

A POTENTIAL ALLY

Lora

The young male that smelled of lavender and earth had been analyzing Lora's side for the past fifteen minutes, since she'd woken in the dark cell, and hadn't glanced at her face once. *Clearly, not a soldier*, Lora thought to herself.

The dark-skinned male with piercing blue eyes, dressed in a clean white tunic and brown breaches, seemed transfixed by her wound, or rather, based on his murmurings, the lack thereof. She had realized almost immediately that there was no pain under her arm or down her side, or on her lip from her teeth. She felt no pain anywhere, except for her head, which was pounding like a blacksmith hammer on an anvil.

The last thing she remembered before waking in this dark, dingy cell, was freezing in the rapids of the river she had jumped in to escape her Drake captor and his dragon.

She wasn't sure if she was relieved or not to find the rider, Garrison, or the dragon, Emir, anywhere in sight.

The male paused his examining, pulling a paper and writing utensil from his pouch. He made vigorous notes, scratching things off and muttering to himself. She squinted in the darkness to try to get a better look at him. He was probably her age, a little younger maybe, dark skinned, with blond hair bound at the nape of his neck. He was probably tall, but she couldn't really tell since he sat on a stool hunched over her. She glanced around the room again, trying to piece together where she might be.

Tied to a cot in a jail cell was the obvious answer. There were three walls of thick stone and one entirely made of bars which, to her surprise, had been left open slightly. *The fool left the cell door open, escaping will be easier than I had originally thought.* Unfortunately, she seemed to be underground. There was a musty scent in the air and no natural light, only the soft glow of the torch outside her cell. How the young man could even see anything *in* the cell was a mystery to her.

She tried to shift her head slightly to get a better angle at the door, when her brown eyes collided with the pale blue of the young male. He shot to his feet, paper and utensil clattering to the floor.

"You're awake," he all but whispered, his gaze never leaving hers.

Obviously, she thought.

"I was merely examining your wound, or rather...your scar," he said, motioning to her exposed side.

Obviously, she thought again, but still did not reply.

The male blinked several times, then took a small, tentative step toward her. "May I?" he asked, again motioning to her side. She gave a slight nod of her head. Whatever he wanted to do—somehow, she knew he wouldn't hurt her.

He returned to the stool next to her cot, one of his sleeves unrolling as he moved closer. He didn't bother rolling it back up, leaving the swirling twin tattoos on his forearm partially exposed. He rubbed his hands together before gently placing one on each side of her tunic and pulling the fabric up. She wasn't sure where or when she'd been placed in these new clothes, but there was a veritable slit that ran the length of her thigh and side, she assumed to allow easy access for healers to the more sensitive parts of the body.

His focus seemed to narrow in on the winding scar, muttering something under his breath. He reached his hand out to touch her side but paused, meeting her gaze again. She said nothing, but gave another slight nod. *What the hell*, she thought, *not much I can do to stop him anyway.*

"Scar tissue," he finally said, his voice loud in her ears after so much silence. "It builds up over time, creating new, fresh skin that often has a waxy or shiny appearance."

He seemed to be reciting from a medical textbook as his fingers gently traced and poked along the ragged line. He stopped at a wider portion, tilting his head, then moved up along the edges of the scar.

"It takes days, sometimes even weeks to form," he continued, moving up along the edges of the scar, "sometimes, it forms but is reopened before it can really solidify, causing the wound to reopen as well." His fingers stopped again over another wide spot, the spot where her stitches had ripped open the most. "The more the scar tissue is damaged, the more visible the scar will be," he said, his hands falling away from her skin. Two heartbeats passed before she realized why he was telling her this. This scar was a forever scar. She would carry it with her for the remainder of her life. Her eyes teared up as she thought of all the scars littering her body. She wasn't sure why she was crying. She didn't care that she had scars, honestly she quite liked them, they reminded her what all she had survived. But still, a tear slipped free and rolled down her cheek.

The young man's attention snapped to her face, to that single tear. Her face burned red as she met his gaze again.

He stood as if to leave, but then turned to her and, again, spoke in nearly a whisper, "Where I am from, scars are to be revered. They are proof that you are a fighter, a survivor. They garner respect, not shame or sadness."

He turned fully, heading toward the open cell door, and Lora's face heated even more. This stranger thought her so shallow that she would cry over a scar, but then she recognized the words, a memory resurfacing.

Her throat was scratchy and dry, but she pulled her tongue from the roof of her mouth and croaked, "You are the third person to tell me that."

At her voice the male turned around, gaze locking with hers.

"So don't feel all poetic and special," she added, though she wasn't sure why she was even bothering to talk to the stranger.

A small smile passed over his lips as he said, "You must have smart friends if they speak such poetry." A dimple in his right cheek appeared as he leaned on the bars.

She lay her head back on the cot and took a shaky breath. "Not really," she countered, keeping her eyes closed, allowing the memories to surface more fully. Only one became clear, the other foggy and impossible to see.

"The first *was* a friend a long time ago. She used to say it to me any time I got hurt. Not the same thing you said, but close." She let the image of Kacey cleaning her back after a whipping come to mind. She had been so gentle, so kind, and then she had been taken away. The memory soured in her mind as anger bubbled in her blood.

"And the second?" asked the stranger, not seeming to notice or care about her growing anger.

She stared at the filthy ceiling. Her head was still pounding and her mouth tasted like ash. She couldn't form words as tears began to sting her eyes again.

The stranger merely shrugged in the doorway. "Well, anyway," he said awkwardly, as if he wasn't sure how to leave the conversation. "It sounds like your friend is really smart if she said anything close to what I said." His attempt at humor was lost on her.

"Was," she said, the lone word all she could muster. It took all her strength to not rip out his throat or burst into tears. Her very soul was crumbling inside of her.

She felt the air in the cell shift as the man's shoulders drooped in realization. He took a step closer to her and, kneeling, bent to where they were nearly face to face. His voice dropped to a reverent whisper, his eyes dancing with age-old grief, as he spoke words so true she felt them etched into her very soul.

"Those we love are always alive within us, even if they are no longer with us."

The stranger then silently picked up his things and left.

She waited until she no longer heard footsteps before she bent over herself, holding nothing back as she let the weight of her situation, her life, settle into her bones, filling her fractured heart. And for the first time in a long time, Lora cried.

***

The sound of boots shuffling across the stone floor had Lora's eyes shooting open. The torch had gone out hours ago and she had drifted in and out of sleep since the strange young male had left earlier.

It was that same young male that now appeared at her cell, a plate of food in one hand and a mug of steaming liquid in the other. A tall female with darker skin than the medic and a shaved head stood behind him, looking not at all pleased to be there. *You and me both*, Lora thought, as the pair made their way to her cell door. The female walked with a feline grace, her onyx-eyed stare so intense it made Lora's stomach sour—she *looked* like a bitch.

"Good! You're awake. I brought food!" the male said enthusiastically. The female pulled a key out of her pocket and opened the door.

He entered her cell and the woman merely stared at him in relative disbelief as he. He didn't seem to notice. "Sorry it took me so long. Had to make sure—"

He was cut off by the woman's loud cough. She was pretty confident the female didn't actually need to cough, rather she had wanted to shut the male up. He seemed to agree as he rolled his eyes, a small smile playing on his lips.

He held up the plate then, and she sat up, pushing herself against the wall and drawing her knees to her chest. The woman tensed, tracking each movement she made. *Oh yeah, she's a soldier.*

"I brought some food," he said again, offering the plate to her. "It's cold, but edible for the most part. I picked at some of the cheese on the way down here and it didn't seem stale or anything."

He held the plate out a little farther toward her, but she didn't move. She just stared at him. The woman outside the cell was basically vibrating with impatience. She did not look like the person Lora wanted to piss off.

Lora pulled her gaze back to the male, who settled himself on the stool. He had changed his clothes and now wore Drake-red trousers and a fresh cream-colored shirt with the Drake insignia—a man kneeling with an open winged dragon above him—sewn over the heart. The woman wore similar clothes, however hers seemed tailored for mobility, whereas his for comfortability. *Ok, so they are Drakes. Good to know.*

The young man still held the plate in his outstretched hand, a pleasant expression settled on his features. No hint of the sadness from earlier.

Lora sighed and grabbed the plate from him. She'd need her strength in the end, and she doubted he wanted her dead, though the same could not be said for the female. *She* was staring daggers at her.

Lora almost scoffed at the idea of any of the Drakes thinking they could handle her, but then she smelled the bread and beans on her plate and hunger consumed her. She didn't give herself time to consider whether it was poisoned as she ate greedily from the plate, beans mixing with stale bread and cheese.

The food was cold, like he had said, but still good. A small whimper left her throat as she swallowed another hunk of cheese. She hadn't realized how hungry she had really been. She couldn't imagine how hungry Garrison must have been when they got here, let alone the dragon. Her shadows danced weakly under her skin at the thought of the dragon but she pushed them down. Better to seem weak, makes it easier to escape.

Her voice was hoarse but she croaked out, "How long..." She paused, not knowing whether or not she should give away her lack of memories.

But the young man spoke before she had to decide. "Garrison and Kalon left two days ago."

Kalon? Who the hell is Kalon?

"They should be back for you soon," he explained, taking the empty plate and placing it on the floor. The woman threw her hands up in annoyance. Maybe he wasn't supposed to tell her that.

The way the guard's eyes nearly bulged out of her head told Lora he definitely wasn't supposed to tell her that. And for good reason. She now knew she had only a few days before the dragon rider and this Kalon guy showed back up, meaning she better have an escape plan figured out before then.

The woman seemed to read her mind, her eyes narrowing on Lora in the dim light. "You said you wanted to bring *it* food, ask questions, and leave," she said indignantly. "You've brought the food, now ask the questions so we can go. I don't want to spend any longer down here with *it* than I have to."

It? The fuck is that supposed to mean?

Yep, the woman was definitely a bitch. Lora sat up, preparing to stand and ask just that when she was yanked back down by the bands around her wrists. For a brief moment she panicked, thinking they were chains, but the male seemed to realize that.

"Rope," he said calmly, holding up the end of it with a knowing look, "not chains."

She didn't know why or how he had figured out her issue with chains, but it didn't really matter. A not-so-small part of her felt grateful, regardless of the situation.

Lora's blood cooled a bit as she sat back down. Limited mobility, that's what the ropes provided her. She could sit or lay on her cot, or inch into the corner on the other side, presumably enough space to see to her needs. But that was still better than chains.

The young man looked at her with a shimmer of something—hope maybe—gleaming in his eyes. She took a steadying breath, which seemed to ease some of the tension in his shoulders as well. He glanced over his shoulder and nodded to the female. She still seemed unnerved, but nodded back, then turned and took several steps back down the corridor before stopping. The male rolled his eyes again, but again smiled softly to himself. Then he locked eyes with Lora and his smile faded, lips pulling into a tight, weary line.

With a deep breath he said, "I would like to know your name." A long pause passed and he added, "Please."

Lora merely cocked her head. *Like hell I'm giving you my name.*

"Look." He sighed, "I am trying to be civilized. I'm the only one here—" Another cough from the corridor, and he rolled his eyes a third time. Clearly, he and the female knew each other rather personally, enough to annoy one another and for her to anticipate his speech.

"What I mean is," he amended, raising his voice a bit so the female could hear, "I am hoping you and I can talk so that you don't have to talk to anyone else." Another cough from the corridor had the young male looking exasperated.

"It's just…" He paused, searching for the right words. "I'm a medic, see, so I know what will happen if I let someone like my friend here be the one to ask questions, and—"

This time his words were cut off by the opening of the cell door and the female's face mere inches from his. She had moved impossibly fast—Lora hadn't even heard her until the cell was opened. *Damn.*

"Enough!" The female seethed, grabbing the medic by the tunic and hauling him to his feet. She was incredibly strong.

The medic was no Garrison but still, she'd hauled him off the stool like he was nothing more than a sack of flour.

His words resonated through her like a physical blow as the realization of them dawned on her. He was trying to keep her from being beaten, or worse, for information.

But why? Why does he care? He clearly thinks of himself as my ally. But it didn't matter what he said they'd do to her. She was trained for it. Welcomed it, really. A small piece of her felt bad for the young medic, gallantly trying to save a woman he thought needed saving. But that small part of her shriveled up and died as she wondered if Kacey was given the same treatment. If a kind medic had offered her the same option. Kacey was gentle and caring, not built to be tortured in dark cells.

A sneer etched its way onto Lora's features as she threw herself at the pair standing in front of her. The ropes caught her before she could sink her teeth into either of their throats. The female jumped in front of the medic and, within a heartbeat, threw him out of the cell.

The female was immediately in her face, and Lora saw the hilt of the sword a second before it collided with the side of her head. Pain erupted through her, and the last thing she saw was the face of the medic, now bracketed with concern and disappointment.

The world went black, and she welcomed the pain.

CHAPTER 6

SARANON, HVAR

Kalon

The Armed Dowager Inn in Saranon, Hvar had seen better days. In its heyday, Kalon supposed, Saranon had been a bustling town in a thriving kingdom, actually in need of a three-story inn equipped with bath houses and not one, but two restaurants in its lower level. But now, with the war waging around the neutral territory, Saranon was mainly filled with refugees and tradespeople hoping to avoid the heavy taxes imposed on them by the Shadow King.

He and Garrison had arrived four days ago, disguised as fur traders from the north. They had each dawned dark breeches, thick tunics, and overcoats that covered weapons strapped over their bodies in various places. While Kalon had sent a missive to Shade Commander Roulinns a day after their arrival, he had not heard anything back, which is why he now sat, sweating his ass off on a small cafe terrace facing the inn, waiting on Garrison to bring out their lunch.

He watched as the people came and went from the tattered, worn buildings, and wondered how many of them had been displaced recently. Though Hvar had remained neutral in this conflict, many of its outlying cities and villages had been ransacked by one kingdom or another over the years. He had personally seen several of them destroyed, although he had tried to warn the villagers of the impending attack beforehand, which cost him several soldiers and a severe whipping from his commanding officer. He still saw the faces of the children that had not escaped the slaughter when he closed his eyes each night. Even now, seeing the children playing in the street made his stomach sour.

Sweat slid down his back, pooling around his waist where his dark, tight tunic was tucked into thick, even tighter breeches. How anyone could wear this getup on a daily basis was beyond him. He'd nearly ripped the pants thrice just this morning from moving in ways he thought were standard for humans. Garrison had merely laughed. Due to his hulking size, the jerk got to wear loser clothes, seeing as the tight ones attracted too much attention from men and women alike.

Kalon flexed his back muscles and squirmed under the oppressive heat. Saranon was at the bottom of the list of places he wanted to visit, let alone stay overnight in, but he was too anxious to receive word about his soldiers, about Jade, to have anyone else wait for Roulinn's reply. Another bead of sweat rolled down his back, and Kalon contemplated returning to his room across the street if only to undress and lay naked on the bed to avoid the sweltering heat of the day. But before he could get up to do just that, a streak of moon-white hair crossed his vision.

His twin sister, Kierra, bobbed across the busy street, her bright hair swept into a high bun on top of her head. Several pieces had protested being locked away, dangling at the nape of her neck and around her face in tight curls, offsetting her dark skin. She wore a dress that was cinched at the waist, causing her upper chest to be exposed in an entirely uncomfortable fashion. The skirts of the dress were large and rounded, moving in unison with her footsteps as she bounded up the stairs. She looked absolutely ridiculous, and she knew it.

Kalon knew, probably more than anyone except maybe Garrison, that Ki was as wild and reckless as they could get—growing up fighting with them, besting anyone in archery. He smiled knowing his sister was just as uncomfortable as he was in Saranon.

Kierra made her way across the cafe, a pleasant smile plastered on her face, as she passed several men who looked at her like she was their next meal. Kalon's smile grew as she threw them a promising wink, though what she was promising was not what they were thinking. By the time she made her way to Kalon, she, too, was covered in sweat.

Seeing his smile, hers dropped instantly.

"You look ridiculous," she stated by way of greeting, removing his feet from a chair and plopping herself into it.

"Good afternoon to you as well, sister," Kalon crooned, his smile still firmly on his face. "You look lovely in your"—he paused, scanning her attire— "is that a new petticoat?"

The biscuit she had picked up was beamed at his face. Kalon caught it with a chuckle and plopped the stale bread into his mouth. He nearly gagged.

Seeing that, Ki's smile made an appearance again. "Serves you right! Making fun of your dear sister who traveled all this way to see you."

Her tone was thick with mockery, but what she said was true. Kierra *had* traveled a long way to meet him and Garrison here. After being rescued from the Shades a little over four years ago, she chose not to reenlist in the Drake army, but rather work with a network of spies and refugee runners here in Hvar. She'd been in the small village just outside Saranon when Kalon and Garrison had arrived and asked her to come to the capital city with them.

He knew leaving the refugees was hard for her, even for a couple of days. She felt responsible for their safety, even though she shouldn't. While some had been displaced by the Drakes, most were fleeing from the Shade army marching southward. Most, if not all, bore some form of scars from their journey, emotional or physical, and Kierra took each scar personally. Though she was relatively unscathed from her near decade with the Shades, sporting only a wounded shoulder and a pretty beaten-up face when she'd been retrieved, he knew she bore hidden scars that were deeper than those he could see—the shadows in her eyes told him enough. While he hated that she had to relive her traumas, her knowledge of the

Shade army was virtually unmatched, which is why he had to rope her into this.

Kalon and his sister had been close growing up, and when she had been taken...

He opened his mouth to say what, he wasn't sure, but was interrupted by Garrison bringing in two huge trays of sandwiches and dried fruits. Garrison placed the trays gingerly on the table before leaning over and planting a kiss on Kierra's cheek, the small act chasing away the shadows in her eyes for a moment. Kalon was so grateful for that little reprieve, he could have kissed Garrison on the mouth.

Luckily for his friend, Kierra got straight to the point. "From what I've seen and experienced of the armies that pass through, none of the other commanders have the power yours does."

She made a point to dab at her mouth with her napkin as she spoke. It was dangerous to have this conversation here, but less conspicuous than hiding out in their room at the inn, where the walls were thin and everything had a price—even silence.

"You said he took down a whole cliffside even while injured, correct?" She looked to Garrison for confirmation. He nodded, biting into his third meat sandwich. Kalon preferred not to eat the meat of Saranon, having seen where some of it had come from while stationed at the outpost just south of the city, but Garrison was unfazed.

Ki nodded again but looked around while sipping on her tea before continuing. "If he is that strong, it's worth figuring out who exactly he is. Shades with strong magic are usually high-ranking officials, not simply commanding officers." She paused again as a group went by, and she smiled tightly at one of the women, who sneered back at her. Ki, to his enormous amusement, stuck her tongue out in response. Garrison smiled at her while he, too, sipped from his teacup. Garrison was a good male. He loved Ki as his own sister, and the thought warmed his heart again.

Ki continued explaining the breakdown of the Shade power system and their army as he and Garrison listened intently, the latter eating another four sandwiches. It was mostly information they knew, but it was worth hearing it all again. Kalon was just finishing his second vegetable sandwich when Ki concluded, "Again, with a commander as powerful as he is, you may be able to barter for more than just the three officers."

Kalon nearly choked. He hadn't considered asking for anything beyond his officers, his mind never straying far from getting Jade back, but that wasn't what had snagged his attention. Garrison was eyeing him with confusion as he wiped his mouth and faced Kierra.

He hadn't told her everything that had happened at the outpost because it seemed less relevant—it was unlikely Ki had interacted with anything like what Liam had described. But now he realized he might have left out *too* much. Kalon cleared his throat awkwardly, his mouth feeling suddenly dry.

"Ki," he said, voice oddly high pitched, "there is something else we forgot to mention about the commanding officer. Something happened and, well to start off, the commanding officer we have in custody is female."

Kalon hadn't thought the gender of the officer had mattered that much, but he was glad he'd told his sister while she was sitting down. Her nose crinkled like she was smelling foul cheese, and then she erupted in laughter.

Garrison and Kalon shared a disturbed look as Kierra looked between the two of them and then roared again.

"I'm confused," Kalon started, his temper beginning to rise. "Is something funny?" The other patrons of the restaurant were beginning to take notice, listening for any information they could glean.

"Kierra," Garrison asked, meeting her now teary eyes, and reaching for her hand. She stiffened at his gentle touch, her mirth vanishing almost instantly. "Did you know a female commander while you"—he paused as a group walked by—"while you were away?"

Kierra's eyes fluttered closed and she tilted her head back, her hands pulling free from Garrison's grasp. Kalon and Garrison both watched as she shook her head slightly, rolled her shoulders, and then looked at them, eyes clear and bright. A shudder ran up her spine, and Kalon watched as literal shadows danced in her eyes.

"No... I..." Kierra took a shaky breath, seeming to wade through her memories before continuing, "Sorry. It's not funny—it's just, there are few female commanders at all. And if they did have that kind of power, they wouldn't be a commander. They would be delegated to breeding."

They all shuddered at the thought, Kalon especially, since he figured how his sister had come by the information. The Shades had always been different from the Drakes, the most prominent differences being in regard to their treatment of women. Kalon and Kierra both, from a young age, had heard the stories of what the king did to his beloved mistress turned wife, Katalina, upon realizing she had betrayed him—though many suspected he simply grew tired of her and had her killed out of boredom. Either way, the man had her burned publicly, stating that she had been with an enemy Drake and so must die in fire as the Drakes would do. A ridiculous notion. Drakes were relatively impervious to fire even after death, but it had sparked the attention the king had hoped, renewing the Shade people's hatred of the Drakes once again. The fact that Kierra had lived amongst them for nearly a decade never ceased to amaze him. And enrage him.

His thoughts drifted to the commanding officer he had in custody, and then to who the Shades had. *Jade.* His stomach clenched as its contents threatened to reappear. He only realized he had zoned out when Garrison kicked him under the table, drawing his attention back to the present. Kierra was looking at him, studying her brother in a way he knew meant she had more information and was contemplating whether or not to tell him.

Garrison seemed to notice the look as well and said to Kierra, drawing her gaze from his, "If there is anything else you know that you think could be helpful..."

Kierra now studied Garrison with the same scrupulous look before leaning in close, her voice no louder than a whisper in the wind, "Have you considered the rumors?"

Garrison and Kalon exchanged a look again, Kalon stiffening at the severity in his sister's eyes.

"The rumor of the Shadowfire, you mean?" Kalon confirmed, leaning back in his chair and running his hands through his hair. "I mean yeah, it's been on my mind Ki, but this girl—I don't think it's her."

"Because she's a woman?" Kierra asked, eyes narrowing and head cocking to the side.

"No," Kalon said pointedly. "Because of where and how she was obtained. I doubt the king has the Shadowfire dressed in a commanding uniform and fighting alongside the grunt soldiers."

Kierra hummed her disagreement as she looked across the now-crowded cafe.

Kalon's jaw hardened as frustration bubbled to the surface. "Ki," he said, drawing her attention, "it's merely a rumor spread around campfires." Apparently there were some abandoned outposts and a near abandoned village that were obliterated to nothing but ashes, and some people reported seeing silver fire within the Shade shadows. It was borderline nonsensical. A way for the survivors to cope with what the Shades had done. Easier to blame one nightmare than a whole kingdom of them.

Kierra didn't look convinced though, as she rose and dusted herself off, crumbs from her biscuits flying to the ground.

Kalon forged ahead. "We have no proof that there is an actual person who could wield shadows and fire—even Liam thinks—"

"Liam doesn't know everything," Kierra interrupted, shooting him an incredulous look as she marched toward the front of the cafe. "I'm not saying the Shadowfire is for sure true—but it's something you should still be looking into. Especially if you now have this powerful Shade in your custody. It's worth asking about."

She glanced both ways and crossed the busy street, leaving Kalon and Garrison behind. They had to jog to keep pace with her steady steps toward the inn. Kalon's temper began rising to the surface again at the nonchalance of her actions.

When they had finally caught up with her, she was climbing the stairs of the Armed Dowager Inn. Kalon opened his mouth, but Garrison shot him a look that had him closing it. Both males remained silent as they followed Ki inside the musty inn and up several flights of stairs.

Kierra made it all the way to her room before she turned to them and said, "I need to get back to the refugee camp." Her eyes went a bit distant and she sighed, leaning her head against the door. "The rumors are already spreading about this and I've written to our aunt, but no one is listening to me."

After several breaths she looked up at her brother, who was still red with a combination of heat and frustration and continued. "The people who come to these camps have nothing, Kalon. They are scared and alone, and sometimes what they remember is selective. Sometimes it's easier to pin all your trauma on a single person, even if that person doesn't exist. It makes it easier to cope with, an easier pill to swallow, I know that. But I also know that Cyrus is evil, and if there was someone who could wield shadows and fire, he'd use them any chance he got."

From the look in her eyes, Kalon knew his sister spoke true, had guessed it himself. The fire that had been his anger banked and completely disappeared as he pulled his sister into an embrace. She froze for a moment before wrapping her arms around him and resting her head on his chest. Garrison stiffened and took a casual step away, giving the siblings some privacy.

"Just promise me you'll look into it?" she asked, unwrapping herself from their embrace. Kalon held on a little longer, still so glad to have her back, before letting go and stepping back.

"I will." He placed his fisted hand over his left arm in a Drake's promise.

Kierra straightened and nodded before stating, "Sorry I couldn't provide any more about your commander. But if she is as powerful as you say she is, you might want to learn more about her. And see what she knows."

Garrison and Kalon both nodded, Garrison offering, "Maybe Nuva's even managed to get her name," as Ki unlocked her door with a heavy-looking key. He added, "She said to tell you hi, by the way".

At the mention of Nuva, Kierra's dark skin flushed, but her lips remained sealed as she went inside her room, all but slamming the door in their faces, a grace of a smile beginning on her lips.

***

Kalon and Garrison left Kierra to change before making the half-day journey back to the refugee camp. By the time she was ready, the sun was setting properly, although the city was still sweltering. The heat didn't seem to affect Kierra, who mounted her mare in thick brown riding breeches, a tunic, a vest, and a long wool cloak. While the route to the camp was relatively straightforward, she didn't want to risk anything by looking 'stealable' in the clothes she'd been wearing earlier.

Kalon couldn't argue with that, though he wanted to argue with her traveling at night in the first place, even though she was more than capable of handling herself. Judging by Garrion's expression as he helped Ki strap on her saddlebag, he shared the same sentiment.

"I'll send word once I know more," she said as she took off toward the dying sun, not even glancing back in their direction.

"I hope the rumors aren't true," Garrison said, breaking the silence at last.

"Me too," agreed Kalon with a heavy sigh, as both males watched and waited until Kierra's shape was nothing more than a pinprick on the horizon, before turning and heading back into the Armed Dowager Inn to continue to wait for the messenger.

***

Lucky for them, they didn't have to wait long. By breakfast the following day, a message had arrived for Kalon, who was more than ready to leave Saranon. The message, however, wasn't what they were hoping for. It was from Nuva and it was brief, only containing two words, an order: *Outpost. Now.*

CHAPTER 7

LET'S MAKE A DEAL

Lora

Lora spit blood right as another soldier rushed her. It wasn't like she could go anywhere since they had her bound in chains, fastened to a grounded stake in the courtyard, but still they ran at her like she could get away. In all honesty, she probably could have escaped, but with her renewed strength, she was having too much fun beating the shit out of the cocky soldiers who took turns trying to best her.

The female from before had returned to her cell, without the medic, to ask questions. The medic had been right in assuming the female and her compatriots wouldn't just ask nicely, and they especially didn't take kindly to being spit on—which she had done after the second question. That's when the bitch had brought out the canthite chains and it had taken six of them—three of which ended up in the infirmary—to hold her down in order to bind her.

After they realized she could fight, they decided to test their skills against hers. She guessed they assumed that if enough of them beat her, she would eventually give in, but they had been oh so wrong. After the first one drew blood, she unleashed herself on them. With the canthite chains clamped around her wrists and ankles her shadows were nullified, but unluckily for the soldiers, she didn't need them.

She spun using the weight of the chain to her advantage as she pivoted and struck the soldier in the leg, causing him to collapse to his knees, where he was at the perfect height for her to wrap the chain around his neck. While in this position it would be easy to kill him, and she *really* wanted to kill him, she had decided after the first guard had attacked her that she wouldn't kill any of them. It seemed unfair to kill a soldier with so much confidence and so little skill to back it up. Plus, if she killed them, they might kill her, and that was something that did not benefit her escape plan.

So, she waited until the man was *nearly* dead then let go, slipping the chain back from around his neck and letting his body slump onto the floor. She blew loose strands of hair out of her face—long hair was really annoying in these scenarios, especially in a shitty braid like the one she'd managed to give herself before the onslaught happened.

Another guard had decided to join the fun, and so she had to sidestep the recently unconscious guard as well as the one who had been trying to sneak up on her from behind. That particular soldier had thought she couldn't see him only to realize too late that she could, a shortsighted issue that resulted in her knuckles stinging and his nose broken.

She only rolled her eyes as she dodged the third attempted blow from the new soldier. This one, a female, seemed better prepared for the fight, holding onto two long wooden shafts used for training. Lora's face broke out into a smile. While the soldier may have brought the weapons, she surely didn't know how to wield them properly. She was down and out before she could even use either of the shafts Lora had disarmed from her. *Shame, she seemed so confident*, she thought, as she watched the sun begin to set over the outpost walls.

She yawned. This had been going on for the past three days. Soldier after soldier, sometimes in groups, would come out to the courtyard where the first female soldier had brought her for questioning and try their luck at fighting her.

The female soldier, who she overheard called Nuva, had told each soldier who approached Lora that if she didn't answer a question, she was theirs to "train with". It had made Lora laugh, earning her a strong punch to the gut from Nuva herself.

The soldiers thought they were training against a Shade commander, getting to see how they moved and fought up close. But little did they know she was only using moves she'd seen them use while training in the courtyard or initially fighting her. She had *allowed* the first several blows in order to see how the soldiers of the Drake army were trained.

Idiots, she thought as she watched the medic from before—Liam—pull the two guards' bodies out of her reach. She didn't feel the slightest bit of guilt over any of it. They were *Drakes*, for gods sake.

Nuva and a small gang approached her, no doubt to ask another round of questions, so she made a show of sitting with her legs crossed on the ground, yawning, like a child waiting for a bedtime story. *Not that I ever really got those unless they were from Kacey about some made-up land.*

The thought of Kacey sobered her mood, and a small wince escaped at the memories.

Nuva smirked triumphantly, mistaking it as a wince of pain. She then stepped aside to reveal who had been walking behind her. Her original captor Garrison and another male. She assumed they had both arrived earlier from wherever Liam had said Garrison had gone. She hadn't seen any dragons, but she felt the earth rumble several minutes ago, so one must have landed outside the walls of the keep. *Smart not to keep the beasts contained in this small courtyard*, she thought as the males approached.

Garrison was just as tall and broad as she remembered, though somehow he seemed bigger—perhaps from finally eating adequate food these past several days. She was sure she looked worse for wear seeing as she *hadn't* been given the best quality food. She could feel herself losing her muscles— another reason she was enjoying these so-called *training sessions*.

But the male standing next to Garrison was not someone she had seen before, though something about him felt familiar. He was tall, taller than Garrison, but lithe. He had a strong frame that seemed packed with muscle. He had dark brown hair that curled on his forehead and around his ears. His face, which had sharp cheekbones above his square jaw, was set in a casual indifference, though his eyes, his glowing amber and black-flecked eyes, danced with amusement.

If Lora was being honest with herself, he was handsome. But she was not in an honest mood.

He seemed to note her roving eyes and smirked as her gaze landed back on his stunning face. "Well, hello there," he purred, closing the gap between them in two paces. "You seem to be causing a bit of a stir out here." He eyed the men and women being dragged away by healers and medics. His voice seemed familiar—but only in that way she assumed all arrogant people's voices sounded.

Lora merely yawned again and picked some dirt from beneath her fingernails, not even deeming to look up at the stranger as she remarked, "Poor Liam seemed so bored when he would come and visit me, so I figured I'd send him something to do."

She glanced up and smirked as the stranger's nostrils flared at her casual use of the medic's name, so she continued, "And Nuva here has been so kind to provide me with playthings these past couple of days."

Anger flashed in those amber eyes and her smirk widened to a full on, fiendish grin. Nuva had the wits to seem a bit unnerved by the casual use of *her* name and leaned in to whisper something to Garrison, who locked eyes with her. She simply winked. Garrison covered a laugh with a cough. Nuva rolled her eyes. Then the stranger cast an annoyed glance back at the two behind him.

So, they all know each other—well, apparently. Oh, this is going to be fun, she thought, drawing her attention back to the stranger in front of her. *Let's see how riled up you'll get,* she thought, placing her hands on her knees, her chin in her hands.

The stranger's gaze was fixed on hers, set with a seedy determination. She yawned again as she said, "Is there something you needed…" She paused, looking him over. "You know, I actually don't know your name. What was it again?" she asked, drumming her fingers on her cheek.

He didn't answer, although a smile crept slowly across his face.

Fine, have it your way. She did the only thing a mature adult woman would do when dealing with an annoying male—she laid on the floor and pretended to go to sleep.

***

After laying on the floor for what felt like a small eternity, Lora lifted her head to find the stranger simply staring at her, his eyes swirling with a mixture of confusion and amusement. She smirked slightly and adjusted her long, annoying braid over her shoulder. *If she was ever allowed the choice she'd chop it all off.*

"Care to join?" She patted the space next to her. "It can get a little cold, but we could always use body heat," she said in a similar purr he had used, even though the idea of being that close to the smug stranger made her want to vomit or stab him. Maybe both.

The stranger's smile fell, telling her enough—he was tiring of her little game. She smiled to herself. *Good.* People get sloppy when they're angry, and sloppy means easier to kill. Though, in the back of her mind, a voice told her she wouldn't kill the handsome stranger. Not yet.

"Probably a good call," she said, scooting up to lean on her elbow, her shoulder screaming in pain from a blow a guard had landed yesterday. She looked up to the sky, basking in the fading sunlight.

"Although, I'll admit," she continued, not deeming to look in the stranger's direction, "you do seem like the type who likes their women in chains—"

She was cut off by a hand grabbing her cheeks and squeezing. Hard. The stranger had moved so fast she had barely seen him, and his eyes were near glowing with rage.

Gotcha.

"You watch that tongue of yours or I will cut it out of your mouth." His words dripped with venom, his breath so hot on her face, it felt like steam. She almost winced—almost.

He let go with such force she felt like she'd been thrown. *Fuck he's strong. And pissed off. Good.*

She merely rubbed at her cheek. "Ow." She pouted. "That hurt."

The stranger turned, heading back toward his comrades as she rose and dusted herself off. "Gods what a threat," she said, adding so much sugar to her voice she could have baked a cake with it. "Who died and made you king?"

Just as before, the stranger turned and reached for her, but this time she was ready. While he lurched straight ahead, she turned slightly to the left so that her right fist would be in line with the stranger's face. The following crunch was one of the most satisfying sounds she'd ever heard, the second being the curses from the stranger and Garrison.

What Lora had not anticipated was the female guard, Nuva, to side swipe her feet from under her while she was off balance, causing her to go crashing down. Her head slammed into the hard ground before her bound hands could catch her. *Fuck, that hurt.* She tried to scramble to her feet but another, stronger blow came to the back of her head.

A loud thud, a burst of light from behind her eyes, then nothingness, again.

***

Lora gasped as cold water splashed over her face and body. Judging by the now-dark sky, she had been out for at least several minutes. Her vision swam a bit as she tried to focus on the figures in front of her. Nuva, *the bitch*, was the one holding the bucket, a smile plastered onto her face.

"Thanks for that, I'd needed a bath," Lora spat, a feline smile of her own dancing across her face as she tried to stand.

Whatever she had been splashed with wasn't just water. The courtyard ground was now slick, causing her to slip several times before finally righting herself by holding on to the stake her chains were attached to. The smile playing on the stranger's face sent a heatwave across her own features. They had taken away her footing—smart, and extremely annoying.

The stranger approached her again, looking rather smug as he did. She scanned behind him to see more soldiers had come into the courtyard, many carrying torches. *Shit. Were they about to burn her alive?*

She spotted Garrison in the gathering group, two steps behind the stranger. He seemed anxious, inching closer to the stranger and the main square, his eyes scanning the crowd and lingering on the torches. Good to know it wasn't just her not *loving* this situation.

A shadow fell over her face and she looked up to see the stranger now standing mere feet from her. He looked relaxed, his shoulders back, hands in his pockets, a neutral expression on his still-bloody face. He was still in his flying leathers, his shirt a little rumpled with the sleeves rolled up.

The stranger cocked his head as if assessing her, and Lora tried to stand up straighter and failed. *This shit is very slick.* She'd need to figure out how to use it to her advantage.

The stranger turned, putting his back to her—*idiot*—and addressed the still-growing crowd. "Fellow soldiers, it has been brought to my attention that most of you here were bested by this creature before me."

Well, that's rude. Lora looked into the crowd again and saw many faces sporting bruises, busted lips, and black eyes. *Shit. Were these all people I beat the past three days?*

A smile danced on her lips as she noted the number—twenty-three. She had beaten twenty-three Drake soldiers in three days while chained to a post. Her smile grew in earnest when she noted the annoyance it brought most of them.

The stranger continued his little speech, still with his back to her. "It has also been brought to my attention that *it* has not answered any of our questions."

It...really? She rolled her eyes as several curses sounded from within the crowd, but her smile only widened. She had barely even spoken while at the outpost let alone answered any questions. The fools here didn't even know her name.

She scanned the crowd again, her gaze landing on a soldier in the very back, dressed in loose fitting clothes with his sleeves carelessly rolled up—Liam. The medic had come only once to attend to her various wounds after she'd lashed out at him in her cell. He hadn't spoken, but his eyes had shone with that quiet wonder when he first examined her without knowing she was watching. What he thought of all the soldiers she had sent to the infirmary, she didn't know or care. He wasn't looking at her now, but rather, he was watching the stranger intently, hanging onto his every word like he was a god or king.

Just like being doused with water, realization slammed into her. Liam had mentioned someone named Kalon when she had still been in the cell. Others had mentioned "the prince", not realizing she could hear. Several soldiers even mentioned that this *prince* had gone away to run an errand with Garrison—and hadn't Liam said Kalon and Garrison would be back soon? Hell, some of the loser lipped soldiers even whispered about Emir being the *prince's* dragon. Or something like that...

Kalon must be the prince of the Drake kingdom, or what was left of it.

Lora tried to remember what she had learned about the history of the Drake royal family, but all she could remember at the moment was that the Drake Queen had killed her Shade husband about thirty years ago, sparking the war. Since they had no children, the next line extended to a smaller clan of the Drakes.

That must be this *Kalon's* family. Before she could think too much into it all, she was pulled back to the situation at hand by laughter from the crowd. Apparently, the prince had a sense of humor. He was looking at her, amusement dancing over every feature of his face. She realized he had asked her a question, and she hadn't replied. She also hadn't realized he'd turned to face her. *Damn, I really must have been hit on the head hard.*

She smiled and, looking as bored as she could, noted, "Oh, sorry were you talking to me? I stopped listening when you opened your mouth."

The laughter in the crowd died immediately, though Kalon's eyes shone with a renewed sense of purpose.

"Interesting," he purred, taking a step toward her, and she found herself leaning back a bit, keeping distance between them. His eyes never left hers as he said, "I would have thought that you would have wanted to hear my offer."

Offer? What the hell is he talking about? When she didn't respond, Kalon's smirk only deepened. He made a grand gesture of bowing her direction before saying loudly so all could hear, "Allow me to say it again, but this time in a way you can understand."

Her anger bubbled to the surface at his condescending tone. She had the feeling that if she got her hands around his neck, she might snap it, damn the repercussions.

The prince merely continued, condescension soaking each word, "Blood equals answer. Knockout equals freedom."

Lora's boiling anger evaporated immediately at the word *freedom*.

He was offering her a shot at her freedom. But why? Was he *that* cocky? Did he not see the *twenty-three* people standing around him that she had taken down? There had to be a catch.

As if reading her mind, Kalon's smile grew. "Of course, it's not just me that you have to answer to." He turned away but spoke loud enough for her to still hear. "It's these lovely folks as well. So, to make it an even playing field, each of the soldiers you have taken down will get to land one blow, and then you and I will have our fun." On the last word, he winked over his shoulder at her.

Oh, he was most definitely cocky. He thought that after twenty-three blows she wouldn't be able to stand, let alone fight him. But he was wrong.

She had to play this right for it to work to her advantage. Twenty-three blows would hurt like hell, and it would render her weakened, and she wouldn't want to use her shadows too much either…

She took a breath, just one, before she found herself striding as steadily as she could on the slick ground, as far as the—thank the gods for the small victory—*normal* chains would allow her, toward Kalon and the soldiers around him.

"Seems to me like you want me weakened, prince," she purred as she halted mere feet from the prince, chains clattering with the sudden movement. "But if you want to fight a weakened opponent, then by all means, let's play."

Kalon's smirk spread into a full-on grin as someone in the crowd, someone who sounded a lot like Liam, said a silent prayer to some god. Kalon's smile never waned as he called several names and the corresponding soldiers stepped forward. She braced herself as best she could on the slick ground, but instead of attacking her, the soldiers grabbed each of her shoulders to hold her in place.

Panic flared in her eyes for a brief moment as Kalon said, in a near whisper, "Can't have you blocking any blows now, can we?" Then, he nodded to one of the soldiers to his left. The soldier stepped forward and it was one of the first she had knocked out several days ago.

She looked into the eyes of the male, smiled, and said "Hello, again," before getting punched right in the face. Her left cheek stung and she could already feel it swelling, but her lip didn't split, so there was no blood she could spit in the next soldier's face.

The next, a female she had headbutted, landed a strong uppercut to her jaw. The next landed a blow to her side that came uncomfortably close to her still-tender scar. Each of the twenty-three soldiers she had taken down took their turn landing an unblocked blow on Lora, and for each one her eyes never left theirs until the next came up to take their turn.

And for each one, she smiled.

***

Kalon

The Shade commander had taken every single of the twenty-three blows given to her, and still she smiled.

She smiled at each soldier who had thrown a punch, and when they were done she turned her eerie smile to him. It was unsettling and not the least bit unnerving.

He had not expected her to still be standing, but when his soldiers released her shoulders, she simply straightened and wiped her bleeding nose on the back of her arm. *Who is this bitch?*

His soldiers, though happy to get to land a blow on her, looked equally unnerved. Many of them had left after their turn, leaving the courtyard empty except for him, Garrison, Nuva, and three other soldiers, which included the ones who had held her shoulders.

Liam had left after the first punch, muttering something under his breath. Kalon had locked eyes with him before he went, and the disappointment in his gaze still lingered with Kalon even now.

The Shade now stood, blood dripping down her face, looking utterly bored. Her half smirk at him had him snapping out of his stupor and marching toward her, temper roiling.

"Ready to play, prince? I was getting a bit bored, I'm hoping you and I can have some fun." Her smile was nothing short of feline. If he was being honest, no, he was not "ready to play". He imagined what exactly she thought fun would be, and a small shiver escaped him. She tracked it like a wild beast tracking the movements of a scared mouse. *Oh shit, does that make me the mouse?* That thought did not sit well with him. He set his jaw in a hard line, frowning slightly.

"Such a confident spirit. It'll be a shame when you lose," he bit out, trying to muster up more bravado than he felt.

Standing preternaturally still, she said, "I'm shaking in fear."

The sound that left Kalon's throat was near animalistic, but the Shade did not move an inch at it. "There he is," she said, and somehow her smile grew.

"Hurry up!" called Nuva from behind him. "This bitch is creeping me out."

The Shade rolled her shoulders at the insult, but after a brief moment of contemplation, settled back into her casual, arrogant stance, apparently deciding it was a compliment.

With a hand on his arm, Garrison stopped Kalon before he could move toward the Shade. "I still think this is a bad idea," he muttered quietly, eyeing the girl not ten paces from them.

Kalon looked at his friend, and before he could respond, the Shade shouted—from *ten fucking paces* away— "That would have been helpful about twenty-three punches ago!"

How the fuck did she hear us? Kalon locked eyes with Garrison one last time, who seemed to think the same thing, before shaking free of his grasp and marching toward the shade. "Someone needs to teach you that it's impolite to eavesdrop," he said, annoyance and promise in each word.

The Shade cocked her head as he stopped in front of her.

"Here are the rules," he started, trying to sound more confident than he felt, letting his annoyance dominate his unease.

"Oh goodie!" she said before he continued. "I just love those."

His eye roll had to have broken a record somewhere. This woman was insane. "As I was saying, the rules are simple. I land a blow that draws blood and you answer a question. You knock me out and Nuva there sets you free." Her eyebrows shot up and she gave a little wave to Nuva behind him. "And no fancy tricks," he mentioned, nodding to the small shadows gathering around her shoulders. She shooed them away like mice on the street.

Her brown eyes returned to his and then narrowed. "There is a catch, right? You just saw how many people I took down earlier…" She smiled to herself at the memory. "I'm not looking a gift horse in the mouth or anything, but—"

"There's no catch," he interrupted. "But I will need an assurance."

Her eyebrows furrowed. "An assurance?"

Tight lipped, he nodded. "Yes, so you don't—"

"Kill you?" It was her turn to interrupt with a wicked smile spreading across her face.

"I was going to say 'lie.'" He leered, his eyebrows raising. "But cute of you to assume you could kill me." Nothing about the predator in front of him was cute.

Her eyes sparkled with amusement. "Cute, you think I'd have a reason to lie, since I won't be answering any questions." She was slowly approaching him, and he did not like that one bit. "But sure, if you're so convinced you need one, what kind of assurance can I offer you? You already have me chained in your outpost courtyard..." She made a dramatic gesture to the space around them.

"A Troth," he found himself saying before he could stop himself. He heard the smallest of gasps from behind him. This had not been a part of his plan.

Her eyes narrowed again, "A what?"

"A Troth," he repeated, trying to act nonchalant. His very bones seemed conflicted, something deep inside him both pushing him toward her and pulling him back. He put his hands in his pockets and strolled the final couple of paces to her. "It's like a bargain between two people," he explained. "You set the terms and then you shake on it."

"You shake on it? That's it?" Her smile faded to confusion as slight unease danced across her features, her eyes dimming with distrust.

"Not exactly," he said, withdrawing a dagger from its scabbard at his hip. She eyed it warily. "I was going to take it off anyway," he said, for some reason needing her to know he was going to fight fair. She only shrugged, as if it didn't matter. For some reason though, it did.

He moved to take her hand, but she pulled away. "You have to share blood during the shake. It'll just be a little slice, it won't hurt," he explained calmly.

She cocked her head in apparent annoyance. "And how do I know you don't have some creepy Drake disease you're going to infect me with?"

Anger stirred in Kalon's blood, his patience waning. "I don't have some '*creepy Drake disease*.'" He paused, trying to reign in his temper. "Do you want to make the deal or not?"

She blinked twice before she snatched the dagger out of his hand. *Damn, she's fast.* "Same rules you have already established, and," she added, "this blood doesn't count." *Smart girl.*

He nodded and she sliced the bottom of her palm open, no longer than a coin. She flipped the dagger in her other hand with expert precision and handed it to him. He took it and sliced his own hand while repeating the rules. "Every time I draw blood you, Shade, answer a question honestly. You knock me out and you get to walk out freely—no more harm will be done to you." He extended his hand toward her, but she didn't take it—just squinted her eyes at him. He rolled his eyes, but added, "And this blood doesn't count."

This time, when he extended his hand she took it, but before she could pull away he smiled and added, "And neither of us can kill the other."

Kalon heard Garrison curse from behind them, but he and his friend both knew they needed to keep this one alive—especially since the other two they previously had were now dead, courtesy of Kalon's temper.

He felt the zapping sensation of the Troth settle in at the same time she ripped her hand from his grasp with a soft gasp. Troths were old magic Liam had told him about once—old and powerful, appearing as a swirl of reds and golds on his palm.

The Shade commander looked down at her palm, at the new mark she would bear until this fight ended—the mark of the Troth.

Kalon pulled a key from within his pants pocket and reached for her chained wrists but paused when her attention snapped to him. Meeting her gaze this closely felt like plunging into a frozen sea. His very blood seemed to freeze in his body. She cocked her head, assessing him. "I was going to take off your chains, unless you'd rather fight with them."

She shrugged as if it didn't really matter, which unnerved him even more. He stared at her a second longer before simply loosening the chains, then placing the key back in his pocket.

"At least this will make it more interesting," she drawled as he moved to step away. "Shall we?" She made a show of gesturing to the physical combat training area where the post holding her chains was. Kalon only nodded, the Troth scar throbbing. *What have I got myself into?*

***

Lora

The prince had been right—the rules were simple, and the *Troth* would keep Lora honest. Unfortunately, after getting hit twenty-three times, she wasn't doing too hot. Which was an understatement since she actually felt quite feverish, and her vision was a tad blurry. But then again, she'd fought under worse circumstances. What made her feel ever so slightly better was the fact that the arrogant prince looked like he, too, might throw up. *Good. His nerves will make him an unsteady opponent.* She had used up almost all her bravado, and when he'd reached for her chains and their eyes locked—she had had to suppress a shiver. Her shadows had even recoiled behind her, thrashing in her blood and under her skin.

But now was not the time to think about that. She stood in the arena, rolling her shoulders and hunkering into a fighting position. Before she could make a plan, the prince nodded once and launched himself toward her.

He was fast. *Fuck, he was fast.* But she dodged his first two blows with a duck and roll set she'd seen two of the guards do earlier that morning. He seemed to notice and threw a third, somehow quicker, punch toward her side. She barely dodged it, the glancing blow he did land causing her to fly sideways. *Gods, he's strong too. Who the fuck is this guy?*

She managed to barely dodge the next three shots, and the prince looked pissed about it.

"We'll start with something simple," he said as he panted and dodged another of her punches. "Like your name, perhaps?"

No way in hell was she telling him her name. If they still had Kacey, they could use her name against her. Plus, she had no intention of losing. She hadn't gotten a shot on him yet but was saving her energy, watching how he moved so she could find her opening. Her shadows pushed under her skin, begging to be used, but she held them at bay. Not the time. She threw a lazy punch toward his left side, and he took it, letting his right arm take the blow instead. *Interesting.* She threw another punch to his left side, and again he turned, letting his right arm take the blow. *Gotcha.*

"A little sore there prince?" she crooned, dodging a sloppy left hook.

Kalon's eyes were blazing with fury now, the look oddly familiar. "I would say you should let Liam look at it…" She kicked out and landed a blow to his right ribs. "But he's a bit busy at the moment." Her smile was nothing short of feral, his frown was deeper than she thought possible. *Good. Stay mad, you'll be easier to knock out.*

She took a steadying breath, preparing to hit him and end this game. But before she could, the world was pulled out from underneath her and her ears were filled with a deafening crunch as Kalon's fist collided with her jaw. *Damn, good shot.* She hadn't even seen it coming.

Lora landed hard on the ground and could hear Kalon's footsteps circling her. She took one breath and as she lurched up to swing, she felt a foot at her back, shoving her down again. This time, her nose crunched and sparks erupted behind her eyes. Damn, this guy might actually beat her.

When she looked up from her sprawled spot on the ground, she expected to see him rushing her, or at least preparing for another blow. But instead he only stood there, two paces away, eyes wide as he looked upon her. Shock and satisfaction mixing on his features. Blood dripped from her now broken nose onto her chin.

And at the sight of her blood, the bastard smiled.

Shit. She had assumed she'd win, and at the least hoped he'd knock her out and not actually draw blood. The surprise on his face had shifted into smug satisfaction as the blood started flowing in earnest; she knew he'd call in her answer—her name.

"Well?" He approached her slowly. "I believe you owe me an answer. And I'm sure many more," he promised with a wink.

She thought about lying, but the Troth on her hand seemed to burn at even the consideration. She would not give them the name *Lora*. It was what Kacey had called her, a name she had given herself when she had seen it in one of the pages of the books she used to read before Kacey had arrived. A name that had snagged her attention because it felt right. She felt like a Lora—not a Collis, as her mother had named her. Collis didn't even make sense. It was old Shade for "dark haired", and she was anything but. Not that anyone here would know it for the lie it was.

She guessed that her mother had given her the name in hopes her hair would be dark—but her mother should have known it wouldn't be, having been raped by a Drake. Or whatever the story Cyrus spun. Lora could not have been born with perfect, raven black hair like her mother, like the king. So, although she was born as Princess Collis, a bastard princess at that, she introduced herself as Lora, the nobody.

No, she decided. *Lora* was hers, and they could not have it. It was foolish she knew, to give them her real name, the one given to her at birth. But, on the off chance they still had Kacey, Collis wouldn't ring a bell. It couldn't be used against her.

The scuffle of boots drew her attention back to the arena, to the prince, whose hand was now extended to her. *Is he going to help me up?*

He didn't wait for her to reach up—he leaned down and grabbed her by the arm, hoisting her to her feet. Shit, he *was* helping her up. *Odd fellow*, she thought, perplexed.

Kalon's face flashed with what seemed to be confusion at his own actions, but it was gone in an instant. "And here I was, thinking you may just win," he said with another wink, releasing her arm and taking a step back.

That perplexed look immediately turned into a frown. "I was winning," she reminded him. "And I would have already been walking halfway back to Shade territory if I hadn't sustained *twenty-three* punches before we even started."

She wasn't bluffing. The only reason Kalon was still standing was because her eye was too swollen for her to use her peripherals. He knew that, and was taunting her anyway. Her shadows pushed to be released but still she kept them hidden.

"Seems like an excuse, but whatever," he said smugly, shrugging as he walked over to his comrades and took a long drink from his canteen. The female guard, Nuva, had a ravenously pleased look on her face—one that Lora immediately wanted to punch away.

Instead of charging the guard, though, she took the moment's reprieve to roll her shoulders. She would not lose again, that, she was sure of.

As Kalon approached her, looking far too casual, she charged. Her palm began burning, demanding she follow through with the Troth, so she did—right as she landed a strong right hook to Kalon's temple. His eyes flared, and she smiled. Before he could demand an answer she leaned in and whispered her name—her true name—and as his eyes flared again she spun, throwing another punch to his ribs. Then another to his back as he lurched forward. She was a whirlwind of punches and kicks that the prince had no chance of keeping up with—or stopping. He doubled over after a nasty kick to the stomach and she grabbed him by the hair, forcing him to meet her gaze. Her palm was on fire now—the terms of the Troth seeming to vibrate within her hand as Kalon was close to unconsciousness. "Your mercy is a weakness, prince," she whispered in his ear, feeling his body stiffen at her tone. "A weakness I do not have."

She took in a too-shallow breath, steadying herself for the final blow that would grant her freedom. But Nuva surged forward and was stopped by Garrison, who said, "The Troth," and apparently that was enough for Nuva to stand down. The look on her face shifted from rage to fear. The Troth was important to them. They honored it, even as the man they seemed to respect so highly knelt, bloodied and bruised before her—they would not intervene.

Something inside her shifted at the sight of their desperate faces. It was a weakness, she knew—but she felt it nonetheless. She should end this. She could end it. She could be free within moments, but something about the way the prince met her gaze made her flinch—he was willing to go down in front of all of his soldiers, his friends, to honor their Troth, but he would go down fighting. It was a type of honor, bravery, and stubbornness she had never seen before. One she hadn't expected to see from a Drake prince. Not to mention, if she did knock him out, would the other Drakes have to uphold his part of the Troth? They could easily swarm her and her freedom would be lost.

She took a shaky breath, just one, and knew what she had to do. She released his hair and swung, loosely, and Kalon caught the punch with his good arm, rotating, causing her to lose balance. She staggered to the left as Kalon swung out to the right, swiping her feet. She fell hard, but rolled so that most of the impact was on her arm. *It'll be harder to escape tonight if my legs are damaged.* Because that is what she would do—lose now and escape later, when no one was looking. Why she decided that, she didn't want to think about as she spun again, barely dodging Kalon's next blow.

He wasn't going down without a fight, and she wasn't going to purposefully lose without drawing a little more of his blood.

They parried once again and she made a show of lagging, delaying her blocks and throws in order to appear tired. She got in a good punch to his jaw, and Kalon spit blood off to the side. He was *actually* lagging, her whirlwind earlier seeming to have truly disoriented him. She saw his next swing coming a mile away, knew how to defend herself against it, but didn't. She let the blow fall upon her, letting her very bones rattle under its power. He had given every last bit of his strength to that punch. She went down, not faking the wince as pain lanced across her face.

Kalon approached her and she dove for his legs, a move she knew he'd counter with a headlock. After a few moments of thrashing about, hitting his legs and clawing at his arms, she went limp beneath him. Kalon loosened his hold and she sagged to the ground, face down in the dewy grass. Darkness claiming her.

***

Kalon

Kalon was panting hard as he used the toe of his boot to roll the Shade onto her back, her body limply rolling over with the force. No, not just a Shade, but *Collis*.

He had won her name fair and square. Well, sort of. It was a name that felt odd, distant from the woman herself. Would his sister know of her? Would she have heard of this wild, brave, albeit insane, Shade? He would need to write to Ki immediately, and hope she could make it here before he received any missives from the Shade Commander Roulinns about the trade deal.

He had hoped to get more answers but she had been fast and strong, even after all the blows he and the others had dealt. She was a force to be reckoned with for sure, a force who had almost beaten him, *should* have beaten him, if he was being honest with himself. He'd seen in her eyes—the moment she decided not to deliver the final blow. *But why?* It didn't sit right with him.

He looked down at her ravaged body lying prone in the grass, and a shiver went up his back. *Collis*. She certainly didn't have raven black hair like her name suggested. The way it had come out of her braid and spilled over her shoulder made it look like a pool of bright red blood. It was creepy, to say the least.

He took another deep breath, wincing at the pain in his sides. Now that the adrenaline was wearing off, everything ached.

Garrison and Nuva were suddenly beside him. His ears were still ringing so he couldn't hear them speak, hadn't even realized they had approached until Nuva snapped her fingers in his face.

He turned, ears clearing a bit, as she said, "And it's a good thing she finally got tired."

"Back off, Nuva. He won, didn't he?" Garrison said, his low voice almost impossible to hear through Kalon's still-ringing ears.

"I need to write to Ki, see what she knows about a Shade named Collis." He walked away before he realized where his legs were taking him. He didn't know if Nuva and Garrison followed him or not, but he couldn't look at the Shade anymore—no, not just *a* Shade, but *Collis*, a Shade who would help him free Jade.

CHAPTER 8

ESCAPE ATTEMPT #2

Lora

Kalon's headlock should have knocked her unconscious. Kalon and his friends surely thought it did, seeing as they left her on the ground where she'd fallen. The fools hadn't bothered to re-tighten her restraints—which was good. If they'd tried to, that arrogant prince would have realized she snatched the key when she'd allowed him to land her in the headlock. It had been all too easy to let the prince think he had the upper hand. Finally letting him win once she had the key.

They may have her true name, which wasn't ideal, but they would never get the chance to learn more. Her temple pulsed as she forced her eyes open, adjusting quickly to the darkness around her. *Good—still dark.* Just like she'd planned. She wouldn't have to use too much of her shadows once she got the chains off, which meant she could conserve them for later.

She worked the key out from under her tongue where she had hidden it, making quick work to unfasten her wrists from their chains. The minute they were off she felt a surge of power, followed by a wave of nausea. She made it all of two steps before she puked, the food she'd been given the day before making a return. She'd need to find food and water once she escaped the outpost. Maybe she could blend in with the people of a nearby village. *Shit*. And she'd need to dye her hair, eventually. Maybe she could find some tree bark or something.

After a few minutes, her nausea subsided, and she began to move. Her joints were a bit achy from her fight, but her body had rebounded quickly enough to where the pain was minimal, mostly in her head and face from the final blow Kalon had dealt. Her left eye was still swollen, but at least she could see.

She noted where the guards were—where they always were at this time each night, based on her previous observations—and began her quick track around the courtyard. If how the guards acted the last several nights was any indication, it was time for a shift change, meaning no one would notice she was gone for a five-minute window. Which was plenty of time to get away.

Loose hair blowing in the wind, Lora took two deep breaths before making a mad dash to the northern wall. She chose that wall specifically for its wrack of daggers and spears the fools always left out. They were dull and meant for training, but they would do the trick either way. She paused before the wrack and retied her hair. The last thing she needed was to worry about being blinded by her own damn hair. Then, she strapped on two daggers and grabbed a spear before pivoting toward her exit and sprinting.

The two main gates of the courtyard were on adjoining walls, meaning the guards could focus their strengths there if there was ever a siege. She smirked—the Drakes really were a stupid group of people. While the guards were all concentrated on the two gates, she would be making her way through the smaller gate she'd spotted two days ago. Most imports of food and supplies were brought in through the main gates, however, any weapons, clothing, or armor was brought in through the eastern corner of the facility, which, judging by the smell of the clothes people wore around here, was near water.

Lora managed to get fifteen paces from the eastern wall before a guard noticed she was gone. An alarm sounded, and she heard the pounding of feet behind her. *Shit.* She paused and pivoted, throwing one of the knives she collected toward the sound. As she turned toward the gate again, she heard the satisfying thud of the soldier going down. Not dead—her stupid promise to herself stopped her from making a fatal blow to any of the guards now swarming her.

Another guard fell in her wake. A small piece of her hoped it wasn't the medic or the dragon rider. A larger piece of her didn't care, so long as she got out of there in one piece. So, she forged on, heading toward freedom and knocking down anyone in her way.

***

Kalon

The young soldier was in Kalon's chambers before he had finished knocking on the door. There had been a commotion from outside the window moments before, but he was too deep into his conversation with Nuva and Garrison to inspect it. In all honesty, he didn't really care what the commotion was about. The day's events still weighed heavily on him like a blanket of lead, clouding his thoughts with images of a wicked smile and blood-red hair. Liam had refused to join them for this conversation— another weight on his chest.

"My prince," exclaimed the soldier, breathing heavily from where he stood in the doorway. Nuva and Garrison both jumped to their feet at the intrusion, the former drawing her short sword. Kalon was glad they were here, if only so he didn't have to worry about getting killed. The young soldier looked nervously between the General and the Commander, now both standing with weapons drawn, and back at Kalon who still sat in his chair, glass in hand.

Another heartbeat passed, the only sound being the deep breathes from the soldier.

"Yes? Did you have something you wished to tell the prince? It seemed quite urgent," Nuva quipped, sheathing her sword. Garrison followed suit, though he shifted a step closer to him. It made Kalon roll his eyes.

The soldier didn't move. Kalon wasn't even sure the kid was breathing. "Speak freely," he said, hoping his calm voice would put the soldier at ease. It did not.

The boy swallowed once then blurted out, "It seems the prisoner is trying to escape!" Then he bowed again, adding, "Sir."

Kalon sat upright, mind racing. The Shade, *Collis*, should still be knocked out. "Through which gate: south or west?" He rose and put his glass down on the side table next to his chair.

"Neither, sir," replied the boy, his face leaching of color as he eyed Nuva's serious face.

"Neither?" Nuva repeated indignantly, as if she, too, had trouble understanding what the boy meant. There were only two ways to leave the outpost—the south or west gate. Unless she was coming here...to him...

"No, ma'am," stuttered the boy, now looking at Nuva. "She seems to be headed toward the docks."

Kalon's eyebrows rose. *The docks?*

"And how does she know the docks exist?" asked Nuva, her temper rising, filling the air with ether.

"We don't believe she actually does, commander..."

Kalon's eyebrows shot up higher, but the boy trailed off as he looked past Kalon and Garrison to the window overlooking the outpost.

The commotion outside had gotten louder, and even Garrison had turned from the soldier in the door to look out the window.

"She should be easily detained." Nuva approached the soldier at the door. "She's in chains, for gods' sake. Get her under control!" When the boy didn't move she nearly threw the soldier out and bellowed, "That's an order!" The poor boy all but ran away to deliver Nuva's orders as the commander slammed the door.

At the mention of chains, Kalon felt his pocket for the key, and a frown spread across his face as he corrected Nuva. "No, she is not."

Seething, Nuva's attention flew straight to his hand and empty pocket. "That little bitch!"

She stomped toward the door as Garrison chimed from the window, "That little bitch is currently armed and running rampant through the courtyard." Apparently, he had been watching the spectacle outside unfold while Nuva had been berating the young soldier. Nuva and Kalon made eye contact before joining Garrison at the window.

From their vantage point, they could see it all unfolding, and Kalon could do nothing but stare in horrific awe as the Shade commander tore through his soldiers—using *his* moves.

"She's wrecking them. All of them," Garrison said with a hint of the same awe Kalon felt.

"And she's using our own maneuvers against us," Kalon added. *Damn, she's good.* "Smart to not let us see any Shade techniques—"

Nuva was in their faces, interrupting their exchange that was hedging toward complimenting the Shade officer below. "Are you two going to get out there and help, or keep drooling here at the window?"

That got Kalon's attention. He and Garrison began re-arming themselves but Nuva was already stomping toward the door. "Alive," he reminded Nuva as she charged out of the room.

Garrison opened his mouth but Kalon said quickly, "I know what you're about to say, but I don't want to hear it." He strapped on his dagger and straightened, heading for the door.

"I wasn't going to say anything," Garrison said, quickly catching up to the prince. He glanced over and noted that his friend had the audacity to look almost offended at Kalon's accusation, his eyes dancing with the words, *as if I would ever say anything that would upset you.*

As they made their way through the corridor, passing a bloodied soldier being carried on a stretcher toward the infirmary, he added, "What I will say is you might hate her, but you've got to give her credit where credit is due. She's kind of a badass." They breached the warm night air and bore witness to just what all was going on in the courtyard.

With a roll of his eyes, Kalon launched into movement, but not before turning to Garrison and admitting, "I'm well aware."

***

Lora

It was almost too easy to disarm and knock out the Drakes at the outpost. Lora almost hoped it was a training facility, because if these were the best and brightest the Drakes had to offer, then they were sure to lose the war. In the six minutes since the alarm had sounded she had knocked eleven soldiers unconscious, eight of which had to have been twice her size.

Three had landed blows on various places on her body, one nasty uppercut had split her lip, and stars were now dancing in her vision from a nasty left hook she hadn't blocked in time. She had to make a point of not getting hit in the head again.

Lora got into a rhythm of twirling and ducking. The Drakes at this outpost all fought the exact same, so it didn't take long for her to figure out how to overcome them.

After what felt like the hundredth dodged swing, Lora paused, coming face-to-face with the prince of the assholes himself—Kalon.

"Fancy seeing you here," she hummed, wasting no time and swinging the now-tipless spear at him. She smiled, tasting the blood between her teeth. She tracked Kalon's shiver, even though he tried to hide it.

He ducked, a lover's smile now on his face. "If you wanted to dance again you could have just asked." A strong hit from her spear had him pausing for a breath before continuing, swinging his short sword, cracking the spear. "No need for all these dramatics."

"Well," Lora crooned, pouting at the splintered pieces of wood in her hands, "it seems you still like to ruin all my fun. No bother." She shrugged, then spun to jab an oncoming guard with a piece of shaft. "Now I have two toys instead of one!"

Kalon swung out again and she took her chance to whack him hard on the arm, causing him to nearly drop his sword. "It seems you have company, dear," she lulled as more guards rushed toward them. "How very rude not to inform me!"

"Shame I can't keep you for myself this time," Kalon said after a strong swing she barely dodged.

They parried twice before splitting again, and an onslaught of guards rushed her.

***

Kalon

As they parried, Collis was terrifying in the best possible way. She landed way more blows on him than when they sparred, and he began to realize she had let him win. Her verbal assaults were just as powerful as her right hook, causing him to lose his footing anytime she called him *dear* or cocked her head at him.

"Are you having fun out here?" asked Nuva, her tone dripping with condescension. "Or can we stop her from knocking any more soldiers out?"

Not killing? Kalon thought to himself. *Why wasn't she killing anyone...*

Kalon paused to consider, and soldiers swarmed the Shade. The look she gave him as he stepped back from the fray was almost *disappointed*. Bored, even.

She could kill us all. He'd realized that the minute he saw her smile, blood streaking her teeth from a nasty looking split lip. She was strong enough and crazy enough to kill anyone who stood in her way. And yet...she didn't. She hadn't even touched her shadows yet, Kalon noticed as he glanced around the well-lit courtyard. Interesting. She was either hiding them from his soldiers, or choosing not to waste them. Either way, all this destruction, all this damage, was raw, unpowered

Collis. But that didn't scare him. What scared him most, was that he *wasn't* scared of her.

Not at all.

***

Lora

While the Prince allowed his guards to swarm Lora, he seemed to be content to just watch, so she did her best to bore him. Never using any of her own training. Never using her shadows, not that that particularly mattered since they lit every torch in the entire outpost, making it look like daylight inside the courtyard.

She took down two large guards who had decided, foolishly, to tag team her. Unfortunately, they both ended up missing some teeth and in desperate need of new noses. Poor Liam would have his hands full again. Not that she cared.

Another soldier came forward, swinging an ax, and she almost yawned. This was getting tedious. It had been almost ten minutes since the alarm had first been raised. If she was right, all exits would be fully sealed soon. She needed to hurry.

A soldier came at her with canthite chains—*fuck*—and she realized it was one of the soldiers from earlier, one she had knocked out right when she first escaped. *Not good. Maybe letting them live wasn't as smart as I originally thought.* Because this soldier—she looked pissed.

Lora analyzed her options quickly. The bitch in front of her had canthite chains, and there was no way in hell she was going back in those. Her wrists still ached from the regular chains—a shudder worked through her as she thought of the bite the canthite would make if they touched her skin.

Never again would she let those chains touch her skin, especially not here. To be so weakened—she didn't want to finish the thought. She hadn't even used her shadows, and they still wanted her power nullified. *If they only knew the damage I could truly do.* Her blood boiled at the thought, her power surging to the surface, demanding to be used.

No. She needed to escape, and that was it. In the process, she might end up hurting someone and would need to deal with it—but why should she care, anyway? These people had taken her, taken her friend.

She smiled a wicked smile, realizing she didn't give a fuck if they were hurt.

Kalon's eyes widened, as if he had realized just that, as Lora ducked under a swing of the chains from the soldier. He opened his mouth but she couldn't hear what he said through the roaring in her ears. She took a deep breath, preparing to unleash, when suddenly she just…stopped. Her whole being froze as a voice so familiar it felt like her own flittered toward her; a voice she heard in her dreams every night, the only one that both comforted and wrecked her. A voice she spent her life trying to find and free.

She looked then, using her shadows to protect herself from oncoming attacks so she could find the source. She peeled away the layers of guards and soldiers with barely a flick of her wrist, the shadows carrying them not-so-gently out of her line of sight.

Her attention snapped to the shadowy corner of the outpost when a familiar voice said a familiar name. And as the speaker finally came into view, Lora froze, her shadows disappearing entirely.

A woman emerged from the southern gate, heading toward the prince a few meters away.

"Kalon? What the fuck is going on?" asked Kacey.

CHAPTER 9

UTTER CONFUSION

Kalon

Kalon could see it in her feline smile: at the arrival of canthite Collis was preparing to do something truly horrible. Then suddenly, as if frozen in time, she stilled, her shadows swarming her, and her head whipped toward a corner of the outpost. Her smile faded to a look of horror-ridden confusion.

In a matter of seconds, she was finally taken down to the ground by guards. Another heartbeat later and she was rechained in canthite, this time, and hauled away to the cells.

"What the fuck Kalon? That was her, wasn't it?"

As much as he loved his sister, now was not the best time to be chastised by her. She had barely missed the onslaught that Collis had unleashed.

"You got my missive, then?" he asked by way of greeting, steering them toward his chambers—and away from Collis.

The last thing he needed was his sister to have to interact with the deranged Shade.

"What? No, I sent word ahead that I was coming, I found out more about the Shadowfire from the refugees. I couldn't risk putting it all in the missive..." Her words trailed off as she looked closely at her brother. "Are you all right?" He could feel her stare on his black eye.

He rubbed the back of his neck, stretching. "Probably payback for the headlock," he said with a shrug, beginning to walk forward again.

"The headlock?" Kierra asked, pulling him back to a stop. "You put the commander in a headlock?"

"Yeah?" he said wearily, pulling free from her grasp and taking the stairs two at a time toward his quarters.

"Why would you do that?" Kierra asked, keeping pace as they ascended the winding stairs.

"Because I thought I could knock her unconscious," he said, trying to make all this sound less ridiculous than it was.

"What... So you knocked her unconscious?" He could hear Kierra's condescension even though he couldn't see her.

He paused at the door to his quarters. "Well I *thought* I'd knocked her unconscious—"

"How the hell do you *think* that?" Kierra bellowed, her tan cheeks flushed with rising anger.

He opened the door, preparing his retort when Garrison chided from inside, "She outsmarted him!"

The jerk was already lounging on the small sofa in the room, nursing a black eye Kalon hadn't remembered seeing him get. He stormed over to Garrison, who simply held up the glass he'd already poured for Kalon. He finished it in one gulp.

A sharp look from Kalon, and Kierra's eyebrows somehow shot higher. "She did, did she? I might like this girl." She plopped down next to Garrison and took a long pull of his drink.

"No, you wouldn't," Kalon stated flatly, setting the glass down on the small table. "And that's not entirely true..." he continued defensively, "she technically outsmarted *all* of us." It was Garrison's turn to raise his eyebrows, and Kalon gestured vaguely toward him. "What? You thought she was unconscious as well! You're the leading general of the Drake army, you should have double checked."

Garrison looked somewhat offended. "And you're the prince of the *kingdom*! *You* shouldn't have entered a Troth with her in the first place!"

Kalon knew what was coming before Kierra's mouth even opened.

"You entered a *Troth* with her?" There was no way Kierra's eyebrows could possibly go higher—her eyeballs themselves nearly bulged out of her head. "Kalon, what the hell were you thinking?"

"I was thinking it would keep me alive when I fought her," he admitted, rubbing his neck again.

Kierra was in his face in an instant. "You *what*? There's no way I heard you correctly."

"You heard him correctly, all right." Nuva entered the room, closing the thick wooden door behind her. Of course *she* was relatively unscathed from the ordeal.

Kierra spun toward the sound of Nuva's voice, but whirled back around to Kalon, her eyes blazing with fury. "Why the hell did you want to fight her?"

"For information," was the only answer he could come up with.

"Normal methods weren't exactly working, and she had sent nearly half the outpost to Liam anytime we questioned her." Nuva was braver than Kalon for admitting that the Shade had wounded anyone on the outpost. Kalon knew Kierra's anger; he felt it, too.

Kierra looked ready to ask a million questions, so he cut her off. "I harnessed her propensity for violence and we made a deal."

"A deal?" she spat. "It was a *Troth*! Those are sacred!"

Shit, she's pissed.

"Yes. It was the only way I could think to learn anything," Kalon admitted, hoping she understood his reasoning. By the looks of it, she did not. He tried a new tactic. "Even you said you might like her...."

That had been the wrong thing to say. He had always had a temper, but his twin could level a building when she was mad. She took one step toward him before Nuva—again, braver than Kalon—placed a firm hand on her arm.

Kierra's eyes never left Kalon's, but she took a steadying breath, her shoulders relaxing a fraction before she pulled from Nuva's grasp. "And what was the deal, exactly?" Her tone dripped with indignation.

"If I drew blood, then she answered a question honestly," he said, matter-of-factly. Kierra gaped, eyes wide.

"Hence, why he requested a Troth to keep her honest," Garrison chimed from his spot on the sofa. The asshole.

Kierra's eyes narrowed on him again. "And what exactly was she to get out of it?"

Kalon and Garrison exchanged a glance and Kierra demanded again, "What would she have gotten?"

"Freedom." Nuva said—she was Kalon's hero tonight.

Kierra's mouth dropped open and her hand had somehow shifted to her side, where she kept her dagger. Her furious gaze met Nuva's, but she asked her brother, "And did you learn anything of value?" The words dripped with venom, and the tension in the air was almost palatable. Kalon hadn't realized how stupid of a deal it was until he had to explain it to Kierra.

He let out a long sigh, running his hand through his messy hair. "Not as much as we hoped," he admitted, red creeping into his cheeks at the admission. "But we did learn her name, which could lead us to learning more about her, so there's that." It didn't feel like nearly enough, not as his black eye pulsed and his side still ached.

Kierra still looked like she'd stab all three of them. For a moment, he wasn't sure she wouldn't, but then she took a shaky breath, and looked at Nuva. "This was your call?"

"Ultimately, you know that everything is Kalon's call. But yes, I agreed that it was a good course of action. Even volunteered to do it myself, but the bastard wanted it more."

Kalon's chest swelled with appreciation for Nuva's unwavering honesty, especially with his sister. Never before had he been so happy his sister and Nuva were together. At least Nuva could weather the storm of his sister's wrath.

Kierra took one more breath then faced him, her eyes a tinge softer than before, though still filled with roiling anger. She crossed her arms, then looked between the three of them. "Well? What's her name?"

Everyone nervously glanced around the room as Kierra stood, hands on her hips, waiting for the answer.

Kierra very well may know the Shade officer downstairs, and Kalon wasn't sure how to tell her that.

"If you are being quiet for any other reason than a lapse in memory, you are one second away from my dagger being embedded in your shoulder," she vowed, locking eyes with each of them. Even right after she had been rescued, Kierra had never wanted to be treated any different than before. Now was no different.

Kalon cleared his throat, straightening the book on the small table in front of him. "Her name is Collis," he said, eyeing his sister carefully, looking for any reaction to the news.

Kierra squinted at him, eyes narrowing in anger once more. "No it isn't."

"What? What do you mean?" Not only was Kalon confused, but now, he was mildly irritated. He had gotten her name through a Troth… and gotten the shit beat out of him. It better be her fucking name.

"I mean, there is no way the Shade officer downstairs is Collis Nightgale," she repeated.

"Maybe not Collis *Nightgale*. But her name is Collis," stated Garrison as he stood at Kierra's serious tone.

She hunkered into a fighting stance Kalon and Garrison both knew all too well. She was dug in on this one, meaning she truly believed what she was saying to be true. "Any Collis would be Collis Nightgale and, like I said, that's not possible."

"And why is that?" he asked, bracing himself for whatever his sister was about to say.

She stared at them both for a heartbeat before saying matter-of-factly, "Because Collis Nightgale is the ostracized princess of the Shades and presumed dead."

Kalon and Garrison both stared at her, wide eyed and mouths gaping open. "I don't understand what you are saying. The girl downstairs said her name was Collis and she couldn't lie," Kalon said.

"Well, she did," Kierra stated flatly.

"Just because her name is Collis doesn't mean it's the same Collis you're talking about," Garrison commented, plopping back down on the sofa. Kalon felt inclined to do the same but resisted. Why was Kierra digging her heels so much at this?

"Yes, it does." She had the audacity to look annoyed at them. As if she wasn't the one being thick headed.

"Kierra, listen to yourself," Kalon said, trying to remain calm. "It's possible there are two Collis's in the entirety of the Shade kingdom."

"Afterall, doesn't it mean dark hair or some shit? That's like every Shade, so it would make sense for there to be more than one," chimed Nuva, who studied Kierra with a mixture of curiosity and mild amusement. Of course she'd like seeing Kierra all riled up.

Kierra shot her a look before she explained, not so calmly, "Yes, it does mean 'darked haired one.' And no, there are no other Collises in the Shadowlands."

"And why are you so confident in that?" asked Kalon, his face inches from his twin's, his temper beginning to heat.

"Because it's illegal," she said, baring her teeth at his tone.

"What is?" asked Garrison, now standing again and inching toward the siblings. "To be named Collis?"

Kierra's eyes didn't leave Kalon's as she replied, "Yes."

"That's absurd. That can't be true, right?" Nuva asked as she, too, inched toward the siblings. Kalon noted that both his friends were now in position to grab either one of them should this turn physical, which, by the glean in Kierra's eye, was highly probable.

"I've heard of weirder rules, but this does feel like a stretch," Garrison said from Kalon's left. This was how their fights would go as children—they would be at each other's throats until Garrison, Nuva, or their grandmother could pull them apart. Then they'd be stuck on clean up duty for a week or two and be fine.

"I don't care what it *feels* like. You are focusing on the wrong shit," Kierra snapped, still not looking away from Kalon. He swore he saw something like hurt flash in her eyes.

His temper eased as he saw that hurt flash again as Nuva reached for Kierra. She was telling the truth, even if it didn't make sense to them.

"I'm sorry—you're right. What do you know about the Collis you're talking about?" He took a step away, and the tension in the room eased. A little.

Kierra noted it and nodded, straightening where she still stood by the door. "Only what I heard from the guards and other Shade ladies," she said, rolling her shoulders.

"And that was?" Nuva asked, clearly not caring if she got Kierra riled up again. Kalon shot her a look, and she held her hands up defensively.

Kierra rolled her eyes and took a deep breath. "Rumor had it that King Cyrus's mistress-turned-wife Katerina was pregnant with their child when she was traveling in Attica. They say her baby died and she stole one from a camp of refugees, killing the mother to hide the evidence. Then, she presented that baby to Cyrus as theirs, naming it Collis for her impenetrably dark hair—almost unbelievably dark. The King was overjoyed and paraded the child around as proof of the strength of his line. But when the little girl was five years old, she fell into a river. Rumor has it that when she emerged her hair was fiery red, exposing the truth—or what the king assumed was the truth—that Katerina had cheated on him with a Drake, and Collis was not his child. Apparently he was so ashamed, he burned Katerina at the stake and exiled the child to some distant land in the north. No one ever saw her again—she was presumed dead until about five years ago when she re-emerged with black hair and with a strong shadow gift, once again parading as Cyrus's prized daughter."

Kierra finished her tale and yawned, as if the information was old news and, frankly, a bit boring.

Everyone gaped at her with wide eyes. Kalon's mind was careening in a million different directions as he worked through everything Kierra had just told them.

Garrison was the first to break the silence. "You heard all that from rumors?"

"And whispers," Kierra added, inspecting her fingernails and shrugging nonchalantly. "You learn a lot when people don't care who you are."

"Clearly," Nuva grunted as she slumped onto the sofa next to Garrison.

"So," Kalon started, pacing in front of the fireplace. "Let's say what all you said was true—"

"It is," Kierra cut in.

Kalon, pausing his pacing, pinned her with a look. She merely shrugged again. "Ok, fine. Since the information about this Collis is true and if the Shade downstairs really is the same Collis—"

"Then you currently have King Cyrus's most prized possession in holding," Nuva finished for him, her eyes wide.

"And could you identify Collis if you saw her? Just to be sure?" he asked his sister.

"No," she answered flatly. "Like I said, no one had seen her for nearly twenty years. and I was gone by the time she resurfaced." She sighed and looked toward the ceiling, her eyes fluttering as if holding back tears.

After another sigh, she looked at her brother. "Based on everything you've said—and what she did to your face—I do not doubt who she is. Which means your trade agreement may have just become a bit more possible," Kierra said as she headed for the door. "But I would be careful, Kalon. The Shades may act one way, but really think and feel another way entirely."

And with that she slipped out of Kalon's quarters and into the hallway.

Nuva rose off the sofa and headed toward the door. She paused, realizing that the conversation might not be over, and turned back to Kalon.

"Go," he said, seeing the pleading in her eyes. "Make sure she gets to her quarters and does *not* go see Collis."

Nuva nodded once and then she, too, slipped through the door. Kalon took a deep breath and glanced up at Garrison, who was staring at him.

"Do you think that she really is the princess?" he asked, gingerly touching his own blackened eye.

"I don't know," Kalon admitted. There were too many pieces to the puzzle he was trying to work out, and Kierra hadn't even gotten a chance to tell them the information she'd learned about the Shadowfire. He let out a long sigh as his mind raced in several directions.

"What now?" Garrison asked.

"Now?" Kalon repeated, rubbing his neck again. "Now I write a very strongly worded message."

"To Commander Roulinns?" Garrison inquired, pouring Kalon and himself glasses of amber liquid.

Kalon, staring out the window into the courtyard where the Shade officer—the *princess*—had been chained. "To the King of the Shades."

CHAPTER 10

A RACING MIND

Lora

Lora had been pacing for what felt like hours and was amazed that her path was not carved into the stone floor of the cell she was in.

The Drake guards who had dragged her into the cell had left her little space for pacing, so the path she could walk was only a couple steps in each direction. Any farther and the canthite would dig in more than it already did.

Kacey– Kalon– Dragons– Fire– Kacey–

Her thoughts were like a relentless torrent of waves crashing against her mind, one after the other. She had tried to close her eyes, to sleep and keep the thoughts at bay, but they came back as images and nightmares. Between the canthite clamping down her power and memories trying to force their way out, she felt like a volcano moments from eruption. The pacing kept her from exploding, so pace she did.

No one had come downstairs since the guards had locked her in the cell. There was no food or water, and even the medic hadn't come down to inspect her or tend to her wounds—or stare at her scars. And that female, whose voice sounded so much like Kacey it made her stomach lurch just thinking about it—she hadn't made an appearance, either.

"It can't be her," she said aloud, her voice echoing off the stone walls. "She would have come for me or left me a sign. Plus," she added to no one, "how would she even be here? Talking to *Kalon*? Shouting at him like she knew him?"

Another piece of the puzzle. If that was Kacey—which she was pretending to steadfastly believe it wasn't—then why did she look so different? The Kacey she remembered had been slim, almost emaciated, with dark, long stringy hair. Pretty, but nothing that ever drew the attention of the guards or other men.

This woman—she was curvy and packed with muscle like Lora. And her hair had been shoulder length and white, like liquid moonlight.

But her face, a little voice whispered. *It was the same. And so was the voice.*

Lora was inclined to strangle that little voice but became distracted by the sound of a door somewhere down the corridor opening, followed by the sound of several pairs of boots scuffing along the floors.

She moved as silently as she could to the back corner of the cell. It was the most advantageous spot in the cell—not that any spot in a dungy prison cell was *technically* advantageous, especially when chained to the floor in canthite.

Lora strained her ears, but heard no voices. Only the continued sound of footsteps. *Long hallway.* Two people, by the sound of it. *Maybe it's Kacey,* that little voice hoped. Again, she wanted to throttle it.

She listened again to the steps that now seemed to be approaching her. If she was a betting woman, which she was, she'd say it was the rider and the prince.

Within two minutes, she nearly smiled when two figures rounded the corner and Kalon and Garrison stood at her cell door. She did smile when Kalon turned in the dim light, revealing the bruise she'd left on his right eye.

"Hello boys," Lora drawled. "To what do I owe this pleasure?" She still stood with her back against the corner, doing her best to look confident and cocky. Stupidly, she glanced behind them, and the prince instantly noted the shift in her attention.

"Expecting someone?" he asked, his eyebrows rising.

Her face fell into a bland, bored expression. "Only hoping your medic would come by. He's my favorite," she purred, drawing her attention back to the males in front of her. Kalon's eyebrows raised in question and she smirked as she explained, "He has *oh* so gentle hands."

Garrison choked. She would have thought it was a laugh had Kalon not remained so very serious.

"You seem happy for a princess who hasn't managed to escape *either* time she's tried," Kalon crooned, walking the length of the bars.

Lora stiffened—*princess*. Well they figured that out fast. Within a heartbeat she relaxed, tracking Kalon's movement like a predator tracking its prey.

She shrugged, feigning nonchalance, "I'm hoping I get the extended stay upgrade if I'm here long enough."

Kalon paused his pacing, glancing up at her.

She smirked, holding up her chained hands, and gestured to the dirty cell around her. "Don't all your long-term *prisoners* get this wonderful treatment?"

A flash of anger in Kalon's eyes was the only reason she knew she'd struck a chord, but it was gone so fast she thought she might have imagined it.

"Enjoying your stay that much?" He eyed her chains. "Perhaps you could take notes and report them back to daddy. He seems to be the only one keeping prisoners long term."

Lora could live a hundred more lives, and Kalon using the term *daddy* would still probably be the creepiest thing anyone had ever said to her—and she'd heard some creepy shit.

"First of all, ew," she said, pretending to throw up. "And second, I have no idea what you are talking about."

Kalon rolled his eyes and began his pacing again.

"What? Are you trying to say I'm the only long-term prisoner you've had?" She asked, moving her hands to her hips. The motion caused both Kalon and Garrison, who had been keen on simply listening, to still. "Yeah, right."

"Yeah. Right," Kalon retorted. "We don't make a habit of stealing enemy people. That seems to be your daddy's department, princess."

Again, with daddy and that title. She thought she might vomit.

"Again. Ew." She made a gagging sound. "You can't possibly expect me to believe you have no long-term prisoners…" Kalon's flat stare caught her off guard, but she covered her confusion with a smirk. "So what? You just kill them all when you have a tantrum?"

Instantly, faster than she thought possible, Kalon reached through the bars and held her by her cheeks. She hadn't even realized she'd migrated toward the bars. *That's a soft spot— noted. So easy to rile up*, she thought, and Garrison seemed to agree as he grabbed his friend's arm and pulled him from her.

"You should get your walls thickened," she said, rubbing slightly at her cheeks. Kalon was still clearly seeing red, but a small smirk started on his lips at her apparent discomfort. She immediately dropped her hand.

Kalon's smirk grew. "But then how would you learn all your misinformation?" he inquired, his tone dripping with sarcasm.

"By asking a million questions, it seems," Garrison finally chimed in. Her attention snapped to the rider, who looked bored more than anything.

"Glad to hear your voice Gar-Bear," she crooned, winking at him. He coughed as Kalon's eyes narrowed. She smiled. "Oh I'm just asking for a friend," she added, beginning her own pacing, her eyes never leaving Kalon.

A short, shrill laugh broke from Kalon. "I truly believe you are incapable of having friends, princess. And I can guarantee you don't have any here."

She smiled again, this time showing all of her teeth. "I certainly hope not."

Garrison had the right mind to look a tad unsettled at her expression, but Kalon seemed unfazed. "Enough chit chat princess, let's get down to business, shall we?" *Again with the title*, she thought, meeting Kalon's amber and black flecked eyes sparkled with determination.

"Aw, man." Lora pouted. "I thought you were just here to hang out." She smiled broadly, then added, "You know, royal to royal—"

Kalon's smirk faltered.

"Oh no," she crooned. "Did I ruin your plan to throw me off by using my title?" She laughed, cold and bitter. "Sorry," she apologized, in no way sincere.

Kalon seemed to be seeing red again, as if steam would soon sizzle from his mouth.

"Want me to be honest, *prince*?" she asked, crossing her arms over her chest.

His eyes softened slightly. "A*lways*," they seemed to say, before narrowing again.

A shiver worked its way up her spine but she stamped it out. "Well," she drawled, "I quite like how the title sounds coming out of your mouth. And you know something else?" She tossed her braid over her shoulder. Kalon tracked the motion, and Lora noted it was disgust that rippled through him as he watched it sway behind her. "I think you like saying it."

Clearly she'd struck another chord because Kalon was all but vibrating with anger now, his eyes glossy with rage. His skin had an odd glow to it and it seemed, in the dim light, like he might have been glowing. He slowly turned, his attention lingering on her for one moment longer—which made her stiffen—before walking back down the long corridor and disappearing from view. Garrison gave her a wary glance and then strode off after his prince.

Good riddance, Lora thought as she plopped down on the floor of her cell.

But as the anger and adrenaline eased, her mind began racing again, the dread of realizations weighing on her. If she was the longest prisoner they've ever held, that could really only mean one thing for Kacey—she was either dead, or wasn't their prisoner at all.

CHAPTER 11

TO FALL OR FLY?

Lora

No one else came into the dungeons for at least another several hours, maybe even a day. Without any natural light, it was hard for Lora to keep track of time. The torches along the walls didn't help either because they lasted unnaturally long—not one had burned out since she'd been thrown down there. She now stared at the long-lasting flame from her spot on the floor.

After the males had left—or stormed off, in Kalon's case—she'd tried to exercise to keep her mind and body sharp. But with the limited space and the canthite chains, she could only do about two movements—not to mention she hadn't had food or water in at least two days, maybe more. She was already having to peel her tongue off the roof of her mouth every couple of minutes.

She needed water. She needed to find a way out, to think of an escape plan. But once the walls began to press in, she hadn't thought of anything. Hadn't even tried.

She'd just curled up in the corner and stared at the cell wall, stared at the golds and reds that danced along them, her mind wrapping around her like her shadows longed to do. At some point she passed out, but was haunted by her thoughts.

Kacey was a prisoner and is now dead. That has to be true. I saw her beaten and taken by the Drakes. But I heard her here, shouting to the prince like she knew him, trusted him, had a relationship with him. Maybe they tortured her so badly that she eventually forgot who they were, who she was? But she looked healthy, strong, even. Maybe she had gone with them willingly. Hadn't she been reaching out to me when she was taken? But if she was here on purpose, by choice, not a prisoner, then why did she leave me behind? Why not leave a note or send a signal to say she was all right? I have spent the last five years of my life looking for my friend. Everything I've done was to get her back, or to get revenge on those who took her. If Kacey had been fine this whole time...then I really was all those things that flashed in my mind constantly: Monster, Murderer, Coward, Freak, Bastard, Weak, Worthless, Monster.

Each thought was like a tidal wave crashing into her mind, battering her conscience until it was nothing more than pulpy foam. She did nothing to stop the emulsification of herself.

***

The prince did not return, but the bitch did.

Lora was too weak to move anything other than her eyes as she watched Nuva enter her dank cell. The rider said something snarky, but Lora couldn't hear her over the thrumming in her head. She needed water. She must have said as much, because Nuva smirked as she tossed a small canteen to the floor. She couldn't stop her desperate crawl toward the leaking canteen, or the whimper that left her as the cool, sweet liquid slid down her throat. She didn't need to look up to know Nuva was enjoying her depravity.

As Lora finished, she chanced a glance toward the cell door, where Nuva squatted, nearly eye level with Lora's crumpled form.

"Time to go, *your highness*," she said, her voice coming out garbled in Lora's ears. Her mind was a muddled haze as she tried to figure out what Nuva meant.

Then, too quick for Lora's weakened body to block, Nuva's fist collided with her left cheek. Her head snapped to the side, her skin splitting near her eye. A spark of anger ignited as Nuva's laughter echoed off the walls of the dungeon.

"Never," Lora tried to say as she lunged forward, only to feel as though she were stuck in thick mud, her limbs barely operating. She locked eyes with Nuva as the soldier's serpentine smile grew. Her vision blurred, panic rising when Nuva gave a quick glance to the water canister, filling in the final piece of the puzzle. As the darkness took her, Lora finally registered why the water had tasted so sweet. It was laudanum.

They'd drugged her.

CHAPTER 12

TO FLY

Lora

There was such peace in this sleep. Peace like she had not known for a long, long time. Here, her mind did not wander to dead friends or lies. It simply floated in the clouds, a summer sweet breeze flowing around her. She could feel her hair rise and fall across her cheeks and as she opened her eyes, she could see the renewing world from above, bursting with the bright colors of sunrise. She was floating through the clouds, the land below nothing more than a green blur, the trees as small as ants. Another soft wind tossed her hair, and she blinked away the tears that had sprung from her eyes.

I must be dead, Lora thought, looking out over the waking world. It was too beautiful to be anything but the last trip across the sky that souls take before entering the Veil. Her chest tightened at the beauty and wonder that was her world.

She could see Liam, the medic nearby, floating amongst the clouds as well, mounted on—

Her stomach dropped as she dipped below the clouds, flying faster with each wing beat. Flying. She was flying. Not a soul dead on the wind, but a girl strapped to a giant fucking dragon hundreds of feet in the air.

The wonder she had felt moments before soured to anxious fear as she peeked over the edge of the black dragon beneath her. She felt her weight shift and she began rolling, pitching over the side—

"Woah there," came Garrison's gruff voice from behind her, his arm wrapping around her waist and righting her in her seat. "I don't think you'd survive *that* fall, your highness." The dragon beneath her, Emir by the looks of it, chuffed what she knew to be a laugh, and she whipped her head around to see that there was a slight smirk on Garrison's face, too.

She wanted to snap at him, wanted to feel angry, but she felt hollow. So, she focused her attention on trying not to think about the plunging death drop on either side of her. Garrison said nothing else as they continued to fly parallel to the rising sun.

Without moving this time, she glanced over the edge of the beast beneath her to see small streams and trees, but no mountains. "Why are we headed southwest?" she asked, not expecting anyone to answer.

For some reason, her mind felt clearer than it had in the cell. Her thoughts still pulled at her, but she didn't feel like she was drowning in them. It was as if they were being carried away by the winds. She closed her eyes as another strong gust tugged more hair loose from her braid. She knew she was meant to be wrecked, but up in the clouds she felt at peace, almost at home—not that she truly knew what that would even feel like. They were descending, it seemed, and her shoulders relaxed ever so slightly as a citrus filled breeze flitted past.

The dragon beneath her seemed to also relax the same time she did, allowing the breeze to lift the three of them up into an oncoming cloud, higher than they'd been before.

Lora glanced down again at the dragon and wondered what its scales felt like. The dragon stiffened under her hand as she stroked his side. He was warm and smooth, not at all what she expected. She felt a bit lightheaded as she stroked the dragon again, trailing her fingers along its spine and out toward its wing. He shifted beneath her, and she felt a rush of warmth between her legs.

"He…uh…doesn't like when you do that," Garrison said, his voice a bit distant behind her. But he was still close enough for the heat of his breath to dance along her neck.

"Hmmm?" she purred, scooting into him as he adjusted himself, putting distance between them, causing her to immediately crave his warmth. She scooted back more, letting her head fall onto his shoulder as she stroked the dragon again.

She ground her hips behind her and Garrison let out a curse as the dragon suddenly dropped sideways before immediately straightening out again. Her insides began to burn, a heat building in her very bones as a citrus and ember scent curled around her.

Garrison squirmed uncomfortably in his seat as she traced a nail on the inside of the dragon's wing, pushing her backside into Garrison's front. There was a low, guttural sound from the beast beneath her and a shaky breath from the male behind her. "The stroking," Garrison choked out. "He doesn't like the way you're touching his wings. They're sensitive."

Like a bucket of cold water had been thrown over her, Lora sat stick straight. What had come over her? The rider and the dragon both seemed to tense in an entirely different way as she tried to keep as much distance between her and Garrison as possible. Which was rather hard, seeing as he'd strapped them together again.

"I— Uh—" She couldn't form words. Heat filled her cheeks as she felt how she had made Garrison feel pushed against her backside.

Could she plead temporary insanity? Garrison was hard as a rock, the dragon nearly dropped them out of the sky when she'd stroked his wing… *What the fuck was going on?*

Garrison's cough from behind her nearly had her jumping out of her own skin. "It's the altitude," he said, his voice still thick, his breath warm on her neck. "For some, being so high and in the clouds can be…"

"*Hard?*" Emir whispered in her head, his voice thick and laced with dark amusement. It sent a shiver up her spine.

"Challenging," Garrison finished, repositioning himself yet again. "It was like a drug the first time I ever flew," Garrison admitted. He continued, awkwardly filling the silence with the stories of his first flight, though Lora was barely listening.

They began to descend and she realized her thoughts had been fuzzy, like she'd been drugged or intoxicated.

The more they descended, the less fuzzy her thoughts, though the more panic and anger and fear seeped back in. The dragon and rider also seemed to tense the closer they were to the ground. Garrison offered her a drink from his waterskin, and she drank the sweet tasting liquid greedily.

"We should camp here tonight," Garrison said, his voice sounding distant again.

But as she turned to look at their campground for the night a wave of exhaustion slammed into her and she was consumed by a rush of darkness.

The last she heard was Garrison's curse and the chuff of Emir before she passed out.

CHAPTER 13

THE REFUGEE CAMP

Lora

Apparently, Lora was being traded back to the Shades for some Drake commanders. Or at least, that's what was briefly explained to her. The trade was to take place tomorrow at dawn, but the Drakes had wanted to arrive early to scout the land and run some errands. Lora had woken as they landed in a small clearing north of where the trade would take place. Apparently, they hadn't been traveling alone—the minute they had landed in the small clearing, several other dragons immediately launched back into the sky, taking their riders with them.

"Where are they going?" she asked, hoping none of them had witnessed her altitude-induced insanity. Her cheeks heated at the thought of it. Her head was still slightly fuzzy, which kept most of her self-loathing at bay.

Garrison came up beside her and handed her a small pack, not even glancing at the fading shapes. "To Ravell. It's a refugee camp not too far from here."

Her very bones were tired, but she found herself curious enough to ask, "A refugee camp?"

Garrison began unpacking in the clearing as he answered, "Yeah, for people displaced from the war."

"I know what refugees are." She thought of the town they had passed over when they had first kidnapped her, the one they had burned to ash—Noor. "Are they mostly Drakes?" she asked, already knowing what the answer would be.

But it was Emir's rumbling voice in her head that answered, "No."

She had almost forgotten about the dragon. He stood mere feet away, tail swishing slightly in the clearing like an impatient prairie cat, eyes locked on the small shapes still in view.

"They are mostly people from neutral territories or those who wanted to stay out of the war on both sides," Garrison supplied, glancing between the dragon and Lora, a hint of confusion in his eyes.

"What are *you all* doing there then?" she asked, following Emir's gaze and searching for the dragons and their riders. She could no longer see them, but it seemed Emir still could.

"*You mean besides creating and maintaining them?*" Emir questioned in her mind, his head slowly swinging toward them. She shot him a look that was meant to be angry but came off as a bit surprised. *What does he mean, create and maintain?*

"They are delivering food and medical supplies," Garrison said, looking increasingly concerned.

"Is that why Liam went with them?" she asked, refusing to meet the gaze of the dragon who was just feet from her face. For some reason, this conversation was pissing her and the giant beast off equally.

Garrison gave a tight-lipped nod. "He's needed most of the time anyway, so he figured he could go and help out before tomorrow."

Whatever that meant, Lora didn't want to know. The shadows that danced in the rider's eyes made her stomach drop again. Her thoughts began to race and her head filled to the brim, nearly exploding.

The numbness she'd felt in the cell was completely drowned out by her anger. Of course the Drakes would set up a refugee camp for people *they* displaced, and of course they would want to instill fear while they *helped.*

"It seems cruel to show up with dragons..." she said more to herself, trying and failing to think about the next morning—when she would be handed over to Cyrus, when she could finally get answers about Kacey.

A hot blast of air that she knew was a laugh came from her left and she couldn't help but whip her head toward the prick. *How could he laugh at something like this?* "What? You don't think that the people who have been displaced by the war *you* people started would be afraid of giant dragons in their new home?"

Emir's eyes narrowed so much she could barely see his slitted pupils. "*You people...*" He seethed, steam rising in his mouth. "*I do hope you are meaning the Shade Kingdom, because the Drakes—*" Emir, paused, snapping his head to the sky.

Whatever he was going to say was interrupted by the approach of a large brown dragon with an unfamiliar rider atop it. Her blood was still boiling, but both the dragon and his rider seemed to disregard her. The dragon was flying incredibly fast in their direction.

The rider dismounted before the dragon even landed, taking two quick strides to get to Garrison. She opened her mouth to speak but stopped, eyeing Lora.

Noting the stress on the rider's face Garrison nodded, "Speak freely, Sireen."

The rider—Sireen—relaxed a fraction, then cleared her throat. "General Damaris, there is a problem in the camp and your assistance is requested."

Damaris? Was that Garrison's last name?

Sireen shot her gaze to the dragons, both now watching the humans intensely—the brown one eyeing Lora like it wanted to eat her—before addressing Garrison again. "Emir is needed as well," she said stiffly, eying the dragon. "It's urgent."

Lora's mind raced with all the possibilities as the dragon rider finished talking to Garrison.

Emir emitted a chuffing sound that had Sireen rushing back to her dragon and Garrison rushing to him. Lora stood there as the flurry of activity seemed to pass her by. What would require Garrison *and* Emir? And where was Kalon?

As Garrison strapped his pack onto Emir's back, Lora asked, "What's going on?"

"We aren't sure, but it's something to do with the refugees," Garrison said, buckling the final straps on Emir. The dragon gave a small flap of his wings as if testing the weight before settling back down with a nod to Garrison. "There has been an influx and many are wounded at the camp," Garrison explained as he extended his hand to Lora, helping her mount Emir ahead of him.

He buckled them in and said, his voice low with apprehension, "Sireen said something is coming."

Lora felt a shiver work its way up her spine as Emir flapped hard, sending her flying back against Garrison, a small yelp leaving her throat.

Emir snickered before he cooed, "*I won't let you fall, princess. It would defeat the purpose of tomorrow.*"

She didn't have time to be annoyed as they raced into the sky. With her stomach in her throat, Lora used every ounce of self-control she had left to keep her body stiff and her mind sharp. The last thing she needed was another bout of altitude-induced insanity as they headed toward—wherever it was they were headed toward.

She was nervous to ask, but needed to know. "What did they say was coming?"

"Sireen didn't say, but she seemed worried..." Garrison trailed off, as if he was trying to think of what would cause Sireen such stress.

Lora began to feel sick. While the soldiers at the outpost weren't meticulously trained, none of them seemed to be afraid. So to see a rider pale at whatever was coming... A shiver worked its way down her spine, and she dug her nails into her palm to keep herself steady.

"Shadowfire?" Garrison half whispered, half asked, causing her to stiffen further.

But Emir let out a low rumble. "*Death*," he bristled as they approached a small clearing to the left of the now-visible camp.

As they banked wide, Lora's attention fell to the east of the camp, where the sun should have been cresting the hills. But instead, all that could be seen was thick, impenetrable darkness.

***

They landed swiftly, Emir taking back off into the skies before she had even fully dismounted. Something tightened in her chest as she watched him fly toward the growing darkness.

Garrison was a forearm deep into his bag, digging around for something. Even from this distance, Lora could hear screams. Her body began to shake involuntarily as she watched Emir's shape disappear into the impenetrably dark sky. Where he completely vanished, the screams grew louder. She needed to get to them, needed to help. She could help them, save them. It wouldn't make up for everything, but... these people were innocent, regardless of who they were.

"We need to help them, we need to—"

The words died on her tongue as Lora whirled toward Garrison, who stood a few paces from her, canthite chains in hand.

She paled.

"I'm sorry," Garrison choked, looking for all the world like he truly meant it.

She reeled back. "What the hell are those for?"

"Collis, please." Garrison looked like he was going to vomit as he made to approach her. She hated the way he said that name—*Collis*. She hated even more that he didn't want to chain her, he was doing it anyway.

"No." It was a command, a refusal that came out with more strength than she had in her. "No," she said again as Garrison made to move toward her. "I'm not— I won't— -"

Garrison still walked toward her. Panic rose in the back of her throat. She could already feel the oppressive weight of them on her wrists and ankles. Her shadows began to writhe under her skin, begging to be released. They were going to chain her here while all that shit went down. She'd be chained and defenseless. She'd be *chained*.

"Look, I know. For some reason I trust you. But the prince…" Garrison advanced another step and she froze, panic gripping her like a vice.

"Please." She wasn't above begging. Not as she could feel the bite of the chains already digging her skin, the feel of her power being zapped away.

Garrison looked like he wanted to vomit even more as he beheld her shaking form.

"Please," she repeated. "I won't do or say anything, I promise. I won't even come with you—you can tie me to the tree for all I care. But please, *please* Garrison, don't put those chains on me."

She felt, more than saw, his resolve dissolve. Slowly, he lowered the chains. "I can't leave you here unchained. You could run away, or worse."

Worse? What would be worse than ruining their trade deal by fleeing?

"I won't," she said, a little less pleading. "Let me come with you." She hoped her earnestness shone in her eyes.

His resolve crept back in as he looked at her. "I don't trust you that much."

"But you do trust me some," she confirmed, taking a small step in his direction. His nostrils flared as he set his jaw in a hard line, watching her move toward him. "Whatever bit of trust you have, let it be the one to hear me. I only want to help those people. So please, let me help them."

She was very near the edge of begging again when Garrison's eyes softened and she knew she'd won—for now.

***

Kalon

At some point, Kalon hoped the deafening screams would stop, but it had been nearly thirty minutes in the blazing camp, and they hadn't faltered. The fire was excruciatingly hot—even for a Drake—and he feared few would survive this attack.

This hadn't been the first time a refugee camp had been hit. Usually it was a small band of unmarked soldiers, though everyone knew it was the Shade army that would lower itself to killing civilians. The Shades would ransack the place, stealing anything they thought valuable, looking for any powerful Drakes, maybe hit a few people—but this? These people had already been displaced by a war they wanted no part of, and now they and their loved ones, plus whatever was left of their possessions, were being *burned* away.

Burned.

Kalon knew of only one person who would authorize this type of cruelty, and he'd all but invited the bastard here—Cyrus.

***

Lora

Garrison and Lora arrived at the top of the hill overlooking the camp just as another wave of fire erupted. She gasped as Garrison pulled her back by her tunic, the flames dancing toward her, nearly singing off her face.

The camp was in chaos. As she righted herself, she saw just what was happening to the refugee camp below. Whatever structures had been built before were now piles of burned rubble. The smoke was thick in the air and smelled of burning hair and flesh, causing her to rock forward with nausea. Garrison looked equally sick, but his attention was darting to the different forms within the smoke and flames—Drakes. There were Drakes down in the fire helping people evacuate, or trying to stop the flames from spreading.

Garrison tracked several forms and took a lunge forward, only to stop mid stride and turn back to her. "Stay here and stay out of sight," he said quickly before turning and sprinting into the fiery mess below.

She bit at her bottom lip. She could help, couldn't she? Before she could reconsider, she found herself hurtling down the hill in the opposite direction Garrison had gone in. She skirted the outside of the camp, following the sound of screams. If she could just get to the survivors, she could help them to higher ground—

She gasped as a Drake darted into a burning building, another appearing and beginning to seemingly twist the fire, pulling it away from the screaming people nearby. *Firewielder.* The title danced in her mind as she watched in awe.

A large post barreled in the direction of the Drake outside and she lunged forward, shoving the Drake out of the way, the post barely missing either of them by inches.

Once the Drake, a rider by the looks of it, was on her feet, she simply nodded in Lora's direction before returning to the burning building.

"Hey—" she called out, but was cut short as her head filled with a roaring so loud and full of fury, her heart nearly stopped.

Another explosion of fire threw Lora sideways, but seconds after she hit the ground, Lora was back on her feet, trying to find the forms she had been watching before through the black smoke. But what she saw had her knees shaking, threatening to collapse beneath her.

In the center of the camp was Emir's giant form, pulling and pushing at the flames. It was as if he was battling the very fire himself, when suddenly a plume of smoke rose above the rest. Not a regular plume, rather a sharpened, directed, patch of darkness, spearing for Emir, who was too focused on the refugees below him to notice. She didn't give herself time to consider what—or who—that patch of darkness was as she threw every ounce of her shadows toward Emir.

A heartbeat—that's how long it took for her shadows to reach Emir before the other, larger and deadlier, shadow did. That heartbeat felt like an eternity. She should have had no voice left to scream, the thick smoke from the fires clogging her throat, but she shouted as loud as she could at Emir to look out, to move out of the way. And, as if he heard her, he did.

A single heartbeat, and the giant dragon dodged the coming shadows, shoved aside by Lora's own power, and let loose a roar that brought Lora to her knees before a wave of smoke-induced nausea had her keeling over. She took a deep breath, trying to steady herself to rise, but the ground shook again. This time, she felt her magic snap back to her in response. She managed to control her breathing enough to lift her head in Emir's direction, only to see a tunnel of fire and smoke spiraling into the sky, swallowing smoke and Drakes alike—as if all the fires were being pulled off the buildings and people, into the vortex in front of her.

And in the center of the spiral of fire was a giant fucking dragon—*Emir*.

Lora couldn't pull her eyes from the spiral of fire as she rose from the ground. The flames licked and twirled as if in a dance, shooting skyward. Every flame in the camp had been sucked into the tornado of fire that Emir was controlling. She was only slightly aware of others running past her, up the hill and away from the camp.

All of her concentration, all of her very essence surged to mingle with Emir's power. She felt herself fall forward, her own power pushing at her skin for release, and for a heartbeat she considered it—loosening herself, allowing her power to flow freely, unhindered, to see just what it could do. There was a roaring in her head that was not entirely her own. As if it sensed her desire, Emir's fire seemed to dance her direction, and she could have sworn she heard a voice in the back of her mind—

One moment, she was watching the fire spiral grow and expand. The next, she was on the ground, Liam and Garrison's bodies covering her as a blast of extreme heat swept through the camp.

She pushed and struggled to get free—all she could think about was the people she had just seen in the camp, how they would be swallowed by the heat. She could still help them. But the males above her held firm, keeping her from reaching those in need, keeping her from Emir's fire.

"Shit mi fia," she heard Liam grunt as she landed a nasty blow to his abdomen, but still he didn't let go. Still, he and Garrison kept their bodies on top of hers.

When the heat finally died moments later and the males on top of her pulled away, she beheld what the blast of heat had, and hadn't, done.

The camp, or what was left of it, was devoid of any fire. Any heat at all actually, as if it had all been sucked up and blown away by Emir's spiral. Few structures still stood, and there were far too many piles of what she assumed were people.

Lora surged forward then, looking for the people she had seen and felt running by her when she had so stupidly stood in the flames. But they were not there, nor were there piles of bodies where she expected to see them.

She whirled, wide eyed, only to find the hill she and Garrison had been on earlier, packed with people all surrounded by Drakes, all, for the most part, unharmed.

"Fireproof, remember?" Garrison chided her from where he stood, covered in soot but also unharmed. Her only response was the collision of her fist on his face.

CHAPTER 14

THE TRADE

Lora

Lora was still reeling from the display of power Emir had shown at the refugee camp as she and Garrison trudged back up the hill toward their camp for the night. Liam had left after a brief explanation about how the Drakes were impervious to fire, which explained why he and Garrison had thrown themselves over her very flammable body. It was very clear to her that they needed her alive for this trade to happen, and she had endangered that. Garrison had mumbled something to Liam, who glanced at Lora worriedly before he jogged off toward the refugees to help the injured. She could only make out one word from the exchange and it was that one word, mixed with Liam's expression that made her drag her feet right now—Kalon.

She knew she should probably be quiet, but adrenaline was still coursing through her veins, so she found herself asking, "What will happen to them?" They weaved through trees toward the spot Garrison had picked out earlier, Lora dragging out each step.

Garrison hadn't looked back at her but once, when she had gotten stuck on a particularly slick spot coming up the hill. He still didn't now, his voice barely audible over their footsteps. "They will be moved to another camp." His tone was matter-of-factly. as if they had done this type of thing hundreds of times. *Had* they done this type of thing before?

"Not this type of thing exactly, no," he said, again barely audible over the sound of their footsteps. She could just see the side of his face, where the punch she landed was bruising.

Her eyes widened. "Did you just read my mind?" *Holy shit.*

Garrison let out a soft, broken chuckle. "No, Collis, you said that out loud."

She released the breath she'd been holding. "That's a relief. I'd hate for you to hear all my secrets," she said, trying to liven the mood. It did not work. Garrison merely kept trudging through the woods in silence, his mind clearly elsewhere. After a few more minutes of awkward silence, Lora was about to ask another question when they finally arrived at an open area. Garrison froze at the edge of the trees at the same time she was hit with a familiar scent—citrus and ember, although now it was more of a raging fire than smoldering embers.

Kalon stood in the clearing not twenty paces away from where she and Garrison had emerged. She scanned his body quickly—and other than looking exhausted and filthy, he was unharmed. His amber eyes were locked with Garrison's, and it dawned on her that while he would be furious, she hadn't thought about the fact that Garrison had disobeyed his orders to chain her.

She paled. Garrison had directly disobeyed the orders of his prince, and now he would be punished—all because of her.

Something in her chest shifted, and she felt the air leave her lungs. She *cared*?

"It wasn't his fault—" The words died on her tongue, and as quickly as the panic swept in, it disappeared. Garrison's shoulders had relaxed and he was now moving toward where Kalon stood. He bowed slightly and both males put their foreheads together. She thought, for a split second, they would kiss, but as quickly as they embraced they released each other, both looking better than they had moments before.

She had no idea what to make of that—except that it pulled at a memory in her mind from when she was younger. She and Kacey had fought over something stupid, and when they made up, Kacey had touched their foreheads together, explaining it was how you show gratitude or forgiveness. The memory danced in her vision, ideas, and thoughts swirling with it, but before anything could be tangible, she was shoved forward by Nuva, who had seemingly just arrived from the camp.

Nuva and Kalon locked eyes, and another secret conversation flowed between them. Kalon nodded and Nuva, after placing her forehead on his, turned and strode back through the trees she had just come from, making a point to knock into Lora again. As Lora drew her attention back to the camp, she noted that Kalon was actively not looking at her, though the ire leaking off of him was palpable.

She went to move in his direction, why, she wasn't quite sure, but he side stepped her, striding across the camp to where Garrison now began peeling a potato.

After everything that had happened—the fires, the death and destruction—he was going to ignore her? Garrison and Nuva got a forehead touch, and she got *ignored*?

But why should it matter? she chided herself. *Of course they're forgiven—or whatever the forehead thing was. They are his people, and I... I'm nothing. But that's not fair, either. I saved Emir, his people, he could at least look at me—*

Kalon's attention snapped to Lora and she felt an inner conflict raging as he strode the few steps toward her, stopping with no less than a breath between them.

She squared her shoulders, refusing to cower in front of such a pompous asshole, no matter his rank or title.

Kalon's eyes narrowed, and although her gaze did not leave his, she felt Garrison stiffen where he sat. "You were meant to be chained to a tree, *your highness*," he spat the last words with such venom, she was surprised he didn't just kill her then and there.

She, too, narrowed her eyes. "Maybe I didn't like the idea of civilians being killed," she spat back with equal rage, her power surging around her like asps, ready to defend, ready to strike.

"Unlikely," was Kalon's only reply as he made to step away, seemingly unfazed by the pulsing shadows around her. But she wasn't finished with the conversation, and like hell would he get the last say.

"Unlikely?" she repeated, moving into his space so that they shared breath again. "What is so unlikely? Clearly I feel a *tiny* bit that way, as I was in the fray saving *your* people from whatever that hell storm was!"

"My people? Those refugees came from *your* kingdom too, *princess*, and yet you were too busy using your shadows that—"

Her heart splintered. "What?" It wasn't exactly a question, spoken barely louder than a whisper.

"I knew you were ready to see your dear ole dad, so ready that you all but flagged him down with your shadows." Kalon was seething now, his words coming out in short pants.

"I was protecting Emir!" she shouted. But she lost her spark of fury as realization after realization hit her.

"Cyrus isn't my father," she said quietly after a heartbeat. She wasn't sure why, but it mattered to her that they knew that. Even though in every other way, other than biologically, Cyrus was her father. He had been the one to exile her and then raise her after Kacey had been taken. He had chosen her path as any Shade father would have. For a time, she had even embraced the idea of him as her father. Weeks ago even, she would have proudly watched as Cyrus's power incited fear in their enemies—but something had shifted. Hearing Kacey's voice, the chance that she might have actually seen her—alive and well—and now the attack on the refugee camp, something had become dislodged in her core, and she couldn't seem to put it back to how it was.

"Why would a dragon need protection from you?" Kalon seethed, meeting her gaze.

"Cyrus is *not* my father," she repeated, needing him to understand.

"I don't care."

Lora flinched at Kalon's harsh words. He bared his teeth before turning and walking back toward Garrison, the conversation clearly over.

She wasn't sure why, but she did care. And it was that thought that had her curling up at the edge of the camp, waiting for sleep to claim her. At least tomorrow she would be returned, even if she wasn't sure she wanted that anymore.

***

A small vibration woke Lora from her fitful sleep, and by the time she was fully awake, the camp was a flurry of activity. Somehow, in her sleep, someone had managed to bind her wrists—in rope, thankfully. She marveled at how deeply she must have slept for someone to have been able to do so, but then again they could have easily slipped her some of the sleeping drought they had used on her before.

Either way, when she sat up that morning, hands bound, mouth dry, and sun blinding, she had one thought in her mind: home. She was going home.

She didn't give any space in her muddled mind to what that home would look like, what kind of welcome she would receive. Only that she would be free of these people and back with her own.

After her eyes finally adjusted to the sun she instinctively scanned the camp, realizing quickly that there were a lot of faces she had not seen before, along with several dragons.

The dragons seemed uninterested in the comings and goings of the Drake riders, so she turned her attention to the group of people clad in Drake crimson, seemingly arguing over a map. Though she only assumed it was a map since she could not rise from her spot on the ground—it appeared, much to her chagrin, that they had bound her feet as well. *Had to have been Garrison*, she thought to herself, remembering how gentle and featherlight his touch had been when she was with him in the caves. *When they kidnapped you*, she reminded herself, and although her original captor stood in the group of Drakes and the dragon, Emir in the small group of dragons, the arrogant prince was nowhere to be seen.

She scanned the camp again, *just to get her grounding*, she lied to herself, her gaze sweeping over the small group—now breaking apart—and finally landing on Emir. The dragon was looking directly at her and she felt her skin prickle, the hairs on her arms and neck standing up. His eyes narrowed, and she could have sworn she felt his chuff from where she sat.

You're welcome, by the way, she thought, squinting her eyes at the black dragon.

Emir cocked his head as if to say, *"For what?"*

Saving your ass yesterday, you big asshole. She rolled her eyes, of course the dragon wouldn't care—he and Kalon were probably in sync with how they felt about her.

Emir chuffed in her direction, causing the other dragons to step away from him. "*Should the actions of yesterday negate all other actions?*"

You don't know anything about my life. She was becoming increasingly angry that she was having to explain herself to a fucking dragon.

"*I know enough.*" Emir's immense form turned then, putting his back to her as the small group of riders began advancing toward them.

She stared at him until a twig snapped behind her, causing her to whirl around, only to be greeted by Liam's smiling face, his hands full of fruits and various breakfast foods.

"Good morning," he said, creeping closer but staying out of reach. "I didn't mean to startle you."

She looked at him suspiciously as Liam placed the fruits and food on the ground between them. She debated arguing that she hadn't been startled, but decided against it, turning her attention back toward the bustling camp, her eyes scanning the riders for the arrogant—=

"He's not here," Liam said, her attention snapping to him as he peeled an orange, his forearm tattoos gleaming in the sunlight.

"Who?" she asked, feigning disinterest as glanced toward the dragons.

"Kalon," Liam replied, matter-of-factly. "That's who you're looking for, right?" He didn't look up at her, but she could see a hint of a smirk making an appearance. Seems he, too, was feigning disinterest.

She rolled her eyes as she pulled her gaze from the now-mounting riders.

"No. Why would I be looking for that asshole?"

Liam looked at her as if he could see straight through her lie, a full smirk now dancing on his lips, but he stayed quiet. The silence stretched between them, becoming uncomfortable. Lora broke first.

"I just figured since Emir is here and someone said they're inseparable..." She tried to say it casually, but even to her ears, it was obviously not.

Liam didn't pause his peeling as he stated frankly, "They are, but Kalon has more important things to do today." She looked askance at the medic. For some reason she felt offended. Kalon had more important things to do than retrieve his comrades from his enemy? What was more important than a prisoner trade?

Another long beat of silence stretched between them as Liam peeled and sliced several more fruits before pushing a small pile of them in her direction.

She looked to the sliced fruit, and then to Liam. She had half a nerve to not eat anything just so that he had wasted his time.

When she made no move to eat, Liam sighed and plopped an orange slice in his mouth before saying, through chews, "You know, as a medic I give all the riders a little snack before they fly—especially the newer ones."

Lora shot her eyebrows up as if to say, *So?*

Liam's smirk shifted to a lopsided grin. "It has long been believed that having food on your stomach can help reduce the effects of the alte-sum." When she raised her eyebrows higher, the jackass didn't explain further.

"And what exactly is an alte-sum?" she asked through gritted teeth—she was done talking to Liam or anyone else in this camp.

"It's not exactly a real illness," Liam explained, now gathering the fruits he'd kept on the side into his hands. "Funnily enough, it directly translates to 'high fly', but many new fliers, at certain altitudes, get a little…off."

"Off?" she asked, deciding at the same time that she didn't actually care what this high fly shit was—she wasn't going to eat his fruit, anyway. Purely out of spite.

"He means horny," came Garrison's gravelly voice from behind her. She nearly startled at how quietly he'd approached, and when he finally came into view, she noticed the greenish-blue bruise blossoming on his cheek.

Lora couldn't, however, stop the heat from flushing her cheeks. Before she could come up with a response, Garrison explained the plan. More to Liam, she realized, but she was happy to know what was going on.

"We will leave in five minutes, once everyone's eaten." He paused and made a point to slide his gaze toward her and her pile of untouched fruit. "And then it's about a fifteen-minute flight to the drop spot." He turned to Liam and said, "Kalon has asked that you remain behind in case things don't go well, or, in the more likely event, we end up wounded."

Wounded? They have a peace accord with Cyrus's general for the day, who is getting wounded?

But she didn't have any time to ask questions, because Garrison was already striding toward the other riders, fruits in hand. "Eat," he called over his shoulder as he himself popped an apple slice into his mouth before passing the rest of the fruit out.

She made no move toward the fruit, but her stomach gave her away with a loud grumble. Apparently it had a stronger will than her mind, and after all, if Liam was right that the food would help with the altitude insanity, then by all means she should stuff her face. In no way did she want to experience that kind of heat again—the embarrassment or the...other feeling.

As she ate a slice of orange that had her stomach doing flips for more, she realized Liam hadn't stopped staring at her since Garrison had walked away. He seemed as though he wanted to say something, but chose not to. He rose, but before he started walking away, he turned to her and whispered under his breath, "You saved my cousin yesterday. Thank you."

Again, before she could respond, Liam was already at the group of riders, checking bandages and speaking softly to the dragons.

***

Lora had barely finished the pile of fruits when Garrison was back in her space and hauling her to her feet. Though she was bound in rope at the wrists and ankles, it had been done in a way that allowed her to move with relative, albeit restricted, mobility.

Within minutes she was on Emir's back, Garrison climbing behind her and tying her to him like he had before. She rolled her shoulders, preparing for the launch upward that always sent her stomach to her toes. Emir seemed to straighten under her in annoyance as she repositioned herself atop him, trying to balance while her hands were tied. *Moody ass dragon.*

As Garrison made the final checks on her restraints, Emir swung his large head back to them, his black scales glistening in the sunlight. She could feel the ire leaking off him as their gazes met, the dragon's eyes narrowing as he let out a chuff of hot air.

"It seems he's decided not to like me now," Lora said, pushing a loose strand of hair behind her ear. Her gaze never left the dragon's as he chuffed hot air at her again.

She raised her eyebrows expectantly. *Not talkative anymore?*

No response from the dragon, other than his head returning to face the forest around them.

"One could argue that he never liked you," Garrison chimed from behind her, bracing his hands in front of her waist as he tied the final strap down. Emir chuffed again, and she rolled her eyes. *Of fucking course a dragon doesn't like me—that's not the point. The point was I saved his ass, and no one besides Liam has even said thank you. A bunch of ungrateful assholes.*

"Well, he can get in line—"

Her words were ripped from her throat as Emir launched skyward, beating his wings fast and hard to get them into the cloud cover before settling into a steady pace.

The clouds were cool against her skin. A shiver worked its way up her spine as Emir banked and caught up to the small host in the clouds. The fifteen-minute flight passed quickly and right as Lora adjusted to the bitter cold of the misty clouds, they began descending toward an outcropping of trees on the edge of a short cliff.

As they flew closer, she caught a glimpse of a small battalion of Shade soldiers, only noticeable as a clump of black in the relatively green forest. They circled the cliff several times, looking for a place to land, she realized, before they were back in the clouds again.

"There is nowhere for all of us to land, so Simone and Tyson are going to go down and get two of our commanders first." Garrison's voice was barely audible over the whipping of the wind. She had no idea who Simone and Tyson were, but she nodded anyway as two dragons fell out of formation and headed toward the cliff edge.

"Once they are back in the air we will land on the edge and do the final trade."

Lora's stomach lurched again as Emir dipped beneath the cloud cover, following the path Simone and Tyson had taken moments before. When they emerged from the clouds, she could make out the two dragons and their riders perched on the cliff edge. Three hooded figures were brought forward and two of them were handed over. Emir grunted as they hovered, and she began to shake as another figure walked into the clearing. The stout, pale, dark-haired figure was flanked by two guards and a tall, gangly male. He paid no heed to the dragons and Drakes in front of him, instead, his attention shot skyward, to the rest of the host.

And she knew, with no amount of uncertainty, that it was to her that the man now looked.

The dragons launched into the air and Emir made to swoop down onto the edge. With another shiver, Lora felt the burning gaze of the man she once called father.

King Cyrus.

CHAPTER 15

THE BETRAYAL

Lora

Cyrus actually came. The King of the Shades left his high tower in the Shadowlands to come here for this trade. She couldn't believe it. Even as Emir landed and she was released to his guards and the hooded Drake commander was sent over to Emir, she still couldn't believe it.

A minute later there was a gust of wind and Emir and Garrison were in the air, hovering below the clouds as the dragons adjusted themselves with the new weight they now bore.

"I see the tall brute had several bruises and a black eye. Do I have you to thank for his current condition?" It was the first thing the king had said to her since the trade had happened, and his gruff voice was like a song she had been hearing since birth. The pride in his voice usually filled her with warmth, and yet now, she shivered as he smiled down at her. She nearly winced.

"Yes, Cyr—" she started, but a sharp look from the man had her clearing her throat. "Yes, your grace. It was while I tried to escape." Not a lie, although it was when she was trying to escape to save the refugees. *But not telling the full truth isn't considered a lie, right?*

"A shame you did not succeed. But alas, we are here now, and you are back with your people."

It was said matter-of-factly, though something in Lora recoiled at his words. This is what she had wanted. The best possible result after being captured by the Drakes. She guessed the *best* possible result would be having Kacey safely with her.

But Kacey is safe, a little voice in her head told her. She hated that little voice.

"Although," he added, noting her hair, "Our people do not need to be reminded of the stain that was your mother and her traitorous actions."

She had completely forgotten her hair dye had washed out days ago in the frozen river. Fitting that she was exposed the first time in a frozen river. Now again, her shame stems from another unpleasant series of events. Events she was still processing. "Also from when I tried to escape," she explained, frowning at her blood-red hair that had come out of its braid. She lowered her gaze, her face tilted toward the ground and palms open in supplication.

The king's attention turned fully to her, his gaze snagging on the faint Troth mark before his voice dropped to a whisper as he leaned in close to Lora, nearly face to face. "I am disappointed in you, *daughter*, that you did not kill them on sight. After everything they have done to you and your people, to your *dear friend*, I would have thought I would be grieving your loss, not trading for your return."

Her blood chilled at the king's words. He was right. She should have killed them on sight, the minute she found out who they were. It should've been her only priority, but something had changed. She had decided against killing any of them. *Why?* A little voice in her head whispered the answer, but she shoved it away.

"I was learning as much information as I could, your grace," she said, eyes lowering further, now fully looking at the ground again. "To be of better use to you, to the kingdom, and to help end the war."

It was what she'd been spoon fed since birth—the war must end. And once she matured, she'd been told *she* was the deciding factor. That she would bring an end to the Drakes once and for all. The King had said it was fate. He said it with such confidence, such conviction, most of the time she believed him.

"Yes, yes. A good reason for you to be alive then," purred Marcus, to her left. *When had he gotten so close to me?* "A shame that none of that information will likely be helpful seeing as they'll be dead." His smile had always unnerved her. There were too many teeth. And they looked too sharp. Of course he came with Cyrus, he was basically a lap dog for her adopted father.

"What?" She turned her attention away from the creep and focused on the king. He was simply staring out to where the dragons were still hovering, the repositioning taking longer than she thought it would. They would need to fly slow and low with the extra weight of their returned prisoners, who still seemed to be hooded.

Her blood sang to return with them. To feel the wind whipping in her face while she rode Emir. Emir and Garrison both had even looked back at her once, as if hearing that same song. Her stomach dropped and she felt a pang of something—disgust? Worry? *They held you prisoner. They beat you. What the fuck are you thinking?*

"Your grace?" she prodded, bringing herself out of her own mind and hoping Cyrus would strike Marcus for his ignorance. The king had made a deal—no harm from him during the trade. She'd seen his signature on the paper and had confirmed its authenticity.

"Yes, Marcus speaks true," the king said, causing her to gape and Marcus to sneer. "They will never make it back to their wretched keep," he concluded, a feral smile spreading across his face as he looked longingly at Emir's hulking form.

"But, your grace, if I may, how will you get around the trade agreement?" she asked, looking around nervously. Something didn't sit right with her. She shouldn't care what happened to her captors. The ones who took Kacey and probably killed her, as the king had just reminded her. They were monsters, murderers, and thieves—and yet she had sworn she'd seen Kacey walking amongst them not two days ago. Only, it couldn't have been her. The girl, the woman she saw, had moon white hair and a silver sheen to her skin. She was in what looked like riding clothes—breeches and a vest—nothing like the Kacey she remembered. And she had been safe and unharmed as she ran through the outpost toward *Nuva*, of all people.

"Shoot them." The demand brought her out of the fog of her memories.

"What?" She didn't think she'd heard him right.

"Did I stutter, or has your hearing been impacted by their particular methods of torture? I said, 'shoot them.'" The king did not turn his attention to Lora, but still she could feel his impatience at her delay. At her reluctance to follow orders. Never once had she refused an order before. Always she had been his dutiful "daughter". His *weapon*. He had traded for her. He loved her in his own way.

She had no idea why it mattered but the question slipped out before she had time to stop herself. "But…why?"

The king turned slowly to her, rage reddening his pale skin, contrasting sharply with his black eyes and blue-black hair. "Why?" he spat at her, his brows rising further than she thought possible.

"I mean," she amended, taking a deep breath. "You promised no harm would come to them. You gave them back their soldiers in exchange for me. I am only curious as to your change of heart. Was it not a fair trade?"

The king let loose a harsh laugh that sent a shiver up her spine, her arm hairs raising in its wake. The soldiers behind her found her comment funny as well, echoing the king's vicious laugh.

"A fair trade? They do not know what they have given up, do they? And for what? Their dead commanders and their own inevitable deaths." The king was again looking after the dragon and its rider, smug victory on his face.

"Fools, your grace," said Marcus, nodding in agreement. She *really* hated that fucker. He always gave her the creeps and was too touchy when he trained with her and her shadows. If he hadn't been so close to the king, she would have killed him by now.

A blink was her only show of surprise at his words—*dead comrades*? Their inevitable deaths? But he couldn't mean now—that the Drakes were *already* dead? He'd promised no harm…

"Dead? Your grace?" Her mind worked as she began to piece her king's horrible betrayal together.

"Of course, they're dead. It has been long established that Shades do not barter or negotiate with these traitors and thieves. It is beneath us, as you do well to remember." The king no longer looked smug as his gaze settled on hers. Her skin crawled with the weight of it, the power behind it. She stared at him blankly.

"Shoot them down and let us leave this festering swamp before the fires start." It was a command, one her blood sung to fulfill but her heart trashed against, and she began to back away. *Fires? What is going on?*

"I …" She straightened to her full height, confidence swelling in her chest. "No."

Marcus's eyes widened. "You dare defy the king's orders?" he asked, making to move toward her. She side stepped him and approached the king's right side.

"No?" He turned to face her fully, his face reddening.

"No," she repeated, her bravado slowly fading as the king's eyes blazed with fury, his shadows growing behind him. Her own shadows seemed to pulse in answer, excited by the challenge. She kept her eyes focused on the king's, her chin high.

"No, what?" He was so close, she could see the lack of soul in his all-black eyes. A vein in his temple bulged and she knew she was seconds away from a lashing. Regardless of who was around, the king would strip her bare and whip her for her insolence. She needed to change tactics. She swallowed the lump of fear rising in her throat. She needed to think, and do so quickly…

"No. I will not shoot them down," she repeated, earning her a somehow sharper look from the king and raised eyebrows from Marcus, who looked excited to see her bleed. She breathed again and, lowering herself into a kneel, continued, praying that it would work. "You swore on your life you would not hurt them, and how could I, as your obedient servant, allow you to be harmed in this way?" The words burned her throat as surely as Drake flames would. She kept her eyes to the ground, knowing the king would like the show of respect, of devotion, of supplication.

He straightened and, wearing a wicked smile of satisfaction, lifted her chin. "Of course, dear child. It is clear now to me where your refusal comes from. Not in defiance, as

Marcus here has suggested, but in concern. How very brave." While his voice was calm, it did not reflect the unmatched rage in his eyes. He may have sounded understanding, but once they were in private, she had no doubt she would bear scars from this interaction. "You have been away for quite some time. It is, of course, understandable that you would be filled with concern." His face softened with his words, but his eyes remained flaming with fury. "However," he continued, loud enough for all those with them to hear, "it is misplaced. I am in no danger of harm in this, my child."

The term would be heard as endearing, maybe even loving, to any around them, but it sent another shiver down her spine. She would *definitely* have a scar from this.

She bowed her head again as he released her chin. Cyrus continued, no longer looking her way as he spoke to the group of Shade soldiers around them. She trembled as he spoke. From fear or shame, she did not know.

"The Drakes believe that we have allowed them and their despicable commanders to be returned to them," he said, opening his arms to gesture to where the Drakes now flew away. She could still make out Garrison riding Emir, the now un-hooded Commander Jade in front of him clinging to the parcel she carried. Something wasn't right. The hood was now removed from Jade, but she couldn't make out a face. *Why doesn't it look like a female...or really even a human? And why is Garrison moving around so much in the air? That can't be safe, for him or Jade.*

Her attention snapped to the King as he said, "When in fact, those hooded are our soldiers; martyrs who volunteered to slay the riders who hold them and take back the dragons that are rightfully ours by any means necessary." *Soldiers, not the Drake commanders. But where are the Drakes?*

"Oh sire," purred Marcus, a feline grin spreading across his ashen features as he stepped forward from the crowd. "Do tell them what is in the parcels that our brave soldiers carry."

A surge of energy pulsed through the group of soldiers as they eagerly waited for their king to reveal the truth. Lora, however, was only filled with dread. Whatever it was, it wasn't good for the Drakes. Marcus was far too happy for it to be anything short of horrific.

Her stomach dropped as her adopted father, the King of the Shades, said, smiling directly at her, "Their comrades' heads, of course."

Jade, Kalon's lover's head, now sat in the lap of a soldier pretending to be her, whose goal was to kill Garrison and take Emir.

She was glad Kalon wasn't here for this. Her blood began to burn, her ears filled with roaring that might not have been solely hers. Cyrus had lied. He had lied, and was now asking her to shoot them out of the sky to make it what? *Easier* for his soldiers to take the dragons? To shackle Emir? The thought almost made her laugh—to shackle a beast that mighty would not only be nearly impossible, but cruel.

"Daughter," the king called, his gaze never leaving hers. "As I have pledged, I will not be the one to harm the Drakes as they leave." A pause before another smile crept across his face—this one promising pain. "But you are not I, and so, it will be you who deals the blow that will allow our soldiers the upper hand. Your blow that will end their lives. This blow will avenge your dear friend, as I know you long to do. For her, Collis, I will command one last time: Shoot. Them. Down." The last words he emphasized as his eyes began glowing, his shadows growing. They were a tidal wave behind him, one her own shadows grew to match in response. *Collis*—her name given by Katalina, and spit as a curse.

Lora swayed where she stood. She was out of options. He had seen her hesitation and cornered her with his speech and demand. To refuse him now was to sign her own execution, regardless of how useful she was. Not to mention the soldiers now being carried away by the Drakes were sure to kill them, anyway. The death she offered would be swifter and painless. But to kill them from behind, to kill them at all—something inside her screamed and raged that it was wrong. Because it *was* wrong. But had that stopped her before?

She didn't give herself any more time to consider as she took a shaky step forward, opened her palm, and erupted power toward the dragons and their riders.

Her shadows exploded from her almost uncontrollably—*almost*. She guided them ever so slightly, and where she aimed, soldiers fell. First, the riders of the dragons cascaded off their mounts' backs, then the Shade soldiers masquerading as the fallen Drake commanders fell next. Her shadows knocked into them and they were rocketed off the dragons, falling to the earth quicker than the riders—letting it appear that the riders were slowed by a soft wind or a shadowy breeze.

The dragons, in their confusion, dove for the riders first, catching them and hurrying away as the unhooded figures collided with the ground, the crunch loud even from where she stood. The parcels they had carried—the heads of the Shade commanders—fell away with them, splashing into the raging river below.

Still her shadows erupted, arching into the sky and draping the dragons and their recovered riders in darkness. Her power flowed and flowed and she was glad she'd eaten earlier. The King bellowed something from her left, but still she funneled all her power into that drapery, praying the dragons had good eyesight in the dark.

Suddenly she fell sideways, her shadows ceasing as fast as they'd burst from her as her face collided with the ground. Two soldiers had tackled her.

"Out of control bitch," spat Marcus as he clamped canthite chains around her wrists. "You hit our soldiers, too."

Lora's remaining shadows vanished immediately as the cold chains bit into her calloused skin. She was hoisted to her feet and was half dragged, but half staggered toward where the king stood, giving orders to his remaining soldiers. Many, she could see, had already sprang into action, charging toward where the dragons had last been seen. Because now… Now the sky was clear, and she smiled to herself as a small bead of hope spread in her. *They must have landed. They had to have*, it whispered to her.

As the last of the soldiers charged away, King Cyrus noted his adopted daughter's smile and slapped it right off her face, snapping her neck to the side with the force.

"You weak bitch," he hissed, picking her up by her hair from where she'd fallen on the ground. "I'd hoped you'd kill the Drake scum on sight, but instead, you developed some sort of empathy for the thieves. Some deranged mercy for the refuse." He dragged her to the edge of the ledge they were on, and her mind raced with every possible outcome.

"It was an accident," she croaked out between gritted sobs, the hair ripping from her scalp feeling like hundreds of needle pricks. "I haven't used my powers in so long—they had the same chains—"

Her explanation was cut short as the king threw her to the ground in front of him. She knew what would come next, but it didn't stop the pain as his steel toed boot rammed into her side, her ribs crunching with the impact.

"It was no accident and you know it," he seethed, grabbing her again and setting her on her knees. "Don't lie to me, girl. I am your king."

Lora's face still stung from the blow he'd dealt her moments before. She could feel her heartbeat in her side, and she couldn't take a full breath. *Yep, definitely some broken ribs.*

"Look at the king when he speaks to you," demanded Marcus from somewhere to her left. Her vision was blurry, but she could just make out his ganglious shape in her peripheral.

The king paced in front of her, considering her punishment. "You have failed me, Collis. I, who put so much faith in you. Who nurtured you as my own daughter."

Lora's mind swam as Cyrus suddenly delivered another blow, this time to her other cheek, snapping her head to the side.

"But what is the most disappointing, is that you have failed your kingdom, Collis."

The words hit her like a physical blow. Her heart pounded. There were good people in her kingdom—

"Innocent people," Cyrus said, interrupting her thought, "who will die now because of your carelessness, because of your *mercy*." The king hated that word, always saying it like a curse. "And we both know what mercy is, don't we?"

She did know what mercy was, especially to her king. A *weakness*. She had the scars to show for it. The scars the men in front of her—the king and Marcus—had both dealt her.

"But don't worry child," the king continued, now looking past where the dragons had been, to the small, cleared area in the valley she knew hid the new makeshift refugee camp. She followed his gaze and saw a trickle of smoke spread over the area. "Your act of mercy has inspired me." He turned his gaze to hers, and another wicked smile presented itself. "My men have been dispatched to a small camp not too far from here. It seems my fires yesterday did not deter them and because, as you and I are both aware, the Drakes would destroy it anyway, my orders to burn it to the ground are *merciful* to say the least. Would you not agree?"

Lora gaped at the King, her blood running cold and then heating back up again. *It's wrong.* He was going to burn the makeshift refugee camp down in spite of her, even after burning down the original the day before. He *was* burning the refugee camp, right now. *It's wrong.* It was a test, she knew, to see if she would stand against him as she had about killing the Drake riders. And in that moment, for the first real time, she hated him. She hated what he had made her into, and she knew this was one of the tests she would fail.

And so, with a shaky breath, she launched herself at the king.

He had been waiting, it seemed, as he caught Lora by the arm and swung her toward Marcus, whose closed fist collided with her temple. She rolled under his grasp and kicked, hard, in Marcus's direction. To her imminent satisfaction, the fucker went down with a loud thud. She spun again, freeing herself from the king's grasp only to be caught in a web of his shadows. Her own shadows stirred under her skin, but with the canthite chains still around her wrists, they had no escape.

She writhed in the king's shadowy grasp, but it was no use—they were as strong as the canthite hanging from her. The shadows swarmed her and grew heavy, forcing her back to her knees. The king dusted off his clothes while Marcus rose from his former place on the ground, a trickle of blood coming from his nose. *Good. At least I got a shot in on him before they drag me to some hole in the ground and leave me to die.*

The king frowned as he wiped his brow of the sweat that had beaded there—at least he'd broken a sweat. A smug smile appeared on Lora's face, despite herself.

The king's frown deepened at that. Marcus, finally righting himself, came to stand at her father's side. She looked to the king, the man who had sent her to Attica as a young child, the man who created her, honed her, and all she felt was hate. The king must have seen that in her eyes, for he merely frowned at her before turning away and saying to Marcus, "She is of no use to me in the Shadowlands. Dispose of her." And then he was gone, striding toward the billowing camp below.

Lora's attention whipped to Marcus as he approached her, the king's shadows still holding her in a kneeling position. But her mouth was able to move, so she asked the question that had been burning in her since the outpost.

"Why did the Drakes steal Kacey?" she blurted, half out of a need to know, and half to buy her some time. Marcus had turned around and was fiddling with something behind him—his back to her was an insult in itself.

Marcus didn't even look up from whatever he was doing as he answered, annoyance filling his tone, "What?"

"Kacey, my friend," she explained, trying to see what Marcus had in his hands. "Why did the Drakes take her?"

Still, he didn't turn to her, but he did pause, agitation in his voice as he answered, "Because of who she was to you, I'm sure."

He made to move but she pushed further, stalling as long as she could while her mind raced. "But no one knew who I was in Attica. So how would the Drakes?"

This time, he turned to face her, an unloaded crossbow in his hands. She didn't let her gaze linger on the weapon, instead keeping her eyes focused on the creepy fuck's face. "Probably because she looked so delicious," he crooned.

Lora's stomach turned. "How would you know what she looked like? You never met her—"

Her speech was cut short as Marcus loaded an arrow into the weapon and smiled. "Enough chit chat. You are a blight to the kingdom. A disgrace and a traitor, and so you will die like one," he purred. And before she could register what was happening, Marcus shot her in the chest and shoved her over the ledge.

The last thing Lora saw as the soldiers tossed her into a pile of refugee corpses was the screaming faces of children as her kingdom's soldiers burned their camp to the ground. Then there was a deafening crack in the back of her head, and she was consumed by flames and smoke and nothingness.

CHAPTER 16

DEAD?

Lora

Searing pain. Wet tunic. Loud shouts and the smells of burning. Strong hands at her side. Stronger hands on her shoulders. Roaring in her ears. Pain, unending pain. Then, nothing.

***

Blinding light. Whipping wind. More pain. Flailing arms, kicking legs. Muffled grunts. Sudden pain. Then, nothing.

***

Quiet. No screams of terror. No smells of charred flesh. Just peaceful quiet, the occasional flapping of leathery wings, and a muted pain in her shoulder and head.

"You have to drink Mi Fia, please." The medic almost sounded concerned as he tipped her head back and let some more hot liquid slide down her throat.

Lora didn't move away as he poured the rest of the mug down her throat. She didn't move when he carried her away or when he patched up her wound. She barely registered the flare of pain. She barely registered anything. The darkness still surged around her, and she welcomed it.

***

Lora peeled her eyes open and thought she may have crossed to the other side of the veil. But upon further inspection, she doubted her room in the eternal halls would have such a comfortable bed, or that Liam the medic would be sitting in a chair across from her.

His eyes fluttered as if he'd been trying to stay awake, but he had just recently succumbed to sleep. And by the looks of it, he had been there for quite some time—piles of plates and cups littered the area around him, as if he'd had food brought in. She took a second to observe her surroundings. Firstly, she was in new clothes, her hair pulled out of her face and braided, and her shoulder and arm were bandaged all to hell. While she didn't see any dirt or grime on her, she still smelled faintly of charred wood and ashes. She noted, too, that she was no longer in the outpost. The air coming from the small window was too crisp to be in a valley. *Where the hell am I?*

The chamber was spacious, the bed she was currently snuggled into occupying a third of the room. Across from the bed was a stone fireplace and a small chair turned toward her, the one Liam was currently sleeping in, a side table beside it.

To the left of Liam was a large door that must have led outside of the room, and to the right of the fireplace, beside a small window, was a wardrobe. The only other door was a small one to the left of the fireplace that she supposed led into a bathing chamber. And based on the sounds, someone was using it.

Her heart rate picked up, causing her shoulder to ache and throb. She shot her eyes to Liam, but the medic was still drifting off. *Not a soldier*, she reminded herself.

Liam may have been unconcerned, but she didn't want to be caught unprepared for whoever would come out of that chamber. And with her hurt shoulder, her shadows seemed inclined to remain hidden, so she needed a weapon in case she needed to fight her way out—shadows or no.

Looking around, she spotted a dirty kitchen knife on one of the discarded plates next to Liam. It looked dull, but it would have to do.

She slowly eased herself from the bed, noticing that whoever dressed her put her in a nightgown that was nearly to the floor. She rolled her eyes—not ideal for running or fighting. But a small smile crept across her face, because it was like the ones that Kacey—

Her thoughts were derailed as her foot made the wooden floorboards creak so loud, she thought the sound might echo.

Liam may not have been a soldier, but he was up and in a fighting stance immediately, the knife in his hand. She rose from her hunched position, and the medic's shoulders relaxed a fraction.

"Sorry, I… I must have dozed off," Liam admitted, rubbing the back of his neck with his free hand. "You look better than the last time I saw you."

She cocked her head. Was he complimenting her, or had she looked that terrible when they had taken her to the trade? Liam's gaze softened and she realized that no, the outpost wasn't the last place he saw her—he must have been the one to heal her after…

Lora swayed on her feet and Liam was there in an instant, grabbing her arm and easing her onto the bed. Her head swum as memories flashed in her mind. Her shoulder began aching in earnest, and she felt a pulling sensation beneath the bandages.

"Shit," Liam cursed, looking down at her shoulder. "I think you pulled some stitches out." He reached up to look but paused and threw his gaze to hers. Lora nodded once. Liam nodded back and, after blowing on his hands, pulled the neckline of her gown down enough to inspect the bandages.

"How long?" she croaked, her throat dry.

"You've been asleep for a couple of hours," he said, moving the bandages and gently touching the wounded area. "But it's been about a month since your first injury."

Lora nearly tipped over again. A *month*. She had been taken off the battlefield, beaten, and then shot, all in the span of a month. Damn.

"They don't look too bad," he said more to himself than her as he peeled back another section of bandages. "But you'll need to be more careful when you move around." He gave her a knowing look. "I don't think the scar will be too bad either," he said, folding her gown's neckline back so that her shoulder and neck were covered again. "Not that you care," he added with a wink.

Lora merely stared at him in disbelief. *Is he making a joke? Does he not know who I am?*

He turned, heading toward the small side table and picked up a glass, inspected it, and poured some water into it, then brought it to her. "Keeping you hydrated is the best way to make sure the stitches heal fast," he explained, handing her the cup. "Which was probably why the ones Garrison put in didn't stay."

She nearly spit out the water she had just decided was safe to drink. *Oh shit.* She hadn't even thought about the fact that she was back in a Drake stronghold, and while this was a far better accommodation than the cells of the outpost, she had no intention of being a prisoner again. Who knew what they planned to do with her now.

Liam noted the panicked gleam in her eye and took a small step toward her.

"Is..." She wasn't even sure what she was going to ask, but Liam cut her off as the door to the small room unlatched.

"Kalon doesn't know you're here," he said quickly, and paused, as if considering his next words carefully. "But someone else does."

Lora could already hear people talking in the hallway, but her attention was fixed ahead as the smaller door in the chamber opened.

A small gasp left her throat as Kacey came stepping into the room.

***

Kacey was exactly as Lora had remembered her, except she wasn't covered in blood and bruises like the night Lora thought she had been killed, and her hair...

"Kacey?" Lora stammered, wincing as she tried to sit up. She pushed through the pain and leaned against the headboard of the large bed. Liam eyed both women warily, the small blade back in his hand.

Kacey took one step forward, and the words came tumbling out of Lora, barely more than a sob, like a damn had broken. "I thought you were dead. I... I saw you get taken... You were all bruised, they'd beaten you and then they had dragged you to that town of sympathizers and I saw them haul you away. I..." The next words faded away as Kacey's lip began to tremble. "Kacey?" she whispered.

Kacey was on her then, throwing herself into Lora's arms. The force of the embrace hurt like hell, but all Lora could think about was her friend, her very much alive friend. The girls sat, hugging, for a few minutes, the only sounds that of their silent sobs.

Liam had backed away but remained close by, between the girls and the main door.

"I don't understand." Lora sobbed into Kacey's shoulder. "What is going on? Are you ok? Why are you here? What happened to you?"

Kacey pulled back and brushed some stray hairs from her tear-streaked face. "I'm okay, Lora. I'm okay." She reassured her over and over again, but Lora couldn't believe it.

"I saw what they did to you before they took you. And then, I thought I saw you in the outpost, but…" Another swell of burning tears had her words dying again. "I don't understand," she whispered at last.

There were shouts from the hallway now, close to the door. Kacey eyed it, then nodded to Liam, who settled into a fighting stance. She tried to get in front of the girl, but Kacey kept her body shielding Lora's. "I'll explain everything, I promise. But I need you to trust me."

"I do, of course I do. But Kacey, what's going on?" She was in a near panic as the voices in the hallway rose.

Kacey turned to answer her, but the door swung open.

CHAPTER 17

WHAT THE FUCK IS GOING ON?

Kalon - Thirty minutes ago

The trade had been a disaster, starting with the burning of the refugee camp and ending with the death of his soldiers. It didn't help that the Shade princess had shot at the dragons after saving several at the refugee camp. Kalon had been at the new camp—which Cyrus had also tried to burn—for the past two days, helping to stop the spread of the fire. There had been few survivors, and Kierra had gone with them back to Castle Pridama to watch over them as Liam worked his magic.

He had just returned to Castle Pridama as the sun was setting. He was covered in soot and grime from head to toe and was in no mood to talk when Garrison caught up with him as he left the aerie.

"You've looked better," he said by way of greeting, falling into step beside him.

"Well, I've had better days," Kalon quipped, wiping some of the soot off of his forehead and onto his equally dirty sleeve.

Garrison had returned to Pridama with Ki and the injured, so Kalon hadn't seen him since everything had gone to shit. He looked over at his friend to see the male in about the same shape he was in. "How is everything here? Are the injured taken care of? How many did we lose?"

He didn't really want to hear how many innocent people had died because of that Shade bitch and her tyrant king, but he needed to know. If anything, so it could make it easier to kill her when he saw her next, because he would be seeing her again. That much he'd promised himself right after he had been informed of Cyrus's betrayal.

Garrison began rattling off the numbers to him, those who had died, those who were injured beyond full repair, the Drakes that were lost in controlling the fire. Kalon was barely listening. He couldn't think too long about what he had heard were in those bags. The thought of Jade's head…no, he couldn't think about that now. It would haunt him for the rest of his life. Jade—his Jade. She was gone and it was all *Collis's* fault. His thoughts spiraled as his blood heated with hatred. His ears rang, blocking out Garrison's voice. His blood was on fire, his vision went red, and his mouth tasted of ash.

Suddenly, Garrison was in his face. "Calm down." It was a command, not a suggestion. Few people had the guts to command him to do anything, and Garrison was one of the only ones Kalon ever tolerated taking orders from.

"Calm. The fuck. Down." Garrison said again, grabbing him by the neck and locking eyes with him. Kalon's breaths came out in short gasps. He was too hot, and his skin felt like it was peeling off of him.

"Someone *will* get hurt, Kalon. *You* will hurt someone, so you need to calm down right now." Garrison's words slowly soaked through Kalon's frenzied mind. Five breaths later and Kalon's shoulders were relaxing, his skin and blood cooling with each passing second.

He looked up at Garrison. "Thanks. I…" He didn't know what to say. It had been a shit past few days, and all he wanted to do was sleep.

He took another shaky breath and, pulling out of Garrison's grasp, started walking again, toward his bedchambers on the third floor. *Fuck. So. Many. Stairs.* His feet were already dragging. He turned to ask Garrison to carry him when he realized his friend was no longer beside him—the male hadn't moved from where they had just been standing.

Even though every fiber of his being was thoroughly exhausted, he straightened at the seriousness etched into Garrison's features. "What's happened?"

His mind raced. What if something happened to Ki? He nearly sprinted the several feet between them as he asked, desperation coating the words, "Is it Ki? Is she okay? What's going on?" He shook Garrison, demanding answers he knew would kill him if they were bad.

Garrison grabbed hold of his shoulders, steadying him. "Ki is ok."

Kalon felt he could finally take a full breath. But Garrison added, "She's been with the injured all through the night, one in particular and..." He seemed at a loss for words.

Kalon, though exhausted, knew his sister must be equally so. "I should go and check on her. She needs sleep, and she won't do it unless it's an order." Kalon changed course and headed toward the infirmary, but Garrison still wasn't moving.

"She won't be in the infirmary, brother," Garrison called after him, causing Kalon to pause and turn.

"Then where is she? You said she'd been with the injured all night, are they not in the infirmary?" He was too tired for these games. Why wasn't Garrison just telling him where Ki was?

"No," he said, still searching for the right words, which was annoying.

"Spit it out, mate. I'm exhausted and I want to see my sister so I can collapse. Is she not with the injured?" The words came out angrier than he'd meant, but he was tired and just wanted to not think about the horrors of the last two days.

"She is," Garrison repeated.

He felt like a broken record as he repeated what Garrison had literally just told him. "Ok so she's in the infirmary... because you said she was with the injured all night and—"

"No, I didn't," Garrison interrupted. "I said she was with the injured, *an* injured actually."

Kalon's temper slipped. "What are you talking about? What's going on?"

Garrison shook his head and made to approach him before stopping short. "Okay, bear with me. I know you're tired, but I need you to listen."

Kalon nodded, though his temper continued to grow.

"I'll take you to your sister, but you can't lose control, okay?"

Kalon's eyes flared. "What happened to her? I swear to the gods—"

"Nothing happened to her, gods Kalon, just listen to me." The seriousness in his tone took Kalon by surprise. Garrison walked not toward the infirmary, but Kierra's chambers. "Remember when Collis told us about her friend who was taken?" Garrison asked as they rounded the corner.

Kalon's responding snarl did not deter him from continuing.

"Well, she had mentioned some towns that had burned down, and Liam said she was muttering the name Kacey when she was asleep. Even talked about her, saying some shit about scars and strength."

Kalon's eyes narrowed as Garrison pressed on. "I did some digging, and while we didn't have an unit in the region Collis mentioned, we did have someone in the area." Garrison paused, right outside Kierra's door, blocking the way.

He was almost at his boiling point with his friend, his patience this as ice. "What, I'm supposed to not kill the bitch on sight because we had one person there who may or may not have accidentally killed her friend? Garrison, you're being ridiculous. We saw what the Shades do to prisoners, and we don't even really take prisoners. So, whatever it is you think you're getting at, I don't care. Nothing will change how I feel about her."

Garrison looked as exasperated as Kalon felt. "Think, Kalon, when you and Ki would run off and join the smaller units, what did Ki always say her name was?"

He was beyond thinking, but the name slipped out almost unconsciously, "K. Sea—like the oceans. But what does that have to do with Collis?" He all but spit her name as he tried to get past Garrison. The bastard merely pushed him back and leaned harder into the door. Kalon bared his teeth, and a lesser male would have turned away, but Garrison merely bared his teeth back.

"We *were* in the area, you asshole," Garrison explained, both males inches from each other's throats. "We *were* the ones at that village, but not as soldiers fighting, as a rescue mission."

"What?" seethed Kalon. His mind was too foggy to process what Garrison was explaining. "A rescue mission for who?"

And as if the gods had a sense of humor, the door swung open under Garrison's weight to reveal Liam standing in front of Kierra's bed, a dull butter knife in his hand, and Kierra sitting on the edge of the bed. But it wasn't either of them that Kalon's attention settled, but on the fiery-haired Shade all but sitting in his sister's lap. *Collis.*

CHAPTER 18

OH SHIT...

Lora

When the door finally swung open, Lora came face-to-face with an irate Kalon, whose attention was fully on her. *Great.* He was the literal last person she wanted Kacey to be around.

Despite her stitches, Lora managed to surge forward, grunting with the pain, and threw herself in front of Kacey. To her horror, Kalon also lunged for Kacey, grabbing her by the arm and pulling her toward the door. To Lora's surprise, Kacey punched him in the face.

"Kierra, what the fuck?" Kalon exclaimed, staggering back, nose already bleeding. His eyes were a molten amber that even she knew meant death was close by.

"Oh shit," came a familiar voice from the hallway. Garrison.

Shit, Lora would have to fight them all off to get her and Kacey out of here. She guessed Kacey could technically help too, the right hook she'd delivered to the prince had been perfect form.

"Kalon," Kacey said calmly, not moving an inch from between Lora and the prince of the Drakes. "You need to calm down and listen to me."

"Kierra," Kalon said to Kacey, mocking her calm voice. "You need to step aside so I can kill the fucking Shade bitch behind you."

Nope. No thank you. That was enough to get Lora moving again. She spun from behind Kacey and grabbed the knife from Liam, who was still standing dumbly between the two at the doorway.

She didn't give a shit that her stitches began pulling or that she was in a night gown, there was no way she would be killed by this fucker, not before she could get Kacey to freedom. "Kacey, look out!"

"Lora!" Kacey lunged for her at the same time Kalon lunged for Kacey.

"Not today asshole," Lora spat, driving the knife into Kalon's arm as she spun and knocked Kacey out of his grasp.

"Shit!" Kalon shouted, pulling the dull blade from his arm. Lora hadn't had the strength to push the blade in very far with her shoulder screaming, not to mention the blade was basically a spoon with how dull it was. So basically, it didn't wound Kalon at all, rather it pissed him off to the high heavens. *Great.*

Kalon made to move toward her but Kacey was in his face, her anger rising to match his. "Kalon, I swear to the gods if you lay a hand on her I will—"

Kalon's eyes widened as he locked eyes with her friend. "You'll what, *sister*?"

Lora froze where she stood, her arm and shoulder throbbing. *Sister? What the fuck?* She looked at Kacey, but her friend's attention was on the prince.

"Kalon," Kacey said, voice deadly calm. "Don't." Kalon saw it for the command it was and sneered.

But before he could open his mouth, Nuva was in the doorway, eyes blazing with hatred. "What the fuck is happening... Get away from her! Do you know who that is, Ki?"

"Do you?" Kacey shot back, seething in the direction of the soldier. Nuva seemed almost offended at the retort, stiffening under Kacey's fiery gaze.

Garrison eyed the room warily, shifting his weight to be better between Kalon and Kacey.

"I think," said Liam from the corner he was now standing in, "that we all have some things to learn about one another and it would be best if we did so calmly."

Kalon whipped his head in the direction of the medic, his gaze glossy with rage. To Liam's credit, he did not so much as flinch.

"Kacey?" Lora's voice had shifted from panicked to something darker, harder. Everyone's attention turned to where she stood near the fireplace. "Why does he keep calling you Kierra? And sister?"

Kacey's eyes swam with a mixture of guilt and resolve. Right when it looked like she would finally get answers, Kacey turned to Kalon. "Liam is right. We have a lot to discuss. Perhaps we should convene elsewhere in the castle."

Lora's mouth gaped open like a fish out of water. There's no way Kacey had just said that—commanded that. Her mind was reeling, and she felt the world slipping from under her feet. *Oh shit,* it really was slipping from beneath her because yet again, she was falling over, eyes closing in pain—

"Lora!" It was Kacey's voice, but Liam's hands as she was caught, blood oozing from her opened wound.

"I'll have to restitch her." *Liam.*

Followed by the gruff response, "Do it." *Kalon.*

"We will wait for you in Emir's quarters." *Garrison. Emir? The dragon? He's here? He has quarters? Do dragons even need quarters?*

The thoughts swirled in Lora's head as something warm settled on her lips. "This will make you sleep," came Liam's voice, the sweet taste of laudanum sliding down her throat.

Then came another voice dragging Lora's attention back to the room. "You'll be okay. Just... Let me figure out what to do." There was a light, warm pressure to her forehead and then a loud clang as the heavy wooden door closed and latched.

The warmth of the laudanum spread through Lora and soon enough, she was drifting fitfully to sleep.

CHAPTER 19

KACEY'S STORY

Lora

Lora wasn't sure how long she'd been asleep, but when she woke, there was no light coming from the small window in the room and a fire crackled in the fireplace. They had clearly learned from their previous mistake and had given her enough laudanum to keep her asleep through her restitching and bandage change.

She took a deep breath, her mind racing. Kacey was alive. It *had* been her at the outpost. And Kalon had called her *sister*. What the *hell* was going on?

There was a sound to Lora's right. She tried to roll into a better position but her arm and shoulder were too tightly wrapped. She could thank Liam for that. Another sound and the wall—*the literal wall*—opened next to the bed.

"What the fuck!" Lora shouted, trying to jump up and immediately collapsing back down in pain. Stars swam in her vision as the pillows and blankets swallowed her.

A hand was over her mouth before she could shout again as all-too-familiar eyes looked down at her. A plait of white hair spilled over Kacey's shoulder, her eyes cautiously darting about the room, a finger held over her lips.

There was a cough from outside the main door and a second later Kacey relaxed, rolling off of her to sit on the edge of the bed. She grabbed a pillow and stared at Lora with unnerving stillness.

"What the fuck, K?" she whispered, still not sure what just happened. "Did you just come out of the *wall*?"

Kacey looked around one more time before a smile spread across her face. "Glad I can still sneak up on you, bean."

Bean. Lora's heart tumbled at the nickname. Kacey had given it to her early on when they were working in the kitchens together. *You're as small as these beans, Lora,* one of the other workers had teased, amusing Kacey to high heavens. The nickname had stuck.

"Only because you came out of the fucking wall and jumped on me like an ice cat!" Lora hissed. Kacey's smile grew, and the girls sat in silence for a second before Kacey's smile faded. Lora's eyes stung at that, her throat burning with unshed tears and unasked questions.

"Your hair," Kacey remarked, reaching up and brushing away a stray strand of ruby-red hair from Lora's face.

"*Your* hair," Lora pointed out, nodding toward the moon-white braid.

Kacey looked down at her hands, a small smile spreading again. "You like it?"

Lora beamed at her friend, still just as gentle as she remembered—*at least something is still the same.* "You never looked right with black hair anyway," she said with a smirk.

Kacey's eyes snapped up as she whacked Lora across the unbandaged arm with the pillow she had been holding, "Well, neither did you!" she laughed back, her voice a whisper.

"Ow!" Lora faked a deadly injury while stifling a laugh, which had Kacey chuckling. A second passed, and both girls sat smiling silently at one another.

"Kac—"

"Bean—" A weary smile spread across both girls' faces, and Lora could tell Kacey had more to say than she did. "No, you go ahead," she offered, nodding to Kacey who was now wringing her hands around her shirt.

"It's just," Kacey started, planting her hands firmly on the bed next to her. "We don't have a lot of time, and Kalon thinks I'm doing research in the library and forgot my room secretly connects to it so..." She trailed off as her gaze traveled around the room, anywhere but in Lora's direction.

"Right..." Lora said slowly, trying to catch her friend's attention. "And he should know that because..."

Kacey paused before looking right into Lora's eyes. "Because we grew up here, Bean."

Lora stared at her friend in disbelief. "What do you mean?" A beat passed, and her mind raced at a full sprint as she tried to sit up. "Why did Prince Asshole call you his sister?"

She feared she already knew the answer, but it still felt like a shock when Kacey said quietly, but not weakly, "Because Prince Asshole is my twin brother."

Lora's jaw dropped. "He's your what?" Clearly, she had misheard her.

"Brother, Bean." Kacey was stiff as a board as she stared, tight lipped at Lora.

"Kalon, the prince of the Drake Kingdom," Lora clarified slowly, "is your *brother*? Like, biologically?" *What the shit?*

"Yes," Kacey nodded. "Biologically." She didn't continue, instead giving Lora the space to figure it out for herself.

"No." The pieces all came together. "Because that would make you—"

"Princess Kierra of the Drake Kingdom," Kacey finished for her, sketching a mock half bow.

"What? What the hell, Kacey? You're a fucking princess and you never told me?" Lora saw red. She clenched her fists to keep from screaming.

"That's what you're mad about?" Kacey said, jumping to her feet in indignation.

"Well, it's one of the things on my list, *Kierra*." Lora spat her name at her, the words dripping with venom.

"Well, it's not like you were up in Attica telling the truth either, *Princess Collis*." Kacey's words, too, were filled with poisonous accusations that Lora felt like a physical blow. She figured she had a point, but Lora wasn't going to let those accusations sink in, or the truth in them—no, she was going to box them away in her mind and stay mad. Being angry was easier than facing the truth.

The girls stared at each other for what felt like a small eternity. Kacey—Kierra—whoever the girl was, was the first to falter.

"Look, I didn't sneak in here to waste our time fighting," she said, moving as if she wanted to sit on the bed, but decided against it.

"Oh, you didn't?" Lora was still riding her temper, her words coming out in short snaps. "Then what exactly did you sneak into your bedroom—*in a fucking castle because you're a princess*, might I add—to do?"

Kierra narrowed her eyes before taking a breath. "To talk to you."

"You snuck in to talk with me? How very thoughtful." Lora's temper wasn't going down anytime soon.

"I snuck in to talk *to* you," Kierra emphasized. "I was hoping you would do most of the *listening*."

It was such a Kacey thing to say, that Lora's retort died on her tongue, her rage vanishing in an instant. This was her friend. The one who had cleaned her wounds and cared for her. Had laughed and cried with her. The one she had done everything for, had given *everything* to get back. Lora could give her space to explain, right? She crossed her arms, sighing out the last of her fury.

"The floor is yours, your highness," she muttered. "My lips are," she made the sealed motion over her lips, going so far as to throw away the imaginary key.

Kierra rolled her eyes and took a deep breath, then began.

"I was born and raised here in Castle Pridama. Kalon and I are twins, which is rare since it's kind of hard for Drakes to have kids, but that's beside the point. When I was really little, my mom took us to the capital to meet the new princess. While we were there, we were attacked. My mom sent Kalon and I away with a guard, and our Aunt Tura found us in the forest between the two kingdoms several days later. She told us my mom had been found by the Shades and was killed. Tura brought us back, and then our grandmother raised us. We spent a lot of time at Garrison's—you've met him, right?"

Lora nodded, and Kierra gave a small smile as she continued. "We spent most of our time with his family. Gamma felt it was a better place for us than being in the musty halls of Castle Pridama. Anyway, when we were old enough we all joined the Royal Drake Army, and that's where we met Liam and Nuva. We were all in the same flying quadrant and—" She suddenly stopped as if she'd heard something outside, her right hand moving to her left bicep, a wince of pain glancing her features.

Lora was immediately alert. "Are you ok? What's wrong?" Despite her pain, she lurched up and reached for her friend.

But Kierra had moved slightly out of reach, as if touching Lora would cause more pain. "Nothing's wrong," she assured. "I'm ok, I'm fine." And, noting the concerned look still on Lora's face, Kierra added, "I promise I'm okay."

Lora relaxed only a fraction after that, as the Drake forged ahead with her story.

"About twelve years ago, when I was fifteen, I was on a practice scouting mission when we were attacked by a group of Shades. I managed to escape and, instead of returning to base like I was supposed to do, I followed the Shade caravan.

I was young and reckless and thought that I could handle it. I managed not to get caught, only to then wind up in a group of refugees. One of the ladies saw my hair and tried to get me in trouble for a little bit of cash, and that's when I realized that all Shades had dark hair. I was basically a walking Drake target, and I had been told about the treatment of Drake prisoners." Kierra paused, and the moment of silence had Lora's insides turning.

Kierra cleared her throat, then continued. "So, I did what I had to do to silence the woman, then used the money I'd stolen off of her to buy dye for my hair. By the time I had a solid plan to escape, I was suddenly standing on a trade block being bought as a kitchen maid for a general in Attica. I was shipped there before I had time to run. That's where I met you. I didn't want to be your friend at first. I wanted to hate you—"

"So why didn't you?" Lora interjected. "It would have been easy to not talk to me that first day."

"Yeah, but...how well do you remember the first time we met?" Kierra retorted, a small smile playing on her lips.

Lora couldn't bring herself to say the truth that lay in her heart—that the first day they met is when she really felt like she had a reason to live. She had felt *seen*. "I mean, I remember that we were on bean-pinching duty together in the kitchens."

Kierra's smile grew. "And you were shit at it. The cook was an asshole to you and I gave you your nickname. That was the first time *you* met *me*, but I met you before that."

"What?" Lora's eyebrows shot up.

"Yeah. Three days before, after you'd been whipped by your training officer." Kierra's smile faltered. "I was the maid who changed your bandages."

Lora blanched. "You never told me—"

Kierra's shoulders, which had tensed throughout her story, relaxed now as she looked at Lora, her features softening. "I had hoped you would eventually open up to me about it all, which you did. But you're right. I never said anything or corrected you about when we first met."

"But why?" she all but whispered, her throat feeling too tight to speak.

"I don't know," Kierra admitted, looking down at her hands. "Does it matter?"

Lora's brows pinched together. In the grand scheme of things, she guessed it probably didn't matter. "I guess not."

"What *does* matter," Kierra said, now looking back at Lora, "is that we became friends." Another, softer smile now played at her lips, and Lora took Kierra's hand in hers, now also smiling gently. It's true, no matter their differences they had instantly clicked. And although they had both been lying—Lora still lying—Kierra was her friend. There was still the same current of energy that connected them, now just flowing a bit differently.

"Every day I was in Attica I dreamt of escaping, of feeling the wind in my face while flying." Kierra tried to hide the wince as she subtly rubbed at her upper arm again, but Lora tracked the movement. "And I could tell you wanted to leave too, so I would drop hints about running away."

"Taking the mountain roads..." Lora thought back to all the times she'd caught Kierra staring out through the outpost windows.

"And heading straight south, yeah," Kierra confirmed, a hint of that strong-willed woman coming back into her voice—the part of Kierra Lora wasn't sure she knew. "Except," she continued, "secretly, I was planning on us going southwest—toward Drake territory."

Lora felt herself blanching again, a cold sweat breaking out along her brow. "Us?"

"Well, yeah," Kierra said quietly, but not weakly. "I wasn't going to leave you behind after everything they had done to you." Lora's eyes stung as something eased in her chest. "I had it all planned out, supplies packed and everything—even managed to get in contact with Garrison and Kalon to come and get us. I just needed you on board. But it all went to hell before I could tell you."

Lora's face pinched as she tried to think about when this planned escape was meant to take place, all the memories of their last encounters dredging to the surface. "Wait, I don't understand. The night you were taken—"

"The night I was taken was the night we were supposed to sneak away," Kierra interrupted. "I had snuck down and drugged most of the guards, but one of them didn't drink what he was supposed to and caught me while I was redyeing my hair." Lora shuddered as she realized how very wrong she had been about the entire situation.

"He was not at all happy to discover what I'd done, and when he realized I was a Drake... Let's just say he was more than happy to share his displeasure with me. Repeatedly." Kierra squared her shoulders, but Lora saw the shadows in her eyes. Though she did not know for sure what the guard had done to her friend, she remembered vividly what Kierra had looked like the night she'd been taken.

Another shudder racked Lora. She would never forget the bruises that had covered Kacey's arms and neck, the black eye and the blood that seemed to come from everywhere and nowhere. The blood on her legs...

Tears that matched Kierra's now spilled down Lora's cheeks, and she grasped her friend's hand again, squeezing tight.

What had been done to her friend, by someone she probably knew...the tears were flowing freely now from both girls as the gravity of the situation settled between them.

Kierra took a shuddering breath through the tears, and Lora tried to stop her, but she pressed on. "I managed to escape from him once he'd passed out but... I couldn't..." She pulled her hand away as Lora realized what happened next. She had run. She had run and left Lora behind.

Her heart broke as Kierra silently wept, shame and guilt filling the air, from both of them.

Lora opened her mouth to speak but Kierra looked up, and her eyes were filled with such sadness that she couldn't bring herself to say anything, her throat clenching with grief and anger. She didn't know how to fix it, or what to say to make it better. Nothing could ease either girl's guilt or shame. So, she just reached for her hand again, letting her unsaid words flow through the touch.

Kierra shuddered at the contact but didn't pull away this time.

She didn't look up but still, she continued. "I managed to make it to the small village where I was meant to be picked up. The locals there were trying to remain neutral and Kalon and Garrison had paid off the ones who were wary. I don't know what happened, but someone told them we were there, and then everything just went to hell."

Lora's stomach dropped, her bowels going liquidy. It sure did. Because while Kierra was running for her life to the Drakes, Lora was leading the charge to fight them.

Kiera's next words had made it feel like the world was slipping away from Lora. "A whole unit of Shades arrived, and they began burning shit. I wanted to stay and help, but there was nothing I could do. And then you were there, and I couldn't get to you, and you looked at the dragons with such hatred... I knew you couldn't come with us, that you wouldn't and..." She took another deep breath. "And then I woke up in the castle, my grandmother and aunt at my bedside. I tried to come back for you Bean, please believe me that I did, but Kalon told me there was nothing left to go back to. The town had been eviscerated. There were no survivors. But I knew in my heart you weren't dead, I could feel it, but..."

Kierra met her gaze. "Lora, I saw the village. I went back and there was...nothing left. I just assumed you had died like everyone else. If I had known..." She trailed off as her gaze landed on Lora's wrists, where the scars from years of canthite chains now permanently marred her skin.

"I'm, I'm so sorry I couldn't save you." It was the new guilt in Kierra's voice that had what was left of Lora's soul fracturing.

But Lora had had enough of apologies and death. Her friend was alive. It was all she had hoped for for the past five years, and here she was—alive and well. So, Lora pushed aside her grief and shame and questions, and embraced her friend.

The girls sat there, crying and holding one another until sleep claimed them both. And for the first time in a long time, wrapped again in the arms of her friend—her sister—Lora slept well.

***

A soft knock at the door had Lora's eyes flying open. She wasn't sure how long they'd been asleep, but the small window in the room was now lighter than when Kierra had come in. There was so much to process, so much to still talk about, but another soft knock had Kierra sitting upright in the bed, putting her finger over lips as if Lora didn't already know to stay quiet.

This time the knock came a bit louder and more urgently, but still the door did not open. Kierra's head cocked slightly to the side and her nose crinkled as if sniffing the air slightly, then her shoulders relaxed as she eased off the bed.

Kierra opened the door and Liam slipped in effortlessly, sliding past her as she closed the door quietly. Lora stiffened as their gazes met, but Liam merely nodded before striding to the small window and peering out.

Kierra turned to him and asked, "Is Kalon—"

"Still asleep," he confirmed, nodding to her as she began re-braiding her hair. "But not for long," he added, pulling a change of clothes from the satchel Lora hadn't realized he'd been carrying. "Same goes for your aunt," he added, and as Kierra took the clothes and began to undress, Liam moved back toward the door.

They worked effortlessly together, swiftly and as if of one mind, and Lora marveled at the comfortability they shared. Liam leaned his head toward the door as if listening for something, still having yet to look at her again, and Lora realized, with heat creeping up her cheeks, that she was only in a nightgown. A very thin, see-through nightgown. And although she wasn't ashamed of her body, she definitely wasn't as comfortable being basically naked as Kierra was, even though she was sure Liam had seen most of her body anyway during one of the various times he'd healed her. Regardless, Lora found herself pulling the sheets around her a bit tighter as Kierra finished dressing.

Lora wasn't sure where to look but the girl—no, woman—standing in front of her was almost unrecognizable. Last night, Kierra had come into the room in a light red nightgown that was by no means matronly, but still elegant and soft. Now, the person in front of her wore tight, black leggings, a tucked-in dark red tunic, calf-high boots, and a waist belt of daggers.

Lora looked from the daggers to the insignia above Kierra's heart—a man kneeling with an open-winged dragon above him—and it dawned on her. "You're a dragon rider, aren't you?"

Liam stiffened. Kierra looked between Lora and the door before quickly coming to the bed. "I'm sorry. I didn't have time to explain everything to you last night, but I have to go now."

Lora started, "But— I— What— There's so much left to say," she concluded, hanging her head. She wasn't sure what to say, and she had known that Kierra would have to leave, but she hadn't mentally prepared to say goodbye this soon.

Kierra looked to the door again and Liam nodded once before going into the hallway. Kierra stepped closer and reached for Lora's hand, "I know, and I'm sorry." She paused, and Lora could smell the tears before they began to fall. "About everything," Kierra added, pulling Lora into an embrace.

Lora looked up to see her friend straightening to her full height as a single tear tracked down her tan cheek. Lora needed to at least tell her, at least explain, but her throat felt tight again, and Kierra pulled away from the embrace.

"My aunt is here and I need to speak with her before Kalon does." Kierra headed toward the door but stopped short, her shoulders tensing. "Liam is going to have to drug you again."

Lora stiffened at the thought of being wrapped in that dark-filled sleep, unable to protect herself—vulnerable, weak.

Kierra looked over her shoulder as if she'd heard the torrent of thoughts and fears in Lora's mind. "I won't let them hurt you, I promise," was all she said before she disappeared from view.

CHAPTER 20

DECISIONS TO BE MADE

Lora

After Kacey—Kierra—had snuck back out, Liam gave Lora some more laudanum and she welcomed the dreamless sleep. Her mind woke faster than her body, both a blessing and a curse. While she was still snuggled in the warmth of the big bed, a good sign that they hadn't dragged her ass to the dungeons, she could hear the torrent of discussions from outside the door.

Her drug-muddled mind began identifying the voices: Definitely Kierra, Kalon, and maybe Garrison, but he was staying relatively quiet. The most vocal participant behind the prince was a voice she couldn't place. She wasn't sure she'd heard it before, but it still sounded familiar. Like something you have a dream about and then you see the next day.

As more of the fog lifted from her mind, the discussion became clearer and the topic, a bit obvious, was her.

Kierra: "Just give her back? Sell her like fucking cattle?" *Sell? Oh shit.* "After everything I've told you about them? About her? Is she nothing more than a commodity to you?"

Great question!

Kalon: "Have you not been listening? She tried to kill us after the trade deal—"

Kierra: "You really believe if she wanted you dead you would still be alive?" *Truth.* "Why do you think Cyrus had her killed? Clearly she didn't kill you like he'd asked her to!"

Yes! That's exactly what happened! Kierra one, Kalon nothing.

Kalon: "Or, she was ordered to shoot down the riders, which she did!"

Okay, also true…

Kierra: "And then what? Because she followed orders so *well* Cyrus had her shot in the chest and thrown into a burning temple? If you send her back there, sell her back, whatever, you are sending her to her death."

Kierra was right. If Lora was sent back, they would kill her…or worse. The truth and reality of those words settled into her very bones, like a weighted blanket laid atop her soul. Kalon's response felt like a physical blow to her chest.

"Good."

"You don't mean that, brother. You can't." Kierra's voice broke and Lora heard shuffling and movement, like someone had tried to step forward but had stopped. "You know who she is to me. You would take her away for something she was commanded to do, something she had no control over? You of all people—"

"How dare you—" Kalon's voice was vibrating with rage. She didn't need to see his face to know it was bright red. Kierra had struck a chord.

Kierra was apparently in his face, as her voice came from the exact spot Kalon's had moments before. "Oh, I do dare *brother*, it is not only you who has lost something in this war. Do well to remember that."

"That's enough," That unfamiliar, familiar voice ordered. "I wish to see the girl before deciding anything. You have both made your cases, but ultimately it is up to me, as crown regent, to decide the fate of the Shade."

Fuck. Kalon's aunt is here—I guess Kierra's aunt too.

The door cracked open and the crown regent dropped her voice to almost a whisper before entering the room. "Kierra, you will wait out here. When I emerge, I will have made my decision and there will be no further discussions. Understood?"

"Shouldn't you at least let her wake up, hear her side of the story—" Kierra began, but then there was a long pause, in which Lora felt certain Kierra was backing down. Based on the silence that followed and then noise at the door again, she knew Kierra had conceded—though her point had been perfectly valid in Lora's opinion.

The door creaked open, and Lora did her best to steady her breathing. She had yet to open her eyes, so maybe she still looked asleep.

Kierra and Kalon's aunt walked in the room, and Lora's shadows pulsed against her skin, then recoiled. She listened to the aunt make her way over to the bed, stopping near where Lora's head was resting on the pillow. *Please believe I'm asleep*, she thought, keeping her breathing even.

Kalon's recognizable footsteps sounded moments later as a citrus and ember scent crammed its way up her nose. She felt the crown regent continue to stare down at her, as if her gaze were a physical brand.

Her voice broke the silence at last, so loud in Lora's ears she almost jumped. "You speak of things this Shade has done, my nephew." A pause and shuffle of feet. "Mmmm," she mused, her voice drifting over her and settling in her chest. It sounded so familiar...

"You have too much emotion involved because of your loss, it is clouding your judgment," she continued, her voice sounding much closer now. If only Lora could see what she looked like.

There was a sound as though Kalon had begun to speak but was immediately silenced. His aunt hummed again, and Lora felt her gaze return to her prone body.

"Such peculiar, bright hair for a Shade," she mused, gingerly picking up one of Lora's loose strands. "Like blood on the pillow."

Lora's hair dropped onto her shoulder. *Well, that's creepy as hell.* She felt a shiver snaking its way up her spine as the crown regent seemed to turn toward the back of the room.

"Medic," she snapped. Several steps, and then the smell of earth and lavender reached her nose—Liam.

"Liam, your majesty," he said, most likely bowing.

"Liam, right." Her tone gave no indication that she cared about Liam's name. "Well, Liam, please describe the injuries of the Shade princess to me, specifically the ones sustained recently."

There was a pause, and Lora felt the tension rise in the room ever so slightly. The crown regent cleared her throat.

"Of course, ma'am," Liam said, moving toward the bed but stopping a few feet away. "It seems Lora was shot in the—"

"Lora?" the crown regent purred, amusement flickering in her tone. "Is this not Collis, the beloved Shade princess?"

"Yes ma'am, it's just, Kierra had called her Lora so I thought—"

"You mean the *Princess* called this"—she paused, probably looking over Lora in disgust based on the next words— "*thing by a different name? How interesting. Continue.*"

Okay, so Kierra's aunt is a bitch. Noted.

"Right," Liam said a bit nervously. "Collis," he amended, "sustained several blunt force blows to the head as well as a single arrow shot to the upper chest and several broken bones."

Damn. That sounds about as bad as it felt.

"Hmmm, and why didn't it kill her?" The crown regent hummed, her attention back on Lora. She could *feel* her gaze through her closed eyelids.

"The arrow seems to have missed her heart by inches— perhaps she turned away or was shot by someone from a distance," Liam explained. "And the broken bones appear to be from a short fall, perhaps off a ledge or short cliff."

Lora's heart raced as she remembered the feeling of the arrow piercing her flesh, the crunching sound in her ears as her bones snapped when she collided with the forest floor.

How she wasn't dead was still a mystery, even to her, but the next sentence made her glad she was already laying down.

"And the fire? Where are her burns?"

Fire? What fire?

"There were no visible burns when she arrived at Pridama, ma'am," Liam replied matter-of-factly.

"But it was reported that a fire-haired girl was the only survivor of a temple burning. Is this not the same girl?" The crown regent inquired, again touching Lora's hair. Images flashed through her mind of guards picking up her feet and arms, of being tossed onto a pile of bodies, of smoke filling her lungs as walls crumbled around her. Of *screams*.

"I wouldn't know, ma'am, I don't receive those reports. I merely help who I can when they are brought to me." Poor Liam sounded like he would rather be anywhere else.

"I see." She seemed to pace slightly, like Lora knew Kierra did when thinking. "It is possible," she said at last, sounding thankfully farther away, "that they did not intend for her to die?"

"How do you mean?" Liam's question was weary and hedging on angry confusion. *Oh yeah, he really doesn't want to be here.*

"I mean that perhaps the tyrant King knew she would survive and that we would pick her up unknowingly," the crown regent supplied. "Maybe he has now planted her here, amongst us as a spy."

Lora could practically see Liam's gaping mouth. What she had suggested was borderline insane, even for Cyrus.

"Seems like an awful lot of trouble ma'am, when she could have died from any one of her injuries. There is no way to know for certain that they weren't meant to be fatal. Maybe she genuinely was meant to die, but somehow survived." Lora could tell Liam was exasperated by the idea. As a medic, he would be the one to know whether or not Lora should be alive or dead. And he'd already explained that she *should* be dead.

"I do not deal in maybes when it comes to my kingdom, boy," she snapped. "She is a threat, Kalon has said so as well." A pause, "Leave us," she commanded, presumably to Liam because it was his long strides that exited the room.

"Aunt?" Kalon asked after a long silence.

"You truly believe she is dangerous, nephew?" she asked, seeming to resume her pacing.

Lora held her breath.

"Yes, I do, but -" Kalon bit out, and she could feel his heated stare burning into her.

"Then we must rid the Drake people of her," the crown regent concluded, closer to Kalon now.

"I agree, we could send a missive to the King and—"

"No," she interrupted Kalon again. "No deals. You handle this tonight. I will dismiss Kierra now. Come."

Kalon sucked in a breath, presumably about to speak, but his aunt spoke again, so quietly Lora barely heard her. "Do remember what this girl did to your lover, nephew. She may be Kierra's friend, but losing one Shade won't hurt nearly as bad as losing Jade did."

And with that, the crown regent made her way to the door, closing it behind her and Kalon, the latch locking from the outside.

Her voice sounded again, now from the hallway, "I have come to a decision. While I know she is important to you Kierra, Kalon is correct in his assessment of the threat she poses to the Drake people. Because of what she was to you, I will not allow Kalon to kill her outright, but she cannot stay here."

A muffled noise, as if someone had started to speak but was instantly cut off.

"Kierra, you are dismissed. You are to return to the refugee camps. We will call you if there are any further developments or problems that arise." A pause, then the sound of shuffling feet. "I do hate that this girl has caused you such distress, niece, I hope in time you can grow from it."

But it was clear to even Lora that Kierra must not have listened to her aunt's feigned apology.

"May I at least say goodbye?" It was not a tearful request, rather one made in indignation, in disagreement with the decision being made.

"I'm afraid she is still very drugged. When she awakens fully, I will personally inform her of your well wishes." Another pause, and then the curt command, "Dismissed."

There was another muffled sound and then the scuffling of shoes down the hallway. If it was possible to tell someone's mood from the sound of their walking alone, she would assume the person striding down the hall was furious.

But she hadn't put up a fight. Kierra had to realize her aunt was going to kill her, and yet she'd just walked away, as if last night was a farewell, rather than the beginning of their rekindled friendship. Like Lora meant nothing.

Then there were whispers on the other side of the door, words Lora could not make out, but she felt the tension again rising between the two people there. There was a long pause, and then she heard Kalon's strong steps walking away from her room, while his aunt called Liam back to the door.

"Medic," she snapped, "I will need you to drug her so that she can be moved to a new location."

Liam's response came too quietly, but the aunt's reaction told her Liam had all but refused. "It does not concern me whether or not her body can handle the drug or the move."

"Yes your majesty, I will need to get more supplies then," came Liam's tight, flat response.

She replied dully, "Just do it, boy."

There was a long pause as Lora heard Liam's steps retreat down the hallway. Then, the crown regent spoke to someone else. "I am leaving Pridama now, I have business elsewhere. Be sure that boy has her ready. The Shade dies tonight." And with that, her slow, light steps followed Liam's.

Lora waited for as long as she could before she sat upright in the bed, mind racing. The weight of everything that had happened to her, to her friend, settled on her soul as she began to process this new set of information.

Kierra had been a Drake the whole time. She hadn't been taken, but rescued, and Lora had been the villain in the story. Maybe not *herself, exactly*, but she was Shade, and so were those who Kierra hated and feared. Kierra had left her, and she had done terrible things to try and get her back, believing her stolen.

Then *she* was stolen by the very people she had been determined, hell, trained to destroy. And now, Kierra's aunt hated her, expected her to disappear and die easily. The bitch planned on drugging her and having Kalon dispose of her like garbage. And if she was drugged, she wouldn't be able to put up a fight.

But she did plan to fight. If the crown regent wanted her gone, she would make sure to be just that once night fell—gone.

CHAPTER 21

ESCAPE ATTEMPT #3

Lora

Lora took a quick inventory of the room she was in, noting the lack of general supplies. *Shit.* She didn't have time to wait until night fell, so she would need to use her shadows. They swirled in her veins, pushing against her skin, but she knew they would be short lived, especially as the laudanum was still wearing off and her shoulder was still wrecked. *Fuck.*

Based on the sounds from outside her door, there were at least two guards. She rose from the bed and quietly made her way to the bathing chamber. The window she had hoped was bigger than the one in her room was, in fact, much smaller. *Not helpful.*

She took a brief moment to glance in the mirror and realized that Kierra and Kalon's aunt wasn't wrong in her general assessment of her—she had looked better, for sure. There were dark circles under her eyes and her skin was paler than normal from the blood loss. But she was able to stand and move without too much pain in her arm thanks to Liam's mending, which meant she could *probably* escape. *Probably is better than probably not*, she reminded herself as she glanced around the bathing chamber for a weapon. No such luck, *of course*.

As she made to leave the small room, she heard a soft click from the bedroom and the smell of vanilla and embers drifted over her. Kacey—well, Kierra.

Kierra stood at the base of the bed in new travel clothes, a small satchel sitting on the edge of the bed next to her.

"What are you doing?" Kierra looked confused as Lora strode toward her from the bathing chamber.

"I could ask you the same question," Lora snapped back, stopping in front of her. It still amazed her every time she saw Kierra. She was alive, and safe, and a *fucking princess*.

"What are you doing up?" Kierra amended. "You could rip your stitches." She made to reach out to her, but Lora stepped back, eyes narrowing on her friend.

"What are you doing here?" Lora snapped, shifting into a slight fighting stance. "Shouldn't you be halfway back to the refugee camp? Or did I mishear the order given to you?"

Kierra stared blankly before her face shifted to a bitter frown, rolling her shoulders as she began unpacking the small bag. "I wondered when the laudanum would wear off. You always were impervious to its effects in Attica."

Lora's temper rose at the casual mention of their shared past, a past that, as of last night's conversation, was going to get her killed. "One becomes rather impervious when they are required to grow a tolerance from a young age." Kierra stiffened and a beat passed before Lora added, a wicked smile spreading across her lips, "And no one here seems to learn that lesson."

Kierra turned to face her, her eyes narrowing. "Not your first laudanum experience with us, huh?" she asked, now seeming to register the fighting stance Lora had taken and adjusting her stance accordingly.

"Nope," Lora said frankly, her eyes never leaving Kierra's. "Sweet Liam keeps it handy and the prince—your brother, right? —he likes to use it when he's bored."

Kierra's eyes narrowed even more. "I did not take you for a boring guest."

"A guest," Lora said with a harsh laugh. "I am no more a guest here than you were in Attica." And the truth of those words settled between them, even if they lacked some truth...

Kierra was stiff as a board now, eyes glazing over in rage the way she had seen Kalon's do. "If someone has laid a finger on you—" she started.

"No," Lora interjected, making to circle the girl slowly. "Just kidnapped me, held me for ransom, physically beat me several times, and is now planning on killing me," she added with a sweet smile that usually had Kalon seeing red. It had a similar effect on his sister.

"From what I was told," Kierra drawled, a small smirk spreading across her face as she too began to circle, "no one actually beat you."

Lora gaped. "Excuse me?" *What the fuck? I'm obviously still covered in bruises from my time at the outpost, is Kierra blind?*

"I'm just saying that based on Kalon's face—and Garrison's, for that matter—you never lost." Kierra wore a feral smile now, and Lora could have sworn her eyes shone with a bit of pride.

What the fuck is going on? "That's not true," she corrected, making to step toward Kierra's weak side.

"Oh, yeah?" Kierra challenged, maneuvering away from her with ease.

"Yeah," she said right back, venom in the one word. "I lost once," she added, settling deeper into a fighting stance.

"That doesn't count and you know it," Kierra shot back, also settling into a deeper stance. "Are we really going to do this here? While you're like that?" She pointed to Lora's bandaged arm. She had a point, but like hell was Lora going to back down.

When she didn't reply, Kierra's face fell into a contemplative expression Lora had seen her make a hundred times when trying to solve a riddle. Finally, she spoke. "Why are you still here? I saw the damage you did at the outpost. You could have escaped at any time. Why didn't you try to flee?"

Lora started—it wasn't what she was expecting her to say. "I couldn't," she admitted, settling back into her fighting stance, not even realizing she'd stepped out of it. It felt unnatural to prepare to fight *against* Kierra when the past five years she'd been fighting *for* her, but she was getting used to her world being turned upside down. Kierra's truth could get in line with the rest of fucked up shit she didn't want to deal with.

Kierra noted her shift in attitude and re-braced her footing. "Couldn't or wouldn't?" she shot at her, eyeing her with disbelief.

"Couldn't," Lora said again, feeling her temper rise.

"And why not?" Kierra challenged.

"Because of you," she said before she could stop herself.

Kierra stood up to her full height suddenly, all negative energy vanishing as she cocked her head in confusion. "Me?"

"Yes, you!" she all but shouted, also straightening. "I may be the villain in your story, but you were a friend in mine," she added, her nostrils flaring as she forced down breath after breath, trying to calm herself down. She was a hairpin away from losing her fucking mind, and no one usually survived that.

"*Were?*" Kierra asked, having the audacity to look hurt. "What the hell is that supposed to mean?"

"It means that, clearly, we aren't friends anymore," Lora retorted, still breathing in through her nose and out through her mouth. Her shadows pushed at her skin and based on Kierra's quick glance to her arms, she had noted them.

"Because I'm a Drake?" she asked, dragging her attention back to her.

"Because you lied to me *Kierra*," Lora shot back.

"Well, it's not like you didn't lie to me, *Collis*."

Both women stood there, fuming, eyes locked in a long-known battle of wills.

"Why are you even here?" Lora finally asked, shoulders sagging. Her shadows had receded and in their wake rose a wave of nausea. She hadn't eaten enough, and her body was now registering it.

"You heard the argument, I'm sure," Kierra said, as if that explained everything.

It did not. If anything, it was even more confirmation that she *shouldn't* be here. "Yeah, so?"

"So," Kierra said, obviously annoyed, "clearly I couldn't let her be the only thing that stood between you and death." She walked past Lora then and began unpacking the bag again.

She straightened, "But she told you—"

"It doesn't matter what she told me," Kierra interrupted. "I know what she told Kalon. And I will not let her kill you." The resolve in her voice sounded so much like Kacey that her throat threatened to close again.

But she isn't Kacey, your friend, she's Kierra, the enemy princess, Lora reminded herself.

But is she really your enemy? that annoying little voice asked in return.

"Oh," Lora finally said, at a loss for words as she walked toward the bed to see what Kierra was unpacking. The role reversal was not lost to her as she looked upon her old friend. Even though Kierra was older, their entire friendship Lora had stood up for the gentle and kind girl—and here she was, a princess defying her aunt to keep Lora safe. Lora had spent the last five years working to liberate her friend, and now she was liberating Lora. The irony was not lost on her, either.

A small sound came from outside the door, and Kierra stiffened. "Shit—they're waking up." She stuffed a couple of items back into the bag as Lora came to her side.

"Who's waking up?" Instead of answering, Kierra thrust a pair of pants and a dark tunic into her hands. "What is this for?" Lora asked, now holding a pile of clothes that smelled oddly of citrus and ember.

"To change, obviously," Kierra said. Noting Lora's confused look, she added, "You certainly cannot escape in a night gown that is longer than your legs…" She made a pointed look at Lora's flowing gown, already tangled around her legs. "Well? Hurry up!"

Lora couldn't argue with that logic and stripped as quickly and quietly as her wounded shoulder allowed. Kierra helped in getting the garment over her head, all but tearing the fabric to get it over her bandaged arm.

Once dressed Kierra pulled out a small piece of chalk from the bag— "hair dye"—and set to work quickly covering Lora's burgundy hair with a dull brown color. "It'll wash out in a day or two, so I put another brick in the bag. They'll be looking for a redhead," she added, as if knowing Lora was going to ask. Lora only nodded and Kierra made quick work of the dye and began braiding Lora's hair into a coronet.

"You won't be able to go out of the main doors—" she began, finishing the braid.

"Obviously," Lora said, rolling her eyes as she adjusted the tunic a little. It was a bit snug, but it didn't hurt her shoulder too badly.

Kierra narrowed her eyes in the mirror before rolling them. "Anyway," she continued, a slight hint of amused annoyance in her voice, "as I was saying, you can't go out the main gate, so you'll need to use the servants' access. I poisoned the guards—"

"You what?" Lora all but shouted.

"They aren't *dead*," Kierra clarified, "Just *really* asleep. Don't worry," she added when she noted Lora's still-widened eyes.

Lora frowned. "I wasn't *worried*," she said, but it came out less convincing than she'd hoped.

Kierra's eyes rolled so far Lora wasn't sure how they didn't get stuck in the back of her head. "Anyway," she continued, "take the next left and it will land you in the kitchens. From there, all you have to do is make it out of the castle." She patted Lora's shoulders when she finished with the hair and made her way back to the bed.

"And you?" Lora asked, following after her. She wasn't sure why she asked. So much was left unsaid between the two of them that she could have cut the tension with a knife.

"I'm headed back to the camp, like I was ordered." A pause. "If anyone catches you and asks…" Her eyebrows rose as she handed the bag to Lora.

"Yeah, yeah, you didn't help me," Lora finished for her, taking the bag and securing it on her good shoulder. When she looked back up at her friend, the wall was open next to her. She took a deep breath as she approached the hidden passageway, and they locked eyes for a brief moment.

A glimmer of long-held pain lanced Kierra's features. She stepped forward as if to hug Lora but decided against it. "Be quick and don't get caught," she said before disappearing down the pathway, taking a different turn than the one she'd told her to take.

Lora watched her go, counted to ten, took a deep breath and repeated Kierra's instructions: *Use the servants' access, take the next left, and it will land you in the kitchens. From there, all you have to do is make it out of the castle.*

Where she'd go after that, she had no idea. But it would be far, far away from this place and the war. With one more deep breath, she stepped into the servant's access, the wall closing behind her with a *click* and cloaking her in darkness. But she wasn't afraid of the dark—especially not as her shadows swirled around her as she charged toward her freedom.

CHAPTER 22

THOROUGHLY CONFUSED

Kalon

The docks were, honest to gods, the last place Kalon would have looked. Clearly, he had underestimated her. How had she made it all the way from the *castle* to the *docks* without *anyone* seeing her? That, and about a hundred other questions, ran through his head as he approached the captain of the... *ale Snatcher*? Ah, assuming the faded area that looked like a capital *G* was to be believed, the boat *used* to be named the *Gale Snatcher*, but this boat had seen better days. Years even, judging by the smell that was already emanating from below deck with twenty-five paces still between him and the gang plank.

His lip curled with a mixture of amusement and utter bewilderment. Presumably, that is why she had picked this vessel to board. Apparently, blending in with the crew of the *Gale Snatcher* was not as easy as she assumed it would be.

Garrison was the only reason he'd even found *Lora* in the first place. Kalon had realized his aunt was going to have her killed and had woken early that morning ready to make a deal with the Shade to keep her alive. As much as he wanted her dead, he needed her shadows, and at least she could be of use to him. But when Kalon found her room empty, he had headed north as fast as the wind could take him, assuming she had headed back toward Shade territory.

Assuming she had traveled on foot, Garrison searched the fortress grounds and caves, spreading the search to the docks once he'd heard a stowaway had been thrown in the brig earlier that afternoon. Smart move to check around the water even before the stowaway news—she had tried to escape using water the two other times, why would today's attempt be different?

"Your grace," the captain said, a quick bow and then a slight nod of the head to Garrison and Nuva behind him. The captain of the *Gale Snatcher* was nearly as tall as Kalon and broader than Garrison with a long beard braided and tied up in loops that were decorated with little beads.

"Captain…" Kalon paused, thinking of the name of the man in front of him. He settled on just Captain. He cleared his throat. "Captain, we were told you had a stowaway."

"You can call me Mullins, sir," Captain Mullins said with a wink. "Haven' had the pleasure to meet your acquain'ince yet," Mullins, said with a hiccup. "Your grace," he added, another bow beginning.

Kalon nearly rolled his eyes. *Oh good,* he thought, *an accent.* How this man had not toppled over already he was unsure—Mullins reeked of alcohol. The kind of alcohol Kalon, Garrison, Liam, Kierra, and Nuva would get into as kids when they snuck down to the docks or into barracks at war camps. The kind that could not possibly lend to good navigational practices. The thought of Lora shoved under deck with the crew who were no doubt in worse looking shape than Mullins here, brought a smile to Kalon's lips.

Interestingly, the man's ocean-blue eyes were as clear as the day was long. With a knowing smile and a quick nod to the captain, he cleared his throat again. "Just Kalon is fine. I know you are off tonight, but it was brought to my friend's attention that you arrested a stowaway recently."

"Aye, that we did sir. Caught 'em hidin in the back of the bow. He's down in the brig now, peekish fella, would've kept 'em on had he not been so green from all the swayin." Mullins eyes danced with amusement—he seemed to really enjoy this persona.

Kalon's eyebrows shot up. "He?" A quick glance to Garrison had the commander's eyes raising as well.

The captain's eyes tracked the motion. "Were you expectin' someone else *just Kalon?*" A smile bloomed across his face. "Perhaps the lady friend you've been seen with around by the Sea Breeze?"

Apparently, Captain *Mullins* missed nothing, but also everything. While yes, Kalon had often visited the Sea Breeze Tavern and Pub on several occasions after a long day or on return from camp. He was usually with Jade, looking to cause a little trouble or win at cards. He was in no way looking for that right now and hadn't since Jade had been taken.

Jade.

He had tried not to think about her since Kierra had broken the news to him last night—Jade's head hadn't been recovered, but the other two commanders' had. Liam said they had probably been dead over a week, at least. She'd been dead for weeks. Weeks!

He had been so sure she was still alive, was so sure he would have felt it if she had died. But he hadn't felt anything, and now all he felt was rage. Pure, undiluted fury that threatened to unravel his very soul. Fury that had had him on the sparring mat with Garrison for hours yesterday trying to blow off steam. It hadn't worked. Now, this mission was the only thing keeping his anger at bay, loosely locked away in his broken heart. His breakfast soured.

He ran his hand through his hair and gave Mullins a tight smile. "While I am always pleased to visit the Sea Breeze and indulge its patrons and staff with my presence I am, unfortunately, on official business now. Perhaps once I've finished my duties I can…extend my pleasure beyond your acquaintance," he said tightly, slowly returning his gaze to Mullins, whose eyes now shone brighter as he surely saw the promise of a chance to beat Kalon at a game or two of cards later on.

Kalon needed a break. A vacation from this wretched place and this war. So did Garrison, Nuva, and Liam.

A cough from Mullins drew his attention back to the present. *Right, focus.*

"Captain Mullins, thank you for your assistance in capturing the stowaway. If you could be so kind as to take us to him, that would be most appreciated." Kalon's formal phrasing had Mullins's eyebrows shooting up, but he gestured below deck nonetheless.

The four of them boarded the large vessel, and Captain Mullins guided them toward a hole in the deck with a set of stairs that would surely lead them to the brig.

"After you, my lady," instructed Mullins, sweeping his arms toward the stairs in a grand gesture and eying Nuva.

Nuva took one glance below deck and exclaimed, to no one in particular, "I think I'll keep watch up here," before all but running back on to the docks.

Mullins chuckled before motioning for Kalon and Garrison to follow him below. The smell ripened as they descended the creaky stairs to the brig. A mix of salt water, sweat, piss, and blood crammed its way up Kalon's nostrils as he suppressed a gag. He was pretty sure Garrison was holding his breath and decided that Nuva's decision to remain above deck seemed like the right idea.

While Drakes had a booming industry on their western coastline, Kalon himself wasn't much for sailing. He never liked confined spaces, and since everything was wooden… it just never seemed to work out when he was younger and learning about the trade. The same went for Nuva and Liam, though Garrison's distaste seemed to stem solely from the smells. The male looked greener than the spring fields of his family's farmland.

The brig, which was in the lower stern of the boat, was no bigger than two people standing shoulder to shoulder and consisted of bars on two of the four sides. The bars were slimy with algae and gods knew what else, making them look easy to break out of if one really tried. However, the pirates had been smarter than Kalon in that they had restrained their prisoner properly, it seemed. Not with chains, however, he noted, seeing the chains tossed into a pile in the corner of the cell.

They were just out of reach of the bound body currently slumped against the back wall, almost completely lost in shadows. The hint of jasmine and ember danced toward him through the thickness of piss and blood, and Kalon smiled slightly—*gotcha*. He looked back at the slumped form and the captain seemed to notice his glance to the chains as well.

Straightening, Mullins explained, "The lad nearly took out three of my best sailors when they went to chain 'em." He nodded toward the blood Kalon could now see on the walls and floor around the cell. "Jayme lost one of his five teeth and Kay left with a broken nose—is why we settled for rope, lad wasn' near as upset about that." With a chuckle he added, "But still wasn' thrilled!"

The body in the corner didn't stir once throughout the conversation, nor as Kalon and Garrison moved closer to the bars, but he felt the gaze under the wide brimmed cap tracking him as he moved—and he swore he glanced a smirk when Mullins had mentioned the damage that had been done to his men.

Garrison made to open the door but Kalon caught his arm, silently motioning him to wait. With a loud sniff in the body's direction Kalon began pacing in front of the cell, as if deep in thought. When the body still didn't move, Kalon spoke. "It seems you were right, captain, the lad is clearly breaking the stowaway law." He made a point not to look at the bundled body. "It's a good thing you called us in—we will have to take them up to the castle to be tried. I know my aunt will enjoy the reprieve from war business to pass judgment." He cut his eyes to the body but only saw a slight stiffening. *Ok, let's get a bit more serious shall we?*

Kalon paced in front of the bars again, thinking about what he could say to expose her, then his eyes snagged on the chains. "Captain," he said, his back now to the cell, "I'll need two of your strongest men. If the lad is so upset about chains, I have a feeling he won't like the ones we brought with us. You're dismissed." It was a low move, he knew, but it worked.

The form on the ground moved, suddenly and wildly, a growl coming from deep within the mass of cloaks, a sneer spreading across a grimy face.

What he beheld as the form rose from the floor was not at all what he expected. Lora didn't just look like a boy—she moved and sounded like a boy, too. Her hair was pulled up under the cap and looked dark brown, from what he could see. She had smeared something on her face and used ash or coal to appear older and dirtier. If he was in the mood to be honest with himself, he would be impressed, but he was in no mood for honesty.

If the chains hadn't given her away, then that sneer would have. He would remember that sneer for the rest of his life. It haunted him in his sleep, and not always in a bad way. *Okay no, he could not go there right now. This was the woman who killed Jade,* he reminded himself, though a small voice in his head pushed back at the lie.

That was, in fact, the opposite of productive, and nothing about this situation garnered those thoughts whatsoever. Not the smell, not the circumstance, and certainly not the way Lora stood, staring at him through the guck on her face as if she wanted to flay him alive.

So Kalon set his face into a pleasant smile that he knew would have her seeing red, narrowed his eyes, and drawled, "Hello, princess."

CHAPTER 23

LET'S MAKE *ANOTHER* DEAL

Lora

Lora sneered at the arrogant prince before her. The fact that he was using her title like a curse word was annoying, and the fact that he had just dismissed any witnesses from below the deck was also not great news. This had the potential to get ugly. She chided herself for her reaction to his chain comment, but in all honesty, it took everything in her not to shake at the thought.

She growled at the prince. His eyes sharpened, and he bore his teeth right back. *Great. This is going* really *great.* She had managed to make it all the way to the small village docks, stolen articles of clothing and some charcoal on the way, adopted an entire boyish persona, all without getting caught and only barely using her shadows to end up face-to-face with Kalon, of all people.

Getting caught as a stowaway was a minor setback, but now the asshole prince was here. He hadn't even tried to kill her yet, which was equally as unsettling as it was reassuring. She rolled her shoulders back, preparing for a fight, as the drunk of a captain came back down the stairs flanked by the two sailors she'd already taken out—his biggest men, apparently, if he had followed Kalon's orders. She was not about to be chained without a fight. The taller sailor, Jayme, they'd called him, had the right idea of looking a bit unnerved when he saw her braced for the ensuing fight.

Kalon tracked her gaze and smirked at her through the cell bars. "I see you are already acquainted with the captain and some of his crew," he drawled. "How very rude of you to sneak on their boat and then knock out Jayme here's tooth."

She cut her eyes to Kalon, and his smile only grew.

"You see," he continued when she didn't respond, "I have half a mind to bring you back to the castle and have you tried, as I've stated before." He paced again, as if deep in thought.

She wanted to throttle him. He had the upper hand here, and he knew it. *Asshole.*

"But," he said, still pacing, his eyes now glowing like pools of liquid gold, "I am feeling merciful today." His smile turned serpentine, and her shadows built behind her at the challenge in his eyes.

"And as I've stated before," she said slowly, tracking his pacing, "Mercy is a weakness." Why she was antagonizing him, she had no idea. But everything about him made her want to start swinging.

"Ah yes, your little personal pep talk before I knocked you out and won our little fight." The amusement in his voice had her seeing red all over again. He knew good and well that nothing about the fight they had in the outpost courtyard was little—and she was pretty sure he knew she'd let him win.

"No matter," he continued, since she didn't respond. "Regardless of what a measly Shade thinks, I think my mercy will benefit you today." He stopped his pacing now and their gazes met, eyes locking in a battle of wills. "Let's make another deal, shall we?"

"No thank you," she gritted out as sweetly as she could, smiling at him from beneath the brim of the hat she'd stolen. "I like my chances where I am." She gestured to the boat around her. "Also," she added with no small amount of sarcasm, "Why would you want to make a deal with a measly Shade anyway?" She let her smile settle into a pout that she knew would have him fuming.

Kalon's eyes narrowed slightly before his false smile reappeared. "While I'm sure that's not true, I thought you would be smart enough to at least *hear* this offer first?" He made a look as if to say, *Gotcha*.

She rolled her eyes and crossed her arms. "Because the first Troth went so well?"

Kalon's smile only deepened as he resumed his pacing. "You see," he said, "the good thing about you being trapped in this dingy cell—no offense, Captain Mullins—is that you have to listen, because you have nowhere else to go." He said the last bit in a sing-song kind of way that had her shadows dancing behind her, her lips tightening to a thin line.

He didn't so much as glance at her as he continued. "I need to retrieve a very special item from an old acquaintance, and I believe you can help me."

"And how exactly could I do that?" she shot at him, still overwhelmingly annoyed that he was even there.

"I've been considering many things since our last encounter," he drawled, paying no mind to the shadows that now danced around him. "And from our first. You know what has really stuck out to me?"

She made a point to look really bored as her shadows snaked through his legs like a curious cat.

"'No, what was it that has struck you, so oh handsome prince?'" He said in a higher and shriller voice. "'Thank you for asking, how very wise of you to be interested,'" the prince replied in his normal voice. While he looked very proud of himself, she merely rolled her eyes. *This dude is insane.*

"As I was saying," he continued, having a full-blown conversation with himself, "I have been considering many things. For example, how does one manage to escape a cliff dwelling castle, make it all the way across town and into the harbor in new clothes without being seen once, in broad daylight?"

"Skill," she offered with a sweet smile, noting how his smile faded a bit at her response.

"A possibility I considered then quickly dismissed," Kalon said, pausing his pacing to inspect his sleeve before continuing again. He and his sister were two sides of the same coin—he the golden skinned, dark-haired side, and she the silver haired, dark skin side, both always pacing.

Kalon's monologue drew her out of her stupor. "Escaping has not been the forte of this particular guest." And it was his turn to sweetly smile at her, which had her baring her teeth half-heartedly. Kalon ignored it and continued. "Then I thought too, what kind of father would shoot his own daughter and leave her for dead?"

Lora stiffened at the truth in the words as Kalon stopped and stepped into her space. It was foolish to be so close to her, even if she was still in the cell and loosely tied.

"And it occurred to me—perhaps maybe, just maybe, the rumors are true. Maybe you aren't as beloved as I thought you were. Maybe, you actually are the bastard daughter of that cuckolded king. But I think you already knew that about yourself. I think that you knew that the king wouldn't actually care about you because you were never his daughter. I think that's why you gave me your name, because you knew it didn't matter if I had it. And in the end, I think you let me win, not out of mercy or pity, but because if you walked free you would be walking right back to that cuckold of a king—"

Her hand stung with the heat of the slap she delivered to Kalon's face through the bars. His prattling hadn't bothered her once until the end. He had no way of knowing the true reason for her actions was his twin sister. She had thought maybe Kacey—Kierra—would have explained it all to him, but apparently not.

But Lora wasn't going to be the one to tell him. She wasn't going to be the one to explain that everything she had done, from the moment Kierra was taken from her, was to get her back. It was of no use for her to tell him, and really, she didn't care if he knew. But she couldn't listen to him say one more false truth about the king and her love for him. So, she had slapped him to shut him up. Unfortunately, instead of shutting him up the bastard was now smiling at her, smug satisfaction blooming on his red face.

***

Kalon

Kalon hadn't realized he had moved so close to the Shade, but apparently he was close enough to get the shit slapped out of him. Apparently he'd struck a chord when talking about Cyrus. But her lashing out meant that she was listening, which was more than he expected her to do after her behavior at the outpost where she'd pouted and laid on the floor like a child.

He cracked a crooked grin in her direction that he knew would have her teeth setting on edge, which was one of his favorite things. He rolled his shoulders and then continued, content to keep talking while she was listening.

"As I was saying before you so rudely interrupted," he continued, making a point to stay within her range but not as close as before, "I came to the conclusion that you are only of value to the tyrant king because you have something he values most of all—power." He noted, with no small amount of satisfaction that the girl seemed to blanch a bit under all the charcoal on her face. He wasn't even sure she was breathing as he continued.

"Seeing as you are a Shade—albeit, an odd one—you must have pretty strong shadow magic to be of use to the king. So," he drew out the word just to irritate her, and it worked instantly. "The offer, as it stands, is this: you help me retrieve my item with your shadows, and I will grant you free passage anywhere you want." The girl stiffened. "Back to the north, perhaps—"

"No." Her voice was quiet but not weak, and full of gravel.

"No?" he couldn't help but ask.

"I don't want to go north," she clarified, her voice still barely above a whisper. *Interesting...* Garrison and Kalon's eyebrows both shot up and they exchanged a glance, a silent conversation passing between them.

"Ok, not north," he repeated with a hint of sarcasm. "In exchange for your help retrieving my item with your shadows I will grant you safe passage anywhere you want, and especially not north. Does that sound fair?"

Lora, to Kalon's chagrin, had the audacity to look as if she would decide against it.

"I'll need money," she finally said, looking him dead in the eyes. "Not a lot, but enough for my voyage and for when I get...to wherever it is I go. Plus, clothes and supplies," she added, nodding slightly.

Kalon made a point to look at what she was wearing—she certainly would need a change of clothes before they left. She smelled of piss, blood, and booze, but her eyes—they shone with a new sense of purpose he hadn't seen since she'd tried to escape. He hadn't realized he had been staring until Garrison coughed.

"Well?" she asked impatiently, crossing her arms over her chest.

"Seems fair enough," he said through a tight smile. "But if you don't want to go north," he drawled, "you could always stay here and earn some money before your travels." He wasn't sure why he had offered, but the words seemed to tumble out regardless of his intentions.

Lora's eyebrows shot up. "And what? Fight? For you? No thank you, I'm tired of war." She had the audacity to yawn a bit at the idea of fighting in a war.

"But what about the people?" he asked, confused at how just a couple days ago she had been willing to fight for the refugees, to stand up to her uncle, and now, nothing.

"I don't have any people," she said sharply, beginning to cut her ropes with a makeshift dagger he hadn't seen her holding a moment ago. He made a mental note to disarm her before he let her above deck.

"What about the Shades?" Garrison asked, since apparently Kalon had started staring again.

"They are no longer my people after their king had me shot in the chest with an arrow," she retorted, finishing the last bit of rope on her wrist and moving to her ankles. "Or did you forget that?" she said through grunts as the rope came free.

"And the Drakes? The refugees? The innocents?" It was his turn to ask.

Lora pulled the last of the rope free and looked him dead in the eyes, a torrent of emotions flashing in them before saying, "Like I said, not my people. I didn't start this war, so it's not my job to finish it."

***

Lora

With the rope finally off her wrists, Lora felt a wave of relief settle over her. She rubbed at where they had been tied, but when Kalon tracked the movement, she immediately stopped.

If this deal worked out, then she would be free. Not free like the last deal had offered, but free and safe, able to go and do what she pleased. The feelings that surged through her almost made her lightheaded. Kalon and Garrison had stood there questioning her while she undid her own restraints, and now Kalon was just gaping at her.

"What? I told you before, mercy is a weakness that I do not possess. I have no interest in the war. Not anymore," she mumbled the last bit. Kalon cocked his head as if he heard it but chose not to broach the subject any further. Garrison stepped forward with a key, and Kalon held up a hand to stop him.

"What now?" she asked with sass, drawing his gaze to hers..

"You know the drill, *princess*," he said with a fake smile. "Your palm, please." He held out his, drawing a knife from a sheath at his side with the other. Garrison stiffened.

She noted the unease leaking from Garrison, her eyes sliding between the Drakes, before reluctantly holding her palm out to the prince.

"I'll say the requirements of the Troth, we do a small slice here and there and then we shake, just like last time," he said, another, more annoying smile blooming on his face.

She nodded tightly in his direction. Garrison, who she wasn't sure had taken a full breath since they'd arrived below deck, now stepped forward, extending the hilt of a smaller, more ornate knife to Kalon. Kalon seemed to like that knife better and traded with the male. Garrison looked to her and then down at her unbound hands and his serious eyes softened a fraction, a tight smile playing on his lips.

She looked away. The last thing she needed from any of these assholes was pity.

Kalon took a deep breath and cut a small slice across his palm, the blood welling immediately. "I, Kalon, Prince of the Drakes, will provide safe passage for"—he paused and looked up at her— "sorry, what do you want to go by, princess?"

She stared at him flatly. "Just Lora."

"Right," he replied, his tone dripping with sarcasm before straightening and continuing. "I, Kalon, Prince of the Drakes, will provide safe passage and needed goods to *just Lora*—" A small smirk played on his face as he repeated back the name she'd given him. "In exchange for the use of her shadow power in retrieving my stolen item. Anything you want to add?" he asked as he finished his little speech.

She rolled her eyes but then nodded. Kalon rolled his right back but handed her the knife anyway. "I, *Lora*, will provide extraordinary shadow services in exchange for *free* safe passage and considerable coin and goods for my journey." She made a point to emphasize the words she felt were important but wasn't sure if it would affect the strange magic of a Troth. She sliced her palm before she gave herself time to reconsider and sucked in a sharp breath at the tingling pain.

Garrison took the knife from her through the bars and Kalon turned his hand over, lining their bloodied palms together. "Let neither one of us break the Troth, nor harm the other," he said and she, though mentally prepared, still gasped as the magic roared through her veins, tying her to the prince for the foreseeable future.

Guess killing him if he gets annoying is off the table, she thought, starting to withdraw her hand immediately after the tingling stopped, but Kalon pulled a small, thin strip of cloth from his pocket and gently wrapped her palm where the Troth mark had bloomed—black, this time.

When he was done, she pulled her hand back through the bars and watched as he did the same to his own hand. Something in the air shifted, the tension between the three of them easing a fraction as Garrison moved to unlock her cell.

She breathed deeply and stepped out of the cell—her first step toward freedom. She looked around, having assumed the world would be a bit different now but alas, they were still in a shit old boat that smelled of piss. At least Kalon had stopped staring at her. "And where exactly will we be going to 'retrieve' this very special item?" she asked, pulling her hat off and wiping some of the muck off her face. Holy gods, she smelled awful.

"You didn't want to ask that before you made the deal?" Garrison said with a slight chuckle, and she pinned him with a look. Garrison only shrugged before making his way up the stairs. She looked at Kalon, who was smiling slightly.

She raised her eyebrows as if to say, *well?* She felt Kalon's responding chuckle in her very bones as he walked toward the stairs Garrison had just climbed. Within a heartbeat, she balled up her hat and threw it at him.

"What?" he asked, looking back at her, rubbing at the back of his head where the wad had hit him.

Exasperation flushed her cheeks. *This is going to be a long journey.*

"Ok fine," he said, lifting his arms in defense. "We are headed to Kretor."

Her jaw dropped. "Kretor? That's miles away from—"

"A whole kingdom away if you really think about it," he interrupted, picking up her hat from the ground.

Lora was, in fact, thinking about it—it would take weeks, months even to get there and back, not even calculating how long it would take to retrieve whatever it was Kalon felt he deserved.

"It will take some time to cross Balaur," Kalon drawled, seemingly having read her mind, "but once we are done you'll be off to 'not north' in no time." He gave her a tight, knowing smile as he offered her hat back.

Her eyes narrowed, fists clenching as she snatched the hat. "When do we leave?"

"Today."

Lora gaped again. "Today?"

"There seems to be an echo in here," he chuckled, moving again toward the stairs. As he reached the first step, he added over his shoulder, "Yes, today."

"Are we taking the dragons?" she asked, still standing by the cell. Kalon stiffened, turning slowly to face her.

"No, no dragons, they…cause too much attention," he said slowly. "We don't exactly want the royal family to know we are coming, now do we?"

"Apparently not," she retorted, slipping her hat into her pocket. "Seems like a waste to not have them with us though… they can do a lot of damage.."

"True," Kalon agreed, and his energy shifted in a way that had her shadows on high alert. "But they aren't coming. Sorry to disappoint," he added, walking up the stairs.

"I'm not disappointed," she said, following after him. "I'm just saying any weapon we have could be helpful."

They made it to the first landing as Kalon said over his shoulder again, "Let's just say they weren't exactly thrilled when they were shot at the last time you were around."

She was mildly offended. "Oh, so they hold grudges?" Her eyebrows rose with the question.

"Better than anyone I know," muttered Liam, who had come from somewhere in midship. She hadn't scented him coming, which said a lot about the smell coming from below deck. "Hiya boss," Liam said by way of greeting. "Ready when you are."

"Great." Kalon nodded, climbing the last set of stairs. "Let's head out."

"Wait, what?" Lora asked, following behind the two males in front of her. "I need to change before we leave. If we aren't taking the dragons then we're...what? Walking across two kingdoms?" She grabbed Kalon's arm to stop them before they got on deck.

"Gods no," Liam laughed as he climbed the stairs past Kalon and onto the deck.

"So..." She waited, no way was she going to be left in the dark about this plan. A plan to get across an entire kingdom without dragons and through Drake territory...

A smile spread across Kalon's face that made her stomach sour. "Much to your enthusiasm I'm sure, we'll be sailing."

She blanched but composed herself quickly. "Well, let me change before we get on the boat."

"Lucky for you, you don't have to go far." Kalon said, pulling free from her grasp.

The look on her face had Kalon's own smile spreading wider. "What do you—"

"*Lora*," he interrupted, saying her name like a curse word. "I believe you've already had the pleasure of meeting our captain, but allow me to reintroduce you to Mullins Finch, Captain of the *Gale Snatcher* and our navigator for the next couple of weeks."

CHAPTER 24

A SEA-FARING SHADE

Lora

The *Gale Snatcher* had been a specimen in her heyday, but now she was a little more than a glorified rowboat. A rowboat that Lora decided, by the first day, she wasn't the biggest fan of. The spaces were too tight, the food was bad, and Lora never felt like she could fully stand up with all the tossing and rolling of the waves.

It had been so bad the first two days that she hadn't left the bucket they'd given her when she'd started vomiting. At least being sick meant she was too exhausted to have nightmares chasing her awake in the night. Especially when so many of those nightmares revolved around the Drake princess. She hadn't dared bring up her and Kierra's relationship with anyone, especially not Kalon. But when the boat pitched and swayed and nausea crept up Lora's throat, her mind would distract itself with images and memories of her friend and their time together.

A small bright spot on the so-far miserable trip was that the Drakes didn't seem to fare on sea much better. She had barely seen Nuva, and when she did the soldier was green with sickness. And Kalon—well, he spent most of his time in the captain's quarters with Finch and Garrison. What they could talk about all day, every day, was a mystery to her.

Liam took pity on her on the third day and gave her some root to chew that made her seasickness a little better. She also took to sleeping, eating—everything except relieving herself—above deck. She didn't care if she was in the way or not, being able to see the sky and the stars made her feel a little less wobbly. Her favorite spot on the whole damned ship was on one of the tall masts that held the tattered sails. She could lay along one of the horizontal beams and sway with the wind, not the waves.

The fact that they would be on the boat for a little over two weeks made her want to throw up again, but the past day she had been vomit free—and she wanted to keep it that way.

The sun was still forcing its way above the horizon, and Lora was again on one of the lower beams that hung over the starboard side of the vessel as figures emerged from below deck earlier than usual.

Kalon and Garrison both strode from below deck to the bow of the boat, the latter pulling his shirt over his head while the former rolled his sleeves.

Lora swung her legs over the beam and sat up, watching curiously.

The males braced their feet in a fighting stance and an unspoken conversation seemed to pass between the two of them. Without warning Garrison swung out at Kalon, aiming for the side he usually protected. Kalon dodged and swept his feet out, catching Garrison in the shins. But Garrison had seen it coming and rolled with the blow, landing a kick to Kalon's leg as he did.

She watched as the two males punched and dodged for at least an hour, sweat gleaming on both their brows and dripping down Garrison's muscled, tattooed back. She noted that the tattoo covered most of his upper back with dark swirls over each shoulder, as if a dragon had blown smoke over them and then settled. There was another, smaller one around his upper left bicep—it was gold and twirled around his arm like braided cloth. How she hadn't noticed them before, she had no idea.

Garrison said something that Lora couldn't hear, and Kalon's attention snapped in her direction, his amber eyes flaring slightly. Garrison's accompanying smirk and then knockout blow had Kalon cursing at a level Lora could most definitely hear.

The broad male helped his prince off the floor, and they made their way to the table that held canteens of water, both drinking deeply. Lora let her attention drift to Kalon, whose muscular body was very much on display. The sweat on his upper body had caused his shirt to cling to the tan muscles of his chest and back, creating a look not unlike statues Lora had seen in drawings in the library in Attica. His hair was wet with sweat, his curls twisting around his ears and on his forehead.

He ran through a series of moves with his short sword, the blade slicing through the air and the invisible enemies he was surely fighting. *Probably her*, she thought to herself as his blade swiped and sliced.

She tracked a bead of sweat as it traveled down his muscled torso before disappearing, soaking into his breeches. She was suddenly very thirsty, her tongue sticking to the roof of her mouth.

"Are you going to ogle him all morning or will you join in the sparring?" Garrison had somehow snuck up on her, his voice jarring her enough that she nearly fell off the beam.

"I wasn't ogling," she said a tad too defensively down to him, quickly adding, "I was judging his form, which could use some serious work I might say. Who even trained him?"

Garrison let out a harsh chuckle. "That would be me."

"I thought you were the same age?"

"We're close enough in age," he explained with a nod. "But I started training before Kalon. So, when he showed up for recruitment, I had to teach him the basics."

"Oh," she said, feeling a tiny bit bad that she'd said his form was shit.

"But you're right, his form is shit," Garrison said as if reading her mind. "Any time he gets injured he tends to favor the other side too much." His gaze tracked Kalon's swordsmanship as the prince continued his exercises.

"I'm guessing it was his left shoulder recently?" Lora observed, remembering their fight in the courtyard and how he'd favored his right side, letting it take the blow.

Garrison let out a chuckle again, this one brimming with wicked amusement. "Yeah something like that, though I wouldn't bring it up with him." The large male was now wrapping his hands with a thin cloth, and Lora twisted on the beam to see better.

"Why?" she asked, noting how careful Garrison was with his wrappings. "Is he sensitive?" She made a point of throwing as much sarcasm into the question as possible.

"Not at all," Garrison said, amusement dancing in his eyes. "It's just that you gave him the injury, so he might want to return the favor."

Lora's eyebrows shot up in exasperation. "Me? When did I—"

She was cut off by Liam's arrival on the bow. He, too, had removed his shirt. He was, as she had observed in the dark cell, quite muscular for a medic, not as big as Garrison but still bigger than Kalon. His dark skin was already shiny with sweat, his tattooed forearms looking strikingly similar to Garrison's—not to mention the same braided tattoo on his bicep. *Interesting.* Within minutes he and Kalon began to spar.

"Like I said before," Garrison chided, clearing his throat and drawing her attention away from the sweaty males "Are you just going to watch, or are you going to join?"

"What makes you think a princess like me could even participate in that?" she said innocently, batting her eyes.

"You're right," Garrison agreed sarcastically. "A princess like yourself would never have the skills or training to spar with a Drake prince." A sly smile spread on his face as he added, "or to take down nearly two dozen soldiers while chained to a post."

The almost compliment had a smile playing on her own lips.

"Perhaps you could *learn* a thing or two," he continued when she didn't respond. "You know, since you couldn't actually participate."

She shot the rider a sideways glance, who had a full-on wicked grin on his face.

"What the hell has you smiling so big this early in the morning?" Asked Nuva, who emerged from below deck. She looked a bit better than the last time Lora had seen her—it had been when they first boarded the boat and she, too, had been given a bucket. But now there was no bucket in sight. The dark-skinned soldier rolled up the sleeves to her crimson tunic, her shaven head already glistening with the spray from the sea.

"Oh nothing," Garrison said innocently. "Just telling Lora here that she is more than capable of learning a thing or two from sparring with Kalon before we make landfall."

Lora rolled her eyes at the insinuation that the prince could actually teach her anything.

The smell of citrus wafted toward Lora and then came a curt voice. "No, she may not." Kalon's steps had been feather light as he had approached them, and even Nuva seemed impressed at his stealth.

"And why's that?" Lora asked indignantly, adding with a sweeter, nagging tone, "Afraid, prince?"

Kalon narrowed his eyes at her but didn't respond. Instead, he took some strands of fabric from the table and began wrapping his hands like Garrison had, but with a lot less skill.

"I wouldn't want to damage your pride anyway," she said, leaning against the beam. "It seems delicate," she added, pretending to yawn.

"That is not how you'll get him to train you," Liam observed from below her, his bright blue eyes dancing with amusement.

"Good. I don't need it," she replied, more than happy to spend some time soaking up the sun. It wasn't exactly warm, but it was better than the ice fields of Attica. She pulled her hat lower on her head to cover her face as she readjusted herself on the beam, letting a leg hang over lazily, her braided hair draping behind her back. At least it was back to its natural wine-red color.

"Then prove it." Kalon's voice nearly startled her—he stood directly beneath her, looking up at her with a look of resolve, his lips a tight line.

"Excuse me?" she asked, looking down at him from under her hat.

"Prove you don't need it," he repeated, leveling a look at her in challenge.

She straightened, pushing her hat back on her head so she could see him better. "Sorry, was sending twenty-three members of your little outpost to Liam not enough proof?"

"Most of the soldiers at the outpost were still new. They were still learning," Kalon retorted.

She snorted. "And I'm guessing you think that's why *all* of them lost?"

"Yep." Kalon's gaze hadn't wavered once. It was annoying.

Lora let out a bitter laugh. "Okay," she said sarcastically as she leaned back on the beam, readjusting her hat.

"Look, I get it," Kalon said, his tone shifting enough to perk Lora's attention. "You're a princess who can wield shadows—how scary. But we need to know if you'll be a liability."

It took all of her will not to straighten at the words. Even Garrison seemed uncomfortable with the phrasing. "A liability?"

"Yes," he confirmed. "You were in chains for a long time—canthite, if I remember correctly."

She immediately saw red but took a breath before responding through gritted teeth. "Yes. I am well aware—"

"And you've been injured and lost a lot of blood," Kalon interrupted. "Based on the look of you, you're most likely malnourished."

Malnourished? She knew she had lost some muscle, but to say she looked malnourished was rude. Then again, she hadn't seen herself in the mirror recently, and she certainly didn't feel strong anymore. But what the hell, even if she was malnourished, it was their fault.

"You know I'm right," he said, pacing on the deck in front of Liam. "We don't have a lot of time, and we all need to be ready for our mission when we get there. We will only be as strong as our weakest link, and that's looking like you, princess."

Before she had fully registered the insult, Kalon and Liam had begun sparring again.

Well, that was rude. Lora swung her legs over the beam and landed on the balls of her feet, rocking with the boat toward the sparring pair. "Fine. You want me to train? Bring it on," she said, standing between the two sparring males.

"Not me," Kalon said, moving around her. "Nuva."

"Nuva?" she croaked.

"Me?" Nuva echoed.

"Yes, you," Garrison confirmed, nodding at Nuva. "You train new recruits. At this point that's what Lora here is—a new recruit."

Nuva looked as insulted as Lora felt. "I am a commanding officer in the Shade army—"

"Were," Garrison said, swiping her hat from her.

"What?" She watched as he began wrapping her hands in the same thin fabric as the rest of them, the motions like second nature.

"You *were* a commanding officer in the Shade army," he clarified, finishing one hand and moving to the next. "Now…" he paused his work to think through his next words, but Kalon interrupted him.

"Now, you're a weak, fragile no-one who thinks she's still big and tough. Don't even deny it—we've seen you training your shadows when you don't think we're looking, and they aren't as spectacular as they have been."

"Oh yeah?" she said, seething, ripping her hand from Garrison's grasp. "Not the grand show you want?" She stepped into Kalon's space. "And yet"—she moved right into his face—"you won't even fight against me. You *coward*." Lora all but spit the last word at him and she saw it hit its mark.

Kalon's face turned beet red. He sank into a fighting stance right as Garrison's voice rang out, "Enough you two." He moved between them. "That's enough," he said again, reaching back for Lora's hand to finish the wrappings.

Kalon took a step back and composed himself before stating offhandedly, "At this point you are mostly swagger and arrogance and being all talk won't get my shit back from Kretor. So, train, get strong, and be of use to me or our deal is null and void." He made to turn away but she was still mad, still reeling from the insults he'd thrown her way.

"What the fuck? You said you only needed my shadows and now you're wanting to train me like some new recruit? This is bullshit!" she shouted after him.

He paused and turned back to her, taking the two strides forward that put them again face-to-face. "You can't always depend on your shadows, you know. What happens if there is canthite? I don't want you using shadows until they are absolutely necessary. Until I say so. That's why I need you to train. Not for your sake, but for the sake of the people on this boat I care about. Which, may I remind you, is not you." He looked down at her with such disgust that her shadows pushed at her skin, swirling just below the surface.

"So what?" she said, trying to take a breath before she did something stupid, like punch him in the face. "When we run into trouble—"

"*If* we run into trouble," Kalon interrupted, "I want you to be as useful as everyone else in this group—*without* your shadows." He straightened himself and quickly strode to the stern of the boat, the door clicking behind him as he disappeared into the captain's quarters.

While he had a point, it was annoying as shit that she had to agree with him. A liability her ass. She would train and get strong again, not for him, but for herself. So, when the time came that she was free, she would never be someone else's weapon to yield.

***

Lora trained every morning for the next week and a half as they sailed through the choppy waves, barely avoiding two Shade patrol ships and a warring pirate gang. While she and Nuva were by no means friends now, they settled into a semi-comfortable routine of training, sparring, and training again each day.

Nuva had even taken to sleeping outside on nights where the sea seemed to roll and drop more, and she'd let Lora show her some tricks she knew with a short sword. Kalon, much to her annoyance, had immediately taken the short sword away, declaring that Lora didn't need any weapons, as she wasn't far enough in her training for it. It took twenty-five years' worth of training to not bash the asshole's head in for the insult.

At night Lora slept while the crew of the Gale Snatcher, as well as the Drakes, drank and sang wildly inappropriate songs. She decided around night six that she may have hated pirates more than she hated Kalon.

Once they had finally passed out she was awake and training her shadows, honing them to various objects and weapons, still not comfortable practicing in front of the others. As much as she hated to admit it, Kalon had been right.

If she hadn't been training, she probably *would have* been a liability once they landed.

This morning had been a particularly strenuous workout. Nuva had landed a solid right hook to her jaw before being called away to the Captain's Quarters to discuss where they would land. Of course, no one told Lora that's what the meeting was about, but she may have let her shadows slip free into the room in order to report back to her. She wasn't a fan of being left in the dark, especially now that her freedom was on the line.

As she lay on the beam she had claimed as her bed and looked out over the relatively calm sea, she noticed a small blip appear on the horizon. According to her shadows, they shouldn't be seeing any land, or other ships for that matter, for another day or two. She sat up, squinting her eyes against the glaring sun to try and get a better view. She had heard some of the sailors the other night telling stories of how the heat and rolling of the sea can play tricks on the mind, but as Lora stared harder she was 100 percent sure she was actually seeing a ship.

An alarm sounded in her mind as the ship grew larger, steadily heading their direction. There was only one kingdom whose ships would patrol this far south, and she was in no mood to see any relatives.

She hopped from her perch, landing with ease on her achy legs and strode the ten or so paces to the Captain's Quarters. She went to knock but the door swung open, an angry Kalon looking down his nose at her.

"This is a private meeting," he said snarkily. He held the door open only a sliver.

Lora narrowed her eyes as she ducked under his arm, trying to get inside. He barely thwarted her. She shot him an annoyed look that he fired right back before the door opened a bit wider, Captain Finch's crystal blue eyes peering down at her. Kalon stepped out of his way, moving back into the room.

"Captain Finch," she said, righting herself. "There's a boat coming."

"We know," Kalon said flatly, not bothering to look up from the map he inspected.

She stuck her tongue out at him before she turned to Finch. "It's a Shade vessel." The black sails had given it away immediately.

"We know that too," Kalon replied dryly, looking at her with disdain.

"They are going to try and board the boat," she said to Finch, having decided to ignore Kalon entirely.

"No, they won't," Kalon said from inside the room.

"Yes they will," she said with a sigh. *So much for ignoring him.*

"No, Lora, they won't." His tone was laced with condescension, and he looked at her like she was a child afraid of the darkness under her bed. Too bad she *was* the darkness lurking under one's bed.

"Yes, Kalon, they will," she retorted with the same tone he'd used. "I know how they operate and if they see you, which I bet they have, they will change course and come and try to board this vessel." She made a point to give him a flat, dry smile.

He advanced on her so quickly she nearly balked.

Finch looked between her and Kalon, who glowered in her face then took a step back. *Coward.* "Have you ever actually been on a Shade vessel before?" Kalon asked, cocking his head to the side.

Her eyes sharpened as her face pinched. "No," she admitted firmly, still holding her ground.

Kalon laughed bitterly, a smug look of victory spreading across his face. "Well, there you go." He made to move back into the quarters, apparently satisfied with himself.

"You haven't either," she pointed out, turning toward Finch again. "The difference is, I am a Shade. So, I know the way they think and how they act."

"As far as I'm concerned, your role here is to help me steal. That's it." He didn't look up from that stupid map as he continued, "So thanks but no thanks for your input on any other matters. It is not needed."

Lora's temper rose, and she took several deep breaths. She needed him alive for their deal...and if she was right about the Shade vessel, then she had to keep pushing. "Kalon, trust me. They will try and board this ship."

"That's just it." He glared at her. "I don't trust you."

Before she could even stop herself, she hurled a dagger directly at Kalon's smug face. It narrowly missed his head, grazing his right cheek before embedding itself almost to the hilt in the wood behind him.

Finch's eyebrows launched sky high as Kalon's reddened face turned slowly toward her. Finch let out a low whistle and Nuva, Liam, and Garrison had the smart idea to take several steps away from their prince, who looked at Lora with nothing but hatred in his amber eyes.

He glanced sidelong at the dagger. "Did you just throw a dagger at my head?" His voice rose with each word as he yanked the weapon from the wall.

"No." She corrected, "I threw it at the wall *next* to your head."

Apparently it *was* possible for Finch's eyebrows to raise higher.

"If I wanted to hit you in the head, I would have," she remarked, straightening to her full height.

"And you wonder why I don't fucking trust you," Kalon said through his teeth, placing the dagger on the table next to the maps.

"Yeah. Newsflash, asshole, I don't really care that you don't trust me. What I do care about is surviving, and we will not do that if that Shade ship attacks us." She felt Kalon's temper rising, and his skin seemed to almost glimmer with rage. She felt Liam, Nuva, and Garrison go taut, and then within seconds three things happened:

Liam was in Kalon's face, turning him from her view.

Garrison was in *Lora's* face and holding her arms very tightly to her sides.

Nuva was at Lora's side, completely disarming her.

When Nuva finished, she slipped back into the room while Garrison moved Lora farther onto the deck.

"What the fuck?" she said, trying and failing to get out of Garrison's grasp. She threw her whole-body weight into freeing herself and yet, nothing, she barely moved out of Garrison's grasp. *Maybe I should be training with* him, she thought as he moved her to midship, right below her beam.

His eyes tracked something over her shoulder before his grip relaxed. "Look, I believe you about the boat, and I'm sorry about Kalon. But for now, you should probably stay out here."

"Where I can't throw any daggers at your prince?" Lora asked angrily.

"Hopefully you don't have any daggers left to throw, but, yes, where neither one of you can put any more holes in the ship."

Lora wanted to retort back, but her mind was full of roaring. Garrison didn't move until she'd taken three deep breaths, and only then did he move past her, heading back to the Captain's Quarters.

"He can't expect me to stay defenseless forever!" she shouted, turning to face Garrison's hulking back as he disappeared through the door and into the room.

Finch still stood at the door, where he'd been through the whole encounter. He glanced around her, toward where the Shade vessel was still steadily cruising their way. "They will try and board this boat," Lora said one last time, hoping someone on this damn ship would believe her.

Finch merely winked before closing the door, leaving Lora alone to watch as the Shade ship approached.

CHAPTER 25

NO MORE WEAPONS

Lora

The Shade ship Kalon was *sure* wouldn't come for them was now blowing full steam ahead in their direction. She would have been filled with smug vindication if she wasn't dreading every moment that passed, bringing the ship closer. *Are they coming for me? Had one of the pirates sold her out when they docked for an hour a couple days ago? Is Kierra still safe at the refugee camp?* Lora's mind raced as fast as the crew below her did.

"The wind is not on our side," Finch said to the crew as Lora watched from her perch on the beam. She had been sitting up there since Garrison had brought her there, and she was glad of it. Everything going on below her looked like mayhem.

While the *Gale Snatcher* was an older ship, it was still outfitted with all the necessary equipment needed to attack and plunder other boats—however, it was not entirely prepared to *be* attacked and plundered. The pirates on deck all moved to assigned positions that Finch called out from his spot by the helm. Kalon and his comrades had come out from the Captain's Quarters when the initial alarm had been sounded, and they were now stationed throughout the boat, given various tasks by Finch and the other pirates.

Lora was more than happy to sit on her perch and not be a part of the hell that was surely going to break loose once they were boarded. Not to mention Nuva had completely disarmed her, so unless she was going to use her shadows, which she wasn't, she would only be in the way.

The Shade ship was close enough now that she could make out faces of the sailors, none of which she recognized, thank the gods. Everyone on the *Gale Snatcher* seemed to take in a collective breath as the Shade vessel came up on their port side. Lora readjusted herself on the beam, tucking her braid into her hat. She leaned around the beam in time to see a tall, thin man dressed in Shade black make his way to the railing of their ship, whose name, ironically, was *Storm Bringer*.

The Gale Snatcher *versus the* Storm Bringer, *this should be fun*, she thought as she watched the Shade sailors part for their captain.

Finch, too, was making his way to the railing—apparently this is what they did before they started fighting. Once both men were relatively eye-to-eye, the Shade captain spoke first. "Good afternoon, Captain."

"Mullins," called out Captain Finch, "Of the *Ale Snatcher*."

Lora's head swiveled to see that Finch, the clear-eyed, no-shit captain was now, yet again, the hunkered, tattered and "drunk" Captain Mullins she had met weeks ago. *Incredible acting*, she thought with an eye roll. She scanned the crew to see that they, too, looked worse for the wear, as if all the hulking men that had been on the ship moments before were now shoved below deck. Kalon seemed to be doing the same mental math as her, and their gazes collided for a moment.

The captain, who was dressed in head-to-toe, tight fitting, finely embroidered Shade black, smiled tightly at Finch as he spoke. "Of course. Unfortunately, Captain Mullins"—the Shade said the name like it tasted sour in his pompous mouth—"these waters are restricted, as they have been recently overrun with sympathizers and pirates."

Mullins made a face of pure shock as the Shade captain's tight smile hardened. "Well, If I see any I will let you know, sir!" he concluded, nodding to the Shade captain.

The Shade's smile dropped. "That is not good enough, sir. We will need to board your vessel and check." Although, as he said it, he nearly cringed after looking at the apparent filth that was the *Ale Snatcher*.

"Check for what, *sir*?" called Mullins, looking as confused as the Shade commander would expect a drunk fisherman to look.

"For pirates and sympathizers, of course," the captain responded, clearly exasperated by having to repeat himself.

"Well, Cap'in," Mullins slurred, making his way over to the edge of the boat, face to face with the Shade. "It's your lucky day."

"And why is that?" The Shade captain asked, clearly annoyed.

"Because we're both." Mullins said with a wicked smile. Then, before Lora's eyes, Mullins melted into Finch, and the pirates launched themselves on the Shades.

All hell broke loose.

***

Kalon

"Aren't you going to help?" Kalon shouted, spinning to deflect a blow from a Shade behind him. Once Finch had declared they were both sympathizers *and* pirates, then all but released the pirates on the Shade sailors, they had been blade-to-blade with them for nearly thirty minutes. Lora, however, had been perched on her beam, fucking watching.

"Who, me?" Lora asked innocently. He couldn't see her as he spun again, but he was sure she was making that ridiculous face of innocence that drove him mad. "Oh no," she said. "See, that's not part of our bargain. I believe I'm here solely to, how'd you describe it earlier? *Help you steal, and that's it.*"

"We could use some help down here," he called again, stopping his fighting to look up to where the bitch leaned against the mast, leg dangling over as she cleaned her fingernails with an arrow that had been shot in her direction. Kalon had actually seen her catch it in midair and, if he hadn't been fighting for his life, he would have been impressed.

"Kalon, look out!" Nuva called from somewhere to his left. He barely dodged the side swipe a Shade sailor took at him.

"So, it seems…" Lora drawled, not even looking down at them from her perch. "Unfortunate that you have no one else who can help you! But you guys are doing really well on your own." She paused, snatching *another* arrow out of the air, and glanced around the raging battle. "Okay," she admitted, "not *really* well, but you'll manage. Or…you won't," she added with a shrug, discarding the first arrow in favor of the newer one.

"You realize if I die, our bargain is void," Kalon gritted out as an arrow whizzed past his own head. *How in the hell had she caught one?*

"You realize if you die, I'll be able to jump ship and go somewhere else?" she purred, and her smile was lethal and feline. Kalon almost shivered. For an average sized person, she could make herself as terrifying as any brute he'd faced on the battlefield.

He couldn't believe she refused to help them. They honestly might not survive this encounter, and she was clearly okay with that. "And what if the Shades find out who you are?" Kalon shot at her as he swung his sword, relieving a sailor of his sword and hand. Another, fucking massive Shade took his place and swung with a sword bigger than Kalon's arm.

Lora's face bleached of all color, that coy smile slipping to a feral grin. "You tell them who I am, *prince*," she spat, sitting up," and I don't care what bargain we made, I'll kill you on the spot." *And we both know I can*, she seemed to whisper in his mind.

Kalon, sweating his ass off as he fought a huge Shade, still shivered. The sheen to her eyes told Kalon enough. It wasn't a threat, but a promise.

He shook his head as he dove under the sailor's arms. "Okay look, help us and I'll add something to the bargain."

Garrison, who had been dicing up a soldier like an onion, whipped his head toward them, eyes flaring with warning. Kalon chose not to pay attention as he ducked again, narrowly missing a dagger to the ribs.

Lora narrowed her eyes before laying back down on the mast, twirling the arrow. "While that is an enticing deal, it seems I would be of no use anyway...seeing as I am unarmed." She lazily rolled her head toward him, eyes bright with amusement. Another pirate went down as shadows grew to his left. *Well, the Captain's still alive*, he thought, rolling out of reach from a Shade that had charged his direction.

"Nope. No way," Kalon argued. The thought of her having a short sword—absolutely not. When she didn't respond he added, hoping to butter her up, "We both know you don't need a weapon to be deadly."

Lora's face lit up in a mockery of a blush. "Thank you for the compliment, princeling, but I believe you told me...again, I believe I'm quoting you exactly here. 'No shadows until I say so.'"

Kalon could feel at least two pairs of eyes on him from the crew of the *Gale Snatcher* as Lora's words carried over the fray. Of course, now, she would be so literal. She hadn't followed any rules up until this point... Kalon rolled his eyes, stabbing his sword through the stomach of a Shade sailor. "Well, I'm saying so! Come down here and fight!"

Lora faked shock at the idea. "Down there? Where it's all blades and Shades? No thank you. I choose life." She batted her eyes at him in feigned innocence.

Kalon was about to say something that would probably get a knife to his throat later, but Nuva's shout stopped him. She'd been stabbed through the upper arm, red blood already spilling onto the deck and soaking her crimson tunic.

Before he could charge in her direction, an arrow flew from behind him, imbedding itself in the throat of Nuva's assailant. Nuva beheaded the male before he'd finished screaming. Nuva gave a curt nod over Kalon's shoulder before she looked at him.

"Give her a fucking weapon, Kalon," was all Nuva said as she tied her arm off and dove back into the fray.

Kalon rolled his eyes and, turning toward where Lora was lounging on the mast, lifted his arms in defeat. "Okay, you can have one small—"

Lora landed gracefully on the deck of the boat, snapping the neck of the sailor to her left and gingerly picking up his long sword, wiping the blood on his trousers.

"This will do," she said, and winked, *actually winked* at him before she, too, was diving into the fray of, as she said, blades and Shades.

***

Once the princess entered the fight, it was all but over. Lora had twirled and spun, almost as if in a dance, as she slaughtered her way through the Shade sailors. And she didn't use her shadows once. It was incredible.

As Kalon watched with a mixture of mute horror and wonder, it dawned on him, and probably everyone on the boat, just how close they all were to death every time they slept near her. How or why, she hadn't killed him and his friends yet, he wasn't quite sure. Wasn't sure he wanted to know.

Nuva pushed the last of the Shade sailor bodies into the ocean as some of the crew of the *Gale Snatcher* began rigging the *Storm Breaker* with explosives so they could sink her before someone noticed she was no longer crewed. As annoying as pirates could be, Kalon was grateful for their expertise in this area.

Finch, who was back to being Finch, ordered the crew around, having some sent or carried to Liam below deck for mending, some swabbing the deck of the gore, and some making minor repairs to the ship.

"We only lost three pirates and no one from our party," Garrison said as they walked the deck toward Nuva.

"We were lucky then," Kalon muttered, scanning the deck again.

Nuva looked up from where the pirate healer repatched her arm. "We were more than lucky, asshole," she chided him, pulling her arm free from the poor soul still trying to sew her up. "I'll do it myself," she barked at him, sending him scurrying below deck. When she turned back to Kalon and Garrison, both of whom now had their eyebrows raised, she frowned. "How has he survived this long on a pirate ship?" When neither male responded she sighed, adding rather grumpily, "And he was taking too long while others needed help."

Garrison finished what the sailor had started as he knelt beside the barrel Nuva was slumped on. While she had kept fighting after being stabbed in the arm, she had lost a lot of blood, and Kalon could tell she was exhausted, although he would never tell her that.

One thing he admired about Nuva—which also drove him crazy—was that she could be on her deathbed, and if he asked her to do something, she would try to do it. It made her a great soldier, but a dangerous friend.

Kalon smiled at the thought, but when he caught her looking, his smile fell.

Nuva smirked and winced as Garrison tied off her stitches. "How?" she asked, no louder than a whisper. There were too many listening ears for them to speak freely about the attack, and it was a good question.

"The port?" Garrison offered, now wrapping Nuva's arm with a clean cloth. Kalon had considered that already, but only Finch's most trusted men had been allowed on the ship when they had stopped briefly at a port to get supplies a week ago.

"Her?" Nuva asked, nodding toward the beam where Lora was usually perched.

Kalon noted with discomfort that Lora was *not* on her perch. He made a note to send someone to find her. At some point, after all the fighting, she had been taking weapons from the sailors' bodies. Much to her chagrin, Kalon had ordered her disarmed. He hadn't seen her since then, but he was sure she was sulking about somewhere.

"No," Garrison chimed. "She seemed really concerned about them coming aboard, it seemed genuine."

Nuva scoffed as she tested her arm, rotating it around and flexing her fingers. "Maybe she's just a good actress. Right, Kalon?"

Kalon's mind had wandered away as he scanned the deck for familiar red hair, but when he looked back to his friends, Nuva was looking at him expectantly.

"Uh...yeah. Right," he agreed, unsure of what exactly he was agreeing to. "I need to, um..." *Need to what? Go find her? Why? You sound insane, pull yourself together.*

Garrison gave Kalon a knowing look as he passed his brother in arms, heading toward the galley. "I am going to look for our Shade princess. I'm sure she has a theory on how that Shade boat found us."

Kalon let his gratitude flow openly. He was too exhausted to deal with fighting with the princess just yet, thank the gods Garrison was falling on that sword.

Nuva chuckled as she watched Garrison go. "He better pray that the princess never finds out who it was, because gods know—"

A scream wrenched through the air just as Garrison made it to the door below deck. Kalon spun, sword already drawn, standing closer to Nuva's bandaged side as she, too, drew her weapon. Another shriek and Garrison dove out of the way as a pirate was shoved from below onto the deck.

The pirate, one of the ones Lora had beaten up upon arriving on the *Gale Snatcher*, and who Kalon was pretty sure was the second mate, was now covered in blood and writhing under the strain of shadows around his wrists and legs, pinning him to the mast. He tried to scream again, but another shadow covered his mouth. Somehow, even in broad daylight, the shadows were strong and apparently tightening. Kalon made to step toward the mass of impenetrable black that expanded from below deck, but was stopped by Nuva.

The blackness pulsed once and then Lora emerged from within it, shadows writhing around her arms and legs, covered in blood, and looking pissed as hell.

CHAPTER 26

A PIRATE'S CRIME

Lora

The pirate had been foolish in the beginning to lie to her when she had asked him if he had sold her out. He was foolish now for thinking he could get away with it. It had taken two precise slices to his arms with the dagger Kalon hadn't taken from her, for him to start bleeding out. He probably had about three minutes left if he didn't apply the appropriate pressure. But Lora wasn't ready for him to die yet.

Her shadows pushed at the gaping wounds, keeping the blood loss to a trickle as she pushed the fucker through the opening to the deck above. She didn't care that he'd sold her out, not really. But the pirates seemed to think that she had summoned the Shade ship as some trick, and that would not do. Oh no, he needed to admit to the whole crew that he was the reason their three comrades had died—then, she'd kill him.

Lora had pinned the pirate to the mast of the ship, her shadows holding his blood in his body, as well as him to the mast.

"What the hell?" she heard someone say as feet shuffled away from the middle of the deck.

"Tell them," she said quietly, but not weakly. She was expending a gross amount of power to keep him in place in the broad daylight, and she couldn't take her attention off him, or her shadows might falter. Because of that, she wasn't sure who all was watching, but judging by the collective inhale, it was a good majority of the crew.

"Tell us what?" *Finch.* Good, it would be easier if he heard it himself.

"The truth," she offered, her gaze locked on the bloody pirate in front of her.

When no one said anything, she pushed a bit harder on the shadows around his throat and wrists. "Tell them," she repeated a bit louder. "Tell them how you sold us all out so that the Shades knew exactly where to find us," she shouted, anger causing her shadows to pulse as she spoke. The asshole just stared at her, refusing to speak.

"It will be hard for him to admit anything if he cannot breathe." Finch sounded closer now.

Lora's hand twitched, but she eased the tension in his throat just a fraction. "Tell. Them." Her temper grew, but her strength began to fade. She could feel people around her shifting into defensive positions, their shadows on the deck from the dying sun telling her as much. Lora threw up a wall of shadows around the boat, and the display of power was enough to have most of the crew gasping and fleeing from the area.

There was movement to her left that put Kalon in her peripheral view. He was calm and collected, and merely nodded, though she wasn't sure what the hell that was supposed to mean.

"Captain," she heard him say, his voice projecting to somewhere beyond her vision. "Lora seems to have done you a service in finding the one responsible for selling us all out, perhaps we could lower our weapons and hear the truth from the second mate."

The fact that Kalon was so calm sent alarm bells ringing. Not to mention he had just alerted her to the fact that the crew behind her had weapons drawn—*not awesome*. There was a long pause, and then the sound of swords being sheathed behind her. Steps approached her, and judging by the gait, it was Finch. A moment later, he stood next to Kalon, tension and anger radiating from him as surely as it was from her.

Another pause and Lora realized they were waiting on her to release her shadows. Instead, she eased the ones from his throat enough for the pirate to speak. The man sputtered and coughed, his head sagging as he took several deep breaths. So *dramatic*, she thought. She could almost hear Kalon's voice in her head agreeing with her, and a small chuckle worked its way up her throat.

The pirate scanned the crowd and when his gaze finally settled on Lora, he lied, "She's lying."

Lora was stunned, unable to move as the lie settled over her skin. With those two words, she felt the air charge with an energy that usually meant trouble.

But the man wasn't done. "She needed a scapegoat—she doesn't care about us, only herself. She *wanted* the Shades to come, to take her home and kill us all."

The words were like rocks being thrown at her, and she felt each blow as she realized the crew was now looking at her with disgust and distrust—they believed him.

Of course, they'd believe their comrade over her. She should have realized it the minute they had drawn their weapons on her. *Fuck, now what?*

But Kalon stepped up to the pirate, just far enough away to be out of range should the guy spit or spurt blood.

"Were you not here when she fought alongside the crew to protect the ship?" he asked, his voice murderously calm, his eyebrows raised. "Why would she call them here, only to assist in killing them all?" His voice rose with the question, so that everyone on board could hear. "And why bring you out here, keeping you alive by the looks of it, if she did not believe in a semblance of a fair trial?"

Lora's pulse quickened as she felt the tension around her rising and falling, as if the pirates couldn't make up their minds.

"Why would she sell herself out, when she has everything to gain from remaining alive?" he continued. The questions were all great ones, and Lora knew the answers to all of them. But the pirates still seemed unconvinced.

"What would I gain," started the man on the mast, a bit pale from the blood loss, "from selling out my brothers?" He contorted his face into what Lora assumed was meant to be innocence, but Kalon wasn't buying any of it. He glanced sidelong at Lora, whose eyes darted to the man's breaches, before reaching out and skillfully slicing the right pocket of his trousers. Coins tumbled out, and Lora saw Finch's expression sour.

"I see." Finch stepped forward, allowing Lora to see him fully. "Thank you for bringing this to my attention," he said, glowering slightly at his second mate. "As this is a pirate matter, it will be handled the way pirate matters are."

He said it in a way that gave Lora the impression it wasn't going to be handled at all.

Apparently Kalon felt the same way, "So there will be a trial?" he asked, moving between Finch and Lora. Garrison, Nuva, and Liam now inched into her field of vision, too. Still, her eyes remained on the pirate she was struggling to keep contained.

While Kalon and Finch argued, the pirate in front of her met her gaze, and, smiling, mouthed, "You lost, bitch."

Lora's vision blurred as her power poured from her, the rest of the ship fading away. He had won. Whatever the judicial system pirates abided by it meant he was going to walk free. Her power pulsed, and she felt attention whip toward her. The man on the mast began to writhe under the pressure of her shadows.

She knew that Kalon was ordering her to stop, shouting to release the pirate, but all she saw were the bodies of the pirates that had died for this asshole's treachery. He could have ruined her one shot at freedom. The shadows around his neck tightened, and the ones containing his blood loosened, coating her in another shower of the fucker's blood. At this point, it didn't matter that he was lying—she would end this herself.

Her power surged as she took a breath, preparing to deliver the death blow, her gaze never leaving the traitor's. One moment, she was looking into the eyes of the pirate, the next an amber-flecked gaze held hers.

"Let go."

Kalon. He had stepped between her and the pirate. Her shadows still whirled, begging to enact justice, but now her palm began stinging too—the Troth. She couldn't harm Kalon, and at this angle, she would if she struck the pirate.

"Please," he said through the roaring in her head. His tone had shifted and his eyes were soft, if not a bit panicked. "Please," she heard again, and this time, her own blood seemed to cool at the request.

Another breath, and her shadows loosened around the pirate's throat. Kalon seemed to register the shift and stepped out from between them. Lora took another breath, her shadows pulling back into her. But then the fucker in front of her choked out a laugh, and Lora knew, in her very soul, that he would get away with it. So, as her shadows continued to recede, Lora stepped in close, almost able to share putrid breath with him, and draped them both in shadows.

She left just enough light so that the pirate, whose eyes were now wide with terror, could see her as she said, no louder than a whisper, "I know you've heard rumors about my shadows, so let me make one thing clear. When you think you are alone, or with friends, or your fellow pirates in some dark corner or alcove, and you whisper of what you've done, those shadows you hide in, they are *mine*. They report to *me*. They tell me of the things you whisper. No secret is safe, no truth hidden. *They* may not find you guilty, but I promise you this; the minute I am free I will find you, and I will kill you for this."

Another choked laugh as the pirate's terror turned to smug victory. "You will *never* be free," he spat, still gasping for breath as her shadows pushed harder onto his throat.

A wicked smile spread across her face as she leaned in closer and whispered, "And you will never know peace. In every dark corner and shadowy alleyway, you'll know I will be waiting. And I can promise you one thing—you will not die of natural causes."

With that, her shadows fully released him, gasping onto the deck below.

"You'll do the right thing," she said to Finch before she walked straight into the captain's quarters and slammed the door.

***

Kalon

Lora had actually let the pirate go. Kalon was still in shock. He thought for sure she would kill him on the spot for lying to them, but when he'd ordered her—no, asked her—to release him, she had. That was, after she'd whispered some creepy shit about her shadows and a thinly-veiled death threat into the pirate's ear. He hadn't heard all of it, but he'd heard enough to know that the pirate was a fool if he thought she'd been bluffing. That man was one of limited days.

Then she'd just released him like a rag doll and stormed into the Captain's Quarters, never even glancing back. Which was risky, since half the crew wanted her dead for beating the shit out of their second mate and nearly killing him. Kalon wasn't sure why, but he had believed her instantly. She had looked more than pissed when she'd emerged, covered in blood, and the fact that she wanted a trial—all but demanded it—settled any doubt in him.

"Dismissed!" Finch yelled over the crowd of men on the deck. There was no way the punishment was already dealt that swiftly. Kalon looked around for any indication of what he missed, but all he saw was a smug second mate and a confused group of Drakes. Nuva motioned for him to meet them under the stairs to the helm and he made quick work of slipping into the growing shadows, his eyes snagging on the darkest point of them at the back before dragging his attention to his friends.

"What the hell happened?" he asked by way of greeting. Nuva blew out a long breath as Liam wrung his hands nervously, looking between the two of them. Garrison was keeping watch, but he could feel the tension in the air radiating from him as well. The sun was almost fully setting now, casting the whole area in oranges and reds, making everything around him seem more menacing than it was.

"Well?" he asked impatiently. No one had gone into the Captain's Quarters, and he wanted to be the one to tell Lora—especially if the verdict was bad. Which, judging by the looks on his friends' faces, it was.

"He's free to go," Nuva said, squaring her shoulders and facing Kalon.

His temper ignited almost automatically. Liam winced.

"What do you mean? He's free to go after getting whipped? Or at least a reprimand?" He looked to each of his friends as he asked, hoping one of them would have some sort of good news, but with each face he peered into he saw only disappointment matching his own.

"Just free to go," Garrison confirmed, now also facing the group.

Kalon's mouth opened to speak but nothing came out. Free to go. As if he hadn't gotten nearly all of them killed—and three of his own crew *had* died.

"But since it was only pirates that took a hit, it technically doesn't concern us," Liam explained, as if reciting from some pirate code he'd read long ago.

"It's still not right," Kalon concluded, seeing that his friends agreed with him. The shadows in the alcove they were in pulsed and Kalon suppressed a shudder, his mind drifting to the surely raging princess next door.

"What do you think she'll do when she finds out?" Garrison's attention had drifted to the Captain's Quarters as well as, having also sensed the pulse of shadows it seemed.

"I bet she'll kill him in the night," Liam said, as if it was the best possible solution to the whole mess.

"Or maybe cut out his tongue?" Nuva provided eagerly, almost as if she hoped the Shade would.

"Or maybe she'll respect the Pirate Code."

All four Drakes spun to see Lora, sitting carelessly on a crate, legs propped up, the dried blood matching her hair. She sat there cleaning her fingernails as if she'd been there the whole time. She didn't look up as her voice dropped to a deadly calm as she added, "But she'll also swear to kill him if he ever steps foot on land, that he will never know peace in this life."

Kalon felt a shudder work up his spine. When she finally looked up her usually bright eyes had dimmed, like the events from today had drained them of life.

How she had gotten into the alcove was a fucking mystery. When no one responded, Lora swung her legs off the crate, stabbed the small knife into the crate where her feet had been, and strode through them onto the darkened ship. She vanished into either her own shadows, or that of the mast, almost instantly.

Kalon watched the spot where she had vanished for another moment before loosing the breath he hadn't realized he'd been holding.

"Well, that was creepy as shit," Nuva said as she, too, tracked Lora's path before grabbing Liam by the arm. "Come on, buddy, you've had a long day and could use a drink!" Her tone was a forced jovial that almost had Kalon wincing all over again— it was never good when Nuva had to be the one to lift everyone's spirits.

They walked off, arms linked, as Liam prattled on about how someone with blood loss really shouldn't be drinking at all.

"You think she'll be okay?" Garrison asked, coming up beside him.

"Nuva's had worse injuries, she'll be fine. It's Liam we should worry about. If he tries to limit her drinking, she'll probably kill him." Kalon chuckled as he watched Nuva punch Liam in the arm for probably just that.

"I wasn't talking about Nuva," Garrison said, his tone dropping. Kalon turned to him, seeing that Garrison's gaze was fixed on the shadowy beam of the mast.

He turned fully to his friend. "What do you mean? Why wouldn't she be okay?" His blood heated, his heart rate spiking.

"You didn't see her? Her shadows?" Garrison asked, concern etched into his face.

Of course he'd seen her. He'd all but gotten himself shredded by getting in between her and the second mate. "I saw her covered in a man's blood, then her shadows holding that man's blood into his body, as well as his body to the mast of a ship. What else was there to see?" *Why am I getting angry?*

"I'm not sure it was all *his* blood," Garrison said, blowing out a long breath, then adding, "and her shadows were shaking."

Kalon's heart nearly stopped. "What?"

"I'm just saying she fought really hard today, then never saw Liam or any other medic—"

"She is a grown woman. If she needs a medic she can find one herself, and she only fought really hard *after* I basically begged her to join the fight." *Yep, my temper is definitely flaring.*

"She wouldn't fight before that because you didn't trust her when she said the boat was coming," Garrison noted, stepping into his space, but Kalon was in no mood to have this conversation. Not now, and probably not ever.

"It's hard to trust someone who is throwing daggers at your head!" Kalon's eyes flared with a renewed anger as he looked upon his friend. "Why are you suddenly defending her? Did you not see what she did today? She could have killed that man."

"She *did* kill the Shades, almost all of them, without a second thought," Garrison reminded him—as if he needed any help remembering Lora shredding through the Shade sailors, her wine-red braid trailing behind her like all the bloodied bodies.

Kalon suppressed a shudder as he thought about how easily she killed so many people—and how quickly. "Exactly. She's their princess, and she still slaughtered them! When she gets what she wants, that could easily be us next. So no, I don't trust her." His breaths came out in pants as his skin began to prickle. Garrison had the audacity to seem offended, his eyes dark with disappointment as he shook his head and walked away, leaving Kalon alone and confused. *What just happened? Why is he so mad?*

Although he knew he should go after Garrison and apologize, he couldn't move. He was frozen to the spot with Garrison's words ringing in his ears as a realization dawned on him; Lora was weakened, and everyone onboard—except him apparently—had seen it.

***

Lora

Lora's shadows were barely more than just that—shadows. She felt the edges of her power under her skin, like frayed cloth. Although she hadn't used them in the fight today, they had subtly kept her wound free, closing any nicks or scraps or slashes until she could mend them.

But now that they were all but gone, she felt the cuts in her arms and a deeper one on her cheek begin to leak fresh blood. She should have gone to see a medic immediately, and she had tried, until her shadows had caught wind of that fucker bragging to his friends about all the money he'd made from selling them out. He didn't seem to care that three of his crewmates had died, he was just happy to make an extra copper—or gold, apparently. She had only changed course when she realized it wasn't her they had sold out, but Kalon.

The Shade army had been looking for him, and that second mate fucker was supposed to deliver him on a silver platter. He had even smuggled canthite chains on board, which was enough to set Lora's pace from a walk to a full-on sprint.

It had taken nearly all of her internal strength not to kill the man on the spot and then it took all her power to keep him alive. Only for him to be set free, not even reprimanded. "Pirates will be pirates," she had heard Finch say as he made his way to his quarters. If he was surprised she was no longer in them, he didn't show it. She had noted Kalon's little group move toward the stairs, so she'd snuck through the Captain's Quarters window and tucked herself in the shadows of the alcove to listen.

Kalon had all but looked directly at her upon entering, but then he and his crew had discussed what happened. Her shadows had wavered too much, so she had to make herself known, and with no small amount of satisfaction, everyone looked sufficiently creeped out at her apparent spontaneous arrival.

She rested her head on the mast behind her and a dribble of blood ran down her cheek, zigging and zagging through the dried blood already caked on her face. She needed a bath desperately. Unfortunately, based on her eavesdropping earlier, they were to make landfall in two days and then hike a good ways before they'd be near civilization. No bath for a while.

Another dribble of blood, and Lora felt her world tilt slightly. Shit. She needed water and food, anything to help her body stay alert and fuel for her power, but she wasn't entirely confident she could get down. And she knew for a fact that she wouldn't be able to get back up. She was fucking exhausted.

Like hell would she sleep below deck. For starters, she barely had her "sea legs" and secondly, she was pretty sure every pirate on this godsforsaken ship now wanted her dead.

So, she would wait until breakfast for food—maybe then, her shadows could provide a little backup since she knew no one else would look out for her. She had thought that maybe

Kalon would…but no, she had been wrong. He had all but screamed it at her when talking to Garrison moments ago.

He didn't trust her. And for some reason, that didn't sit right with Lora—even though he *shouldn't* trust her. She sighed, her chest feeling too tight. *That's from the kick to the chest*, she reminded herself. She cataloged it with her other injuries, deciding none of them would kill her by morning, so her best option now was to sleep. She looked to the stars, wondering briefly how her life had come to this. But Kierra was safe, and that's all she ever wanted. And so, she decided today while fighting her own people, that her new goal was to leave this continent and be free. Free of the war, of Cyrus, of all of it. Looking at the night sky she prayed to the long sleeping gods that the pirate had been wrong - that he *would* be free, one day. And so, lonely on the mast, darkness claimed her.

***

Kalon

Lora's thinning shadows had flickered for the first couple of hours he watched her sleeping, but now they were gone. The only visible one left held her to the beam, as if she kept one kernel of power for self-preservation. He didn't know why, but after his argument with Garrison, Kalon found himself propped against the rail of the deck across from Lora's beam. Watching for what, he didn't know. For her to go kill that sailor? Not likely, since he'd already be dead if she wanted him to be. For her to fall off the beam, dead, herself? That seemed more likely. Garrison had noticed that she had been injured, and Kalon scented fresh blood mixed with *her* every time a breeze blew past.

But she was alive, he knew that much based on his Troth mark still faintly glowing on his palm. He was pretty sure if she died, it would disappear...

A creak caused his wandering mind to snap alert. From where he was positioned, he could see Lora's beam as well as the stern entrance to below deck, out of which three large forms now emerged.

Whoever it was had clearly been drinking and as they swayed with and without the boat. Kalon stiffened as he caught the familiar scent of the second mate. *Oh, shit. Maybe they're just getting some air?* But the three forms quickly scurried across the ship, two of them producing small daggers as they came upon the mast where Lora slept. *Nope, definitely not just out for a stroll.*

The second mate, who's still-bloodied face appeared in the moonlight, carried chains. Canthite by the look of it. *Shit.* All three were now directly below Lora, and Kalon wondered how they hadn't noticed him sitting there, or how they couldn't hear his heart racing.

Another gust of wind gave him the answer—alcohol. While all three men seemed bound and determined to, at the bare minimum, harm Lora, they were too drunk to notice their surroundings, which was about to be tremendously useful to him.

Sticking close to the shadows like he'd seen Lora do when chained, he managed to rise to his feet and draw his weapon. But that was where his luck ran out. Two steps later, and the deck creaked so loudly, it was a testament to Lora's injuries that she hadn't woken up. It did, however, alert the three very-drunk pirates that he was there, which was…less than ideal.

Kalon straightened and adopted a casual stance, hoping to talk his way out as he'd done with men of this sort hundreds of times.

"Good evening gentlemen," he said, stepping into the moonlight and toward the mast. "Out for a stroll?" he asked, slowly trying to ease himself between them and the beam where Lora slept.

The men swayed as the second mate stepped forward, stammering from drink. "Nothin' that concernz you, *prince*."

Kalon winced at the use of his title. Clearly, the crew was not as tight-lipped as he'd asked for.

"Of course," he said tightly, assessing just how hard it would be to keep this civil. Maybe he could just ask them to go back downstairs… "It just seems like a precarious place to be after having such a day."

Kalon tried to lock eyes with the second mate, but the asshole had managed to slide behind his friends, angling his dagger as if to throw it up at Lora.

"You know," Kalon said, taking two slow, deliberate steps in his direction, "it isn't nice to try and kill someone while they sleep." Another step as the two idiots clambered to keep themselves between him and the mast.

"We don' care 'bout that shit," spat the one on the right, the one on the left sinking slightly into a fighting pose. The second mate was now in a good position to throw his dagger and Kalon was nowhere closer and now out of options.

Kalon struggled to find a way out of this diplomatically—he needed time. "Perhaps there would have been a better deal than the Shade?" he suggested, straightening to his full height. They all paused, attention now on Kalon as a shadow passed over the deck. "If you sold her out for gold, imagine what you could get for me? I'm a much better price," he offered. Why? He had no idea, but the three men all began to chuckle, the second mate now turning to him.

With a wicked grin through his blood crusted face, he merely said, "We know."

Within a heartbeat the man to the left of the second mate swung out at Kalon with his dagger, just barely missing his arm.

"Shit!" Kalon jumped back and drew his short sword, readying for the fight, when suddenly the man pitched forward, crumpling to the deck, unmoving, a small dagger sticking out from his back. All three spun toward the direction the blade had come from.

Out of the darkness emerged Lora, somehow off the beam, her shadows swirling around her. She had to be close to burnout based on the slight flicker in her power, but her face was set with resolute fury.

Good, anger will fuel her adrenaline—keep her standing. Fighting.

A heartbeat was all the second mate needed to determine he wanted Lora extra dead. He charged her immediately, aiming for her side which, through her unbuttoned shirt, Kalon could see was pretty bruised—*shit*.

Lora dodged the blow but swayed as the boat pitched. Kalon lurched forward to catch her, but was cut off by the other pirate, now keen on killing him, apparently.

Kalon spun and sliced sideways, his blade sinking deep into the flesh of the pirate who had charged him. Bone crunched and he felt the blow reverberate up his arm before it all just stopped. The arm at which he had swung was now laying on the ground, still clutching the sword, and the pirate in front of him was screaming bloody murder and clutching the stump of what was left.

Fuck fuck fuck, now that makes one dead pirate and one without an arm. Fuck.

He didn't give himself any time to consider the consequences, not when a small shriek tore through the night. Kalon whirled toward where he last saw Lora standing, only to see the second mate, knife in hand, standing over her. The smell of her blood cramming its way up Kalon's nose.

Lora, now covered in blood that was definitely her own, was crumpled to the floor, not unlike the first time he saw her on the boat. This time, however, she wasn't hiding who she was. Shadows arched from above, forming tight, sharp blades that rained down in one fluid action.

The second mate didn't even have time to scream as he was shredded to pieces by her shadow blades. Lora, however, wasn't done. It seemed she had lost all control as she bled out on the deck, loosing a cry of pain.

Kalon launched to cover her body—her shadows seemed only to know they were meant to harm, not caring who they hit. Seconds passed and Garrison, Liam, and Nuva pulled him off of Lora, her breaths wet pants. The shadows had sliced parts of the deck and some of his clothes, but luckily nothing major.

As quickly as it all happened, it was over. The handless pirate was still screaming, setting off a series of alarms, but Kalon didn't care. His focus was solely on Lora.

"What's going on?" Garrison asked, but before he could answer, the Captain's Quarters door swung open and heavy footsteps sounded on the deck behind them.

"What the hell?" It was Finch, who was pissed by the sound of it. "Did you kill two of my crew members and..." He faltered slightly when he saw the other man, now with one less appendage. "What's going on?" He looked toward where Kalon was kneeled over Lora, Nuva and Liam both helping her to sit up. Finch's eyes flared with fury as he saw the new blood on the deck, covering both Lora and Kalon.

Once Kalon was sure Liam and Nuva had a good hold of Lora's relatively limp body he spun, coming face-to-face with an enraged pirate Captain. Garrison was at his side instantly, positioning Lora and the others behind him, out of Finch's line of sight. Finch opened his mouth to speak, but Kalon cut him off.

"Some of your crew saw fit to deliver a punishment to one of *my* crew, so seeing as it affected me and mine, I exacted the appropriate punishment for the crime. Unfortunately for two of your men, it meant the loss of life, though they did choose that course of action for themselves."

"And the man's arm?" Finch asked, clearly still outraged.

"A casualty in a way, but he'll survive," Kalon said coolly, putting his hands in his pockets. Finch's face pinched in rage—he had used the same phrasing when excusing his second mate earlier that day. And Kalon knew that Finch would lose the respect of the crew if he argued the point any further.

"Of course," Finch said, narrowing his eyes in the dim light, then huffed loudly before shouting to one of the younger crew members to clean up the mess at first light. He turned back to Kalon and a whisper of deadly promise crossed his features. "Let's hope this interaction doesn't happen again."

Kalon returned the look and said, loudly enough for everyone on deck to hear, "It won't. Because next time someone threatens Lora, or even looks at her wrong, they will lose their eyes and lives. And when Lora is done with them, I'll throw the pieces that are left into the water for chum."

And with that, he turned and strode with steady feet to where Liam patched a nasty looking slice to Lora's arm.

Stubborn Shade. Stubborn, brave, lucky Shade.

CHAPTER 27

KINDNESS UNCOVERED

Lora

Two days had passed in a blur of activity, and everyone had, thankfully, given Lora a wide berth. She was finally feeling able to train again when the call for land rang out across the deck.

The Drakes really made a party out of everything—especially when they, too, seemed more than thrilled to no longer be on that godsforsaken boat. They had landed near nightfall, and after meeting up with Garrison's two cousins -Erik and Toke- had decided to camp for the night and hike inland the next day, landing them at the front gates in a week or so.

Or, at least, that was Lora's understanding from the rapid dissemination of information Kalon had delivered to the group hours before as they prepared to make port. The plan, Kalon had reminded them as they offloaded the ship, would be best laid out tomorrow so there was no need to rush inland. Hence the makeshift campsite they had erected in a small clearing in the otherwise dense-as-shit woods.

Lora wouldn't have tried to escape if she'd wanted. The woods felt ancient. Creepy. She was glad they had decided on a fire tonight—hopefully she'd be passed out before it died. Though, she'd take the woods over the rocking of that ship any day.

With that being said, she did wish she had her weapons. Kalon had seen fit to strip her of them on the ship after the battle, which was extremely annoying. At least she'd caught the fucker who had sold them out. The looks on their faces as she'd held the asshole to the mast with shadows had filled her with both smug pride and crushing shame. Either way, the pirate got what he deserved, even if it wasn't by her blade.

While Kalon had mentioned in passing the relative severity of this mission, he seemed more than okay with the several instruments the others had dug out of their packs. He did nothing to stop Garrison and Nuva as they began singing a rather bawdy tune about two lovers and a heated moment under a full moon. If she had been a lady, the tune would have turned her cheeks the color of roses, but Lora was no lady so a small smile spread across her face, instead.

Her stomach lurched slightly as a twinge of sorrow-tinged jealousy swept through her at the group of friends. She missed Kierra.

Her stomach grumbled, pulling her from her thoughts. She had used her shadows all day to keep the group relatively hidden, and even now, they were being used to shield the camp from anyone passing by. No one had thanked her, and

Garrison had merely called it a "party trick". She moved to take a sip of her canteen only to find it full of rum instead of water.

"Damn pirates," she cursed, recapping the canteen and facing the fire again. They were off the boat yes, but she still felt a bit nauseous from all the swaying. She was ready to be rid of this whole continent once this mission was done, but she was not looking forward to getting back on a boat anytime soon.

"I agree," answered Liam, who plopped himself down beside her on the moss-covered ground. He offered her his canteen. "It's water, Drake's promise," he said, closing his hand in a fist and placing it over his left arm. She almost told him that a Drake's promise meant virtually nothing to her, but it seemed to mean something to him, so she let it be.

She took a long sip of water before turning in Liam's direction. "Can I ask you something?"

The medic looked thrilled as ever and nodded fervently. "Sure, anything. I'm an open book. Unless..." he added, now looking a bit nervous as he looked around the fire at the group. "Unless it's about this song. I have absolutely no idea what it is about or where they learned it, though I do have an educated guess." He made a point to look at her canteen, and she figured he meant the pirates were to blame for the obscene songs as well.

A small chuckle left her. "Damn pirates."

Liam smiled. "Indeed."

They sat in silence for a couple moments more before Lora worked up the courage to speak again. "Why are you so nice to me?" It came out softer than she had anticipated, but she felt lighter for saying it.

Liam studied her before answering with a shrug. "What's not to like?"

She wasn't sure if it was a rhetorical question or not. *There's a lot not to like. For starters, I'm a Shade. Then there's the whole killing Drakes thing, not to mention the other horrible shit I've done...*

Liam seemed to notice the direction of her thoughts. "The answer isn't what you think it is," he said softly, pulling her attention back to him. The fire danced a little in her direction, shadows scattering around her.

"It's just..." She couldn't form the right words. "I've done some pretty fucked up shit," she admitted, another weightlifting ever so slightly off her shoulders. "Not to mention I tried to kill you. Several times. And—"

Liam's laugh caught her off guard. It was loud and full, as if she'd told a hilarious joke. She looked around to see if anyone was paying attention. No one seemed to notice, except Kalon who gave her a puzzled look as if to ask, "What's that all about?"

Liam still chuckled softly as he said, "Lora, if you wanted me dead I have no doubt in my mind I would be on the other side of the veil already. Not here sitting amongst my friends." He made a point to nudge her knee with his when he said *friends*.

She blushed, slightly, at the inherent compliment at her skill and definitely not because he implied they were friends.

"That's true," she said, again trying to find the right words. "But I did hurt you and many others, and not just while I've been here, I mean." Her cheeks burned with a shame she had not felt in a long while. *Why am I saying all this to him? Why does it matter?*

Liam considered her words, thoughtful amusement dancing in his eyes. "You did what you thought you had to do to survive," he concluded. "How can I fault you for that?"

Her shame deepened, her skin flushing pink.

"Though it did hurt," Liam continued. "So, if you don't mind, I'd love it if you never did it again." A smile played on his lips, his eyes were near sparkling with amusement.

"As long as you don't put me in chains," Lora said decisively, unable to match his jovial attitude.

Liam's smile softened. "Deal."

She sighed and, casting her gaze to the sky above, wondered what in the world she was doing there. She felt Liam scoot closer and track her gaze above. They were silent for a time before he spoke, the words thoughtful and soft.

"When you first arrived at the outpost, you were in pretty bad shape. Garrison had sewed you up the best he could while you were traveling, but all your stitches had torn out, causing you to lose a lot of blood, and you were near frozen." A pause, and she knew he was considering his next words carefully. "Initially, I had tried to save you in the dirty clothes you were wearing, fearing that by the time I got them removed you would be dead. But I was already too late. You died in the infirmary, Lora, and I felt it. Saw you take your last breath, and in my heart, I knew you were gone."

For some reason, she hated that he had had to see her gaping and festering wound. *He's a medic, he's probably seen worse.* Another pause, and Liam shuddered. What happened next had never been told to her, but she had picked up enough to realize she had somehow come back, and then tried to kill Kalon and a handful of soldiers. But not Liam, not then.

He continued with a steadier breath than before. "When we took you down to the cells, you were completely naked."

She froze then, anticipating the next sentence with so much dread she could have sworn her stomach was on the ground next to her.

"I had Nuva bring some clothes for you to change into but..." his attention fell upon the female soldier, now drinking deeply from her canteen. "You met her. At the time, she wasn't really amenable to dressing you herself, so they left me to do it."

Lora hadn't given much thought to the clothes she had woken in—she had been a bit more preoccupied with the fact that she had woken at all.

"As you know," he forged on, "I examined your scars while you were asleep. I," he swallowed, "I examined *all* your scars." It dawned on her then just what other scars he was talking about. It wasn't just the new one snaking down her side, but the old ones as well, marking her wrists, ankles and back. She shuddered and she could feel Liam's gaze drop to her. She remained looking at the night sky.

He didn't speak, so she cleared her throat, shame and embarrassment burning her face. "So, you are kind to me because I have scars? Because I was wounded? Because you," she choked on the last words, "because you pity me?"

She didn't know why it mattered that she knew why he was kind to her, but hearing the reason somehow left her feeling disappointed. Tears, hot and salty, stung her eyes, and she tried to blink them away.

Liam had grabbed her hands before she had even realized he'd moved. He was mere inches from her face as she drew her gaze to his. "No." He answered firmly. She couldn't bring herself to look the male in the eyes.

"Lora, I do not pity you. We," he said, glancing around, "do not pity you. It's just that I know what made those scars, or at least most of them. Many of us here, Kalon included, have similar ones." He had paused to take a deep breath, but her attention had snapped to Kalon. *Kalon had scars like mine? How have I not seen them? He hadn't exactly hidden his body, but then again, I've never seen him with his shirt off...*

Before she could really look at Kalon, Liam continued. "Scars like those, they don't warrant pity, Lora. They warrant awe. I don't know if you remember, but when I was in your cell and you woke up, I told you—"

"You told me where you come from, that scars are to be valued, revered. That they show to the world that someone is a fighter." A small smile danced across Lora's face at the memory.

Liam was smiling too, as he met her gaze. "It proves you're a survivor, Lora. And how could any of us pity or hate a survivor like you?"

She smiled in earnest. It didn't fully reach her eyes, but it was broad enough to warm her cheeks, the previous moment's disappointment dancing away with the flames.

"You know," Liam said, a smile dancing on his face, too, "you tried to kill me shortly after that."

Lora chuckled a bit as she remembered *that* part of the conversation. Then another memory came crashing through, as if jostled by the retelling of the story.

"I told you I'd heard that before, once from Kacey—Kierra," she corrected. "And another time, from when I was wounded."

Liam nodded then shrugged. "But you couldn't remember who the other wise sage was."

Her eyes widened and she turned, facing the medic as she explained, "That's just it. It's still a little blurry, but I remember. It was while Garrison was sewing me up on one of the ledges. He was trying to keep me alive, but it was the other person, the one holding me down, who said the thing about scars." It was all coming into focus now as she told Liam. "The man seemed frustrated at me squirming and, I guess he assumed I would care about having a giant scar there." She laughed at herself—was he ever wrong. But as she thought harder, a face began to come into view in her mind.

"That doesn't sound right. It was just you, Garrison, and Emir. Do you remember who it was? Maybe it was the dragon," Liam said nervously, glancing around the fire and rubbing at his arm.

She eyed him suspiciously, tracking the movement. "Liam," she started calmly. "Was there someone else with me? Other than Garrison and Emir?"

Liam sagged with relief before responding. "No, mi fia, it was just you three." Her attention snapped fully to him as the words rattled something else loose in her memory.

"Mi fia," she said, feeling the words on her tongue. The hairs on her arm stood at attention and her skin prickled with goosebumps. She felt Kalon's gaze on her, and she didn't have to look toward him to know he was on the move in her direction.

Liam looked like he was going to be sick.

"Mi fia," she said again, feeling the attention of the whole camp shift to her. "You said that once before, after I...after I died." Her thoughts and memories were going too fast to focus. "What does it mean?" she asked more of herself than Liam.

"Maybe you were hallucinating?" Liam offered as Lora continued to piece her memories together.

"I mean, that is a possibility, but it feels like a pretty crazy thing to hallucinate twice." She looked up to see Liam's attention no longer on her, rather it was fixed on something behind her, and he had turned a shade of red she had not known was possible. Kalon came into her peripherals a heartbeat later.

"Who's hallucinating?" he asked in a forced jovial tone. Neither Lora nor Liam answered. Nuva made a terrible retching sound that snapped Liam out of his red-faced stupor.

"Liam," Kalon said with enough forced enthusiasm that the medic winced. "It seems Nuva has gotten herself quite drunk and may need your assistance." Lora looked over Kalon's shoulder to see Nuva, sure enough, needing assistance as she emptied the contents of her stomach into a nearby bush.

"Right," Liam said, having already jumped to his feet. He opened his mouth to say something as he glanced down at Lora, but after glancing back up to Kalon, changed his mind. He left without saying another word. *Weird.*

"You two seemed to be having a deep conversation," Kalon noted, tracking the medic until he was by Nuva before plopping down in Liam's vacated spot. She didn't detect the smell of rum in the canteen, but Kalon's eyes had a glaze to them that was probably attributed to the amber liquid.

Lora rolled her eyes. "We *were*," she emphasized, "until you came and shooed him away." She made a point to take Kalon's canteen before he could protest. He opened his mouth to object as she put it to her lips, but she gave him a rude gesture that had his mouth closing again.

She took two heavy pulls before handing it back to him. *Yep, definitely some type of alcohol.* Her head spun a bit.

Kalon placed his hand over his heart and feigned injury. "You wound me, princess. That you would think me capable of shooing at all." His movements became more dramatic and Lora raised a brow at him.

When he finally finished, she took his canteen again and, taking another long pull, merely said, "You'll survive."

The way he was eyeing her had her taking another drink from his canteen.

"You know," he said, snatching the canteen back, "it's quite rude to steal a male's drink."

"Oh, is it now? Well, cuff me good sir, for I have committed the most egregious crime of rum snatching," she said dryly, holding out her wrists and throwing her head in his direction. *Shit, that rum was strong.* She could barely see straight and her hands and arms were growing heavy. *And it didn't taste like rum, it was sweet...*

"You see," Kalon said, his words sounding muffled as Lora's vision danced with the flames in front of her, "you should always know what it is you're stealing, princess. Because that wasn't rum."

Lora's eyes flared wide before closing completely, her body careening forward toward the forest floor. *Holy shit,* she thought, *the asshole drugged me.* It was her last thought before nothingness claimed her—she was out before she even hit the ground.

CHAPTER 28

A LITERAL RUDE AWAKENING

Kalon

Waking up to a knife at his throat was not exactly the way Kalon wanted to start his day, however, seeing Lora's irate face did bring a smile to his own.

"Good morning, princess," he said through a yawn.

Lora had him pinned to the ground, her strong legs straddling his chest and abdomen, knees holding down his arms. The knife at his throat, he suddenly realized, was made entirely of shadows.

Her deep-brown eyes were near luminous with rage. "You fucking drugged me," she spat, pushing the knife a little harder into his neck. A bead of blood formed. "You swore no harm would come to me while we had our little *bargain*, and yet you drugged me."

He noted, with no small amount of satisfaction, that there was still some moss and leaves in her hair from where she had collapsed face-first onto the forest floor the previous evening. The fact that she was already awake, apparently before everyone else at camp, was a testament to her will—or her training.

Kalon tried to wiggle under her, but she was a solid weight on top of him. She was dangerously close to realizing what his, and most males, mornings were like if she leaned any lower. Kalon smiled. *This should throw her.* "If you wanted to get on top of me you need only ask," he purred as they locked eyes.

Lora's eyes flared and she dug her knee into his side a little harder for emphasis as she said, "Trust me, *prince*, you and I both know I have no *desire* to be on top of you. But when you drug someone, you should expect them to be a little angry. Or do all the women you sleep with simply thank you—"

He tried to roll her over and flip them. In her defense, her positioning was solid and even with his considerable strength, he was stuck. The move did, however, slide her a little bit lower on his body, so that she now sat at the edge of his breeches.

He glanced down at where their bodies touched, the friction of her not helping the situation. "If you don't mind," he said, pulling his attention back to her. "As much as this is exciting, I would greatly appreciate you removing yourself before either of us become uncomfortable."

"I'm quite comfortable, thanks," she seethed, pushing even harder on his side, her ass grazing the top of his—and her eyes flared in surprise.

"I'm sure you are," he said with a wry smile, "but you slide any lower, and I can guarantee the positioning won't be ideal."

Her eyes flared again, but this time in anger. Still, she didn't move. She did, however, remain inhumanly still.

"Though I could probably make it work," he added, noting how her cheeks seemed to flush ever so slightly. *Has she ever been with anyone?*

Woah, what the actual fuck? Where had that thought even come from? And why am I thinking about it now?

She seemed to think it over, and, deciding against his offer, rolled off of him with feline grace, flipping her shadow dagger before it vanished completely. *Fuck.*

He took a shaky breath, rolling his shoulders as he sat up. "To be fair," he said, finally stretching his arms—the right one was numb from all her weight. "I did not drug you. You drugged yourself."

Her scoff made his blood heat in a completely different way than before. "You think I believe that? That you just happened to have a canteen of god-knew-what with you when you came over to sit next to *me*, specifically?" Her arms were crossed over her chest, and she looked so indignant he almost wanted to laugh.

That was exactly what had happened.

"It was laudanum, a plant-based tea you could call it—"

"I know what laudanum is," she cut in softly but not weakly, an emotion Kalon couldn't place flashing in her eyes. "Why were you carrying it around with you in your canteen, and why did you let me drink a good half of it?" Her eyes were near glowing again.

"First of all, I do not *let* you do anything," he corrected her. "You are your own person, and second, but more importantly, you didn't ask what was in the canteen, which wasn't my personal canteen by the way," he added, feeling the need for her to understand there was no malicious intent in this scenario.

"Then why were you carrying it around so just anyone could take it and drink out of it?"

"I was carrying it around so no one would drink out of it by accident." At her incredulous look he continued, his blood now near boiling, "You saw how they got last night. I didn't need a whole camp of very powerful people drugged all to hell today. If you recall, we have quite a lot to do!" His voice was near a shout now and other people around the camp began to wake.

Lora didn't seem to care—she looked equally as furious as he felt. "So, what, you just have an extra canteen full of a sleeping drug that you just carry around with you all night? For what purpose other than to drug me?"

"It's not all about you, *princess*," he hissed. "If you *must* know, it's for the guards once we get to Castle Trintel." She cocked her head, assessing his words. "It was Liam's idea," he added, "so we don't have to kill them and have a war on another front." He hoped she saw the truth in his eyes.

She seemed to consider what he said, but still seemed pissed. "Well, if you weren't trying to drug me, why didn't you stop me?" The words were clipped, and her eyes flashed with a hint of hurt.

"I *did*," he countered. "You flipped me off when I went to say something."

"And you didn't think to say something anyway?" Lora shot right back.

"No," he admitted. "I didn't. I decided that if you were going to make your bed and be an arrogant asshole, then by all means who am I to stop you from sleeping in it?"

Lora's face pinched in disbelief, And Kalon noted that the entire camp was now very much awake.

"*You're* calling *me* an arrogant asshole?" Lora's temper matched Kalon's as his very blood seemed to boil. He tasted ash in his mouth. Lora pressed on, undaunted by his glowering gaze, "*You* kidnapped me. *You* tried to *sell* me back to Cyrus, knowing full well he'd probably kill me. Then *you* tried to kill me yourself when he didn't do the job you so desperately hoped he would. Even after I saved you are your friend's asses at the refugee camp and afterwards. So don't stand there and call me arrogant. You fucking jerk."

Kalon was actually speechless. As fast as his blood had boiled, it had cooled at her words. *Saved.* His voice was deadly calm, well aware that all but Garrison had eased into a semicircle behind him in a protective stance. Garrison, per usual, stood between him and the Shade. "What do you mean saved?"

Lora's face, which had been red-hot with anger moments before, had blanched of all color now. She stiffened, rolling her shoulders back as she, too, took note of the people around them, of Garrison ready to jump between them. A breath, and then Lora merely shrugged. "It doesn't matter." Her voice was flat and emotion flashed in her eyes as she looked to Garrison, then to Liam. *Disappointment.*

She made to walk away, and everyone in the group's shoulders relaxed as the tension dissipated from the area. *Like hell this is over*, Kalon thought, tracking her movements. She simply walked to her pack and began packing things up, readying for the day of travel.

The others followed suit, but Kalon just stood there, a bit numb as he watched the Shade pack up then re-braid her hair. When they fought her skin had been like a living flame, the tan flushing in golds and reds in the sun, but now it looked ashen, more gray than anything. *What the fuck just happened?*

Garrison asked just that as he brought Kalon's pack over to him.

"You mean besides me waking up with a knife *made of shadows* at my throat?" Kalon asked, still piecing together everything Lora had admitted.

Sell. She had thought he had wanted to sell her back to Cyrus, like she was cattle to be sold off. Damn, that didn't sit well.

Garrison's eyebrows shot up, his attention flashing to the thin slice on Kalon's throat, the blood drop that had long crusted over. So close. He had been so close to being killed, and yet she hadn't done it. She could have. She could easily have killed him and ran away.

She may not know the woods like Garrison's cousins did, but with her shadows, she could disappear and likely not be found. But she hadn't. She'd only drawn blood because he had refused to answer her question. Because she had felt threatened and, apparently, betrayed. *You swore no harm would come to me.*

Garrison still eyed him with concern. "She could have killed you, you know."

"Well aware, thanks," Kalon replied dryly, snatching his pack from Garrison.

"But she didn't," Garrison added, a hint of knowing in his tone.

"Well aware of that too," he said under his breath. He could still feel Garrison's attention, even with his back to the male.

"The two of you..." Garrison let out a long breath. "I hope you both make it out of this bargain alive," he added before making his way over to his cousins, both still packing their supplies.

Me too, thought Kalon as he strapped on his pack. But Garrison's words rang hollow in his head. There are far worse things that could happen between him and Lora, things he was infinitely more concerned about.

CHAPTER 29

SURPRISE

Lora

The group traveled mostly in silence the entirety of the day, which was fine with Lora. After waking up from her drug induced sleep she nearly killed the arrogant prince. She had needed the quiet to calm down. Apparently Garrison's cousin had a map in their mind, because she couldn't make out any apparent path.

While the journey wasn't exactly pleasant, the forests and plains they roamed through were beautiful. Growing up in the northern territory of the Shadowlands, Lora hadn't seen a lot of color other than white snow, white ice, and blood red. The variety of greens that the trees displayed took Lora's breath away.

Liam had noticed Lora's fascination with the woods, after the first couple of quiet gasps, and had spent the better part of the last several hours telling her as much history and information he could about the ancient woods and the territory they were in, Garrison chiming in every now and then. While the others seemed to be mildly annoyed by the history lesson, she was enthralled, each new detail painting a picture in her mind that had her desperate to stop and explore.

She had said as much to Liam about an hour ago and he was only now just finishing his lecture on reasons one should *not* go wandering into the woods.

"Then you have to worry about the oglemans, they are said to be so vicious they'll rip your arms clean off before you can even draw a weapon." Which earned him an incredulous look from Garrison and a gag from Nuva.

"Can't you two talk about something more positive?" asked Kalon from the front of the group.

"And less graphic," chimed in Nuva, truly looking a little green.

"And what, pray tell, would you like to hear about?" asked Liam, clearly pleased they wanted him to continue at all.

"How about some history?" suggested Garrison's cousin Erik, his brother nodding in agreement. They never really spoke much, though Lora was inclined to like their cousin a bit more, she respected their privacy enough not to ask about Garrison as a young child. She was wildly curious about *when* he had become so massive.

She turned her attention back to Liam who seemed to be contemplating, "I know several histories. Which one do you want to hear about? I know the history of medicine, the history of herbs and spices, the history of herbs and spices in medicine, the history of the first Drake rulers..."

That one she was really interested in, but Nuva made an exasperated noise and he continued on.

No one seemed to want to hear any of the plethora of histories Liam had memorized. He continued listing them until Nuva grabbed both sides of her head, exclaiming, "Please make it stop! Kalon, make it stop!"

Kalon let out a soft chuckle she hadn't ever heard before telling Liam over his shoulder, "All right, bud. I think another history lesson may be off the table. We don't want poor Nuva's head to explode."

Liam looked a little disappointed so Lora spoke up. "I heard a story from Ka—I mean, Kierra once."

Kalon stiffened at the casual mention of his sister. Lora didn't care. Not after this morning.

"But the details are all foggy. Maybe you know it?" She looked over at the medic who was smiling broadly at her. She didn't know why she cared if he was happy, but she was glad at the smile that had indeed returned to his face.

"I may know it!" he said eagerly. "What do you remember about it?"

"It was when I was really young." She thought a bit more, the memories thickly coated in the haze of trauma. "I think it was about a missing kid, two lovers from different kingdoms, an evil wizard or something, and maybe a place or thing called Amberdona? It was so fantastical I knew it had to be a myth, a bedtime story Kierra had been told. But she had told it with such conviction. Every time I heard it I was in awe."

She could see them now, her and Kierra sitting on Lora's bed in Attica, Kierra dabbing a solvent on Lora's wrecked back while telling her the grand story. It had all seemed so magical, it had almost made the pain from the lashing dwindle. It was one of the first times someone had truly cared for her. Lora blinked away the memories to see that everyone was now staring at her, even Kalon, who had made it a point not to look at her at all the entire day.

"What?" she asked, unnerved by so many staring faces. "I know it sounds crazy, but it was just something Kierra used to tell me when…" her words died off. She wasn't really ready to admit to the entire group the exact reason Kierra would tell her stories. "When I was having a bad day," she concluded, cheeks flushing slightly.

"They're only staring," said Garrison from behind her, "because they didn't know Ki could even tell stories."

The others seemed to shake loose from their stupor. "Right," Nuva said, turning back to face the front. "Kierra always ruins the story when she tells it, it's like she forgets the punchline is supposed to go at the end." Lora could hear the smile on Nuva's face—she knew exactly what she meant.

"I know," Lora whispered, more to herself than to anyone else.

Kalon seemed to stiffen even more, his eyes still trained on her. She locked gazes with him for a brief moment and the air seemed to electrify before he broke the connection and turned back toward the front, leading the charge again, shoulders a bit more relaxed.

Liam hadn't seemed to notice anything that was going on and was busy mumbling the details she had given him, as if he was looking on a library shelf within his mind.

"I looked it up in the library at Attica," Lora said, grunting as she climbed over a small boulder in their path. "But there wasn't any mention of anything like that in those books so I assumed it was make believe...if that helps," she added, noting Liam nodding to himself as she talked.

"It could be," Liam surmised as he too climbed over the boulder. "It could be the story of the lost princess of Ambrosia. But there are no evil sorcerers in that story, per say. Does that ring a bell?"

"Ambrosia..." she mulled over the word and something settled in her chest. "Yeah, that sounds familiar, but like I said, I don't really remember much about the fairytale."

"That's because it's not a fairytale," Liam said, now suddenly serious.

"And there's a reason it wasn't in your Shade history books," Kalon added, having stopped again. The air around them felt charged and Lora's hairs stood on end. Just as Kalon opened his mouth to say something else, an arrow whizzed through the air, striking Kalon in the chest, knocking him back, his head hitting a rock—knocking him out cold. *Fuck.*

"Fuck!" shouted Garrison. "Scatter!"

At Garrison's command everyone dispersed, heading in different directions. The shot had come from across the boulder field and they were about seventy paces from the tree line. Erik and Toke dove behind a large boulder and Liam and Nuva were on their bellies, assembling mini crossbows.

Garrison was nowhere to be seen, but Kalon was now on the ground, relatively exposed and completely unconscious.

Lora didn't have time to consider her next move as she dove for Kalon, covering his body with hers as another arrow whizzed by. Lora's shadows swatted it from the air, the arrow shattering on a nearby rock. She cast her shadows out, covering Liam and Nuva and even Garrison's cousins. *Where the hell is Garrison?*

As if in answer, the male emerged from behind the rock next to them, a couple of paces away. He was dirty but seemed uninjured.

"How many?" asked Lora, still covering a slowly squirming Kalon with her body.

"There *were* about two dozen." A wicked grin spread across his face. "Now it's about a dozen or so left, all with crossbows and swords." Garrison was reloading his own crossbow, though he didn't seem to have a lot of arrows left.

Good, he managed to kill some already. "Who are they? Any visible crests?" They were really exposed in this field, and if anyone had seen them coming, this would have been the perfect ambushing spot.

"No. Not that I can see. They seem to be mercenaries..." he paused, reloading. "Or thieves."

Mercenaries would not be good. "Let's hope it's the latter," Lora managed to say, grunting as another arrow bounced off her shadow.

Kalon's shoulder was bleeding in earnest now, and Lora knew she needed to remove the arrow protruding from his collar bone. She looked over to where Liam and Nuva were, contemplating her next move.

"We're too exposed here," said Kalon drowsily, through gritted teeth.

"Shut up, I'm trying to think," Lora snapped. At least he was awake now. That made movement a bit easier. Then it dawned on her; it didn't matter if they were mercenaries or thieves because whoever they were, they clearly were not expecting this group to survive the encounter. They also likely weren't expecting a Shade to be among them. *Which is probably why none of the Drakes were using their fire wielding*, she thought. Smart of Kalon to insist they don't expose themselves, but at this moment in time, it was fucking them over.

Lora jumped to her feet, pulling her shadows back to her. If they recognized her shadows, they would know who she was. Then they might decide they *do* want her alive. Not gonna happen.

"Maybe we can try to make a break for those trees," Garrison said over the whizzing of arrows and shouts of people, now rushing toward them by the sound of it. They might not make it out of there alive. *Fuck.*

"Garrison when I say so, I need you to cover me," Lora called, looking over the boulder field again to find the perfect spot. She looked back to see Garrison watching at her expectantly, eyebrows raised.

"And then?" he asked, firing another shot over the boulder.

Lora smiled. "Duck."

With that, she ran.

***

Kalon

Through blurry vision, Kalon saw Lora run into the fray of whizzing arrows. He lurched. She was running away, leaving them defenseless. He had felt her shadows drop away from and then she'd just taken off into the fray. But she wasn't running toward the safety of the tree line. No, she was running toward a large boulder in the middle of the field, right in front of their line of defense. *What the hell is she doing?*

He tried and failed to lean up, to see where she had gone, if she was hit, but his arm was useless and any movement sent waves of pain rippling through his body. He could push through the pain if it weren't for his vision going in and out of focus.

Garrison shouted something and another volley of arrows shot by them, several landing close. Too close. *Where the hell did Lora go? And why do I care so much?*

***

Lora

Garrison was right—no crests or insignias were visible on any of the people marching through the tall grass in the boulder field. It didn't matter who they were, because they were all dead to Lora anyway. The minute they shot Kalon, their time on this side of the veil had become limited.

No, she chided herself, *I'm doing this because I don't like being shot at. It has nothing to do with the insufferable prince.* She didn't care about these people, she needed them alive only for her passage to the southern continent.

Leaping over another boulder, she heard Garrison shout a string of curses. *Shit, he's out of arrows.* She didn't give herself time to reconsider as she launched herself onto the largest boulder, right in front of their line of defense, took a steady breath, and covered the world in darkness.

***

Kalon

Everything got really dark, really quick and Kalon knew who that was thanks to. Lora was still alive. Not that it really mattered to him. He needed her alive for the mission they were on—then she'd be off to wherever she pleased. *Good. Less drama, less annoying sensations in my chest.*

His shoulder throbbed hard, a spike of pain lancing down into his hand, bringing his thoughts back to the present. He could not see an inch in front of him and only knew Garrison was there by the heavy breathing to his left.

Then he heard Lora shout something, and suddenly Garrison threw his body over his. There was a flash behind his eyes and when Garrison finally crawled off of him, Kalon could see again. As he blinked, his eyes adjusting to the sudden brightness of day, the wind carried a familiar smell—burnt flesh.

Garrison rose, looking across the boulder field with wide eyes as Kalon tried rising to his feet. He swayed a bit but steadied himself on the rock in front of him. The grasslands they had been walking through moments before were gone. At least the immediate area surrounding them was. In its place was charred earth, still smoking from the fire that had ravaged it.

Across the field, where the enemy had been firing from, there was nothing. No bodies, no weapons, nothing. As if the fire had been so hot, it had wiped away all evidence of people even existing in that area.

Kalon saw Nuva and Liam crawling up from their position to his right, Garrison's cousins emerging from behind a rock a good fifteen paces behind him. What he noticed then was the small patches around the rocks he and his comrades had been hiding behind. There were definite circles where the fire seemed to have stopped, not breaching the space where they had been hiding.

As if there had been a shield around them. But it was fire, so they would have been fine, there was no need to shield... *Lora.* His mind began racing. Did she know that Drakes were all but fireproof? As he made a mental note to let her in on that secret so she didn't waste her energy next time, he looked to the large rock he'd seen her running to, to find it empty.

Shit. He staggered forward a step, but Liam was already there, pack in hand, examining the wound. Kalon looked around the area of the rock but he couldn't see her. She was gone.

Shit. Maybe she'd run away like he'd originally thought. No, he'd heard her shout out moments before the fire erupted.

Shit. Drakes may be impervious to fire, but Shades definitely weren't. He became frantic, his heart beating uncontrollably. Garrison tracked his gaze, noting his worry. His eyes widened as they returned to his prince's and then he was running the direction Lora had gone.

He tried and failed to see what was happening, Liam continuously pulling him back so he could wrap his arm.

Where is she? Where is she? Where is she?

It was a song in his blood, ash coating his mouth as his skin began to heat.

Kalon. Someone said his name. "Kalon," Liam said again, grabbing him by the cheeks. "I need you to calm down so I can wrap your wound."

He tried to turn his head back toward Garrison. Liam slapped his face, drawing his attention back. "Do you hear me? You can't help her if I don't wrap your arm."

Help her? Help who–

Garrison was now in front of them, a too-bloody body limply hanging in his arms.

Lora.

***

Lora

She had been thrown off her feet when the fire erupted. *I should have paid better attention to my footing,* she chided herself as she was catapulted through the air. She landed on a rock with a sickening crunch, and the last thing she thought before darkness claimed her, was that her friends were okay now.

That Kalon was okay.

***

Something hot and thick slid down her throat, and Lora was gasping for breath. She had a metallic taste in her mouth and she took a few heartbeats to assess her injuries before opening her eyes.

By the feel of it, her arm was only mildly injured and her whole body was cold and covered in thick ash. Her head hurt and her mouth felt like she'd eaten a handful of ash, but other than that, she was relatively unscathed.

When she finally pried her eyes open, she saw several concerned faces above her. For a moment, she forgot what had happened and merely stared back at them in equal confusion. Then her head began to throb and with it came the memories of the last twenty minutes.

She blinked a couple of times, allowing her eyes to adjust to the sudden brightness. "Definitely concussed," she heard Liam say. "Can you see me okay?"

"Which one of you?" she asked, her throat scratchy and tasting of blood, her lips cracking as she tried to smile. No one laughed. She cleared her throat as her vision finally came into focus. "Yes, I can see you just fine."

"What happened?" Erik asked, kicking about the ashen ground.

"I must've hit something flammable they were carrying," she explained, wincing as she tried to rise. *Oh shit, I'm going to throw up when I can finally stand.*

Garrison looked at her with an expression she couldn't quite place, but it quickly faded as Kalon came into her field of vision.

"Hey," he said, dropping down into her space, his tone calm and almost too kind. "What the hell were you thinking?"

There he is. "A simple thank you would suffice, asshole," she muttered, trying again to rise, but felt another wave of nausea roll through her. She had expended a lot of power and needed something to eat, or she may very well pass out. She said as much and Liam had Nuva rummaging through his pack.

Lora rolled her shoulders as she sat forward, taking a sweet cake and some water from Nuva. Everyone tried their best not to stare, but it was clear that they were.

"I'm fine, really," she assured them, taking another sip from the water. A shiver worked its way up her spine as a breeze blew past, coating her skin with a cold wind. Her skin—her very much exposed skin.

Nuva let out a low whistle as Liam pushed in front of Kalon with a blanket.

"Damn, girl." Nuva butted Liam out of the way and clapped Lora on the back gently. "No wonder you weren't worried about the scar from Garrison's shitty stitches," she chuckled, throwing a feigned side eye at Garrison, who rummaged through a bag, presumably for clothes.

His head whipped up at the accusation, "Hey! My stitches were just fine! She's the one who kept moving!"

Nuva's laugh echoed through Lora's bones, and it dawned on her that Nuva had somehow been the one to take away any shame. In that moment, she felt included, normal. One of them.

"You'll have to regale us with stories someday," she said, guiding Lora to her feet. "I'm sure more than one of those scars was well earned." She smiled, and Lora felt a pang within her soul.

She was nothing like these people. They had gotten scars in battle, saving lives. Lora got hers from taking them.

She tugged the blanket tighter around her chest as her knees wobbled. She swayed as she stood, and Liam was there under her other arm, helping to ease her to her full height.

"I don't have anything that wouldn't swallow her," Garrison called, all but emptying his pack on the blasted earth.

"I have a pair of breeches," Nuva offered. Adding with a gentle elbow jab, "Now that you've got meat back on your bones, you might just fit in them."

Lora tried and failed to smile, so she just nodded in thanks as Nuva handed her the pants.

"Well, she can't go around without a shirt, she'll freeze," chided Garrison, now looking around like he was going to make her a shirt out of the very grass they stood on.

"Technically it would take several days for her to come close to freezing," Liam said, "and at this altitude she could be warmer—"

Nuva shoved him to shut him up and the pair tussled in the earth a bit. Lora guessed Nuva was annoyed at his constant lectures and Liam was tired of being pushed. Garrison just rolled his eyes and pried the two apart, reprimanding them like children.

Lora took the pause in attention to try and slide on Nuva's pants. A crunch in the ashes had her head whipping up, causing her vision to blur a bit as Kalon's outstretched hand clasped her shoulder.

"Whoa there, let me help you." He pulled off her wrecked shoes with his one good arm and helped guide her feet into the pant legs. He shimmied the tighter fabric all the way up her legs until he got to her thighs, making to keep helping—

"I think I have it from here," she breathed, suddenly feeling both hot and cold.

Kalon's little laugh skirted down her spine and across her skin. "It's just skin, princess. If you need help, I don't mind this one time."

"It's fine, really," she assured him, stepping back slightly and pulling the pants all the way up before buttoning them twice at the top. Surprisingly, they did fit her, and she noted with a bit of pride that her legs felt strong despite being blown off a rock. And kidnapped, and shot, and almost killed by pirates. She began adjusting her chest wrappings, which had miraculously survived the blast, and caught Kalon staring.

Her eyebrows shot up. "You aren't going to offer to help?" she asked teasingly.

Kalon's smirk deepened, a bit of heat flaring in his eyes. "I would need two hands for that, princess, anything less would be a crime."

The promise in his voice had Lora's mind picturing him stripping her back down... but her heat sputtered out with another gust of wind. "Gods it's cold," she said, pulling the blanket tight.

"Shit, right, yeah," Kalon began digging in his bag. "I came over here to bring you this." In his outstretched hand was a dark tunic, not pure black like she was used to wearing, but dark enough that it might as well have been Shade black.

"It may be a little big, but not as big as Garrison's," he added, passing it to her.

"Thanks," she said, taking the tunic and making quick work of pulling it on over her head. Her arm still ached and she winced as the shirt caught on the stitches Liam had sewn in.

"Here," Kalon, who had been tracking each movement, now stood so close they were sharing breath. He picked up her uninjured arm and rolled the sleeve of his tunic up while he spoke. "We were originally going to bypass a small town, but I'm thinking now we should probably stop in and get supplies." He finished the first sleeve and began the second.

"Because I blew up all our supplies?" she asked, her eyes wandering to the ashen field. She heard a voice in her mind say, *no, because the assholes blew up our stuff*. She chuckled softly as she looked back at Kalon, but his smirk was gone.

Kalon opened his mouth for a retort, but then closed it suddenly. He looked confused and then concerned as he stepped back. He gave her a full look over, his face twisting briefly into an unknown emotion before returning to his calm and precise mask. "There. Ready to keep going?"

She took a deep breath, swallowing all the lies and truths that were sitting on her heart. "Yes." Another lie, but hopefully one that wouldn't get her killed.

CHAPTER 30

THE GORA MOUNTAINS

Kalon

Kalon had woken from a fitful sleep expecting everyone else to be ready to continue on. Instead, he woke to the camp all but empty, save for the two cousins of Garrison's who were still conked out on their bed rolls. Everyone else—Liam, Garrison, and Nuva—all stood at the edge of a clearing just outside the shadows Lora had put in place the night before.

He hated to admit it, but the shadow work she could do, even wounded, was impressive. They could take a solid form, whisper to her of things said across a courtyard, or, like now, protect the entire camp from being seen or heard from the outside.

He looked over to where he had seen her fall asleep next to Garrison, but the spot was empty. *Shit.* Pulling on his boots he all but ran to the clearing, sword drawn before he stopped short. What he saw was not at all what he expected.

Lora's shadows had extended to this little area where she was currently in her breeches and her—correction, *his*—black, unbuttoned tunic, throwing several large sticks at her own shadows. The largest stick she threw, a veritable branch, ricocheted off her shadow and plunged back at her.

He started forward, but the Shade was faster than he could even see, dodging the projectile before rolling to her side and launching it back. It seemed like she was fighting an invisible opponent as she ducked and weaved, throwing sticks and lashing out at them with her shadows.

He was awestruck. He'd never seen anything like it or seen anyone move like that either.

"How long…" the question faded on his lips as Lora hurtled past a small grouping of trees, swinging her weight around the last one as her shadows sliced through the other three. She didn't even look back at the debris field she had created as she continued her moves, strands of her fiery hair blowing in the breeze.

Kalon cleared his throat. "How long has she been…well, doing whatever it is she's doing?" he asked, his eyes never leaving the Shade's solid, moving form.

"She's training," answered Garrison. He, too, was tracking the girl's movements, eyes sparkling with an emotion he couldn't quite place. "*Their* kind of training," he added, making a pointed look over at him.

"And she's been at it for about an hour or so," chimed Nuva, who was leaning against a tree, not quite impressed but definitely intrigued. Lora hadn't ever really let them see her train her shadows—he wasn't even sure up until now it was something that was trained, more just honed.

"At least that's how long we've been staring," added Liam, who looked nothing short of delighted.

Kalon rolled his eyes at the perverse medic. Of course he'd think this was so interesting. Kalon was honestly surprised the male wasn't taking notes. He'd probably ask her a million questions when she was done.

Kalon drew his attention back to the princess as she ducked from another stick, but this time it caught her in the shoulder, causing her to stagger backward. He looked to his friends expecting at least Nuva to laugh, but they all stood there watching her, only awe glancing their features as Lora righted herself, readjusted her bandages, and began again.

"Why is she using those sticks?" Kalon asked, now turning to Garrison, who still stared at Lora. But after a long pause, he finally turned to his friend, a smile spreading across his face.

Suddenly, two smaller sticks, about the size of a short sword, were tossed at his chest. "Because you took away my weapons, asshole," Lora said, having snuck up on him on quieter feet than he was comfortable with. "You got a little drool," she added, pointing to his cheek, before continuing back to camp through the trees, aiming for where Liam packed his bag. *When had he left the clearing?*

"You still have that dagger you nearly killed me with!" he called after her, regretting it immediately as Nuva's eyes widened, Liam's brows shooting up in question. It was a shadow dagger, but still...

Lora simply shrugged as she walked, not even deigning to respond.

"Honestly," Garrison said chuckling, turning beside him to watch her walk away, "after watching that, I think anything is a weapon in her hands."

"Yeah," Kalon agreed, something sinking in his chest like a weight in water. "That's what I'm afraid of."

"Careful prince," the girl drawled from over her shoulder, not looking back at them. "That *almost* sounded like a compliment."

Garrison let out a soft chuckle before slapping him on the back and making his way back into the campsite.

Kalon stood there a couple seconds longer, looking back at the debris field Lora had left behind. Although it wasn't charred, it made him wonder about another debris field from the day before.

***

Lora

Once they were all packed, Garrison's cousins led the group through another thicket and into yet *another* boulder field. At some point, she felt like they were climbing a literal mountain.

Liam talked less today. Everyone talked less today. The events of the afternoon before hung in the air like the mist that swirled around her feet.

"How tall is this mountain?" Her question broke the silence, echoing off the rocks around them.

"You don't recognize them?" asked Garrison, coming up beside her as the path widened.

"No? Should I?" She looked around again to make sure.

Garrison gave her a quizzical look before explaining, "The other side of these mountains lead to Attica. These are the—"

"Gora Mountains," she finished for him. A heartbeat passed and she added, "They're haunted."

"They what?" Even Nuva seemed intrigued by the nonchalance of the statement.

"Haunted. Kierra and I once snuck down to the barracks and heard them tell the stories of these mountains," she explained. She glanced up to see that everyone, including Kalon, was now looking at her. "What?"

"You want to tell us *why*, exactly, they're haunted, princess?" Kalon asked from the front of the group. He stopped, and Garrison's cousins took the opportunity to drink from their canteens, Liam and Garrison following suit.

"It's just a story, an old wives tale passed around a fire to scare children," she explained further.

"And soldiers, apparently," added Nuva, a shudder working its way up her spine as she glanced around the area, more alert than before.

"Yes, well, I would like to hear it," crooned Kalon, eyes gleaming with amusement and curiosity. She hated it, and yet, she couldn't look away.

With a frown, she said, "Since you asked so nicely…" She had to dig deep into her memory to remember the major details. "Okay, so, from what I remember, which isn't a lot, there were two dragons who were running rampant in Attica and Angora."

Kalon's eyebrows shot up as if to ask, *Angora?*

"Anyway, they were these hulking beasts who were burning villages and doing what dragons do and no one could stop them. Well, one day, a brave knight set forth to stop the mighty dragons. When he arrived in these mountains he found the mother dragon's nest being guarded by the father dragon. He slew the father dragon where it stood and peeked into the nest, but there was only one, small egg. The dragon that sprung forth from inside that egg was small and deformed. He knew that the only way to capture the mother dragon was to steal the baby dragon. So, he took it and hid it away. When the mother dragon returned to find her baby gone and her mate slain, she roared out, causing an avalanche that wiped out nearly half of the mountain dwelling people. The mother dragon searched and searched for her baby, but never found it or the knight who killed her mate. They say, even now after all these years, the mountains are haunted by the beating of the mother dragon's wings and her roar of sorrow as she searches the mountain caves for her lost baby." She finished her tale and felt rather pleased with her memory, but as her attention returned to the group in front of her, she noted that even Liam seemed skeptical.

"What a picture, you weave princess," Kalon said, the words dripping in sarcasm.

"I said I barely remembered it! Just like that princess story from yesterday," she chided, crossing her arms defiantly.

"Asshole," she added after the arrogant prince merely took in her stance and chuckled.

"I'm not saying it wasn't real," Kalon said with a growing smirk. "It just sounds more like a story from *Fables of Fire and Flying*, that's all."

The group all nodded in agreement.

"What's *Fables of Fire and Flying*?" Lora asked as the group started moving again.

"It's a selection of fables and old stories from the Drake kingdom," Liam answered enthusiastically, though the rest of the group seemed to go a bit rigid. Liam didn't notice as he continued explaining. "Some say that our most sacred rituals stem from the book because it's actually more of—"

He was cut off by an elbow to the stomach from Nuva. They gave each other stern looks, Nuva nodding toward Kalon before another pulse of energy swept through the group.

Nuva straightened, "Let's talk about something else. Aren't there supposed to be hunting cabins or something along the route?"

Everyone seemed to relax at the change of subject. Lora felt the energy shift again as she explained, "Oh yeah, they say that once all the dragons left these mountains, it became a perfect spot for hunting wild game. The sides of the mountains are littered with foxes, deer, and even bears."

"Did you ever visit them as a child?" Asked Liam, his mood seemingly renewed with the change of subject.

"No," she replied. "I was kept in Northern Attica, on the Ice Plains of Taiga. But Kierra and I dreamed of running away—a lot—and one of our many plans was to escape to these mountains. Though the thought of running into a giant dragon used to scare me senseless." She chuckled to herself at the memory, but Kalon stiffened ahead of her, causing her smile to fade.

"Yes well, dragons are rightly scary," Garrison said, clapping Toke on the back as he passed him by. "Onwards!"

Lora couldn't shake the feeling that she had somehow offended Kalon, and maybe even the whole group. But when she walked up to the front to ask him, she was struck speechless by the path up the mountain that emerged before her, and suddenly she had little space in her head to worry about anything other than surviving.

CHAPTER 31

THE SPLIT

Lora

The rest of the hike around the Gora Mountain Range was uneventful and had surprisingly only taken two full days of hiking, since they had skirted around the edges. Still steep as hell though, making her wish dragons weren't so damn noticeable or scary.

The views from the varying heights of the valley they were crossing through had been enough to have her gasping several times. But the cold that seeped in as they settled for bed had them all ready to keep moving by morning. As they eased down one of the final hills she froze—just beyond the tree line below them was smoke on the horizon.

"Gods!" Nuva exclaimed, slamming into Lora's back abruptly. "What the hell are we stopping for?"

Nuva stepped around Lora, who was still frozen in her spot, as Kalon looked back from the front of the line, confused. "We aren't." Kalon took the four steps back to her then tracked her gaze to the tendrils of smoke.

"Lora?" Liam asked, concern etched into his face, but still Lora's gaze remained fixed on that smoke, her body unable to move. She felt like the world was closing in on her, her breaths coming in short pants. No, *not another village burned.* She could already smell the bodies, feel the heat pull at her skin. Her shadows began twirling around her, ready to protect her from the unseen enemy.

"Lora," Kalon's voice was soft and calm, his face blocking her view of the smoke. "Lora, it's okay. That's just Skipton, it's a small trading village." Kalon reached out but seemed to decide against touching her.

She could barely breathe, barely think past the roaring in her head. Skipton, she knew that village, had seen it burn to the ground, knew its tragedy—it was her own. The world tilted and she found herself falling toward the grass beneath her feet, but just as she braced for the impact, strong hands caught her shoulders, gently easing her to her knees.

"Woah there, I've got you."

That's Garrison, her mind told her as she tried to control her breathing. She needed to pull herself together, needed to get through this valley and away from the village. Her eyes wandered back to the smoke, but her view was obstructed by Kalon again, his harsh features softened, making his amber eyes sparkle like liquid gold.

"You okay, princess?" His tone was light, but concern bracketed his face.

Lora took a shuddering breath. "Yeah, yeah, I'm okay," she assured everyone. When she looked back to Kalon, she could tell he didn't believe her. None of them seemed to except for Garrison's cousins. "Really," she tried again. "I think I just need some water."

Nuva nodded seriously as Liam brought over his canteen.

She drank deeply, breathing through the crushing nerves that threatened to pull her under. When she finished the canteen she handed it back to Liam and, taking Garrison's outstretched hand, rose to her feet. Kalon was studying her intently, his eyes sparking with concern and understanding.

"You sure you're alright?" Liam asked again, trying to examine her from a distance.

"I'm sure," she assured him again, batting his hand away as he reached to lift her arm. "Truly. No need for an inspection," she added, trying to lighten the mood.

"Then tell your shadows," Nuva said warily, eyeing the growing mass behind her with a mixture of intrigue and apprehension.

Lora rolled her shoulders and took a deep breath in, closing her eyes. She pictured her shadows settling along her skin, then sinking in. When she opened her eyes again the shadows were gone, and the Drakes were looking at her like she had grown a third head.

"They just...sunk into you..." Liam said, staring at her with nothing short of excitement blossoming in his eyes.

Garrison and Nuva seemed more perturbed by the display and Kalon...his features had smoothed into a calm mask again.

"Yeah," Lora said, pulling her attention back to Liam as she dusted herself off. "They do that."

"Incredible," Liam marveled, now looking at her like she was a book he wanted to read.

"Creepy," Nuva added with a dramatic shiver.

"Useful," chimed Garrison before he clapped her on the back and strode to the front of the line with his cousins.

***

Lora had thought the village was close by, but as they walked and the sky grew darker, she realized she had been wrong. As the sun finally set, casting the world in stunning shades of pinks and oranges, Lora found herself alone with Kalon, collecting wood for the fire, while his friends set up camp in a small clearing by a brook.

They had been walking in a comfortable silence as they collected sticks and other kindling, but Lora could tell Kalon wanted to say something.

"I—"

"You—"

They both chuckled, heat blooming on Lora's cheeks. "You go first," she insisted, leaning over to pick up another stick to add to her growing pile.

Kalon nodded, smiling slightly, then took a deep breath. "Today, before, when you nearly fainted, I know it wasn't because you needed water."

She froze but composed herself quickly. "What do you mean?"

Kalon had stopped at the edge of the clearing they were in, setting his pile of wood down. "I saw you looking at the smoke."

Lora willed her heart rate to settle, to stay calm. "And?"

"And it's the same reaction I sometimes have when I see smoke, or hell, even a hole in the ground," Kalon admitted.

Her eyebrows pinched together. "A hole in the ground?"

Kalon faced her then, devastation in his eyes. "I'm going to tell you something, but you can't panic." The way his voice had shifted had her definitely panicking.

"Okay..." She wasn't sure if she could take a full breath if she tried.

Kalon took another, steadying breath. "Just listen, okay? A couple of years ago, when Garrison and I had been scouting this area, it had just suffered a pretty bad fire—like most of the villages in the area. There hadn't been enough survivors from the raids yet, so we were still trying to figure out what was going on in the neutral territory. And the refugees had started reporting something called a Shadowfire - a new weapon of Cyrus's. And, well, we came upon a camp of Shades who wreaked of—it's actually hard to explain—it was like smoke, but not dragon smoke, more like the embers of a fire."

"Or the ashes..." Lora mumbled, looking away from Kalon's face, her mind wandering to the village below. Kalon had been there all those years ago.

"Yeah, just like the ashes," he said, taking the two strides that separated them, and took her chin in his hand. "Lora, we watched the camp for a couple of hours and it was relatively uneventful. Then, as we were about to leave, I had the urge to stay and wait."

They were so close together in the clearing that they shared breath.

"Why?" She asked, her voice barely above a whisper, her eyes meeting his.

"I don't know," he admitted, his eyes dipping to her lips before he released her chin. "But something made me stay a little longer and that's when I saw a girl—a woman, really. She had this dark, muted black hair, and these stunning brown eyes. I know that's crazy, but they were this maple bronze color."

Lora broke her gaze from his as he spoke, looking anywhere but his amber eyes. She felt herself begin to shake again so she rubbed at her arms, and Kalon seemed to track the movement as he spoke.

"This girl, she was weak, not her body—no, it was strong and muscled—but her eyes... They were so tired and empty." Lora shifted where she stood as a shiver, not entirely from the cold, working up her spine.

"I thought she might be a prisoner or something, but she moved about the camp like a commander. A wraith commander. The men seemed to respect her, or at the very least, respect the smug man I saw walking with her. She definitely had an air of superiority, but it was all but lost behind those dead eyes. I was about to walk away when I saw him chain her in canthite and toss her in a hole in the ground like she was garbage."

Lora felt her body stiffen, the memories of those chains around her wrists and ankles threatening to suffocate her—stifle her. The world seemed to close around Lora as she remembered the hole. The slick, muddy walls pressing into her back, the smell of the dampened earth stuffing itself up her nose. She knew Kalon was watching her, and she wasn't sure he was breathing.

He took a too-shallow breath, and nothing Lora could have done would have braced herself for his next words.

"I lost it then," he all but whispered.

Her attention snapped back to Kalon. He wasn't looking at her anymore. "What do you mean?" she whispered back.

"I nearly ran all the way into camp to set her free. Garrison had to hold me back, keep me from getting myself caught. He dragged me out of there." Kalon's attention was now solely on her, and she felt it like a brand on her skin. She could barely make out the lines of his face as the sun continued to descend, but she could feel the pain and struggle radiating from him.

"You didn't know her. Why? Why would you do that?" Lora asked, holding her breath for his response.

Kalon looked at her a moment longer before shaking his head, looking to the night sky, and the stars that were sparking to life. "I don't know, I couldn't stop myself. All I do know is that I couldn't leave someone in chains." He let out another shaky breath. "And Lora, if I had known it was you—"

Lora's breath caught in her chest as a small part of her heart chipped. "They were for protection," she interrupted, eyes going vacant as she began to dissociate from the conversation, from the memories it dredged up.

"To protect you from what?" Kalon asked, his temper seeming to rise.

"No," Lora corrected. "Not protecting me. Protecting the men *from* me."

She wasn't looking at him, but she felt Kalon's gaze narrow in worry on her before saying gently, "That's not what it looked like to me."

"Well that's what it was," she snapped, tired of his back-and-forth opinions on matters he did not understand. "The canthite nullifies power. If…if I got out of control, I could have killed the whole camp. At least in the hole I'd only kill myself—though the canthite helped prevent that as well."

Kalon's eyes had widened and he sucked in a sharp breath. "What do you mean?"

When she made to turn from him, he caught her by the arm gently and looked down at her wrists, and, despite herself, she did not cover them.

From the corner of her gaze she saw Kalon's gaze soften. "If you think for one second that you, or anyone, deserves that—you are wrong."

The pity in Kalon's voice sent a flame of rage through her, pulling her shadows from their slumber. "Liar," she bit out, spinning out of his grasp to face him.

Kalon's head jerked back like the words were a physical blow. "What?"

"I said you're a liar," she repeated, letting the fiery anger fill her until she no longer felt the phantom canthite around her wrists, or heard the pity in his voice.

"Oh yeah? How's that?" Kalon countered, a little bit of his temper rising to meet hers as he tried and failed to catch her gaze.

"Because you sit here and preach to me about how I don't deserve that after having me chained for nearly a month!" she hissed.

Kalon's eyes narrowed further. "It was for the protection of my men, Lora. I didn't know you then—"

"Oh, I know. This may come as a shock, but I've actually heard that before." She threw all her venom into the words, her anger igniting inside of her, pulling her further from the despair that memories had brought to the surface.

"It's different," he retorted, his temper now rising to match her own.

"It isn't and you know it," she spat. And then she delivered the blow she knew would keep him at arms length. "You're no better than him."

Lora saw the words land like an actual punch. Kalon's face crumpled and he took a deep breath, and she wondered if he was counting to ten to try and stay calm.

"Cyrus and his Shadowfire have killed innocents," he said, a lot less angry than she expected.

But she wanted him to fight, to be angry, to hate her. It was easier that way. "And you haven't?" she shot back.

"This is war, Lora. People die," he started, condescension dripping in each word.

Like she didn't know that? Like she hadn't done terrible things under the excuse of warfare? "That doesn't make it right, Kalon," she said, meeting his gaze.

His amber-flecked eyes were wide with increasing anger. "Lora, I have done horrible things. I know that. But I feel remorse. Cyrus? He doesn't. All he feels is power, death, and destruction. Do you think his little weapon, his *Shadowfire*, feels remorse for the lives it takes?"

"Yes. I do," she said shortly, choosing not to look at him, though she could feel his gaze on her.

"You're being idealistic," Kalon said, his tone shifting toward the kind you'd have when talking to an angry child. "That Shadowfire—it could never feel remorse."

Her temper exploded, stirring her shadows and pulling her power to the surface. "It does. It feels remorse, and guilt, and hate, and love. It feels all those things because it is not an *it*, not a little *weapon* who is thrilled by taking life and destroying homes."

Kalon's eyes flared wide. "You can't possibly believe that," Kalon's tone was set in determination, his mind resolved and unmoving.

But she had had enough, she was tired and knew that this conversation would cause more harm than good. Kalon wouldn't change his mind, and that thought alone had her wanting to run far far away from him—because, for reasons she didn't want to admit, she had grown to care what he thought of her, and that could only lead to heartbreak. So she stooped to pick up her pile.

"Where—" Kalon started.

"Away from here," she said curtly. *Away from you*, was left unsaid, hanging between them. She collected the last of her wood and as she made her way back to camp, she could feel Kalon watching her as she disappeared into the trees.

***

By the time Kalon made it back to the camp, wood in hands, Garrison had already started the fire and assigned Lora potato peeling duty, which she was doing without looking at Kalon at all. Garrison's cousins had caught some type of woodland animal and Lora was thankful she hadn't seen them gut or clean it—it had far too much hair to be something she would *want* to eat.

While Garrison and Liam prepared the meaty parts of dinner, Kalon paced in front of the fire, muttering things now and then to Nuva who was pouring over a map.

"Then tomorrow we will split up," Kalon said to Nuva, who seemed to disagree briefly, but after re-examining her map, changed her mind again.

"Why are we splitting up?" Lora asked, directing her question to Nuva. Splitting up meant she was farther from heading south, from being rid of these people and this continent, and that is not what she wanted.

Kalon gave her a once-over. "First of all, you need new clothes. Secondly, a group this size would be odd wandering around. And lastly, because I said so," he added with a shrug, as if that was a good enough reason.

She narrowed her eyes. "Fine, I want to go with Garrison and Liam then."

Both males' eyebrows shot up, but neither looked at the prince directly.

"Too bad, princess," Kalon drawled. "You're coming with me."

"Why?" It had to be impossible for her eyes to narrow any further.

"Because—"

"You said so?" she interjected with a sassy headcock.

"I was going to say because you need new clothes and I don't know your sizes, but let's just stick with what you said," he concluded with a wink. The way he cut his eyes at her made her think he also wanted to keep an eye on her after earlier today. Either way, this was less than ideal.

Garrison gave Kalon a sly look that she couldn't quite place, but Kalon was ignoring him. And since she was ignoring Kalon, she decided not to press it any further. The faster they got to town, the faster they could be done with this whole "mission" and she could be on her way.

They all ate their dinner in veritable silence, only speaking when ensuring everyone knew the plan forward and backward before Garrison put the fire out. They wouldn't risk any bawdy tunes tonight, as they were too close to the village, so Lora found herself laying silently against the forest floor, her thoughts a torrent in her mind.

But the forest was quiet. And although she was surrounded by people, in that silence, she had never felt more alone.

CHAPTER 32

SKIPTON VILLAGE

Kalon

After their fight in the woods last night, Lora had barely looked at Kalon. She had only spoken to him because she didn't want to be partnered with him in the split, which made today's hike into the town even more tense than it should have been.

They had decided they would enter the town in small groups over the next two days, never staying while another group was there, then make separate hikes to the meet-up point in three days. That meant three full days with Lora in this foul-ass mood.

As they had approached the large gates of Skipton, he had advised Lora to keep her head low and eyes averted. Lora had flipped him off but put her hood up anyway. *Gods, it's going to be a long day.*

Skipton Village had suffered from a series of fires and attacks over the years, leaving the people hardened and relatively wary of strangers. Kalon had expected as much as they approached the gate. What he hadn't expected was Kretain soldiers asking questions and looking under caps.

"Mix in some truth," Lora whispered, noting where his gaze had drifted.

He glanced sidelong at her. She too slid, her eyes to his. "That will make the lies more believable," she explained before squaring her shoulders and facing the soldiers again.

Mix truth with the lies, he repeated to himself—a very unsettling piece of advice from the Shade princess next to him.

"Next," the soldier called, eying Kalon and Lora as they stepped up. "What brings you to Skipton?" he asked, surveying the pair.

"Just passing through on our way to the capital." *Truth.*

"And what's the reason for your visit north?" The soldier asked, almost bored.

"Work," Lora replied, plastering a sweet smile to her face.

The guard's gaze sharpened, but Lora batted her eyes.

"Enjoy your stay," was all he said as he waved them through.

"Work?" he hissed under his breath.

"Sort of the truth," she shot back, looking up at him from under her hood. He rolled his eyes.

"Go buy a change of clothes for yourself," he ordered, passing her a small amount of coins.

"Aye aye sir!" she mocked, stepping into the dull city square as rain began to fall.

He grabbed her arm before she could walk away. "Meet back in an hour," he said quietly. "I want to be in our rooms by nightfall."

Lora's eyes narrowed and she looked to where he touched her arm. "Grab my arm like that again," she seethed, "And I'll cut it off." She shook out of his grasp and stormed into the pouring rain.

"An hour!" he called after her, drawing too much attention.

She merely flicked him off over her shoulder and kept walking. How she knew where she was going, he had no idea.

***

Lora

Lora had kept Kalon waiting for a half hour longer than he'd asked. Judging by the way he was looking at her as she sauntered across the courtyard, he was pissed. It wasn't entirely on purpose. She had bought a new tunic as instructed, but as she was making her way back to the village center she saw two soldiers throwing rocks at the windows of a burned-down house. She had tried to ignore it, but then one had begun to pee on it, and well…she stopped ignoring it. It had taken the extra thirty minutes to tie up both soldiers from the rafters of the house.

"You're late," he spat by way of greeting, his eyes flaring as he took in her soot-covered face.

"Good to see you too," she purred, tapping him on the chest as she walked by.

"Where the hell were you?" he asked, coming up to walk next to her. The rain was coming down harder now, luckily washing away the soot, but her clothes would need several hours to dry once she washed them thoroughly. They needed to find rooms quickly before anyone noticed how dirty she still was. "And why are you so dirty?"

"Worried about me?" she asked coyly, rounding a corner into a seedier part of town.

"Not in the slightest," he bit out, though she noted his voice had been edged with concern.

Two soldiers considered them as they walked across the city square, the rain obstructing most of their faces. She noted that they spoke briefly to one another before they pushed their way off the wall and began to follow them.

Kalon stiffened as he too noticed the two soldiers making their way toward them.

Her thoughts raced in anxious anticipation. Maybe they recognized her. They weren't the ones she'd strung up, but maybe those men had already gotten down and alerted their comrades. She had hoped they would have more time to get out of the streets. An idea flashed in her mind and suddenly, she was grabbing Kalon's hand and guiding him down a covered alleyway.

***

Kalon

"What are you doing?" he whispered, keeping his hood up despite the covering now stopping most of the rain. Lora had arrived late to the meet-up point, covered in dirt and smelling like a fire. Now she was dragging him down an alleyway and—

Lora was stripped off most of her weapons, stashing them in the crate to her left. "Do you trust me?" she asked, now pulling off her tunic from under her jacket and stuffing it in the crates well.

His eyes flared wide. "What?" *What the hell is she doing?*

She locked eyes with him then, the rain making her curls stick to her face, framing it in red. "I think those men are looking for me, and if they find me, it won't end well. So, do you trust me?" She bit out the words, and the emotion that flared in her eyes made him pause.

"Enough I guess," he shot back, now realizing the soldiers were about to turn the corner into the alleyway. *What the hell had she gotten into?*

Lora smiled tightly. "Enough will do." And then she grabbed him, pulling him on top of her as her back slammed into the brick wall, just as the soldiers rounded the corner. "They can't see my face," she whispered and he propped his arm on the wall, covering most of her face.

"Excuse me," one called. "What are you doing down there?"

Lora didn't take her attention off of him as she drawled from under him, her voice no longer her own, "Give me a few minutes, boys, and I can help you next."

Kalon stiffened at the promise and implication in her voice.

"Told you," he heard one say. "It's not her, it's just some common whore." They both laughed, but then one kept walking in their direction.

"He seems almost done with you," the same one called out again, now laughing with his buddy. "Come on man, share with the rest of us."

Kalon's heart raced as his eyes darted back to Lora. She looked at him, and his gaze dropped to her lips.

"You hear me boy?" The soldiers were closer now, and if they thought he was "done" with Lora, they'd take her.

Panic flared in Lora's eyes for a heartbeat, and then he crashed his lips to hers.

At first he was worried she'd jerk away, but she only melted into him as his kiss deepened. The soldiers stopped a few feet from them. Still he kissed her. She tasted like honey and wind-kissed mornings. He slid his tongue into her mouth, and she opened for him, her tongue tangling with his. His blood heated as he slid his hands down her sides, feeling every curve she had exposed now that her tunic and weapons were gone. He pushed her into the wall a little harder, letting her legs straddle him, and she moaned a little at the pressure, him swallowing it with another kiss. *Gods, this feels good.*

A cough from his left had him pulling away only slightly, Kalon's breathing matching Lora's in heavy pants. "You almost done?" one of the soldiers asked, looking at what he could see of Lora with hunger in his eyes.

He nearly ripped out the soldier's throat then and there, but Lora's hand wrapped around the one he had on her waist. He took a deep breath then peered over the arm he had against the wall, blocking Lora from them. "Not nearly," he growled softly, his eyes locking back with Lora's.

Her body went rigid underneath him, and his hand tightened on her waist.

The soldier frowned now, his friend looking a mixture of displeased and disgusted. "Well, you can't fuck in the streets," the soldier said, almost angrily—as if he wished they could.

"Then point me to a fucking tavern," Kalon all but growled, his voice not fully his own. He did not like the way the men were looking at Lora.

"My apologies boys," Lora drawled, peeling herself from Kalon. He, however, did not let go. "Point us to the closest tavern and we'll be out of your hair." And then she winked, *fucking winked*, at the soldiers.

The one who had looked at her like she was meat was now all but drooling. "At the end of this alley ma'am," he replied, his tone dripping with hopeful lust.

Kalon growled but Lora simply smiled at the soldiers before grabbing his hand and guiding them down the alley.

"What the hell was that all about?" he asked after the soldiers had gone. He was suddenly very angry and very cold. Lora paid him no interest as she grabbed her weapons from their hiding spot, strapping them all on efficiently and quickly.

"Lora," he demanded. Her eyes shot back to him, and he noticed that her hands were shaking slightly. "Why were they looking for you?"

Lora sighed through her nose. "I saw some of their men messing with an old burned-out house, and when I asked them to stop, they didn't."

He felt the color drain from his face. "So what did you do?" He almost didn't want to know.

"I didn't kill them," she snapped, and his anger banked with the disappointment and slight shake in her voice. Her body began shaking along with her hands. "I just strung them up in the ashes, as a warning."

He felt like a total asshole. Of course she hadn't killed them. What was he thinking? She looked so cold and frail in her soaking clothes, her eyes distant and glossy. "Maybe you should have killed them," he offered, remembering the way one of the soldiers had looked at her.

She looked around the alleyway slowly, then toward the village. "This town has seen enough death."

He felt the words like a blow to his chest. *Damn.* He smiled faintly and offered her his arm. "Shall we head to the seediest of taverns, oh lady of the night?" he asked, trying to bring a smile to her face.

It barely worked. She nodded slightly, looping her arm through his as he led them the direction the soldiers had pointed.

***

The small room Kalon was shown to was on the third floor of a rather derelict looking tavern. The room was barely big enough for two people, with just one bed pushed against the wall and a small nightstand that the door hit when he opened it.

Lora rounded the corner moments later, still drawing out her steps as if she were following up a customer. But her steps faltered when she beheld the room.

"I said two beds," he said, surveying the small space. "But I guess since you're a courtesan now, they just assumed…"

The whack he received from Lora as she walked past him into the small room was hard enough that he rubbed at his arm.

She threw her belongings onto the bed haphazardly as she began peeling off her soggy clothes. He hadn't realized he was staring until his gaze landed back on her eyes. She smiled tightly at him, faking a lover's expression. "Won't you just be a doll and get this courtesan something to nibble on?" she purred.

Despite himself, his blood heated. He shook his head slightly, sending water droplets across the floor. "Right, yeah, I'll, uh, see if they have anything downstairs that looks even mildly edible." He cleared his throat.

To his horror, Lora smiled slightly before resuming her undressing, which she did painfully slow. Kalon shook his head again and quickly exited the room before he did something stupid, closing the door behind him as he made his way into the hallway. He stood there momentarily, trying to get his mind back together.

They had kissed. He had kissed her. And now, she was undressing in the room they were to share. And…she was attractive, if he was being honest. She wasn't classically beautiful like he'd seen in paintings or how he'd heard other males discuss. No, Lora was wild, like a fire or a hurricane. A kind of beauty that could either kill you or make you new.

Why was he thinking about how beautiful she was? He needed to get his mind to stop listening to his cock and focus. They had to spend the night together, and there was no way they were doing anything other than sleeping.

***

"Knock, knock," Kalon called as he rapped on the door a few minutes later. "I found something that seems to be a beef stew, but I didn't ask too many—"

His words died in his throat as he entered the room where Lora was currently facing away from him, her shirt and chest wrap completely off. He couldn't help but falter a step as he gazed upon Lora's ravaged skin. He had seen pieces of scars peppering her arms and backs, knew of the ones around her wrists and he presumed her ankles, but never had he imagined what he was currently looking at.

There was not a spot on her back that was not scratched and scarred. It had to be years' worth of damage. He felt his temper rise as his voice dropped to a deadly calm. "Who did that to you?"

Lora didn't even glance over her shoulder as she pulled her new tunic out of the bag she'd shoved it in earlier. "It doesn't matter." She sounded exhausted, the events of the day already tugging her toward sleep.

"It sure as fuck does." He wasn't even sure he was breathing, he was focusing so hard on keeping his anger in check.

"Not anymore it doesn't." And with that she slipped on her new tunic and, pulling the thin blanket up to her neck, fell asleep.

***

Lora

Lora hadn't even thought to cover up her back before Kalon walked into the small room. But then he'd seen her back and, despite his people's view on scars, she had seen the way his face had twisted into disgust.

She blew out a slow breath, trying not to wake Kalon, who was currently sleeping on the floor.

She had originally assumed they would sleep in the same bed, but after she'd all but dismissed his questions about her scars and crawled in the bed, he had simply blown out the candle and laid on the floor, using a towel as a blanket.

The bed creaked as she rolled to her side. She wasn't sure what to make of their kiss today. It had been her idea to pretend to be a courtesan, but Kalon took it a step further in kissing her. Deeply. Her toes curled without any consent as she thought back to the way he'd pinned her against the wall of the alley, his hands roaming up and down her side.

She rolled onto her back, trying to focus on breathing. That line of thought was only trouble, and she needed to get some good sleep before they started hiking again. Lora rolled again to her side, pulled the sheets up around her chin, and took three deep breaths before she willed herself to sleep.

***

There was only pain as the whip ripped through her skin again, the gruff voice of the Drake commander inaudible over the roaring in her ears. Then there was blood and smoke and she felt her soul shredding as she watched her friend get ripped away by winged beats. Then her side split open, blood funneling out of the wound as wings beat above her. Then there were arrows flying her direction and red blood and a prone prince-

"Wake up, princess."

And there was smoke and her body hurtling through the air. She was dying. Over and over again, she was dying in every possible way.

"Wake up, I've got you. Lora, wake up."

Lora's eyes burst open, her body gasping for the air she couldn't choke down in her dream. As she looked around in the impenetrable darkness she realized she was completely ensconced in shadows. A moment later she felt a strong hand on her back, making soothing circles as she continued to gasp for air.

Two heartbeats later and her shadows were sucking into her, receding into her skin as light flooded back into the small room. Kalon had come right to her—even in the shadows he had found her.

She didn't stop herself as she crumpled into his arms, shuddering as she folded in on herself. Kalon climbed into the bed then, his arms pulling her in close as he positioned her between his legs, cradling her in his lap. He continued rubbing her back until Lora was lulled into a sleep that had no nightmares, but something far more dangerous— dreams.

***

Lora had one of the most peaceful sleeps she'd had in years wrapped in Kalon's arms. When she had awoken and her eyes still adjusted to the bright stream of sunlight coming from the small window, she breathed in his citrus and ember scent, letting it curl around her, settling in her skin.

Then it all came crashing back. She had had a nightmare and he had reached through her shadows, soothing her. And now…they were intertwined on the bed like lovers. Which was only kind of funny, since she was supposed to be pretending to be a courtesan.

She slowly pried herself from his grasp, easing herself from the bed. She was still only wearing a loose tunic but she feared putting on more clothes would wake him up. So she pulled on his pants, belting them heavily, as she scurried out the door.

She re-braided her hair that had come loose in her sleep as she made her way to the small bar on the bottom floor. "Hello, do you have any breakfast?" she asked, surveying the dirty, empty room. When her gaze landed back on the barmaid, the woman had a knowing smile plastered on her face.

"Worked up quite the appetite huh?" she asked, her smile growing. "I'll get you some bread and cheese."

Lora gave a tight smile back. Within minutes the woman was back with a small plate of cheese and bread and Lora took it silently, nodding her thanks as she dashed up the stairs back to their room.

The door creaked as she opened it and any hope that Kalon would still be asleep was dashed out when she saw his sideways smile.

"Well good morning, princess. Nice outfit," he drawled, stretching and tousling his messy curls.

"I got breakfast," she said by way of greeting, thrusting the plate in his direction.

"Oh! Yum!" he chirped, picking up some cheese and bread and making a small sandwich.

She sat on the bed, feet tucked under her as she, too, picked at the food. "The lady downstairs asked if we'd worked up an appetite."

Kalon let out a short, roaring laugh. "Of course she did. Did you tell her all about it?" His eyes sparkled with amusement as he spoke, little dimples appearing in his cheeks.

"No," she shot back, though she smiled a bit as she took another bite.

"Well eat up, princess," he said, taking a deep breath before jumping out of the bed. "Because today...today, we will definitely work up an appetite."

CHAPTER 33

THE BEAVIERS

Lora

Kalon was right. After they'd redressed, he'd had Lora marching out of the small town and back up into the hills before the rest of the town was even awake. The hike itself was hellish. They had to cover a lot of ground if they wanted to make it where Kalon said they were to camp that night. Which he assured her was worth the grueling, out of the way, hike.

She had decided that no matter how great of a campsite it was, she was very much over all the hiking. Next time she would demand they take a dragon, but she would settle for a horse.

After several hours of companionable silence, Lora asked Kalon about him and Garrison. She assumed they were an item when she first met them, especially with the forehead thing they'd done by the refugee camp. Kalon's ensuing laughter had her ears burning. He had explained, through his laughs, that while they had tried that out once when they were young and drunk, they had decided being "brothers" was better for them.

"Although," he added, "being more than friends has really seemed to work out for Kierra and Nuva." When he looked up and saw Lora's cheeks flushed with heat and confusion, he had roared again, earning him a strong nudge from her. She hadn't considered that Kierra may like females. It wasn't surprising—not after she'd called to the soldier at the outpost—but still, how had Lora not known? She let her mind wander through all the time she spent with her friend, a mixture of jealousy and anguish churning through her as they continued to walk. Kalon must have sensed it because he simply walked beside her silently, giving her the space she needed.

They arrived by the end of the day, just as Kalon had said, to a small cottage in an open grove, about twenty paces from the small trail they'd been following. The cottage was stone, older than she thought possible in this area, and completely covered in thick, thorny ivy.

There was a chimney on the left next to a small, broken window, but it was crumbling. Even the front door, which was curved at the top and had carved dragons and symbols on the frame, seemed like it had been kicked in ages ago. Whoever used to live there hadn't returned in a near century based on the state of disrepair, making it a pretty good hideout.

"Come on," Kalon said excitedly, not seeming the least bit worried as he made his way toward the dilapidated home.

When she didn't move from her spot by the tree, Kalon glanced back at her, a small smile playing on his lips. "Do you trust me?" he asked, parroting her question from before.

She narrowed her eyes, throwing him a crude gesture before muttering, "Enough I guess," as she picked her way through the tangled ivy and branches.

"Enough will do!" Kalon called over his shoulder, a chuckle in his voice. He paid no heed to the piles of rubble or brambles in his path as he marched through the front door, the darkness of the house swallowing him instantly.

She was still five paces from the door when she heard a commotion in the house, causing her to surge forward, her heartbeat turning to a steady gallop as she rushed the last steps.

Then, suddenly, the house changed. Literally. It shifted, right in front of her. The window no longer broken, the front door back on its hinges, and the stone chimney fully intact and producing a string of white smoke that smelled of bread. The ivy was still there, but now it had sweet smelling flowers blooming through it. Even the path beneath her feet had been cleared of branches and weeds to reveal a series of intricately decorated steppingstones.

Lora twirled where she had stopped, watching with eyes wide as the space around her adjusted into a far more welcoming view. The weather even shifted from a cloudy, gloomy day, to a warm autumn afternoon. When she finally faced the front door again Kalon was there, a smile—a genuine smile—playing on his lips. His hands were in his pockets as he simply watched her take it all in.

"What the hell?" She was still watching as the house literally put itself back together brick by brick.

"Come on," he chortled, motioning for her to follow him inside. The front room of the cottage was cozy. It had a small sofa with two worn but comfortable looking armchairs on either side. The rug was of various colors and shapes, and on the walls hung paintings and portraits of various animals and landscapes.

Kalon hadn't stopped in the living room, but instead had rounded a corner to what she assumed, based on the smells, was the kitchen. She walked gingerly through the house as objects still righted themselves on shelves and into drawers.

When she finally made it to the corner, Kalon stood in the entryway, his smile still in full bloom. Behind him, in the small kitchen, stood a short woman, no taller than Kalon's stomach, with wiry brown hair and skin the same color. She was dressed for work in the kitchen, with a mid-length skirt covered in flour and a blouse, with its sleeves rolled up, to match. Beside her stood a man, not an inch taller than she was, wearing similar clothing—except in lieu of a skirt, he wore trousers. He, too, was covered in flour, like perhaps the two of them had rolled in it moments before Kalon had barged in.

"These are the Beaviers," Kalon said, introducing Lora to the stout couple in front of her. "Willow and Birch."

It didn't go unnoticed that their name and their looks both resembled that of actual beavers. Even their eyes were a deep, beady black, not unlike the animals she'd seen damming rivers in the south of her kingdom—*no, not your kingdom anymore,* she chided herself.

"It's nice to meet you," she said, trying not to notice the way the woman stared at her. "I hope we weren't interrupting anything," she continued, trying to fill the silence.

"Oh, nonsense dear," the man said, dusting off his hands and walking toward Lora. "We were making Kalon here's favorite bread, for dinner. We'd just hoped to be done before you arrived."

Lora's eyes widened. "You knew we were coming?" She whipped her attention to Kalon, but he was too busy stuffing several dinner rolls in his mouth to notice.

"Yes child," the man continued. "Ortega saw it yesterday."

Kalon straightened and Lora must've looked as confused as she felt, because Birch Beavier simply laughed before explaining, "You'll understand when you meet her."

A moment later, as if summoned by the mention of her, a tall, incredibly beautiful blond female came busting into the room, flying past Lora, squealing like a newborn pig.

The female launched herself at Kalon, who only had a heartbeat to prepare. "I just knew you'd come!" she said into his neck as she continued hugging him. Her loosely curled hair bobbed as she spoke.

"She's been saying so for days now," Willow said, nodding to Kalon. It was the first thing she had said since Lora got there.

"I'm sorry I didn't send a missive ahead," Kalon apologized, finally freeing himself from the female's grasp. "I didn't want to risk it."

"No trouble, love," Willow said, patting Kalon's cheek endearingly. "Like we said, she showed up a couple days ago and said you'd be arriving shortly."

"Wouldn't shut up about it, really," Birch said over his shoulder while he pulled plates down from a short cupboard.

"Oh, you stop!" the female said, whacking him playfully on the shoulder.

Lora was so confused, and she felt a pit in her stomach at the familiarity between them. "Sorry, but how did you know we were coming?"

The female helped as Birch brought down cups and silverware from an apparently endless cupboard. "I saw us all here eating and—"

"What do you mean, saw?" Lora interrupted.

"Ortega is a seer, princess." Kalon said, taking plates of food from Willow.

"A seer?" Lora's thoughts swam, thinking back to books she had read. "I thought seers were always tucked away in temples and palaces." *Or extinct*, she thought, but chose not to say that part.

"We do, or at least my sisters do. I got out."

She said it so matter-of-factly, Lora almost didn't turn to look at her as she asked, "Why?" But she did—and where the female's eyes should have been were two gaping holes, with scarring on either side of her pale, bright face. It took years of training for Lora to not startle at the sight. How she hadn't seen it sooner, she had no idea.

The female, Ortega, gave a tight-lipped smile, "Too boring, of course. I much prefer being on the road." She seamlessly carried her plates and cups into the dining room next door, her hair and long pale pink dress flowing behind her.

Lora couldn't help the expression on her face. How could this female survive on the road? She was small and lithe and seemed to have very little muscle on her. Not to mention her eyes...

"Oh Kalon," Ortega chirped from the next room, "I've found the best traveling circus. I took a couple of days off after seeing you lot coming here. Left a note that I had business elsewhere and hauled ass here."

"You traveled here alone?" Kalon's stunned face whipped to Ortega as they walked out of the kitchen.

Lora followed behind the pair into the small dining room. The table was half the height of a normal one, and she had to sit on the floor to sit comfortably. "You work for a circus?" Lora asked, equally confused.

Kalon and Lora exchanged looks, a silent conversation passing between the two of them.

Overprotective ass.

Oh, now you're curious?

When her attention returned to the table, Lora realized everyone had turned to stare at her. Ortega was beaming, near bursting, as she looked between Kalon and Lora.

Kalon coughed, and Ortega snapped out of it, launching into tale after tale about the circus and life as a fortune teller, but Lora barely listened. She couldn't stop thinking about the unpleasant emotions that had boiled to the surface when she saw the girl hug Kalon. Try as she might, she could not focus on anything but the way the girl spoke to and about Kalon, their familiarity. She felt her smile sour as she listened to yet another story from the girl, a story that sent Kalon into a roaring fit of laughter.

Lora stabbed at the potato in front of her, only to meet the beady gaze of Willow Beavier when she looked back up. The woman cleared her throat and asked over the chatter at the table, "Lora dear, would you mind helping me with the dishes?"

Ortega immediately jumped up, offering to help, but Willow merely patted her on the cheek and insisted she and Kalon spend more time catching up.

Lora collected as many plates as she could hold, though not as many Ortega had carried in, she noted with annoyance, and made her way through the archway to the sink by the window.

Willow motioned for her to put the plates in the sink, handing her a towel to dry them after she washed them. Lora did the work diligently, her mind drifting to when she and Kierra would work in the kitchens in Attica together.

"You know," Willow's voice broke the silence, pulling Lora back to the present, "Kalon and Ortega have a long history."

She nearly rolled her eyes. "They do seem close," she admitted, forcing herself not to glance into the dining room where she could hear Kalon roaring with laughter again. It seemed he had a string of romantic partners.

"She was born a seer," Willow continued, her hands never faltering on the dishes. "She and Kalon were friends when they were little, but the minute she showed the gift, they swept her away. He and Garrison had been stationed near the temple when they reunited. They were always getting in trouble, those two." Willow sighed as if remembering a simpler time. "When he went to the academy to become an officer, is when they broke up."

Jade. The name made Lora's stomach turn to lead. "So he broke up with Ortega for Jade?" she asked, her gaze locked on the plate in her hand.

She felt Willow's beady eyes turn to her, but still Lora continued to focus on drying the plate. "Ortega's story is hers to tell, but I will say this—when Kalon heard of what happened to her eyes he had gone for her, but she had moved on, joined a coven of women. She left him a note telling him to challenge a girl with green eyes once he got back to the academy. That's when he met Jade."

"Jade is gone." Lora wasn't sure why she said it, but it slipped out.

"I know." Willow's eyelids fluttered. "Nice girl, strong—but sometimes too strong. Not a good match for Kalon, though no one ever said so."

Lora's shoulders tensed. "Why are you telling me this?" she asked, feeling heat creep into her cheeks.

Those beady eyes turned back to her. For a moment the woman looked so much like a beaver she wanted to laugh, which would have been incredibly inappropriate.

"Because everyone has a story, and those stories, they make us who we are, but they are in the past, and the past is just that—the past. Ortega has overcome tremendous odds, Kalon too, but here they are, laughing. Living."

Maybe this woman is actually the seer. Damn.

"Kalon wants to do right, to protect and save, but he doesn't trust easily."

Something in Lora shifted at the woman's wise words. Willow cocked her head and smiled slightly. "You better get in there before they eat all the tarts." She took the towel from Lora's hands and shooed her out of the kitchen. "And Lora," Willow called after her. "Don't forget to live, dear."

Lora stared after her for a moment before her arm was grabbed and she was yanked onto one of the cushions that acted as a dining room chair. Ortega beamed as she tossed another tart into her mouth before saying around the food, "Kalon was about to make you go to bed with him but I told him I insist on getting to know you!" She laughed as Kalon's eyebrows rose, a slight blush flushing his cheeks.

"And where, exactly, am I meant to sleep?" Kalon asked, laughing anxiously.

"On the floor for all I care!" Ortega joked, stuffing another tart into her mouth before handing one to Lora and hauling them both up off the floor. She was much stronger than Lora had originally given her credit for.

"You can sleep on the couch," Birch said to Kalon, as Ortega pulled Lora to a tiny stairwell at the back of the house.

"See you in the morning!" Ortega called to Birch and Kalon, stopping to kiss Willow on the cheek. "Dinner was spectacular as always, Willow."

"Of course dear, get some good sleep you two!" She called after the girls, but Lora didn't have time to respond as Ortega pulled her up the stairs and into a small bedroom.

"I'm sorry, I just had to get you alone," Ortega said breathlessly, flopping on the bed. "It's so rare to have a vision of someone I've never met." She pulled her top layer off to reveal long, pale arms and a light blue undershirt.

"How did you see me then?" Lora asked, taking her boots off and setting them by the bed with care.

"I didn't," she explained, now fully wrapping herself in the blankets and beginning to braid her hair. "I saw Kalon, but it wasn't *fully* him. He was blurry, and I could feel someone with him. Sometimes people can be blurry if they are in danger or have canthite on them—but he was happy and smiling when I saw him, so I figured he must be bringing someone very special with him. I really only see that with... Well, I really don't see it often unless there's a bond." She finished her braid and patted the bed next to her. Lora had no choice but to crawl in next to the girl.

Heat flooded her face. "We are Trothed to each other, could that do it?"

Ortega seemed to ponder the idea for a few moments. "That could certainly be the bond I was sensing. It must be a strong Troth if it's blurring your forms. That's probably why I couldn't scent Kalon until he was in the house..."

"What do you mean?" she had no idea how the girl saw so much without fucking eyes.

But before she could answer, Ortega's attention snapped to the doorway right as Kalon popped his head in.

"Good night, ladies," he said, his crooked smile making an appearance. He nodded to Ortega who blew him a kiss, and then his attention drifted to Lora.

Their eyes met, and she felt a little jolt through the Troth. He smiled again before turning back the way he came. She stared at where he had been standing several moments after he had left. When she finally freed her gaze, Ortega was staring at her—she guessed, anyway, she was since she had no eyeballs.

A small, knowing smile bloomed across Ortega's face, but she kept quiet as she burrowed under the sheets. A tense silence fell between the two females before Ortega rolled on her side, facing her, and whispered, "I know you didn't kill Jade."

Lora froze. *Oh shit*. She didn't know what to say.

"I saw it," Ortega admitted, sighing deeply. "I saw it when I first saw him meet her."

Lora tensed again. *Oh, shit*. "But you still sent him to her?" she asked cautiously. She wasn't sure just how much of Ortega's past she was meant to know. And also—that was kind of messed up.

"He looked so happy when they met and then, when I saw her…" she trailed off for so long, Lora didn't think she'd continue. But then she said, barely audible, "I saw him happy afterward."

There was another pause and Lora felt Ortega shift again, getting comfortable. "Thank you," she whispered.

"For what?" Lora asked, still puzzled.

"For being the reason he's still smiling," she said as if it were true. It was not.

"I'm not—" Lora stuttered as she tried to explain. "We have a deal, I'm just helping him get back something he lost."

Lora felt the girl smile. "I know. But he doesn't trust easily."

She almost rolled her eyes. "So I've been told."

"He trusts you," Ortega said, her voice full of an emotion Lora couldn't place.

She almost laughed, "No, he doesn't." If she knew one thing for certain, she knew Kalon did *not* trust her.

Ortega merely shrugged and rolled over. Her next words were barely audible though she heard them loud and clear. "He trusts you, Lora, I've seen it."

He shouldn't, she thought to herself, as she pulled the sheets up close to her chin.

Although, she secretly hoped Ortega was right.

***

Lora woke up to a hand over her mouth to stifle her scream. Her eyes took one heartbeat to adjust and found it was Ortega, her other hand over her lips. Outside was still very dark, so Lora assumed she'd only slept an hour or so.

Ortega slipped her hand from Lora's mouth, her attention focused on the door. "Kalon is coming," she breathed, her voice no louder than the wind outside. "Get dressed."

Lora was pretty sure she was dreaming, because Ortega's eye holes were glowing a slight blue in the dark. But that didn't stop her from following her order—something about her voice was off. She sat up, quietly swinging her legs over the bed, and slid on her breeches and tunic that were in a pile on the floor.

Ortega hadn't moved in the two minutes it had taken Lora to get fully dressed. There was a creak outside the door just as Lora laced her second shoe.

Lora jumped up then, her shadows covering her and the girl, making the room impossible to see in. "It's Kalon," the seer whispered, and her shadows sucked back into her as a citrus and ember scent came through the doorway.

Kalon looked straight to Lora as he spoke, his voice barely audible, "We have to go."

She didn't wait for an explanation as she grabbed her pack, reaching for Ortega. But the female had slipped between Lora and the bed. She looked directly at Lora as she said quietly, "I'll see you soon!" Then, nodding at Kalon, she rushed from the room and down the hall, to where Lora assumed the Beaviers slept.

"We need to go," Kalon repeated, pulling Lora out of the room. "Someone is coming for us."

She shook off his grasp, keeping pace as they walked down the small landing. "What about—"

"Ortega will handle it."

They hurried down the stairs and out through the front door, turning down a small path she hadn't seen yesterday. She was half running, half being dragged by Kalon.

She pulled herself free from his grasp again. "We can't just leave them there. What if whoever it is finds them? They could get hurt." Her heart was beating wildly, her shadows swirling to protect her from the unknown enemy.

"They won't," Kalon said, making to pull at her arm again.

"And how do you know?" she asked, stepping out of reach. It didn't feel right to run away.

"Lora, please," Kalon's eyes were dull, muted by the moonlight and lack of sleep. "I wouldn't be leaving if I didn't think they were safe. But we have to go. We put them in more danger being there."

She looked back toward the house, as if she could see it through the dense woods. "Fine. But if we see smoke or anything—"

"We come right back," Kalon agreed.

And they were off.

CHAPTER 34

ON THE TRACE

Lora

Lora and Kalon ran as fast as their feet could carry them, dodging branches and bounding over rocks.

"We need to put as much space between them and us," Kalon said between breaths, as they paused their sprinting to catch their breath.

"Who even is it?" she asked, trying and failing to get enough air into her burning lungs.

"Ortega didn't say…" Kalon trailed off as he looked around the dense woods.

"We need a plan," she breathed, leaning against a tree briefly for support. Her lungs felt like there were shards of glass in them.

Kalon looked around one more time before he began pulling off portions of his clothes, stashing his other items in a hole in the tree next to him.

"What are you doing?" she asked.

"Take off your shirt," was his only response as he began rubbing soot from a fallen limb on his cheeks.

She reared back. "What? Why would I—"

"Do you trust me?" His eyes were sparkling in the moonlight as he looked at her.

She took in a steadying breath. "Enough," she said, pulling off her shirt and passing it to him. He quickly handed her back one of his, rolling the sleeves for her once it was on.

"There is a town right around here that burned years ago," he said quietly, pushing soot onto her face. "I get the feeling that whoever is after us doesn't know that."

Her eyebrows rose expectantly. "So, what? We pretend our house just burned down?"

"Exactly," he said, as if that made any sense at all. When Lora didn't respond, he rolled his eyes. "Whoever it is is going to expect us to be running or laying low, not walking down the path in plain sight."

She understood now—they would hide under the disguise of two refugees whose home had just burned down. She nodded, handing Kalon her small pack.

"Ready?" he asked, giving her a once-over to be sure she looked the part.

"Truth with lies," she reminded him, and they walked calmly down the moonlit path.

***

Within fifteen minutes they were stopped by two males on horses. Both men wore several layers of thick, black clothes, as well as several observable weapons. The taller one smiled at her like she was his next snack. She surveyed them as Kalon stepped slightly in front of her.

"Good evening," the taller one sporting a mustache said, his accent not of the area—Kalon was right so far.

"Hello," Kalon responded, nodding to each man. "May I help you?"

"We are looking for two runaways from a local prison," grunted the smaller one. "You wouldn't happen to have seen anyone running through these woods, have you?"

"No, I'm sorry." Lora shook her head. "We haven't really seen anyone at all."

The smaller one narrowed his eyes as the taller one cocked his head. "Seems you're the only ones out at this time of night," he observed, looking now around the dense woods. "Why might that be?" His eyes lingered on Lora, who stared daggers at him.

"Our village was burned, and we are making our way to a refugee camp," she said, her voice still hoarse from all the running. *Maybe it sounds believable*, she thought, trying to calm her heart rate. "We were separated from our caravan."

"Right," drawled the tall one. "And who exactly are you?" His eyes lingered on Lora in a way that made her skin crawl.

"My name is Adolphus," Kalon said, stepping between them to draw the man's attention. "And this is my wife, Maria."

"Wife?" one asked, looking at them both, as if he thought Kalon was lying.

"Yes, of course," she snapped, trying to bring forth images of what a wife should act like—not that she'd seen many married couples. Her mom had been burned at the stake by her adopted father, so...

"You're married?" the shorter man asked. "To her?" he clarified, pointing to Lora and surveying her again.

"Yes." Kalon said again, this time more resolute, grabbing for her hand. "Now if you don't mind—"

"We actually do mind." Kalon had tried to move them forward, only to have the smaller male step in their path again.

"We'll need to see some proof," purred the tall one. "Your paperwork will do, if you'd be so kind."

"Our paperwork was lost in the fire that took our home," she retorted, filling her voice with manufactured sadness.

"No bother," chimed the short one. "It should be easy enough to prove that you're married."

"Of course it will," Kalon said, a bit uneasily, not taking his eyes off the men.

"Simply tell us your love story," the taller male said, a smirk spreading across his face.

"Our what now?" Lora asked, her eyes darting between the men and Kalon.

"You know, your love story. How you met, fell in love, each other's likes and dislikes. Sampson here is a sucker for a sappy love story, so I hope yours is good."

Lora knew that what they said in that moment would determine what happened next.

She inhaled, preparing to lie her ass off, but Kalon spoke first.

***

Kalon

"It's the very best, if you ask me," he began, smiling tightly. He had thought about what Lora had said earlier—that every good lie has truth sprinkled in, and this needed to be a hell of a lie. "Well, we didn't get along at first." *Truth.*

He heard a soft exhale and knew Lora was trying not to chuckle. "A bit of an understatement actually," he continued. "There were several times she even tried to kill me. And vice versa, of course." *Also a truth.*

Another exhale from behind him, this time a bit exasperated. "I mean, I deserved at least two of the times for sure. But over time I began to see her strength and grace and kindness."

"Kindness?" one of the guards asked, eyebrows raising as he looked over Lora, whose shoulders were now squared, her stance more for fighting than being a disheveled refugee. He tried not to roll his eyes.

"Don't get me wrong," Kalon said, smiling tightly at Lora. "She's mean as an adder at times, but when she cares about someone, she's willing to risk everything to protect them. That's something I admire in her. It's one of my favorite parts about her actually, her stubbornness and resolve in standing for what she believes in."

He felt, more than saw, Lora stiffen.

"We were a little love/hate for a while, but she tolerated me enough to travel with me and my friends, which gave us time to get to know one another better. I got to see her kind side, and she got to see mine. So one day, we were traveling and got into a pinch and she did what she did best, which was simultaneously kick and save my ass. I saw it then, the gleam in her bright eyes, and I knew that what I felt was more than friendship. It was like something in my chest opened up, and a string connected my soul to hers. I felt the tug and pull to her as if it were a very real string, and I didn't want to, but I realized it then and there what she was to me. Is to me."

"And what's that?" Sampson asked, eyes narrowing on Kalon in distrust.

"The love of my life," he said frankly, hoping it sounded believable. He wasn't sure Lora was breathing. "Which is why this fire has been so hard on us," he added for good measure. "We were both so ready to settle down, to finally start a life off the road." He made a show of looking at Lora and tucking one of her stray strands of hair behind her ear. Her glowing maple eyes never left his.

Sampson smiled then, but it wasn't one of kindness or affection—it was cruel and wicked and promised pain. "That was a lovely story. Touching, even. Unfortunately, lying is never the right thing to do in these scenarios."

His heart ratcheted up a pace. "I wasn't lying," he ground out, squaring his shoulders in defiance and moving slightly in front of Lora, who had somehow managed to maneuver in front of *him*.

The other male smiled now too, his eyes lingering on Lora. "The love may be real," he said, his voice dropping to a creepy octave, "but that village burned down years ago."

Two things happened simultaneously: The larger one lurched for Lora, and she pulled a knife Kalon didn't know she had from her boot. Within seconds, the four of them were punching and kicking, Lora and Kalon fighting for their lives as the two men fought to take them.

They were strong, both carrying several weapons that he, and surely Lora, had noticed almost immediately. And they were skilled, blocking punches and kicks from them with ease. Lora took a strong punch to the face, her head snapping the opposite way. She was slower in her responses, and to his horror, he noted his shirt was so big it was keeping her from making exact punches, restricting and hindering her movements. He saw shadows dance in the tree line, but they did not make an appearance. *Interesting.* They made eye contact and he swore he heard her voice in his mind, as her eyes twinkled with mischief *"Do you trust me?"*

Kalon only nodded slightly, sending thoughts that had no way of reaching her to her anyway. *"Enough, I suppose."*

As if she had heard, she gave a quick nod. *Enough will do.*

Lora jumped back from a sword swipe from the mustached soldier, as he dove under the swing of the shorter male. They weren't trying to kill him, Kalon realized, as the guy swung another punch in his direction. He took that advantage and landed a barrage of blows onto his opponent who began to sway—*good*. He spun, building up energy for the final blow when a scream cut through the air. *Lora.*

The mustached soldier had slashed her arm and her side, right where her old scar was. Dark blood was already beginning to soak through his shirt, like shadows under her arm.

"Come now, girl," the taller one spat. "Let's get this over with."

They may not have wanted to kill Kalon, but clearly they had no such qualms about killing Lora. "Stop!" he shouted, turning toward where Lora swayed by the tree line. But he was too slow. The soldier swung again, and Lora crumpled to the floor, her blood pooling on the forest floor.

Kalon didn't get a chance to react as the smaller male used the back of his sword to knock him unconscious.

***

Kalon woke up to the sounds of angry shouting, finding himself bound in rope on the forest floor. There was a small fire in the center of the clearing, which he recognized immediately. The men hadn't bothered to take him out of the clearing where they'd fought, meaning, if he looked to his left, he'd see…

Lora. He almost couldn't bring himself to look, but that was the direction of the shouting. And if she was somehow still alive…

He took a deep breath, turning his gaze to where he'd seen her fall, crumpling like a rag doll—but there was nothing. No body, no blood, nothing.

The men were standing right where she should have been. He looked around the clearing again to be sure it wasn't a different one, but no, it was the very same. And still, there was no sign of her. No blood trail like she'd lived or been dragged away.

The shorter male noticed he had woken up, an angry smirk spreading on his face.

"What have you done with her?" Kalon asked, his voice scratchy from yelling.

"Seems your *love* fooled you, prince." He spat in the dirt where Lora had fallen, his face twisting in mild disgust.

Bodies don't just get up and walk away, he thought, reprocessing the incident. He had seen her dark blood spread out over the ground. So dark it had looked like...shadows. She had used her shadows to fake her own death.

He felt the color leach from his face. The shadows in the forest seemed to mock him, dancing as the realization hit him. He searched the shadows again, trying to find her like he had on the pirate ship. Surely, she hadn't left him. But why wouldn't she? She owed him nothing, not really. She had said so herself—he had kidnapped her and tried to kill her. Why shouldn't she have fled at the first true opportunity?

"Seems she fooled us both," he corrected, though a little voice thrashed against the idea.

The males were discussing their next move, the taller one now looking through Kalon's pack. He cocked his head. *How did they get my bag?* Again, the smaller one noted his attention as he looked from the bag, which he had hidden in the woods, back to the males.

"Looks like your girlfriend wanted to give us a gift before running off into the woods." He held up the bag triumphantly. "Murphy, here, followed her scent all the way back to this bag before it vanished on the wind. Thanks to her, we now have your weapons." Both males began laughing then, returning their focus to the bag and the map Sampson had brought out.

If it was his map to Kretor, Lora really had screwed him. His thoughts began swimming as he tried and failed to think of a way out of this. But how did they have his bag? When escaping, Lora would have taken everything in the bag, any extra supplies, but here his bag was—fully intact. Something didn't feel right, especially with how dark the clearing had gotten. Though the moon was high above them, the forest remained impenetrably dark.

A small smile played on his lips as an idea occurred to him. "You don't know who she is, do you?" he asked, catching the male's attention. The forest around him seemed to still at his words.

"Why should we care who that bitch is?" Murphy asked gruffly, his eye already swollen from the punch Lora had landed.

"I just figure if you're in this for the money then you'd want more of it, that's all," he drawled, pretending to sound mildly interested, if not a bit bored.

"What do you know?" Sampson asked, marching over to Kalon and hauling him from the ground.

"It's hard to say when I'm bound so tightly," he drawled, looking down at his body.

Sampson's eyes sharpened and he just shrugged, sitting back down on the ground. One nod from Sampson had Murphy bringing forward a knife. "Just the upper body," Sampson said, watching a few steps back.

Right as the last rope slid off of his shoulders his vision blurred, like a shadow had danced over his eyes. When they cleared, Sampson was on his knees, shadows swarming his body.

And behind him, with a wicked grin on her face, stood Lora.

***

It took Murphy two heartbeats to realize his partner was no longer beside him, and in those two heartbeats, Lora took Sampson's head in her hands and snapped his neck.

Murphy's attention quickly shifted from Kalon to Lora as the brute ran at her, knife in hand. Kalon took the distraction as a chance to untie the rest of his bondage before grabbing one of the daggers the males had dumped from his pack. His pack that Lora had led them to, knowing they would bring it back with them, providing him with a weapon at this exact moment. Gods she was brilliant.

He launched into action, striking Murphy from the back as Lora swiped at him from the front. Her shadows, which were now fully in play, stabbed and shot at the brute. She was slow though, not at all full-strength like he'd seen her before. He caught Murphy's jaw with a strong left hook while also slicing his upper arm.

The man cried out and sank to his knees. Lora was over him in an instant, her breathing heavy as she made to kill him.

"Wait," Kalon gasped, choking for air. "Wait." He took a steadying breath. "Who sent you?"

Murphy's eyes narrowed, but he remained silent. Lora swayed slightly, but her shadows held the man firmly to the ground.

"Who sent you?" Kalon asked again, his voice full of raw command.

Murphy's face twisted into hatred. "Fuck you, Shade bitch." Then he spat on Lora, hitting her in the neck and chest.

Lora's whole body froze, ire radiating from her, but she did not strike him. While Kalon nearly killed the male right then and there, it was Lora's restraint at the insult that had him pausing.

Her gaze shifted to Kalon, and he looked at the man one last time as he pulled out his dagger. "I will only ask one more time," he said, pushing his dagger to Murphy's throat. "Who sent you?"

The man moved to spit at Lora again, and this time she did not wait for permission as her shadows swallowed him whole, his broken body slumping to the forest floor seconds later.

Lora only blinked once at the crumpled form before wiping her neck, her shoulders sagging as she swayed with the movement. The forest was instantly lighter, the moon providing light enough for him to see several meters in front of him beyond the glow of the fire.

While he went for his bag, Lora wiped her dagger on Murphy's pants before sheathing it on her thigh.

"I thought you were dead," he noted, packing his bag.

"And I thought you were going to sell me out," she said back, unceremoniously rolling Sampson over to retrieve his sword. She twirled it twice before sheathing it.

"I kind of figured out your plan," he admitted, now making his way over to her, eyebrows raised as he noted the new weapons she was sporting. "I thought I said—"

"There's no way you're taking my weapons now, prince," she interrupted, pulling out a sack of gold from Sampson's pocket as well. When she noticed Kalon's eyebrows still raised, she smirked. "Just practicing my thievery, that's all."

He chuckled as she rose and began walking toward the forest. "You okay?" he asked, the moonlight highlighting the exhaustion in her eyes.

"Let's just be glad that Murphy, here, only followed your scent to the tree," she said by way of responding.

He looked puzzled so she added, "Because apparently, my shadows can only carry a shirt so far away."

He gaped at her. The realization of her fast thinking and creativity was almost overwhelming. But before he could even think of complimenting her, she pushed the gold sack into his hands and walked past him onto the path.

"We should keep moving," she said over her shoulder, and so keep moving they did.

***

"The sun is still an hour or so from rising, so we have some time before the others get here," Kalon explained as they sat on a fallen log that overlooked the valley below. They had walked the path in silence for about an hour and a half, and if his map was right, the others would end up in this same area soon.

"Want me to look at that?" he asked, motioning to her arm. While she had faked the deathblow and most of the swipe before, the sword had still nicked her skin, the blood now crusting over.

"If you insist," she said, holding her arm out for him.

"I do," he said, pulling out his medic kit—or what was left of it—from his pack.

"Thanks for saving my life," he said, cleaning off the wound.

"I'm pretty sure I'm quoting you here— 'You're no use to me dead.'" A smile played on her split lip, causing some blood to leak out.

Silence fell as Kalon cleaned and wrapped her already healing wound. It didn't need much, but if he was being honest, he just needed to touch her—to know she wasn't dead.

"So what else, exactly, can your shadows do?" he asked, breaking the silence again.

"You mean besides helping me fake my own death?" she asked, smiling in earnest now.

"Yes, besides that, smart ass." He jabbed at her with his elbow, and she swayed with the motion.

Lora took a breath that seemed to go nowhere. When she finally spoke, her words were distant. "That's for me to know and you to hopefully never find out."

"And why's that?" he asked, trying to bring some of the amusement back.

Lora turned away from him then, her eyes glossing over and dimming. "Because that would mean I'm trying to kill you."

A shiver worked its way up his spine as the truth of those words settled in. She *had* tried to kill him—or at least proved that she could several times, all of which but one wasn't even with her shadows.

There was another long pause and he flexed his hands, the bruises on the knuckles already going down. Lora looked out over the valley, her eyes fluttering closed every so often.

"A truth for a truth?" he offered quietly.

"A what?" Lora asked, her eyes flaring open as she surveyed the valley again.

"A truth for a truth," he repeated, looking at her. "It's something Kierra and I used to do as kids. We would each ask a question and the other would have to answer truthfully."

Lora slid her eyes to his. "Why not just enter a Troth with her and beat her up for answers?" she asked straight faced, though her tone had a hint of teasing.

"This is a bit lower of stakes than that," he admitted. "It was really helpful after"—he paused, looking at Lora nervously—"after she came back. It was a way we could talk to each other."

Lora's shoulders relaxed a fraction. "What kind of questions?" she asked.

He beamed at her piqued interest. "Anything. So long as the other person answers truthfully."

Lora seemed to consider the idea for a moment. "Ok," she agreed. "But only if you go first."

He smiled in earnest then. "Okay, fine—do your worst."

Lora turned then to face him, humming as she thought. "Okay...what is...your favorite color?"

His jaw dropped. "No, no! You ask too much!" he exclaimed, clutching his chest dramatically.

Lora let out a small chuckle, and he felt himself track the movement. "So, not that deep of a question," she noted, smiling while she looked back over the valley.

"Light purple," he admitted, following her gaze to the valley, the sun about fifteen minutes from cresting the mountains on the other side.

He felt her gaze on him like a brand. "Really?" she asked. No judgment, just genuine curiosity. "Like Kierra's lips when she's cold?" she asked in a teasing tone.

"No, no," he chuckled softly. "More like the first rays of sunrise as they break through the night sky clouds." Lora hummed as he explained it. "It's best seen from the air," he added, as two birds fluttered past them. "Now it's my turn," he explained, pausing at the look on Lora's face. "What? What's wrong?"

"You mean I don't get to answer my favorite color?" she looked at him with mock offense.

His smile spread. "My sincerest apologies my lady, please, to what color do you pledge favoritism to?" He sketched a bow and Lora chortled, air rushing from her nose in short bursts.

"Thank you good sir," she said smiling. Then after a deep breath she said, "Orange, like the sunset or a dancing flame."

"Hmm," he purred. "Seems we both have an affinity for the sun." He watched as the very first shred of light came over the mountains. His very bones yearned to be flying over those mountains, soaring on the winds he knew blew through them.

He cleared his throat, shaking his head slightly. "Right, well, my turn."

Lora's eyes sparked as she turned to face him again. "Do your worst," she whispered, crinkling her nose.

"What do you like to do for fun?" he asked, studying her closely for her response.

"That's all you got?" she asked, her eyebrows rising before answering, "I like to cook." It was his turn to raise his eyebrows, but Lora was barely paying attention to him. "In Attica I was on kitchen duty sometimes, and if the cook was sick, I would get to work on the food. There's just something about the way you can make something dull and boring like plain rice taste like food fit for a king."

"I happen to love plain rice," he chimed, earning him a teasing nudge from Lora. "I've heard," he added, glancing at her sidelong, "that the southern continent has a plethora of spices, and even a school that teaches people to use and mix them."

"Is that so?" Lora asked, a small smile playing on her lips, but she did not look over at him.

"Just food for thought," he said in a tuneful way.

They fell into a comfortable silence for several moments, the sun beginning to crawl from behind the mountainscape, painting the sky in pinks and purples.

"That was a boring one," Lora chided him, facing him again.

"No more boring than favorite color," he pointed out, turning to face her.

"Touché," she said, another small smile playing on her lips.

"Fine. You want a hard one?" he asked with a nod, his eyebrows raised. Lora's amused gaze was zeroed in on him. "What happened to your back?"

Her eyes narrowed, but she asked, far too casually, "What happened to yours?" He tried to keep the shock from his face—how she figured out about his back, he had no idea.

"I asked first," he said, offering her a small smile. Lora opened her mouth to interrupt, but he continued. "I know you say it doesn't matter anymore, but it still matters to me."

Lora's gaze hardened, her eyes glossing over. "Why?" she croaked, her voice sounding far away.

"Because scars are to be revered, their stories make us who we are." He parroted what Liam had told her around the campfire, what had been told to all Drakes long before the war started. "A truth for a truth," he reminded her gently, holding his breath for her response.

She took a shaky breath, her eyes now settling on her palms as her shoulders slumped. "It is not a good story," she said quietly.

He swallowed the lump farming in his throat. "Then give it to me, let me carry it with you."

He wasn't sure why it mattered to him, but it did.

***

Lora

"When I was young," she began, "I was sent away to the ice plains in Attica. There, I was a nobody, meant to train with the troops as a grunt."

"They train females?" Kalon asked, not judging but genuinely curious.

"No," she explained, "but I was eight and they didn't know what else to do with me. So they threw me in with the junior boys, hoping they would kill me, I guess."

"Clearly they underestimated you," he muttered, and her cheeks flushed.

"Yes, they did," she said with a wicked smile. "I was stronger and faster than most of them. And when they realized I had potential, they moved me up in the ranks, pissing off a lot of people." She paused, a shadow falling across her face as she remembered the things she'd done to the boys who had tried and failed to harm her.

She cleared her throat and continued, "Anyway, I was moved into a stealth division because of my shadows, and part of the training was called *withstanding*." Kalon audibly swallowed, and she took the moment to push her hair out of her eyes, his gaze tracking the strands of crimson hair. "They would take you and show you what would happen if you were ever captured—they wanted to ensure you could endure what the enemy would do to you."

She thought she felt Kalon shudder.

"They took Kierra and me both one day, to show me that anything could be a weapon. The leader said—said he was going to demonstrate on Kierra—" Her voice broke as images flashed in her mind of Kierra being dragged to the table. She wasn't sure Kalon was breathing next to her.

"She—she was the only friend I'd ever had and—and I couldn't let them hurt her. So when the man lifted his arm to strike her, his arm fell one way and his body the other." She let out a shuddering breath as the memories burned her eyes.

"You saved her," Kalon whispered. And she couldn't bring herself to look at him. Couldn't bring herself to admit that all she had ever done was to protect her friend.

"Anyway," she continued, shaking off the memories of the past like a loose blanket, "they didn't take to having their leader maimed, so they brought in this captured Drake commander who explained the type of torture the Drakes prefer for Shades— then proceed to show me. It took sixteen days before I blacked out. When I woke up, I had been out for a week. My skin took ages to heal and even now it is weaker in some spots. But Kierra was there after training every day to change my bandages and clean my wounds."

She could feel Kalon's attention on her. "Luckily I was only thirteen, so my body rebounded much faster," she added, trying to make light of the heaviness that sat in the air.

After a long silence Kalon took her hand in his. "You saved my sister."

"And I'd do it all again," she admitted without hesitation, still not meeting his gaze.

"Lora," Kalon said, reaching gently up to her face, but stopping when she stiffened. "Lora," he repeated, her name on his lips causing a shiver to run down her spine. "That was very brave." Then after another pause, "You were very brave."

She let out a soft exhale, no more than a whimper, the sting of tears filling her eyes. She looked up to see him staring at her, his eyes filled with an unknown emotion. "Your turn," she managed to croak through a broken smile.

But then she heard an uncommon bird call and Kalon was on his feet in an instant, his sword drawn. Moments later another bird called, and Nuva and Liam emerged from the tree line, Garrison and his cousins from the brush below them.

Garrison looked between the two of them, noting Lora's split lip and Kalon's head wound before whistling low. "Seems like you all have a story to tell."

Kalon's smile was genuine as he clapped his friend on the back with a swift hug, nodding to Erik and Toke. Liam smiled as he looked between them all, and Lora felt awkward in her own skin. Nuva began ranting to Garrison about Liam, and soon they were all gathering together to follow Erik and Toke down into the valley to where they would camp and prepare for the mission.

Kalon, though walking between Garrison and Nuva, glanced back to Lora, his eyes sparkling as if to say, "*I owe you one.*"

***

As Lora sat by the fire that night, the Drakes around her all speaking quietly about their own travels, she felt a sense of peace wash over her. She had never been so open with anyone, other than Kierra, in her whole life. It had felt strange to tell the whole truth of what had happened to her to someone else. It scared her that she had given the story so freely, with nothing in return.

But what scared her the most is that it had felt good. Not just to tell it, but to tell Kalon.

CHAPTER 35

THIEVERY WITH SHADOWS

Kalon

Kalon barely slept the night he and his friends had met back up. The thought of his sister and thirteen-year-old Lora being subjected to torture had him tossing and turning.

But Lora had been so brave. She had defended his sister, having only known her for weeks. Kierra had been taken to that camp when she was sixteen. So she had just arrived when Lora was tortured, meaning Lora had chosen to be whipped herself, rather than let a girl she had just met endure it. Not to mention it was a Drake who had beaten her.

No wonder she hated his guts when they first met. If he ever found out the man's name—his mind was still reeling at the mental math as he ate breakfast the next morning, noting that Lora seemed to have slept for most of the night without a nightmare, despite their conversation.

"All right," Liam said, finishing the last sip of his drink. "What's the plan, boss?"

The attention of everyone in the camp turned to him and Kalon straightened to his full height as he addressed them. "The southern entrance to Castle Trintel is about a half mile southeast of us. There is a caravan of eligible women currently making its way into the city proper. Our plan is to infiltrate the caravan to gain entrance to the castle."

"And then steal some stuff?" Lora asked from her spot between Garrison and Liam.

"Correct," he said with a tight smile. "Then steal our stuff."

Everyone around the fire nodded in agreement, and his shoulders relaxed a fraction. This was going to work, it had to.

"And how will we be getting into this caravan of women?" Lora asked again, stuffing her face with what looked to be the rest of Garrison's porridge.

He gave her a broad smile before answering, "You, of course."

***

Lora

The way Kalon smiled at her had sent a shiver up Lora's spine, memories from Skipton Village flashing in her mind, causing her toes to curl. Lora had locked gazes with him and tension built between them, the rest of the world fading away. One of Garrison's cousins coughed and Lora's attention snapped to the present, a blush creeping up her cheeks.

"The parade will pass by the guard gate here, where only certain people will be selected, before heading up to the castle," Garrison explained to the group, pointing on a map to the different locations everyone was to be stationed.

Lora refocused her attention to the task at hand, looking at the drawn-out plans in front of her. Garrison continued, "Once chosen, we will have easy access to the castle grounds and rooms."

She looked at Garrison, confused. "The castle? Why would we need access to the castle?"

"Because what we need is inside," Nuva answered matter-of-factly, cleaning her nails with a small dagger.

She gaped. "We are stealing from the king?" When no one answered, she turned to Kalon. "The King of Kretor is neutral in the war, and I'm pretty sure your kingdoms are allies so why not just go up and ask him for whatever it is?"

"Let's just say the King and I don't have a strong relationship at the moment," Kalon said, his eyes sliding to hers.

Lora rolled her eyes. "What? Lover's quarrel?" She had meant it as a joke, but the whole camp seemed to suck in a breath.

"You could say that," Kalon said shortly, jaw ticking.

"Oh my gods!" she exclaimed, barely registering the way the others were looking at Kalon. "So what? You and I will—"

"Correction, princess," Kalon interrupted her, coming to her side, his hand brushing hers slightly, leaving a wave of goosebumps in their wake.

It took all of Lora's willpower not to look up at him, to keep her breathing steady.

"*You* will be going in with Erik and Toke."

She felt like someone had dumped a bucket of cold water on her head. "What? Why?" Then, realizing she was in a group, smiled sheepishly to Garrison's cousins. "No offense."

Erik simply shrugged, Toke looking unphased.

"Because," Kalon said, drawing her attention back to him, "I will not be going in the city or the castle."

Her nostrils flared. "What the hell do you mean you aren't going? Aren't we stealing something of *yours*?!"

"I physically cannot enter the kingdom without the King knowing. The *lover's quarrel*, as you put it, makes it impossible for me to even set foot in the city proper—hence our meeting on this hill, and hence my need for your shadows." Kalon ended his speech in her face, so close they were sharing breath, but there was nothing sensual or thrilling about this up-close conversation. It just pissed her off.

"Fine," she said after several seconds. She moved a step away from him, pulling her attention back to the map. "So we get in through this parade, and then what? How do we know where to go or where it is?"

Kalon stared at her a second longer then he, too, was looking at the map, then pointed at a tower in the castle. "It'll be in this room on the top floor. They know what it is," he added, nodding to Erik and Toke.

"And what am I supposed to do?" Lora asked indignantly.

"Your little party tricks with shadows of course," Kalon purred, Lora's toes curling against her will. "In and out before sundown," he assured her, pulling his lingering gaze from her and looking over the group.

"Wouldn't it make more sense if we waited until dark?" Lora asked, her face twisted in confusion. "It makes the party tricks much easier to perform," she added, twirling a shadow through her fingers.

Kalon tracked the movement before seeming to recover from a daze. With a shake of his head he explained, "The castle is spelled to lock at first dark—no one in or out. So unfortunately, this is a daytime activity." He tugged on her braid as he said it and she batted his hand away as the plan settled in her mind.

Lora wrung her hands, feeling slightly underprepared for this endeavor. But before she could open her mouth to ask more questions, Kalon straightened again, making him look older as he continued explaining the plan. "Garrison and Nuva will be waiting to pick you up outside the back entrance to the castle where you"—he nodded to Lora— "will provide coverage to the small, wooded area here. It's close enough to the edge of the city that I can meet you there, and we can be gone before the king notices."

The group all nodded and within five minutes, Lora was dressed in a too-big gown Garrison and Nuva had gotten on their rotation in Skipton. Lora looked between the group as they walked straight for the caravan. Liam and Garrison helped Nuva strap on extra weapons while Garrison's cousins discarded their most obvious ones. While everyone else was busy, Kalon was looking at her.

Lora narrowed her eyes as he made his way over. "Still mad I'm not going, I see," he said, his nose crinkling.

"What if something goes wrong?" Lora asked, raising an eyebrow. His eyes roved over the dress and his face twisted into what Lora guessed was polite disgust.

Lora rolled her eyes—of course the asshole was more worried about what her dress looked like than if the plan failed. Kalon brought his eyes back to Lora's and smirked. "Nothing will go wrong, princess."

"And if it does?" she shot back, still not fully believing it could possibly be this easy. "What if your friends need you and you are not there?" she quipped, realizing she'd struck a chord as his body stiffened.

Kalon was in her face in a second, their breath mingling as he stared down at her. "If they need me," he breathed, no louder than a whisper, "I will always be there."

***

Kalon's plan had mostly made sense, though she was peeved at herself for not pressing him for more details. Garrison's cousins stopped abruptly in front of her and she fidgeted with the dress. It probably would have fit Kierra better, but Lora was trying to make it work. It wasn't exactly her style, and the color washed her out. Not to mention it made it almost impossible to have weapons, only allowing for the dagger at her thigh to remain concealed. Lora felt virtually naked, save for her shadows, which writhed just beneath the surface of her skin.

The caravan of eligible women was huge. As they approached a small gap she noted that the women were of all shapes, sizes, and colors. Apparently the King of Kretor didn't have a type. The guards traveling with the women, however, all looked the same. They were tall, broad shouldered, with longer hair and a sharp jawline. Just like Erik and Toke. Apparently the king *did* have a type when it came to his men. Lora wondered if they noted the similarities too, but kept the question to herself as they blended seamlessly into the caravan.

It took about fifteen minutes of walking before the parade made it to the city gates. No one checked papers as the women and their guards were let through. Lora tried and failed to see what was happening at the gates.

"What are they doing up there?" she asked, standing on her toes yet again to try and get a better view.

"The groups are being selected," Erik answered curtly, his hard gaze seeming to say, "So *stand still.*

"And how are they selecting them?" She stood still after another hardened gaze from Erik.

"The king likes to collect …treasures," Toke explained, nodding toward two broad-shouldered guards standing next to a small girl. The girl was unimpressive, but the males radiated power and strength.

"So he's basically sniffing out who he thinks the king would want?" she asked, not bothering to keep the disgust from her voice. This all felt a bit perverse.

Erik snorted. "It's more about power, but yes, I guess you could say that."

Their party was two groups away, and Lora took the time to compose herself. Of course Kalon had ended up in a relationship with this guy - he was stunning and powerful, and if rumors were true, so was the king. They probably made a beautiful pair. She could now add the King of Kretor to Kalon's ever growing list of lovers. Her stomach soured at the thought.

Before she knew it, they were in front of a group of guards, all stocky and clean shaven. The two at the front nodded to the brothers before waving them through.

"We've been given access to the castle," Erik mumbled to Lora as they were marched across the bridge.

"You must be very proud," Lora muttered back, looking to see if he laughed at her attempt at a joke. They both glanced down at her before smirking.

The city beneath Castle Trintel was packed full of citizens and traders alike. While the glistening castle loomed in the background, the city's lower quadrant was derelict at best. The parade wove through the slums before finally arriving at the bright, colorful city center.

The gates to the castle grounds were higher than any she had seen or even heard of. The parade circled the brightly decorated square before trumpets blared and the gates were opened. Women and their guards were then paraded in front of someone who emerged there, hand-choosing who made it inside the castle grounds.

"Another test?" she whispered to the brothers, looking to see just who made it inside.

"This is the king's man," Erik explained with equal quiet.

Lora hummed. "The bloodhound who will sniff out your power." Her nose crinkled at her own joke, but the brothers both cut their eyes to her.

"I think it's your power he'll sniff out," Erik said under his breath as they approached the front. Lora didn't have time to react as she came face-to-face with the king's man. He was small, shorter than even Lora, with dark, pin-straight hair that hung at a chopped style to his chin. He was an overall odd-looking man, his face too long and head too small, but his beady black eyes gave her the absolute creeps.

A shiver ran up her spine as the man looked upon the brothers and, sniffing the air, gave a saccharine smile before nodding them through the gates.

"You must be very proud," Erik parroted as they walked into the castle proper.

Lora rolled her eyes. But before she could answer, her breath was taken away. Castle Trintel itself was a very classical castle in that it was built with shining stone, square in shape, with four rounded towers in each corner, and a tall, gated entrance. The only thing that really stood out about the castle, other than everything painted in bright whites and golds, was the two tall towers in the center of the large building. One had an ornate drapery hanging from its banister, the other, if Kalon was right, held the item to be stolen.

It took them no time to be shown to the large banquet hall within the castle and inside everything was just as busy as the city below. Servants and courtesans alike bustled about the building, all stopping and bowing as the selected women and their guards made their way into the grand entrance hall.

Once everyone was in the large hall, also clothed in golds and whites, a hush fell over the crowd. She couldn't see over the hulking men in front of her, but someone began speaking. She assumed, based on the nasally voice, it was the king's man from the castle gate.

"In an hour or so you will each be shown to your rooms where your guards will stand watch while you change and retire. When his majesty is ready to meet with you, you will be summoned. Until then, please, enjoy a refreshment, courtesy of our gracious king."

The women amongst her all began to speak to each other in low whispers, some excited about meeting the king, others nervous. Lora focused on the soldiers around the room. According to Kalon's plan, Liam would have already slipped into the barracks early and placed laudanum in the canteens that were now at their sides. She hadn't asked how exactly he was planning on doing that, nor how to be sure it had worked. Now she wished she had. Also, how was she supposed to ensure that they even drank from their canteens?

One conversation snagged Lora's attention as a taller girl with luscious strawberry blond curls and large breasts explained to three younger girls that they should really just leave now.

"I have a plan to woo the king," she said, moving her shoulders about in a way that showed off her ample blossom. Lora almost laughed out loud. The only way for her to get the king's attention is if she had different parts moving around below her skirts.

One of the younger girls beamed up at the taller one, eyes wide with reverence. "Perhaps one day we will toast to you as our queen." She shrieked with glee, the other girls following suit.

Then the idea struck Lora—how would they ensure everyone drank? By making it rude not to.

She leaned over to Erik, who looked almost bored. "I need a drink," she said, her voice low.

"This is no time to turn to alcohol," he cooed, a small smile playing on his lips.

She gave a rather flat look that had Toke smirking. "I want to make a toast," she explained, "to the king."

The brothers looked at each other before Erik nodded in understanding, peeling off to get her a drink.

He returned within seconds and she lifted her glass into the air, clearing her throat.

As much as she didn't want to be the center of attention, this was the only way she could ensure the guards drank from their canteens. Lucky for her, the tall girl noticed Lora a moment before the rest of the party and within a heartbeat she was on a chair, shouting across the room, "A toast to our most honorable host! To the king!" And everyone in the room, including the soldiers, took a sip from their cups.

Lora smiled.

Moments later, the doors to the great hall opened. The girls and their guards were instructed to follow the soldiers to their respective rooms. Those aforementioned soldiers worked their very hardest to stand upright as they marched through the halls, a team of eager and nervous women in tow.

No one even noticed as Lora, Erik, and Toke slipped from the group and headed up a spiral staircase toward the towers. Not that they would have seen anything other than shadows moving along the floor.

They didn't pass a single soldier or guard, though she kept them shrouded in shadows anyway, and none of them spoke as they wound their way to the top. The doorway at the top of the stairs was small and plain, not at all what she was expecting. The two soldiers guarding the door were slumped over, clearly knocked out from the sleeping drug.

The brothers glanced between themselves briefly before Erik knocked three times then twice on the door. They waited a moment and then a smaller two knocks sounded from the other side. *They have someone on the inside? That would have been helpful to know*, she thought as they pushed open the door.

Lora followed suit, careful not to step on the slouching soldiers. The room on the other side of the door was not at all what she expected. Instead of piles of treasure, or maps, or really anything of value, there was only a bed, a chair, and a trunk. It was a bedroom. And by the looks of the toys and drawings, a child's bedroom.

Erik and Toke, now crouching, spoke in hushed tones to someone in the corner of the room. She heard a small voice reply faintly and then Erik was rising, his hand wrapped firmly around that of a nine-year-old boy's.

"This is Lora," he explained to the child. "She is going to help us leave, okay?"

The little boy cocked his head, regarding her, before nodding. That was apparently enough for Garrison's cousins, the two immediately setting into motion.

"We will need shadows as we edge through the castle interior, and then shields once in the exterior." Erik's voice was distant as she processed what was happening. They were stealing a child—kidnapping a living child. *What the fuck?*

"Did you hear me?" Erik asked over his shoulder, moving quickly down the stairs.

"Yes," she confirmed, her gaze now focused on the little boy firmly holding onto Erik's hand.

They had just made it to the second story when Toke cursed, stopping to look around a corner.

He came back over to where Erik, the boy, and she now stood, glancing to his brother and then to her as he spoke, "There are about six soldiers blocking the way out, can you handle it?"

She nodded sharply, her gaze darting between the brothers. "I don't know what is through the doors, but whoever it is, handle it." Toke instructed Lora and Erik, both of whom nodded in unison.

She inched to the edge of the landing, and, peeking around the corner to get a good angle, cloaked them all in shadows. The cousins and the boy moved silently through the hallway, staying in alcoves as her shadows strained to keep them concealed against the streaming sunlight. She pushed her shadows farther out, making the soldiers blink several times as the darkness crept into their eyes, their vision blurring.

Once they were in the alcove by the door, she slipped past the guards easily, making her way to the door in a shroud of shadows. She muffled the sound of its opening, and held the door for the others as they slipped in the room. Lora followed behind them, the door making a soft click as they entered the next room...which happened to be a rather long hallway. The four of them crept silently down the hall, making it halfway before an alarm sounded throughout the castle. "Shit," Erik cursed, nodding to his brother as they made a run for the end of the hallway.

Soldiers suddenly poured in from the rooms on either side of the hall, looking around for the cause of alarm—and their gazes settled on her. She threw her shadows toward Toke and Erik, shielding them and the boy as they continued to run. Lora engaged several soldiers as she too pushed forward, making her way to the door. A small dagger nicked her leg, and her shadows faltered.

Toke, now holding the child, made a break for the door at the end of the hallway. "Cover me," Erik called over his shoulder as he followed behind, leaving Lora alone in the hall. Lora dodged a blow, her legs feeling heavy as she made a shield of shadows to cover the four of them as they careened through the opening into an ornate room.

Lora slid across the floor, colliding with one of the soldiers as Erik, the child, and Toke, already on their feet, ran for the back of the room. More soldiers poured in, separating Lora from the group. She pushed her shadows out around her, but a blue tinted sword caught her in the arm, sending her shadows to dust. *What the fuck?* The nick to her arm hurt like hell as her vision swam. She searched the room, finding Erik's gaze as he climbed through a window at the back, unnoticed by the soldiers as they swarmed for her. She sent the last wave of shadows she had in her toward them and through the darkness she saw Erik look back, his eyes filled with an unsaid apology, as he disappeared and left her behind.

***

She had been drugged. The tip of the sword must have been coated in sleeping drug, which is why she had fallen so quickly. At least that's what logic dictated as Lora pried her eyes open to find herself face down on the floor.

She tried to stand, but a boot was at her back, her arms still too heavy to move on her own.

"Lift her!" came the shrill voice of the short man from before, and Lora was being hauled to her wobbling legs beneath her.

"Laudanum was clever, girl," spat the dark-haired little man from the gate. "But it seems we outsmarted you at your own game." The King's man held up a blue tinted blade and smiled wickedly. Whatever the blade was made out of, *it* had a drugging effect. *Awesome.*

She didn't respond, only surveyed the room and found that she was grossly outnumbered, with more soldiers pouring in from all sides. The room itself was almost a throne room, but too small to be the main one in that sized castle.

The door in front of her opened and her eyes swam as a tall, golden-haired man entered the room.

CHAPTER 36

ESCAPE ATTEMPT #4

Lora

The man now standing in front of Lora, cloaked in golden robes, was nothing short of beautiful. But his was a beauty of wicked lethality. She could tell that he had had extensive work done to make his bone structure sharper, his eyes bigger, and his nose smaller. It made Lora curious as to what he looked like before the menders changed his face.

"Now what do we have here?" he drawled, his voice skittering over Lora's skin as he made a slow circle around her. She made no move to speak, only surveyed the soldiers now filing in behind him. *Oh shit*—she realized too late that it was, in fact, the king himself who circled her.

The king regarded Lora in a way that told her he was not looking at her body on display in the dress, but instead looking around her, as if for someone else.

"If I'm being honest," he started, though she wasn't confident he'd been honest a day in his life. "When I was told someone had stolen my prize, I was hopeful to find someone else standing here."

Kalon. The name clanged through her mind.

"No bother," he drawled again. "Based on your scent alone, I'm sure we will have another guest arrive soon enough. Let's not kill you just yet!" She wasn't sure what to make of that. *Her scent? What the hell does that mean?* Her face must have given her away because the king smiled as he approached her, his flowing robe trailing behind him.

"Not one of many words, are you dear?" he purred in her ear, now so close she could smell the wine on his breath. "When he comes for you, I'll be ready." His breath sent a shiver down her spine as he waved his hands and guards grabbed her under her arms. "Let's put her in an obvious spot, shall we?"

And then she was being drug down a hallway, the soldier's grip incredibly tight as her arms slowly regained feeling. The king walked ahead of them, his robes flowing, and Lora felt a pang of hatred radiate within her that was not entirely her own. Moments later the window next to her exploded from the outside, the soldiers holding her crumpling to the floor.

Kalon had appeared so suddenly next to her she thought for a brief moment she had been hallucinating. His citrus and ember scent wrapped itself around her, steadying her as she tried and failed to stand on her own. Whatever was in that blade had her vision blurring slightly, even now.

Kalon paid no heed to the advancing soldiers as he gently held her in his arms, steadying her. "Are you hurt?" his eyes were swimming with too many emotions for Lora to place. "Are you hurt?" he repeated, giving her arm a slight squeeze as he searched her face for any sign of injury.

"N-no," she grunted, shaking her head, her body still not fully alert yet. That seemed to be enough for Kalon as he spun, still holding her up—and came face-to-face with the King of Kretor.

The King's smile grew to a wicked width, showing too many teeth and not enough lip, as he beheld Kalon. "Hello pet," he purred.

Lora's blood ran cold as she realized just what kind of *relationship* they had had.

"Hello Damyan," Kalon said through a tight smile, now facing the king. He had angled himself ever so slightly in front of her.

"What a pleasant surprise," the king cheered, raising a glass to Kalon before downing the burgundy liquid. "I was so sad when you left the last time, how kind of you to return to me."

Lora felt Kalon's body stiffen ever so slightly. Her power began pulsing under her skin, as if Kalon's arrival had caused them to return quicker. *I am here*, she thought, hoping he understood as she brushed her knuckles against his. His body shuddered at the contact. The king tracked the movement, his eyes narrowing, then hardening at Lora.

"I've changed my mind," he said over his shoulder. Lora tried to sink into a fighting stance at the malice in his voice. "I think I will have you kill her now." The soldiers needed no other command as they drew their bows, arrows aimed at

Lora, but Kalon was quicker, lashing out with a short sword and angling himself in the line of fire.

"Ugh! Stop!" The king shouted, looking exasperated. "I can't have you harming my little friend. Kalon darling, step aside please."

Kalon did not move a muscle. The king had the audacity to look offended. "Kalon! This is getting boring, stand aside so we can kill the little thing."

Lora stiffened slightly, scanning the soldiers around her. They had to find a way out of this.

Kalon's hand wrapped around hers and squeezed gently before letting go. She swayed, but managed to stay upright on her own. Kalon's voice was deadly calm as a tight smile spread on his face. "I actually have a gift for you, Damyan."

"Oh wonderful!" chirped the king, clapping his hands together. "Another trade perhaps?" he asked, looking now at the hand Kalon had held. Lora froze in horror. *No. He cannot trade himself for me.*

But Kalon was one step ahead of her. "How about you go fuck yourself?"

Before the king could even register the insult Kalon had thrown a dagger at the soldier closest to him, causing the others to swarm the king in order to keep him safe.

Lora smiled as she withdrew the small blade Kalon had passed her moments ago and began slicing her way through the soldiers.

***

She and Kalon ran down the halls of the great castle, Kalon guiding them toward a small terrace. How they had managed to not be captured or killed yet was an honest to gods miracle—that, plus Kalon's forethought in bringing Lora a weapon.

"We should leave the castle grounds," she grunted, rolling out of reach of a particularly pissed looking guard.

"Working on it," Kalon retorted, all but throwing her out of the room they had been running through. "Up ahead," he breathed, and Lora turned her attention to the small opening in the wall—a servant's entrance.

She nodded and pumped her legs harder, passing Kalon as he slowed to give her cover. An arrow whizzed by Lora's head and she began zigzagging toward the door, not giving the archer a clear shot at her. An arrow barely scraped the edge of her arm as she dove into the servant's door, Kalon flying through moments later. They both used their body weight to hold it closed while Kalon jammed one of his daggers in the hinge. Lora's power surged within her. *Good—it's coming back. The arrow hadn't been the same as the blade.*

They raced down the narrow hallway, knocking over quite a few trays on the way through before arriving in the lower kitchens. They paused, both breathing heavily as the servants looked at them with mute shock.

"Sorry," Lora said through breaths, noting the wave of destruction they had brought with them. "We were...uh... running late."

Soldiers shouted from somewhere to their right and Kalon was jumping into action, pulling Lora behind him as he raced from the kitchens. They burst through another door, landing them in the gardens and face-to-face with the fucking calvery.

"Shit," Kalon muttered as the soldiers surrounded them.

"You trust me?" she asked, cracking her knuckles. She didn't wait for him to respond as she threw her now returning shadows in every direction, coating the sunlit garden in darkness.

Several people screamed, many beginning to panic, but she grabbed Kalon's hand and charged through the fray, heading toward the small gate she had seen moments before. Arrows began to whizz by as archers shot into the darkness, hoping to hit them in the darkness.

Her legs and lungs were burning, but she held the shadows in place just long enough for them to make it to the garden gate, and then she collapsed through the small door, her shadows sucking into her as she took a gasping breath.

But Kalon was already on the move, pulling her along behind him as they charged through the city.

"Neat trick," Kalon admitted as he dodged another arrow. "Got any more?"

She gave a sly, albeit wary, smile. "Oh, yeah."

***

While she did, in fact, have more "neat tricks," they were running out of time to do them. The soldiers chasing after them did not give rest, and Lora was running low on energy. Whatever those blades had been made with had zapped both her power and energy.

They were now out in the crowded streets below Castle Trintel, dodging people and animals alike. She threw a pointed shadow toward a soldier running along a tall wall to her left, only to have it barely knock the man down. *Yep, I'm almost out.*

Kalon seemed to realize it too, slowing a bit as he navigated them through the cramped city. "We need a new plan," he said after dodging a man with a stall full of cabbage.

"I'm open for any suggestions!" she shouted, barely missing the cabbage guy and instead rolling under a rather tall table of shiny objects.

Kalon looked around as he ran, clearly on the lookout for something specific. "Do you trust me?" he asked, grabbing her hand and pulling them into a small alleyway.

"Enough," she retorted, gasping down air as Kalon picked up his speed, his hand still firmly grasping hers.

"Enough will do. Now, jump when I say so."

Kalon took another sharp turn and then they were suddenly back on a crowded street, a large, framed hole on the bottom of the wall to their left. The smell emanating from it gave her the inclination it was a trash chute of some sort, or maybe even sewage. Unfortunately, Kalon was running right for it.

"Kalon—"

"Jump!" His shout broke off her plea and before she knew it, she was being thrown headfirst into the small hole, consumed instantly by darkness and the horrible stench of shit and decay.

Somehow, Kalon had known that this particular trash chute would land them in the main tunnel on top of a small trash boat that was both fortunately, and unfortunately, very soft. The timing had been impeccable, as the boat was about to clear the small gate keeping it under the city.

She gagged as the fluid from her trip down the chute slid down her face and over her lips. Something under her squished and then squirmed and she would have shrieked had she not felt Kalon's hand around her waist a moment later, his body pressing hers into the garbage. She looked up and their eyes met.

Kalon mouthed *sorry* before smearing her face with even more debris, the smell shoving its way so far up her nostrils she thought it might be in her brain. *Stay still*, his eyes seemed to say as he slowly lifted his head. He hunkered back down immediately, eyes wide as he buried his face in her neck.

"*Soldiers*," he whispered, his breath tickling her neck. She simply gave him a slight nod in return, his cheek warming the side of her face.

She heard loud voices shouting out and she stiffened, trying to remain as still as possible on her pile of debris and trash. After a few minutes the boat moved and she saw the light at the end of the tunnel. She held her breath as she passed the voices of the soldiers, only exhaling once she was in the fading daylight overhead.

They'd made it.

CHAPTER 37

RETREAT TO GARRISON'S FAMILY FARM

Lora

Before Lora could formulate any words, Kalon jumped from the small trash boat and strode in the shallow waters toward the tree line. She hauled herself out of the trash and launched after him. *Like hell is he walking away while I'm covered in shit and garbage.*

"You didn't tell me we were stealing a child!" she fumed, splashing through the water, debris and sludge falling from her in chunks.

"You didn't ask," he said with a roguish grin accompanied by a wink before he was, again, striding off toward the trees.

"You can't be serious! A literal child! That's kidnapping, Kalon—"

He clasped his hand over her mouth, muffling the rest of her rant.

"What the hell!" she exclaimed, ripping free from his grasp.

Kalon wasn't listening though, his attention had snagged on a tall tree ahead of them. At his stillness she stiffened, listening for anyone approaching.

She lowered her voice to a whisper. "Kalon, what the fu—"

He held up his finger to stop her, "One sec," he said, turning from her toward where Garrison had appeared next to the tree. He took a step and paused, then turned back to her. "Look—I know you're angry and you have every right to ask questions, but can it wait?"

"Wait? For what?" she asked, her temper rising again.

"Please, Lora. Yell at me all you want, but wait five minutes."

And then he was gone, rushing toward Garrison and the child who poked his head out from behind the large male.

"EMI!" The child squealed, pushing past Garrison and rushing into Kalon's outstretched arms. Lora made her way to the shore slowly, gaping at the pair as they embraced. Kalon's face lit up with a smile she'd never seen, and her temper cooled.

"Jade's little brother," Garrison said, having made his way over to Lora as the pair spoke in whispers, tears flowing from each of them.

Her mouth dropped open even wider but she didn't speak, only stared at the pair in front of her. Any remnants of her anger were doused at the sight. She felt like she was violating their privacy by watching, so she turned back toward the beach and began walking along the shore, sludge still falling off of her.

"What was"—she paused, not sure if he should use Jade's name or not— "what was her little brother doing in this kingdom?"

Garrison, who walked alongside her down the beach, waited several heartbeats before explaining. "Several years ago, Kalon and Jade had been traveling when she got word her family's village had been ransacked by Shades."

Lora tried and failed to hold in her wince.

Garrison pretended not to notice and continued. "Obviously she and Kalon headed there, and when they arrived, Theo was all that was left. He had hidden in the fields outside their home and the Shades didn't know he was there." He took a deep breath as he gazed at the horizon, the setting sun illuminating the skies in vibrant pinks and oranges.

"How did he—Theo I mean—come to be here then?" Lora asked, still trying to understand how the family's tragedy played a role in the child's initial kidnapping.

Garrison turned to her, his eyes blazing with an emotion she couldn't quite place. If Kalon and Jade had been so close, Garrison must have been close with her, too. "Jade loved her brother very much," he said at last. "She never let Theo out of her sight for more than a couple of hours, always leaving him with either Kalon or Liam."

"Ouch," Lora said. "Not good enough?" *Why am I making jokes about this? It's serious! Get it together!*

Thankfully, a small chuffle left his throat. "Not exactly… there would never have been a reason Kalon and I were apart, so I was lumped in with him." A small smile spread across his face as if in memory—the truth still in it.

But something pulled at Lora's memories, too. "If you two were always together, are you both Emir's riders?" She was still trying to figure out the dynamics between dragon and rider, but it seemed unlikely, no matter how big Emir was, that Kalon *and* Garrison could ride him together. A nervous laugh bubbled up at the thought, but she squashed it down—totally not the time.

"Er, it's a bit complicated," he stammered, not meeting Lora's gaze. "And also not the point," he added, shooting her a sideways glance.

"Right, sorry…" She took a deep breath and settled onto the sand. "So how did Theo get kidnapped if he was always so well-guarded?"

Garrison took another deep breath to match hers, sitting down beside her. Whatever the tale, it wouldn't be a pleasant one. Lora knew not to pry. It had to be painful to think about, especially with Jade gone.

"Kalon and I were on a scouting mission near the border of the Kretor about ten months ago, and Jade was back at base camp. While we were away, Kretian soldiers captured the camp and took hostages—Jade and Theo being two of them. The King of Kretor likes power, and powerful people—he collects them, really. And if anyone doesn't fit the bill, he usually sells them off or outright kills them. Jade wasn't of any interest to him…but he probably would have liked Theo. We are at peace with the Kretians, but when Kalon and I came across their caravan, we knew we couldn't beat them and save the hostages. So Kalon did what he does best."

"He wasn't here by choice. He sacrificed himself for Jade, didn't he?" It wasn't even a question—Lora knew the answer.

"Yes, he took her place knowing full well the ramifications. He kept the King's attention so it wouldn't turn to Theo for nearly three months."

Lora shivered. Three months of enduring gods knew what, all to protect the brother of the woman he loved.

"We made a plan to free him, you know," Garrison continued, looking out over the waves. "The crown regent's hands were tied so Nuva, Kierra, Liam, and I, the whole gang, planned the whole thing. A key portion of our plan depended on the pirates, and they asked us to wait for the weather to be right. It pained us all, but we knew it would be better, safer, if we waited—so we agreed we would delay the rescue by a month to give the pirates time." He shook his head, clearing his thoughts. "But Jade couldn't wait. She tried to free them alone. It's how she got captured, trying to free her brother and Kalon. She never even made it to the border. The Shade Commander Roulinns captured her outside of Saranon, at the docks."

Lora's stomach dropped again, a sour taste filling her mouth. "But Kalon is here?" She was having a hard time tracking the timeline.

Garrison's eyes were teary, but he nodded. "Yes, he is. Jade getting captured forced our hand, we had to start our plan early and the pirates weren't ready—the sea was still too choppy to get close to shore, but we tried anyway.

"When we got to Kalon, he was in pretty bad shape, and Theo—we couldn't find him. Kalon refused to leave without him but we were running out of time. *He* was running out of time." A single tear dripped down his cheek. "It was the hardest call I've ever had to make."

"You saved your prince, Garrison," Lora noted, reaching out to place a hand on his arm—but upon seeing her own filth, she decided against it. "And now you've saved Theo."

Garrison smiled tightly down at her. "But the damage was done. When we got back and Kalon found out the Shades had Jade he lost it—went crazy."

Understanding washed over Lora. "That's when he killed those two Shade commanders, wasn't it?"

"He thought she was dead." While it wasn't an excuse, it was a damn good reason, even Lora could admit that.

"A missive came a day later from Commander Roulinns, saying that he was willing to trade Jade and two other soldiers for the generals we had of theirs."

She was going to be sick.

"Our hands were tied. And Kalon—he flew straight to the camp and demanded to see Jade, said he needed proof of life before he would enter into any negotiations or trades."

"Gods," she breathed, "he could've been killed or captured—"

"I just had to see her." The sound of Kalon's voice startled her, causing her to jump slightly. He had snuck up behind them, so quietly she hadn't noticed. His tone was calm, a bit remorseful, but resolute—like he still believed he made the right call.

Kalon angled his head over to the tree line where Theo threw rocks at a crab, and Garrison rose from where they'd sat on the sand. Without looking back he strode to the boy and they began sword fighting with sticks. The child laughed, and Kalon's face lit with a small, devastated smile.

"Did you get to see her? Did they let you?" Lora asked.

"Yes."

The desperation in that single word threatened to draw tears from her eyes.

"She asked." He loosed a shaky breath, running his hands through his hair. "She asked where Theo was. Because if I was free, he had to be, too. When I told her we didn't, we couldn't get him, she—"

The grime on his face was streaked with tears. Lora wanted to reach out and touch his shaking hands, but decided against it. His eyes didn't meet hers as he wiped his filthy cheeks.

She suddenly felt a wave of shame. Why was she forcing him to relive this memory? "It's okay. You don't have to tell me—"

"No, it's important you know, that you understand why this mission—why it is so important to me. To all of us." His eyes glowed slightly as he looked at her.

"Okay." She nodded, not knowing what else to say.

"I begged for her forgiveness. But I had promised I'd keep him safe, and I had failed her. She told me she hated me. It was the last thing she said to me. She was right to be angry, she was right to hate me—" His voice broke and a piece of Lora's soul fractured with it. This selfless male had sacrificed himself for her, and for others his whole life.

"That's not fair. You didn't control what happened. Garrison said you were near dead when they got to you—

it wasn't your call." Suddenly, she was angry. Angry at this woman for making Kalon hurt, even now. He had saved the child, and that was more than she had accomplished.

But Jade was dead, and she had died at the hands of Lora's king. And Kalon—he still loved her.

The girl Kalon loved, the girl he'd begged for forgiveness from, the one whose brother Kalon still felt responsible for, was dead. All because of Lora. And that realization was like a bucket of cold water to her boiling anger.

Kalon stared at her, his devastation still raw with the spoken memories, but another emotion akin to hope fluttered in his eyes.

A childish laugh from over her shoulder had her clearing her throat.

"Does he know about his sister?" she asked, hoping to break the tension rising between them.

"Yes," was Kalon's only reply, his attention over her shoulder, presumably on where the boy now played. She couldn't help but wonder at the boy, who was still able to smile after everything he had been through.

"I'm sorry," she said to Kalon. "I didn't realize—"

He cut her off with a dimpled grin. "I know princess, don't sweat it. How would you have known anyway?" Lora almost startled—his mask had slipped back on so effortlessly.

"I mean that I'm sorry about everything that's happened to you, and to Theo," she amended, not letting this moment pass without saying it. His smile faded, shadows clouding his amber eyes. She hated to see that. "I am not sorry for yelling at you though. You should've told me what we were stealing."

His eyebrows perked up, and a small smile returned. "You should've asked, princess."

She jabbed him in the side with her elbow, eliciting a soft laugh.

After another deep breath, he looked at her, his eyes pinching slightly before he smiled tightly.

"I, uh" he started, clearing his throat. "I spoke with the pirates, and they aren't entirely amenable to transporting you at the moment."

Her stomach simultaneously dropped and launched into her throat.

"I know our deal was that you would leave right after you helped me, but…" Kalon's words died on his tongue as he turned his gaze to the sand at his feet. His swallow was audible as he tried to find the right words. "It's just, you'll need to lay low, and we could probably use your shadows in transporting Theo to safety, and—"

Lora tried and failed to hold in a smile. She let him ramble a moment more before rising to her feet and offering him a hand.

Kalon's surprised gaze met hers and she nudged him with her elbow again as he rose beside her. "Consider it free of charge," Lora said with a wink. *He wants me to stay, to help with Theo, yes, but still. And what's a couple more days delay? Honestly, I haven't even thought about leaving in days.*

Kalon's eyes were near luminous. She held his gaze for what felt like an eternity, the air around them going taut with tension, but she broke away when he opened his mouth to speak, asking instead, "Where to now? Back to Pridama? Traivisa?"

Kalon, who had remained looking at her a bit longer, looked over her shoulder. She followed his gaze, spinning slightly, as Garrison and Theo, now accompanied by Liam and Nuva, approached them.

"The two of you smell funny," Theo said, staring at Lora as he approached. The child's bright eyes danced with mischief.

A smirk worked its way across Liam's face as she eyed Kalon and Lora, still in their sewer-coated clothes.

"You're being too polite Theo, they smell like shit," Nuva said from behind him. She, too, looked at their clothes, her face rumpled with a mixture of disgust and amusement.

Kalon's feigned annoyance. "If you don't wipe that smirk off your face, I'll—"

"You'll what?" Nuva countered, hunkering into a fighting stance.

"I'll hug you!" Kalon shouted. At Nuva's terrified face, Kalon chased her down the beach, flailing his arms around, and, all and all, making a scene.

Nuva shouted something about germs and threw small rocks at him while dodging his attempted hugs.

"Nuva never was one for germs," Liam commented as they all watched the two take another turn around the beach, Lora simply gaping.

After about three minutes of Kalon and Nuva causing a ruckus Garrison intervened and separated the two of them. It was time to keep moving before it got too dark, and Garrison had to remind everyone that they were probably being searched for. Nuva and Kalon straightened at that truth, both resuming their usual antics of pouring over maps and discussing routes with Garrison's cousins, who had been avoiding eye contact with Lora since she'd gotten back.

***

"It's a four-day hike to Garrison's family farm if we don't stop," Nuva explained as she packed her small bag with some extra fruits from the market.

They had slept on the beach for a couple hours the night before and had headed into the village to stock up on supplies before leaving. Lora had almost cried tears of joy when she'd donned her new tunic, discarding the old one immediately. She and Kalon had tried to rid of the smell as best they could in the water, but the stench clung to her hair and skin. She still needed at least five baths to rid herself of the scent of sewage, but at least now her shirt was clean, her hair in a fresh, long braid.

Liam and Garrison had gone to get medical supplies and other food, and Theo was currently asleep on Kalon's back— where he'd been since they'd woken up. Something about the sight had made Lora's chest tighten, but she'd shoved the emotion away.

"It will go faster if we ride," Kalon noted, now looking at the map Nuva had splayed out on a crate.

Lora's skin prickled in anticipation. *Are we finally going to fly?*

Nuva, however, looked sick. Before anyone could say anything, Garrison and Liam arrived, supplies in hand.

"Nuva, are you all right?" Liam asked, concerned.

"Yeah," Garrison added. "You look awful."

Nuva scowled at them, snatched the map up, then stormed away, toward the city center. "We will need six horses please," Kalon called after her, a smile tugging at his lips.

Right, Lora thought, *of course we aren't taking dragons. That would be way too cool.*

***

Nuva, as it turned out, did not like riding horses—at all. It had taken the female several minutes to even climb up onto the small beast, and once in the saddle, she nearly fell off on three occasions just sitting there. The beast underneath her, though she was assured was gentle, looked equally as unexcited to have Nuva as her rider.

While Lora herself wasn't extremely comfortable on a horse, it was easier and way faster than walking.

Kalon had passed Theo to Garrison for a bit so he could go and canvas the area ahead. He had offered for Lora to join, and they rode in comfortable silence up the wide trail.

"It's said," Kalon started, breaking the silence at last, "that some strong shadow wielders can even conjure up images or people and things."

Lora nearly jumped out of her saddle at his voice, having been so lost in the vibrant colors of autumn around them she'd forgotten he was there. "What do you mean?" she asked, having half-heard his question. They were at a slow trot, giving everyone else time to catch up and Lora time to admire the trees.

"They can manipulate the shadows to where they look like people or places." Kalon's gaze was heavy on her.

"Is that a real thing?" she asked. It sounded ridiculous.

"I've never seen it," Kalon admitted with a shrug. "But they say the old king, Cyrus's brother, could do it—that their family line was strong in that way."

Lora simply shrugged, still not really paying attention.

Kalon hummed, seeming to be thinking something and deciding not to tell her.

"What?" she asked, her attention now annoyingly on the smirking prince beside her.

"Oh, nothing..." he drawled.

"That didn't seem like the face of someone who thought nothing," Lora observed, pinning Kalon with a glare.

"Well thank you princess," Kalon said, bowing slightly at the waist.

"That wasn't a compliment," Lora snapped half-heartedly. "And don't call me that."

"Why?" Kalon looked genuinely confused for a moment.

"Well for starters," she explained, "because I'm not a princess."

"But you are," he retorted, his eyebrows raised.

"But I'm not," she shot back.

"You're the King's daughter."

"Technically I'm not."

"Technically, you don't know who your parents were."

"What do you mean? Katerina—"

"I always heard she had little to no shadow magic," Kalon interrupted.

"So?"

"So?" Kalon's tone dripped with condescension. "So, you seem to have way more than little to none." His eyebrows were almost at his hairline.

Lora narrowed her gaze incredulously. "Again, so?" *Why does any of this matter?*

"So..." Kalon drawled, doing the mental math in the air for her. "It's unlikely you got the gift from her meaning your dad would have to be a pretty strong shadow wielder for you to have the gift like you do."

"Be careful prince," she teased. "It sounds like you're complimenting me."

"Forgive me princess, that was not my intention." Kalon's eyes danced with amusement as the pair entered a staring contest.

Kalon opened his mouth but was interrupted by Garrison rounding the corner to join them. Theo was now awake, and he and Nuva both looked worse for wear.

"I know we are close," Liam said as he arrived from the back of the party. "But in my medical opinion, we should rest for the night." He nodded his head conspicuously over toward Nuva, who was barely seated in her saddle, her skin a sickly green color.

Kalon nodded once before announcing to the group that they would camp up the road in a clearing between some trees. Each member of the group was given a task in order to set up, and everyone went right to work.

Garrison took the horses to a small river for them to drink from while Liam tended to Nuva and Theo in the clearing. Erik and Toke took first watch at the north and south side of camp after the small dinner of dried fruits and fish. Lora suddenly found herself seated next to Theo, both watching the fire dance.

Garrison had fallen asleep several minutes before, Liam and Nuva before him, so only Lora, Kalon, and Theo were still awake.

"You should try to rest, buddy," Kalon said, ruffling Theo's shaggy brown hair.

Theo gave him a tight smile but whipped his head toward the darkened forest at the sound of a twig snapping. Lora's heart ached at the fear radiating from him.

Kalon seemed to note it, too, as he pulled the boy close. "You see all that darkness?" Kalon asked him, pointing out into the woods.

"Yes?" Theo answered weakly, his eyes still darting around the small lit space.

"It's especially dark because of our friend here," Kalon explained, pointing to Lora.

Theo tracked his point, his eyes widening as he beheld her. "You're doing that?" he asked, wonder dancing in his eyes.

She smiled softly as she nodded, wreathing her hands in small shadows that danced and pulsed.

"Wow!" the boy exclaimed, leaning forward to see them better.

"Incredible, isn't it?" agreed Kalon, who also watched her shadows dance in her palm.

She felt a small blush creep into her cheeks. "Is the whole place really covered?" Theo asked, his eyes now darting back to the dense woods.

"To the rest of the world," she explained softly, "we are currently invisible."

The little boy's eyes grew wide again as he processed that.

"She's protecting us, so you don't need to be afraid," Kalon said gently, softly smiling down at the boy, who looked up at him before looking back over the pulsing darkness.

"What if," he started, his face twisting and his pale cheeks turning pink, "what if I'm still afraid anyway?"

Kalon seemed struck dumb, so Lora scooted close to the boy, a soft smile settling on her face as she admitted, "I'm afraid all the time."

"Really?" Theo asked incredulously. From her peripherals, she saw Kalon shift slightly.

"Really," she confirmed.

"Even now?" His face twisted again in disbelief.

"Even now."

He observed Lora. "But you don't look afraid."

"That's because I do not let fear control me," she explained, looking into the fire. "I control it."

"How do you control it?" he asked, now also looking at the fire dancing.

"Well." she let out a deep breath. "You have to harness it into something useful."

The boy peered at her through such innocent eyes as he asked, "What did you turn yours into?"

She felt her chest tighten. "For a while, anger. I harnessed it to anger."

Theo still looked at her with such wonder and hope, she thought her heart would crack. "Wouldn't that mean you were angry all the time?"

She let out a distressed chuckle. "Yeah, I suppose it would. I suppose I was," she clarified.

"Sounds awful," Theo noted, turning his attention back to the fire.

"It was," she admitted, more to herself than anyone else.

"What is it now?" he asked through a yawn.

She smiled, watching his eyes begin to droop, "I don't know," she admitted again.

The boy yawned one more time. "I think I'll choose chocolate," he said as his eyes closed and did not reopen.

"What a wonderful choice," she said, though she was sure he was asleep already.

When she finally pulled her gaze from Theo, she was met with a pair of amber eyes sparkling in the firelight.

"Thank you," Kalon whispered, glancing down at the sleeping child.

"We made a deal," she said matter-of-factly, adding, "but I still wish you would have told me."

Kalon's smile grew. "You should have asked."

Lora rolled her eyes, resting her head lightly on Kalon's shoulder. "Ass."

A comfortable silence settled over them as they watched the fire dwindle and before she knew it, Lora drifted peacefully to sleep.

***

Liam had been right. They had been really close. The ride the next morning had only taken two hours before Nuva was near giddy with anticipation, which was saying something since Nuva was rarely, if ever, giddy.

"Thank the gods we're here," she exclaimed dramatically from behind the group. Lora and Kalon, now with Theo, had taken up the front position again. The group rounded a corner and were suddenly looking at the largest estate Lora had ever seen. From where they were positioned on the small hill, the house and its manicured grounds took up most of the horizon, the late afternoon sun painting it in oranges and golds.

"What the hell is that?" she asked. The whole party seemed to have relaxed upon seeing the estate.

"Garrison's home," Kalon said, gently waking up Theo, who had fallen asleep in front of him after watching Lora's shadows for over an hour.

"But you said your family were farmers." Lora gaped, turning to look at Garrison, whose smile was broad.

"They are," he said with a shrug.

"Garrison, that is an estate!" she all but shouted, pointing at the veritable palace in front of them. He merely shrugged again. Her eyes were so wide, they threatened to pop out of her head. "You didn't say you were rich!"

A sly smile broke across Garrison's face at that. "You didn't ask."

He galloped away before she could hit him. *These fucking people and their questions*, she thought to herself, as she watched Garrison and his cousins ride toward the gates of the giant estate. For a moment, it was all Lora could do to just sit there and stare. She really needed to ask more questions, apparently.

Nuva and Liam had started to ride that way as well, but Kalon paused, looking over Theo's head.

"You coming princess?" he called, a genuine smile making an appearance.

Lora rolled her eyes as she clicked her heels, her horse surging forward, following the rest of the party to Garrison's family estate.

CHAPTER 38

GAMMA

Lora

Although it had been late afternoon when they first saw Garrison's house—which was called Damaris Estate—they didn't make it to the stables nearly until sunset. Lora's legs felt like wet noodles, and she was amazed she could even stand, let alone walk once she dismounted her mare.

The doors to the estate burst open moments later, and a stream of white came careening down the stairs. Kierra's form crashed into Nuva moments later, the soldier reviving instantly as Kierra planted a kiss to her lips.

"What took you all so long!" Kierra shouted, now whacking Nuva's arm.

The female swayed but smiled as she pulled Kierra in for another kiss. Lora's eyebrows shot up at the show of affection.

"We had a bit of a hiccup on the way, but—" Kalon was cut off as Theo dismounted and launched into Kierra's arms.

"Ki!" he shouted. Both of them were in a puddle of tears before anyone could stop them.

Kalon came up beside Lora, his eyes lined with silver as he looked at his twin and Theo.

"He's safe, brother," Garrison said, patting Kalon on the shoulder. The group merely sat in that moment, all teary eyed as Theo whispered nonsense about fires and growing to Kierra. Lora felt like she was intruding and made to turn away but then she too was being pulled into a bone crushing hug, Kierra's scent wrapping around her.

"Thank you bean," she whispered into Lora's hair before pulling away and taking Lora's hand. "Come on everyone," she said, smiling at the group. "Gamma has been waiting all day to see you!"

And with that, the group was making their way into the estate proper, Erik and Toke leading the way.

"Gamma? What's a Gamma?" Lora asked as they entered a formal hallway. The size and sheer magnificence of the estate had Lora's jaw dropping.

"You mean, *who's* a Gamma?" Nuva corrected, pushing past Lora, who had stopped to stare at the vaulted ceilings, which were painted to match the morning sky.

"Gamma is Kalon and Kierra's grandmother on their dad's side," Liam explained, now also moving past her.

"You'll have time to gape later," Kalon whispered, pulling her along. "But you don't really keep Gamma waiting." His voice was soft and teasing, which pulled Lora fully back to the present.

"She's basically everyone's grandmother," Garrison chimed in, holding a door open for the group to walk through. There was so much to look at Lora felt overwhelmed, but she was pulled quickly into a smaller, warmer room—a kitchen.

"She sure bosses us around like we belong to her," Nuva called from the hallway to Lora's right.

"I heard that, young lady!" came a velvety voice from behind a swinging door at the back of the room.

"Sorry G! You know I said it with love!" Nuva shouted in the direction the voice was heard from though Lora still couldn't see the woman.

"She brought us here after mom passed," Kalon explained, picking up a small cookie off the sheet in front of them. An old lady suddenly appeared from seemingly nowhere, snatching the cookie out of his hand and batting it with a wooden spoon.

"No eating unless you help! You know the rules. Now all of you, out! Unless you plan on helping!"

Lora nearly jumped back at the sight of the old woman. She had a head full of wiry gray and black hairs that were tied into a messy bun. She wasn't very tall, only coming to Kalon's waist at her full height. By the looks of it, she had to be in her eighth decade of life at the *earliest*. If Lora could have picked a grandmother for Kalon and Kierra, this would be her antithesis.

"Hello, Layla. You're looking scrumptious as always," said Garrison, leaning in for a kiss. He was immediately thwarted by a rather hard whack from the woman—Layla's—wooden spoon.

"None of that, boy. Now put the cookies back you just swiped—" she may have been small but she was holding the spoon like a weapon. Everyone in the kitchen seemed to lean back when she swung it toward them. "That goes for you too medic, and you, soldier girl."

"Now, now, Layla, you know their names," Kalon said innocently with a devilish smile. "They've been around for ages—"

"I don't care who they are, they're in my kitchen stealing my food! What's a cook to do!" She swung her spoon again, flour coming off of her apron in clouds as she stormed off.

"*That* was Gamma?" Lora asked, now gaping for a whole other reason.

A soft laugh left Garrison and Kalon. "No, Lora."

"I am Gamma," came that same velvety voice, except this time there was a face to match it.

Standing in the doorway to the kitchen was a woman about Lora's height with rich, tan skin. Her eyes were the same amber as Kalon's and her hair was the bright white of Kierra's. She was strongly built, even for an older woman, and the way she held herself, even covered in flour, demanded respect. While she appeared rather imposing with a slew of cooking utensils strapped on her waist like Lora wore weapons, her eyes were soft and kind. She looked them all over, and then her gaze landed back on Lora.

"You must be Lora. I've heard such wonderful things about you," she said, smiling warmly and stepping toward her.

"All lies then I'm sure," Nuva snorted, sounding *mostly* kidding.

Gamma waved her away and pulled Lora in close, her voice a soft, lilting whisper. "Kierra told me all about her Shade sister."

"Ki—" Lora stammered, her voice barely above a whisper as she glanced at Kierra, who was busy eating a tart. "She talked about me?"

"Of course child, you were her only friend for nearly ten years. It took some time, but once she was willing to talk about her stay in Attica, you were the first thing she mentioned." The women's eyes were bright and clear, and Lora felt immediately at ease.

But her throat burned. She hadn't thought that Kierra would have said anything about her, especially since it was Lora's people that had beaten her for nearly ten years. But hearing it made their bond feel real.

"Hey Gamma," called Garrison, his hand hovering over one of the cookies he had tried to steal earlier, a pleading face plastered to him.

Gamma's face softened into another deep smile. "Of course child, but don't eat to many or—"

"We'll ruin our supper. Yeah, yeah, we know," echoed the five friends, all now digging into the cookies and tarts.

Lora's eyebrows shot up—all five Drakes looked seven years old again. Lora almost laughed as they, in unison, plastered on the same pleading look Garrison had dawned moments before.

"What we meant was, thank you Gamma, for your ever-growing kindness," said Garrison, planting a kiss on Gamma's cheek.

"Any chance you've got any pump-pastries, G?" Liam asked between bites. It seems he was unconcerned about the cookies ruining his supper as he shoved two more in his mouth.

"Pump-pastries?" Lora asked, and everyone's attention snapped to her, as if they all just remembered she was there.

"She makes the *best* pump-pastries," Kierra exclaimed, shoving a tart in her pocket and a cookie in her mouth. "So if she's got 'em, you'll have to fight Kalon for 'em," she said between chews.

"Not yet, I'm afraid," Gamma said to Liam, now making her way toward the big table in the middle of the room, Theo in tow. "I've been a bit busy making sure everything else was in order for the festival."

A round of laments echoed throughout the kitchen. Nuva looked as if she might cry.

"But perhaps," Gamma started, lifting her finger to her face as if deep in thought, "if my sweet grandchildren asked for them so nicely—" She surveyed the group gathered in her kitchen and everyone, including Nuva, to Lora's surprise, immediately began cooing and batting their eyes.

A series of, "Oh please Gamma?" and "It would mean the world to me!" and "They are my favorite." rang out as the group of friends rushed the old woman.

Gamma laughed, rich and smooth, the lines on her face wrinkling. "I would never deny my lambies anything," she said, patting Liam's full cheek rather hard. "You know the drill," she said, turning sharply, her demeanor changing to that of a commander. "Layla was right. You wanna eat 'em, you gotta cook 'em."

Everyone immediately began donning aprons, even Theo, and moved about to different areas in the kitchen. Apparently, this wasn't uncommon. "We're going to cook?" asked Lora, trying to stay out of the way.

"Afraid to get your hands dirty, *girl*?" Layla spat. She had somehow managed to arrive in the middle of the group undetected. Lora was starting to think she might be a wraith the way she vanished and reappeared.

"Lora actually loves cooking," Kalon said, donning an apron and handing one to Lora. "Isn't that right?"

Lora stared at Kalon. How and why he remembered that random detail from their split trip…

Gamma's smile grew, "I thought Ki had mentioned something about that, let's see what you can do." And with a wink she was donning another, cleaner apron before striding off into the kitchen proper.

***

Cooking with Gamma had been one of the most fun experiences Lora had ever participated in. The woman had boundless patience as she guided each of them through the steps in making her pump-pastries, and even after showing them how to fold the pastry several times, hers were still the only ones that looked right. Though, much to Lora's amusement and Nuva's chagrin, Gamma had used Lora's fold as an example to the others.

Lora had smiled about it all through dinner with the Damaris family, who was just as lovely as she had expected them to be. Mr. Damaris was kind and gentle, like Garrison, and Mrs. Damaris was somehow kinder.

Before dinner, the matron had shown each of them to their rooms. Lora's connected with Kierra's, and she even offered Lora a bright blue dress to wear to dinner. Lora had politely but firmly declined. But still, when Lora had emerged from her bath, the matron had had several dark tunics and dress pants sent to the room and displayed on the bed.

The dinner itself had been lovely. The food was rich and everyone had had at least two helpings of everything. Lora still felt a slight discomfort from the fullness in her belly, a good sign, Gamma had assured her after dinner.

Although the house itself was ornate and nearly nine hundred years old, the Damaris parents were generous and down to earth, eating family style with everyone together.

After dinner, everyone had looked like shit, according to Kierra, and so they had all dispersed to their chambers in order to be ready for the events tomorrow.

Whatever that entailed.

***

Lora had tried to sleep. She had managed to close her eyes and drift away briefly, but her memories and thoughts chased her awake even in the unbelievably comfortable bed she was in.

After taking several sips of water from her nightstand, the shadows that had erupted in her room seemed to ease. Realizing she probably wasn't going to fall back asleep, Lora donned a robe and her boots and crept out of her room, her shadows concealing her as she walked through the halls, trying to shake the eerie feeling that had crept into her chest days ago and had spiked after her nightmare.

She wandered the halls, following an ever-familiar scent as it wove through the estate. A noise sounded to her left and Lora pushed herself into the wall, her shadows concealing her while her shoulders dug into the molding.

"Lora?" Kalon's voice echoed through the long hallway.

Lora let out a soft sigh. Of course the prince was also wandering around. Her shadows vanished and he was looking directly at her, as if there hadn't been shadows in the first place. "What are you doing up so late?"

"I..." Lora paused, thinking of an excuse that sounded less pathetic than the truth. "Well, I realized I never thanked Mrs. Damaris for the clothes."

"So you thought to tell her at midnight?" Kalon snorted—he clearly didn't buy the lie.

"No. That would be rude," she said with a frown.

"Yes and you are anything but rude," he said, pulling on her loose braid.

"Exactly."

"But..." he drug the word out. "That still doesn't explain why you're creeping about the estate so late at night."

"I'm... I wasn't *creeping*," Lora said indignantly. "I was.... I am...just going for a stroll."

"Going for a stroll?" Kalon parroted, eyebrows somehow higher.

"Yes," she confirmed. Then, feeling foolish, she added, "And maybe I couldn't sleep."

"Why couldn't you sleep?" He was suddenly serious, concern bracketing his features. He was so close to her now they shared breath, not a short sword between them.

"I didn't say that I couldn't sleep." Lora took a step back, but only managed to bump into the wall.

"Yes you did," he said, a smirk building on his face.

"No," she corrected. "I said *maybe* I couldn't sleep."

"Maybe you could use some," he offered.

"Well that's awfully rude," Lora shot back, her face souring to a scowl.

"You misunderstand me," Kalon said, smirk still firmly in place.

"Oh I think I understand you perfectly," she snapped, making to move around him. "Now excuse me as I return to my bedroom." After a moment, Kalon let her pass and she stormed off down a long hallway.

Kalon chuckled, and it skidded over her bones. "Why are you headed that way?" he called after her quietly.

"Because it's away from you," she said hotly. "And as you've so kindly established, I need my sleep."

Another laugh, and suddenly Kalon was at her side. "Again, not what I meant. But if you're so dead set on getting to bed then why are you going *that* way."

She looked at him suspiciously as he pointed down the hall she had been marching toward. She didn't move, only narrowed her eyes.

"Oh my gods." Kalon gasped dramatically. "Are you lost?"

"No," Lora said flatly, but too quickly.

"Yes. You are totally lost."

"I am not. I just got a bit turned around on the staircase," Lora admitted, shoulders relaxing a bit as amusement danced in his amber eyes.

"Which staircase?" He looked around.

"The spiral one," Lora noted, squaring her shoulders.

"The spiral one?" Kalon repeated with a nod. "How very… specific. Do you remember which of the six spiral staircases on this side of the estate you come down?"

Lora saw a flash of red. "If I could, I wouldn't be stuck here talking to you now, would I?"

Kalon chuckled again, but this time there was no malice in it. Only amusement. "All right, come on," he sighed, motioning for her to follow him in the opposite direction.

"What?" Lora asked, dumbfounded.

"I'm going to take you back to your room," he responded over his shoulder.

"Oh, well, if you're headed that way…" Lora tried to make it seem casual. It didn't work.

"I'm not, but I can put it on my route," Kalon said with a smile, extending his arm for her to take. "Shall we?"

Lora rolled her eyes, but didn't bat his arm away. Kalon took it as an invitation and looped her arm through his for her. "My lady," he said in an annoying high-pitched accent. "Shall we take a turn about the estate?"

Lora chuckled and Kalon's attention didn't leave hers as she cleared her throat and responded in kind, "Well, thank you good sir. It would be my pleasure."

They walked in silence as he guided her down the hallway, taking more turns than she realized she'd even taken.

"Why were you out and about so late?" she asked, breaking the comfortable silence they'd fallen into.

"Oh, I was lost," Kalon admitted, still striding about as if he was of the utmost importance.

"Really?"

"No," he chuckled. "I grew up here, remember?"

Her face heated. "How would I know that?"

"You weren't listening when I said it earlier?" he asked, glancing sidelong at her.

"I try to rarely listen to you," she teased.

"Well then, you are missing some vital information," he retorted, guiding her down a spiral staircase.

"Oh, I'm sure." She rolled her eyes again.

"As I was saying," he continued, straightening more. "I grew up here."

Lora lifted an eyebrow, "That still doesn't explain why you were, what did you call it? 'Creeping about the estate so late at night.'"

Kalon let out another chuckle and Lora smiled, proud of her joke. "Truth for a truth?" he asked, now looking down at her.

"You owe me? Remember?" She wiggled her eyebrows, causing Kalon to smile at her.

"I couldn't sleep," he admitted, his smile wavering slightly.

"Really?"

"Really," he confirmed, nodding his head as they continued walking. "I've spent the last year working on saving Theo, and now..." He paused their walking, running his free hand through his brown curls.

Lora's mind was a torrent of thoughts and ideas. They walked silently for a few minutes until he stopped again. She looked at him quizzically.

"This is your room," he nodded toward the familiar door. She frowned.

"I hadn't realized how many halls look the same here," she admitted, releasing herself from his grasp.

"Damn," he said with a smile. "You really were lost."

Lora tried and failed to smile back. Their gazes met, and Kalon's was filled with such sorrow, such emptiness her knees threatened to collapse under her.

"Good night," he said, making to turn away.

"Wait," she called after him, halting his movement. He swiveled back her direction, his face set in an amused confusion. "I didn't get to say my truth," she blurted, meeting his gaze.

His eyebrows shot up. "My sincerest apologies princess, please..." He motioned as if to say the floor was hers.

Lora looked around nervously, as if the very walls were judging her. "I'm not really tired," she said, finally meeting his gaze again.

"Really?" he asked, parroting her from earlier.

"Really," she said flatly, not offering an explanation.

"Good," he said, coming toward her. Her heart jumped into her throat as he came so close they were sharing breath.

"Good?" She breathed, "That's rude." She was trying to be funny, but it came out as a whimper.

Kalon's eyes darkened as they dipped to her lips and back up to her eyes. Then he took a step back, taking the air from her lungs with him. "I want to show you something," he said, holding out his hand.

Her eyebrows shot up but she nodded, taking his hand. It was warm and calloused and her fingers fit perfectly between his.

They wove through the castle, taking hallways and stairwells she hadn't noticed existed. They stopped in front of a wall and he glanced over his shoulder at her. "Don't freak out," he said, as he let go of her hand and reached up to the picture frame hanging sideways on the wall.

"I'm not going to—" but Lora's words died on her tongue as she watched as the wall, *the literal wall*, opened up. "Holy shit."

"I said don't freak out," he chortled, taking her hand in his again as they wove down the stairs that had been a wall moments before.

At the bottom of the stone steps was a small door, heat radiating from the other side of it. Kalon released her hand and she instantly felt its absence. He also seemed completely unperturbed by the heated door, as he was merely rolling his sleeves up, a faint smile on his lips.

"Here," he said, leaning over and rolling up her sleeves too. "It's going to be really warm in there."

He pushed open the door to reveal a smaller version of the kitchens from above, only this one was decorated with children's drawings and necklaces made of noodles and beans.

"A little late for a midnight snack..." she hummed, slowly walking around the room, taking in every detail from the worn rocking chair by the fire, to the large, rectangular table in the middle of the room with three mismatched chairs on one end.

When she looked back at Kalon, there was a sheepish smile playing at the corners of his lips. "This is one of my favorite places in the whole estate," he admitted.

"The kitchens?" she asked, still confused.

"Not just any kitchens," Kalon corrected. "This is my grandmother's kitchen."

He explained how, when they were little, it had been hard to find time for just the three of them—him, Kierra, and Gamma, so she had brought them down here late at night to bake cookies and read them stories.

Kalon had smiled at the memories, and Lora couldn't help but smile, too.

He pulled out some cheese and an apple, offering it to Lora as they sat around the table. She rolled her shoulders and a small knife of shadows appeared in her hand that she used to cut the apple into equal slices, offering the first to Kalon as he placed a bottle of wine between them.

"So you always have a knife on you?" he asked, taking the apple slice and plopping it in his mouth.

"Always," Lora replied, slicing another piece of apple and placing it on the table.

When he didn't respond, she glanced up to find him staring at her.

"What?"

He shook his head, taking a bite of cheese. "Nothing," he said through chews.

After another long pause, Lora found herself staring at him.

"Now you're the one staring," he said jokingly, taking a swig from the bottle.

"So you admit that you were staring earlier," she teased, also taking a long pull from the sweet wine. Kalon's laugh warmed her insides just as much as the liquid. "Tell me something," she said, leaning on her elbows.

"Like what?" he asked, and she felt his gaze on her, though she remained looking at the fire.

"Anything," she said, feeling her smile fade. "Something real." It must have been the wine talking, because she almost sounded like she cared. Like she wanted to know more about him, like she wanted to connect.

She felt Kalon's gaze like a brand before he cleared his throat and, looking into the reds and oranges of the fire, began his tale.

***

Kalon

Kalon and Lora had stayed in Gamma's kitchen for nearly three hours. They had drunk two bottles of wine and eaten most of Gamma's fine cheeses. He had done most of the talking, mostly about growing up with Garrison and how the group all met. Lora had chimed in occasionally with questions, or comments about how her life in the frozen ice plains of Attica differed from his here, in the lush forests and gardens. He was beginning to understand why she wanted to go south. Why she gasped at all the trees and flowers and streams—they were all new to her.

He regaled her with the different stories of scars that peppered his body, and she had shown him some of hers until they were both drunkenly laughing at their own misfortunes. Until they were sitting side by side on the worn patterned rug by the dwindling fire, leaning on each other as they spoke. After his last tale of how he had broken his arm fighting Nuva, he noted that Lora had fallen asleep, her head leaning on his shoulder in a way that pinned him to the spot. With none of her usual swirling shadows in place, she looked so peaceful laying there, her crimson hair draped over her shoulder and cascading to her waistline, framing her olive face. Apparently her time these last weeks in the sun had kissed her face, taking the usual paleness to a nice tan.

He hadn't ever realized just how long her hair was, or how, in the firelight, it seemed to brighten, changing hues with the flickering flames. He titled his head more to get a better look at her and she squirmed in her sleep, scooting closer to him and settling her weight on his side. Kalon didn't dare move again as he prayed to the gods that she would enter a deep, dreamless sleep, not plagued by nightmares like she pretended she wasn't. Like the one that had sent her roaming the halls tonight.

He hadn't lied when he told her he couldn't sleep. He couldn't. He had been pacing in his room, adrenaline from the past several months still coursing through him, but then he'd felt an overwhelming surge of fear and panic that he knew didn't belong fully to him. He had followed the tug until he saw the shadows pulsing from her room and he almost burst in had he not seen them recede. He heard movement and by the time he realized Lora was going to emerge, he had darted down the hall, not wanting to seem like a creep. It was happenstance that she wandered the same direction he had. A very pleasant happenstance at that.

He took one more glance down to Lora's sleeping form and gently pressed a kiss atop her head, her jasmine and ember scent swirling around him as he, too, closed his eyes and drifted off to sleep.

***

Lora

Lora's peaceful sleep was filled with scents of embers and citrus, and she was confident upon waking up that last night had been a dream. She had a vague memory of a velvety voice and strong hands carrying her to her room as the sun had begun to peak through the hall windows.

Rolling over, she noted she was in her large, plush bed. Maybe she had dreamed of going down to the kitchens with Kalon, of sharing stories and laughing and drinking wine. She sat up and her head throbbed slightly. *Okay, so the wine part wasn't a dream, at least.*

As she lay there, replaying the parts she wished had been real, a soft knock came at the door. Lora rubbed at her eyes, her vision swimming slightly at the quick movement so early in the morning.

"Come in," she called, trying to sound more awake than she was.

The door opened slightly and a small, round woman peeked her cherry-red face around the corner. Lora tried not to look disappointed.

"Pardon me miss," she said, her rosy cheeks deepening a shade as she took in Lora in the bed still. "I didn't mean to wake you."

Lora smiled awkwardly at the woman. "You didn't!" she lied, hopping out of the bed and coming to the door.

The woman pushed the door fully open with her back as she entered the room, tray in hand. "Emir instructed me to bring this to you, ma'am," the woman said, smiling broadly.

Lora looked at the woman confused, as she took the tray, "A dragon instructed you to bring me breakfast?"

The woman's face changed from bright pink to ashen and back to pink in a matter of seconds. She smiled tightly, her eyes flaring with surprise only briefly. "There is a note," she said, as if that cleared everything up.

"A dragon wrote me a note?" Lora pried, placing the tray on the table next to her bed.

"I believe it was the prince who penned the note my lady," the woman said, clearly ready to leave the room.

"Right," Lora nodded. "Well, thank you…"

"Martham, ma'am," the woman—Martham—supplied.

"Yes, well thank you Martham," Lora finished with a smile as she turned her attention back to the breakfast. But a thought occurred to her as she picked up the note, scrawled in Kalon's handwriting, "Martham—" but the question died on her tongue as the click from the door sounded. Martham had all but run from the room, apparently.

Lora sighed softly. She couldn't blame the woman—Lora was a stranger. A stranger no one had given really any reason for her being there, other than she'd helped them with retrieving Theo. But of course no one could know the extent of her helping, and while they may not know she was a Shade, they certainly knew she wasn't a Drake.

Lora sighed again, plopping on the bed and popping a grape into her mouth as she opened the note from Kalon:

Good morning! I didn't want to wake you up when I left this morning. We are out flying and will be back soon. (Don't be mad—you'll get to fly again soon enough, I promise!) Gamma found us in the kitchens last night and suggested I let you sleep in after I put you to bed.

I know you're probably already hungry, so I had Martham bring up some breakfast for you. Also, I had Martham lay out some travel clothes for today. We are going to go into town when we get back. You'll love it.

Yours truly,

Kalon

P.S.
Thank you for listening last night.

It was no love letter by any means, but it was sweet and gave her all the information she needed to know. Not only were they going into town today, but last night had most certainly *not* been a dream.

CHAPTER 39

INTO TOWN

Lora

Avalon, the village adjacent to Garrison's family estate, was bustling and busy that morning as Kalon and Lora walked through the village center. The streets were filled with vendors and people already celebrating the holiday, their food stands rich with flavorful spices, other vendors calling out their items and their prices.

The whole crew had come with them as well, including Ortega, who had arrived that morning with bread from the Beaviers as a gift. Apparently, she had seen them all there and knew when to arrive. She had also assured Lora, without being asked, that the Beaviers were perfectly fine.

When they arrived in town, Kierra had given Lora a knowing wink before peeling away with Nuva to browse some shops, while Ortega made her way to the dress shop on an errand. Liam and Garrison hung around a bit longer, the former explaining all the different celebrations and their meanings, the latter stuffing his face with anything he could find. Both had vanished within minutes of the group actually reaching the city center, leaving Lora and Kalon alone to wander the winding streets.

The town was small with four major streets leading to the city center, which was decorated with bright oranges and golds. Every corner they had passed had an open cafe or a food stand selling delicious-smelling treats and candies. She had eyed one that was selling apples covered in a brown, sweet smelling sauce Kalon had called caramel, and he insisted they eat one. Despite the stickiness of the caramel, Lora had devoured her candy apple—that's what the vendor had called it—within minutes.

Another stand they passed sold sticks with spun sugar on them. She had spent several minutes simply watching the vendor create his treat, mesmerized by the way the vendor heated the flavored sugars turning it from grains to a cottony substance that dissolved on her tongue.

After eating her fill of cotton candy and candy apples, Lora felt like she should be rolled out of the town square.

Kalon had run inside a small shop to buy a gift for Gamma, and Lora found herself simply enjoying the bustling village. Another delicious smell had Lora's gaze wandering around the small square until she found the source—a small shop next to an older home.

"This smells delicious," she said to the shopkeeper, smiling brightly at him.

He was an older man with eyes a little glossy and a slightly humped back, but his smile was genuine as she spoke to her. "Would you like to try some pralines?"

"Yes please, thank you," she said, taking the small parcel he gave her and tasting the rich and crunchy insides. As she chewed her gaze drifted to the old house behind him. "Is this your home?" she asked, marveling at the intricate designs on the door and windows.

The old man cocked his head slightly before smiling sweetly. "No dear, that house has been under renovation for many years now. Your prince can tell you all about it." He nodded behind her to where Kalon had walked up, hands in his pockets.

"He's not my prince," she said quietly as Kalon approached.

"Oh, but isn't he?" the old man said knowingly.

"Thank you for the pralines," she said as she stepped away from the vendor, his knowing look making her suddenly quite warm in the chill autumn air.

"What can I tell you all about?" Kalon asked, eyeing Lora suspiciously.

Great, he heard everything that old man said. Lora gave him a tight smile before nodding to the old house. "He said you could tell me about this house."

Kalon stiffened slightly. "What do you want to know?"

Lora shrugged. "I don't know…anything? It's cute. I just wanted to know more."

"Hmm." Kalon thought for a moment before he spoke. "It's been under construction for a couple of years now."

"So the man said," she observed, now making her way to the front door. There were intricate carvings all along the door frames of dragons, fields, and mountains. "These look a lot like the carvings on the Beaviers house," she said more to herself.

"Well I'd hope so," Kalon said from behind her, now inspecting the carvings as well, "I did them to match."

Lora whirled to face him, "What do you mean *you* did them?"

***

Kalon

Kalon shrugged, putting his hands back in his pockets, "I carved the ones for the Beaviers, then once I got this place, I wanted to put the carvings here as well." He said it so matter-of-factly, Lora whacked his arm. "Ow! What was that for?"

"You didn't tell me you had a house!" Lora exclaimed, eyes wide in disbelief.

"You didn't ask, princess," he drawled, a sly smile playing on his lips as he watched her cheeks flush.

She whacked him again, this time chuckling softly. Her face contorted into confusion, and he stiffened as he waited for her response. "Can I go inside?"

He loosed the breath he hadn't realized he was holding at her request. "You don't want to know why I have a house in Avalon?" he asked, heart still pounding. Most everyone, including Jade, had mocked him for wanting this little cottage.

They had said it was a waste of time, that he would have several castles and rooms at estates he could stay in. None of them understood. Maybe only Gamma had understood his need for his own space, but even she couldn't fully understand.

Lora cocked her head at him. "I'm assuming because you'd want a place of your own, but it doesn't matter why."

His jaw dropped. She mocked his gaping right back at him, her milk-chocolate eyes pulsing with understanding. "Are you going to let me in, or am I going to have to crawl through a window?"

He snapped out of it, rummaging in his pocket for the key he always kept there. "I bought it with my first year's pay," he explained as he opened the door.

"I didn't realize they paid princes," Lora murmured as she entered the small living room. He took two steps inside, lighting one of the small lanterns that sat on the side table so Lora could see.

"They pay soldiers," he explained, taking her hand and guiding her into the main living area.

"Ah..." Lora hummed, her eyes scanning the small space.

He felt the need to explain more. "My aunt is the queen regent until the war is over. When the crown passed to my family, Ki and I were still kids, and we didn't have any parents. By the time we were old enough to take the throne, Ki was gone, so I abdicated until the war ended. With everything going on... I wanted to be able to help."

His gaze landed on Lora, but there was no resentment or disappointment in her expression, just understanding and a soft, comforting smile. *I see you,* her eyes seemed to say before she lifted her eyebrows, scanning the room again in a silent request.

"When I bought it, there was a really bad leaking problem in the back, but I've almost fixed it," he explained, rustling his hair nervously as Lora slowly made her way through the den.

"Can I get the grand tour?" she asked, looking at him expectantly.

"Do you want the grand tour?" he asked apprehensively.

"Yes." She nodded, and there was no hint of teasing or hesitation. She genuinely wanted to see his house, to hear his thoughts.

"Well then by all means, please follow me," he said as he picked up the lantern and walked through the den. "Off to the side over there is a small study, but it's mostly covered because I'm not done with the roof just yet."

Lora nodded, following his point to the small, shrouded room behind the front door.

He continued, moving into the kitchen. "This is the kitchen—it needed the most work." He explained the different construction and remodeling projects he had done and planned to do, all the while Lora listened attentively, asking questions and offering ideas.

When he finished the tour, Lora took one final look at the cottage and smiled. "This home is well-loved already," she said, and then she was off to buy more pralines and cotton candy, swearing she was already hungry again with a loud laugh that had him smiling deeply.

They walked around the rest of the day in comfortable companionship, something Kalon hadn't realized he had missed. She smiled as he paid for another cotton candy, this time with two flavors swirled together. She begged him to try it, and although he knew the taste, he did anyway, if only to see her smile at him again.

He would buy her any and everything she wanted, he'd give her the world if she asked, so long as she kept smiling and laughing and listening. Because today, in his house with Lora, was the first time he had felt truly heard or seen in a long time.

CHAPTER 40

PRE-FESTIVAL

Kalon

The preparations for the harvest festival were almost done. After going into town, Gamma had requested that the group come together before any activities and help her in the kitchens. Which of course they had, and after about three hours Gamma had shooed them all out after she'd put the last round pastries in the oven, claiming they were officially having too much fun and making too much of a mess to be helpful anymore. Kalon couldn't argue—by the end, there had been flour everywhere and half a batch of cookies on the ceiling from Lora and Garrison's "accidental" food fight.

Kalon smiled to himself as the images of Lora covered in flour, throwing it onto Theo danced in his mind. After kicking them out, Gamma had said something to Lora to make her smile. He had been struck dumb by it. It was a true smile, reaching her eyes and showing a little bit of her teeth. He had wanted to know what Gamma had said but Lora was pulled away by Kierra and Ortega, and reluctantly Nuva, to get ready.

When he tried to argue, Kierra merely reminded him that the pre-harvest festival activities still counted as activities and thus they needed to prepare, before dragging Lora down the hall and slamming the door in his face.

He turned to Theo who merely giggled then ran away, joining Gamma back in the kitchens. Garrison and Liam, who shared a knowing look, proceeded to drag him down to the sparring ring and beat his ass for nearly a half hour, before Gamma came and made them all go get washed up for the bonfire.

Within an hour the three males were clean, dressed and ready, the fires outside already beginning to glow in the afternoon sun. By the time the females re-emerged from their rooms, the sun was gracing the horizon, splashing the sky in vibrant reds and oranges. The small group of girls made their way to the alcoves within the gardens, where the fires were set up and Kalon found himself looking for Lora.

Nuva still wore a version of her uniform from before, but had at least relaxed enough to roll the sleeves. Kierra was in one of her old cream sweaters and a pair of navy breeches she must have stolen from Nuva. Ortega rounded the corner next, and her bright hair was splashed with the shadows the fire cast on the alcove walls.

As if hidden in one of those shadows herself, Lora stood several paces behind the others. The fire cast her bright hair and soft orange tunic in a glow that made it seem it, itself, was made of fire. She was resplendent, and he couldn't even move.

His attention snagged on Kierra, who made her way through the group over to him. She had a look on her face that gave him a feeling she had been watching him as he stared, and so he made a point to look anywhere but Lora as his sister approached.

That did not deter her in the slightest. A smirk spread across her face, and then softened when she followed where his gaze had been. Lora was still standing on the edge of the group, but Garrison and Liam were with her now and she seemed more relaxed.

Kierra's voice snapped his attention back from staring again. "She picked it out herself," she said, now looking toward Lora and the others as they moved to sit around the fire.

"Oh?" he attempted to sound confused but, instead, his words came out soft and slow, more dazed than confused. Kierra eyed him before returning her attention to Lora, who was now sandwiched between Liam and Garrison on a log.

"We were getting dressed and Nuva noticed she was donning her traditional battle black," Kierra continued. "We told her black wasn't allowed at the pre-harvest festival bonfire, so she had to pick something else. She nearly threw up," Kierra was laughing as she said it, but he only stared at her. He was *currently in* all black. He made a point to look down at himself and back up at Kierra who looked at him with another knowing smile.

"What?" She shrugged. "We lied. We were bored with seeing her in black all the time." Kalon felt himself become irrationally angry. They had lied to Lora. She was a guest, his guest—hell, Kierra's guest—and they had made her uncomfortable in making her choose another color. That had to be why it irked him so much to think of Lora nervous and uncomfortable. Why the thought of her unhappy squeezed his chest to the point of pain. Kierra snapped her fingers in his face, drawing his attention, yet again, back to her.

"She chose orange." She said it so matter of factly, but there was a hint of sadness in it, and he remembered their traveling conversations when they were waiting for the others to arrive in the valley.

His anger banked, and a new sort of heat crept through him. "When we were on the road, waiting for the others to join us, I taught her 'a truth for a truth'. We started small and she told me her favorite color was orange. Fire and sunset orange." Just like the sweater she had picked for herself.

Kierra tensed, seeming to see the direction the story was going, but he continued anyway. "I didn't think anything of it, really. We all have favorite colors, but I have never seen her outside of black. It...it caught me off guard."

"She wasn't allowed to wear any other color," Kierra said so quietly, he almost didn't hear her.

He paused, realizing Kierra had gone so still beside him, he wasn't sure she was breathing. He turned then to face his sister, finding her eyes glazed over with tears.

Kierra remained facing the fire, its warm glow making her hair look like moonlight. She seemed to remember something and smiled softly before saying, "In those years I was there, she was my only friend. We weren't allowed much, her especially. She was not given a choice often, and when she was, it was usually a trick. If she didn't choose correctly..." Her voice trailed off as a shiver snaked its way up his spine. He had known it had been bad for his sister, traumatizing to say the least, but he had not let himself consider the horrors Lora had had to face without any friends but his own sister. Once Kierra had left, he wondered if Lora had anyone at all.

"We didn't lie to be mean," Kierra continued, eyes now a little less glazed. "It's just—" She took a shaky breath and turned to her brother, her eyes sparkling with a myriad of emotions. "She has had little chance for choice in her life and I wanted her—I wanted her to pick a color *she* liked, not one she *had* to wear."

He smiled at his sister, that place inside him warming more. "I didn't think you were being mean. I know she means a lot to you. I just hate the idea of her not being..." He was at a loss for words. He wasn't sure what it was he hated about her being, well, anything other than happy. Because, who was he kidding, he cared for her.

That realization shocked him. And by the way Kierra was looking at him, he thought she might have realized it too. He cared about Lora for a long time now, and that scared the shit out of him.

***

Lora

The night progressed as Kalon's friends gathered around the fire, ate sweet treats they'd pilfered from Gamma's stash, and drank sweet apple wine. Kalon had been in a heated debate with one of Garrison's other cousins over the outcome of a sporting event when Nuva and Garrison began singing a bawdy tune.

It was not the type of song she assumed Kierra knew, but soon enough, she and Kalon had joined the fray. Everyone but Lora was singing and swaying as Garrison led another round, this one more absurd than the last. Nuva and Liam danced with Toke and Erik, and soon no one was standing still as they moved freely around the fire. No judgment. No stress. Just friends content on being together, on sharing this night.

Lora listened from her perch on the log, her heart swelling as she watched the friends enjoy their time together. A feeling she could not place swelled inside her and she felt the need—no, the *want*—to laugh and cry. She *wanted* to join in the song. She *wanted* to dance by the fire freely surrounded by people who would not judge. She *wanted* to be included, to be a part of it. And it scared her—that wanting. She had not had anything close to what these people had. At the best of times she had Kierra, but she had never really been hers. She had been a borrowed friend.

Her joy soured as she realized she would never have this. She would never experience what it was to be loved and wanted. Not in the way these people loved and cared for one another. She pulled her eyes from the dancing bodies and studied the flames in front of her. Her shadows danced around her shoulders, comforting her aching heart.

Leaves crunching drew her attention from the flames and there was Kierra, with Nuva close behind. Their faces were red and dotted with sweat from dancing, but their eyes were bright and full of joy. Kierra extended her hand in silent request. Lora froze. Kierra waited two heartbeats before rushing the girl and, pulling her to her feet, thrust her into the dance.

"It's a warm-up for tomorrow," Kierra shouted as she moved and twirled around her. Lora had never danced like this before, but the music had her moving her legs and twirling her arms above her head. It felt strange to be so open with relative strangers, but it also felt good. And they weren't truly strangers, not really. She spun and twirled and on the next round of the song, she joined in on the singing.

The back of her neck tingled, and she knew Kalon was close by. Even over the smell of smoke from the fire, she could smell his ember and citrus scent curling around her. She was passed from Kierra to Nuva and then to Garrison, who merely beamed at her before twirling her into strong hands. Her eyes fluttered open to meet those of amber flecked with gold.

Beautiful. She nearly said it aloud, but Kalon held her hands as he spun and moved her to the next dancer who continued twirling her until she was back to Kierra.

The song finally ended, and she found herself rolling up her sleeves to cool off. Kierra and Nuva had plopped down and were whispering. Toke called for another song, and this time Kierra looked straight at Lora as she volunteered...*her?* Lora's face lost all color.

"Lora and I know a tune," said Kierra, now striding her direction, Nuva again close behind.

All attention turned to her as Kierra whispered to Erik and another one of Garrison's cousins who had instruments.

"What are you doing?" she whispered to Kierra as she came back her way.

"Singing, duh," she said, sounding exasperated for having to explain it.

"But I don't know any songs!" Lora protested quietly, her voice no louder than a whisper.

"Sure you do," Kierra corrected her. "We both know that one about the three kings. *You* taught it to *me*."

Lora blanched. It was one of the only songs from the Shadowlands she knew, and she was confident this crowd wasn't going to like it. "Are you sure that is the best thing to sing here?" she asked, gesturing to the group.

Kierra beamed at her, and her smile became wicked, "Well seeing as it's actually a Drake folklore song, I think it'll be just fine."

Lora didn't have time to process that or reconsider as the music began and Kierra and Nuva started humming the opening lines.

Lora took a deep breath, scanning the small group. She could do this. She'd faced worse. Another breath, and then she opened her mouth and sang.

The song poured out of her and in its place her heart warmed, her soul knitting itself back together. She sang the story of the three brothers, their fates, and their destinies, and then the song ended and another began, one she didn't know but caught onto quickly, linking her arms with Kierra as the bawdy tune rang on.

And she smiled then, a true smile, that had her chest warming. *Happiness*—that was what she was feeling. Happiness and a sense of belonging.

Home, a little voice whispered to her, and this time, she didn't bat it away.

***

Kalon

Lora had woven a story as she and Kierra sang and danced around the fire, and then she'd joined in on the next song. He had thought little else could astonish him after hearing her sing, but then she had smiled and his heart had stopped. It was a true smile, one that reached her eyes and made them sparkle. Then Kierra had said something to her and Lora let out a sound he had never heard before—a laugh. She was breathtaking.

Garrison came over and made her laugh again, and it sounded like a symphony to his ears. She smiled up at Garrison and that smile, it undid him. It was like a fine wine and all he could think about, all he could focus on, was making her smile again. He wanted to drink it in, wanted to get drunk on her laugh and the sparkle of her eyes. He felt her smile in his heart, his very soul, as an intrinsic part of him he thought long lost settled into place.

And in that moment he knew, as she stood around the fire laughing and smiling with his friends, embers dancing around her, that he would do any and everything for that smile—for her.

For as surely as it undid him, her smile was his salvation. An ocean that he so desperately wanted to drown in. He was made, he knew, for that smile, and his whole being seemed to vibrate with the need to be near her, protect her, protect that smile.

His, his heart seemed to sing. *She was his.*

CHAPTER 41

HARVEST FESTIVAL

Lora

Lora had seen the way Kalon had looked at her. His eyes had sparkled like gold, the little flecks of black all but swallowed by their shine. She had felt an odd pulling in her chest, so intrinsic, like the need to eat or sleep.

Kierra had grabbed her a heartbeat later, declaring that it was a girls night and that they would see the boys in the morning. Nuva and Ortega were already at the base of the staircase that lead back to the house.

She had hoped to get to dance with Kalon one last time, but the songs had ended as quickly as they had started and Kierra was pulling her one way, Garrison pulling Kalon the other. Apparently, the night before harvest festival, they went to sleep rather early in order to be ready for the festivities the next day.

Kierra had explained all of that on their walk back up to the rooms. She also explained that the boys liked to go and play with the fires and sleep outside while she, Nuva and Ortega would come back inside to get actual rest.

"That's why we always look better than them in the mornings," Kierra claimed, throwing herself onto the bed in her room. The bed was a massive four poster with curtains draped all around it. The room itself was lit up in every color imaginable. Bright pink flowers decorated the deep green walls, and a bright yellow rug spanned most of the wooden floors. It was an overwhelming amount of color, but not displeasing.

Ortega, who was now lounging on a sofa by the fire, was already in her sleeping gown, the thick creamy fabric flowing to her shins.

Nuva tossed Lora a pile of her clothes and Lora donned them swiftly. Apparently they were all to sleep in the same room, "per tradition".

And even if she didn't fully believe it was their tradition, there were two extra beds in Kierra's spacious room, one for her and one for Ortega.

"What will tomorrow be like?" Lora asked, crawling into her bed while Kierra braided Ortega's hair. Kalon had tried to explain what the festival was for—some sleeping god of plants—but she had never experienced a festival before.

"Well, there is still a lot to get done," Nuva explained, coming from behind the changing shade. "We'll need to help set up the greenhouse and light the next bonfires."

"Do they not stay lit all night?" she asked, looking between the friends.

"Not if those boys have anything to do with it," Ortega chortled, now snuggling under her blankets.

"So who lights the fires?" she asked absentmindedly.

Kierra smiled sweetly. "We do, of course! It's all good fun!"

"And way better than being in the hot kitchen all day," Nuva added, earning her a chuckle from Ortega and a sharp look from Kierra. "Not that I don't love watching your cookies burn," she added with a wink to Kierra, who, now standing near her bed, threw a pillow at her.

Both girls ended up laughing as several more pillows were thrown across the room, and after several minutes, it turned into all-out warfare. Ortega had tipped over her own mattress as a means to protect herself, while Nuva was on the offensive, throwing an astonishing amount of little pillows and pairs of socks from over by Kierra's armoire.

Lora and Kierra had ducked behind the couch, both laughing as another volley of pillows and clothing rained over them.

"How many pairs of socks do you have?" Lora asked over the muffled sounds of pillows bouncing off every surface in the room.

Kierra rolled her eyes. *So like Kalon.* "Let's just hope she doesn't get into—"

"Are these undergarments?" Gamma's velvety voice sounded from over by the door. The girls shot up from their hiding spots, all of their cheeks deepening to a rich crimson.

"Sorry Gamma," Kierra chirped, clambering over the messy room to her grandmother's side and taking the lacy underclothes from her.

"We were just getting ready for bed, ma'am," came Nuva's voice from still behind the armoire.

"I can see that," Gamma said, glancing knowingly around the room. Even Ortega had the right idea in looking innocently away.

"Perhaps you could get ready for a bed a bit quieter," she added, pinning a knowing look at Kierra. "Layla has the unfortunate luck to sleep below this room, and it would be unfair to keep her awake, would it not?"

"Of course Gamma," Kierra assured her, nodding eagerly toward the woman.

Gamma patted Kierra's cheek twice before winking over at Lora. "I'll see you girls at the festival," she said as she turned to leave.

"Goodnight, Gamma!" The girls all chirped, a deep breath rushing out of Nuva as she pulled herself from behind the armoire.

"At least she warned us before we actually did wake up Layla," Nuva said as she crawled into the big bed.

"Indeed," agreed Ortega as she righted her mattress and she, too, crawled under the covers.

"I don't even know the woman and she scares me," Lora admitted, now helping Kierra to lift the final mattress from the floor.

"And for good reason too," Kierra said, smiling at Lora. "Let's just hope we didn't wake her," she added, making her way to the bed with Nuva.

"Fingers crossed, ladies!" chimed Ortega from her bed.

***

Apparently they should have crossed more than their fingers, because right after sunrise, Layla was at their door demanding all four girls start building the fires. Helping with the fires had been cool for the first three, but after the twenty second, even Kierra and Nuva seemed to be lagging.

Apparently in previous years it had been way easier, but something this year was making it harder—or at least, that's what Nuva had grumbled after fire number nine. Luckily for them, the boys did manage to come back from whatever errand they had run and offered to take over.

Kierra hadn't wasted a moment before she was pulling Lora back into their room and started teaching her the dances for that night. She and Nuva took turns between showing Lora the steps and guiding her through them. To her surprise, Nuva was an incredible dancer—though they were both awful teachers.

After about an hour there was a knock at the door that Kierra told her meant it was time to get ready. Lora went back to her room for a bath, per Kierra's instructions, but her friend made it clear that she, Nuva, and Ortega would be in her room to get ready in fifteen minutes. She had rushed off to bathe then, the excitement for tonight prickling and dancing on her skin. When Kierra burst into her room exactly fifteen minutes later, her mood soured. Both she and Nuva began getting ready, donning makeup and special clothes. Ortega was somehow already dressed and was helping Kierra. Lora just stood there awkwardly as the flurry of activity passed her by.

"Why aren't you getting ready?" Kierra asked, brushing through her still-damp hair before beginning to plait it.

"I am ready," she said with a shrug, looking down at her clothes she had worn into town the day before.

Kierra had stopped her primping and was staring at Lora in the mirror. "You can't be serious, bean," she exclaimed, making a point to widen her eyes in exasperation.

"I think she looks nice," chimed Nuva from behind the changing curtain.

Kierra narrowed her eyes in the commander's direction. "First of all, you can't even see her," she snapped playfully. "And second, you wouldn't know nice if it hit you in the face!"

"That's because," Nuva said, coming around the corner in a sharp dress uniform, "I would have caught it, of course." She planted a kiss on Kierra's cheek, and Kierra batted her away. Nuva only smiled and took over braiding the rest of her hair while Kierra applied rogue to her cheeks and lips. How Nuva knew how to braid was beyond Lora, seeing as the Shade's head was closely cropped.

"I'm serious," Kierra said again, now turning to look at Lora. "Go put the dress on."

"Ki, I don't have a dress to put on!" she all but shouted, feeling annoyed for having to explain that to her friend.

Ortega simply winked at her—if it was possible for someone without eyes to wink.

Kierra's eyes widened in the mirror before a smile spread across her face. She whirled to face Lora again, biting her lip with apprehensive excitement. Her braid was ripped from Nuva, who looked exasperated. She shrieked, waving her hands in the air as she wiggled in her seat.

"What is happening here?" Lora asked Nuva who was also smiling, albeit far less aggressively. Even Ortega looked less innocent than normal.

Kierra took a steadying breath and schooled her features into a sly smirk, though her eyes were still alight with amusement. Nuva rolled her eyes but finished braiding the rest of Kierra's hair.

"Kierra?" Lora asked, coming to stand next to the vanity where Kierra had taken the finished braid and was now putting it around her head like a wreath. Kierra's gaze darted between the girls in the room and then back to Lora's in the mirror.

"Ki, do you know something I don't?" Lora asked as if she were addressing a small child.

Kierra made a face in the mirror as if to say *maybe*, then subtly mentioned, "Perhaps, dear princess, you should check your wardrobe." She closed her eyes and lined them with dark liquid and Lora all but ran into her room, ripping the door to the wardrobe nearly off the hinges. What lay inside was a nicely wrapped box, with a notecard sticking from the top. Lora made quick work of opening the note, smiling softly when she read the inscription, written in familiar handwriting—

For not thinking my cottage was a waste of time. At least now you'll look like a princess.

"Why do you think Kalon went into town yesterday?" Kierra cheered, clapping her hands in front of her with glee as she looked at the box in Lora's hands. "Isn't it lovely?"

Lora's mouth was still hanging open as she pulled out the gown Kalon had bought for her from its box. She had never seen anything so beautiful in her entire life.

"Go put it on!" Kierra demanded enthusiastically, now putting earrings in to complete her look. Of course, she already looked stunning.

Lora nodded and quickly went behind the screen, stripping off her clothes from the day. The dress was lightweight, but not too breezy. It had a black underlayer with a pale orange tulle overlaid with flashes of gold and red, as if she was a living, breathing ember. It had one shoulder covered in a gauzy red fabric, the other shoulder open to the world. The bodice was form-fitting but left room for maximum mobility, and while it went to the floor, there were slits on either side, allowing her full range of motion. She couldn't have picked out a more perfect dress if she had tried.

"Hurry up!" Kierra called, clearly still excited.

Lora smiled again as she came around the corner and Kierra gasped, nearly falling out of her chair. Even Nuva gave her a nod of approval.

"Holy shit, I might rip it off of you!" Kierra bellowed enthusiastically. "You look incredible, Lora!"

And despite herself, Lora felt it. "What are you going to do with your hair?" Kierra asked, guiding Lora to the vanity. She looked between Kierra and Nuva nervously. She'd been contemplating it for a couple weeks now, but hadn't found the right time.

Ortega beamed at her in the mirror, as if she already knew her idea and approved.

"I have an idea," Lora said, looking between the females, her gaze landing on Nuva's. "But I need your help."

***

Kalon

"What are we doing down here?" Garrison asked, pulling at the neck of his fine shirt. Kalon and all the males in the military were outfitted in dress uniforms or black-tie finery. Since it was Garrison's home, he was stuck wearing black tie.

"Waiting for the girls," Kalon responded, barely paying attention to his two comrades as they adjusted their clothing next to him.

"But we never wait for the girls," Liam observed, now helping Garrison adjust his tie. He and Kalon were in the same military dress uniforms, though Liam's was medic maroon and Kalon's was commander burgundy—not that they looked *that* different.

"That's not true, we sometimes wait for the girls," he said over his shoulder, his eyes still glued to the top of the stairwell. "And they are usually waiting for us," he added, after Garrison and Liam both let loose a dramatic sigh.

"Are we waiting for the girls? Or *the* girl?" Garrison asked, his eyes sparkling with amusement.

Kalon shot him a sideways glance the same time the doors at the top of the stairs swung open. He whipped his head too quickly to be casual, and Garrison chuckled as Gamma made her way down the stairs, accompanied by Ortega. It took all of his willpower not to look disappointed.

"Good evening boys. My, don't you all look strapping. But what are you doing here in the corridor? Did you not hear? They are hosting the festival in the greenhouse this year." Gamma's eyes sparkled with amusement as she surveyed the males at the foot of the stairs.

"Gamma, don't you look marvelous," Kalon exclaimed, offering her his hand as she descended the last several steps. The older woman was draped in a rich purple, making her white hair stand out even more. The dress seemed to wrap around her several times before cascading to the floor to pool on the ground around her feet.

"Ortega, you as well," he said quickly, now taking the seer's hand as well and bringing her beside Gamma. She had opted for a pale-yellow dress robe with a loose tie around the waist. Her hair had been braided neatly and, probably thanks to Kierra, a bit of rogue was on her cheeks.

"Kalon's making us wait for the girls," Garrison chimed in as he kissed the elder woman on the cheek, and then Ortega.

"Well isn't that polite," Ortega chirped, wrinkling her nose in Kalon's direction. "You must have learned some manners since the last time I saw you," Gamma chortled, making her way past the males and into the grand hall, winking at him as she passed. Ortega, trailing beside her, merely patted his arm, giving him a knowing smile.

The doors to the upper level opened again and his attention whipped its direction, only to collide with his sister.

"Don't look so disappointed brother," she said by way of greeting, making her way down the stairs to Garrison's outstretched arm.

Kalon recovered quickly. "Disappointed by you? Never." He gave her a quick kiss on the cheek before making a point to not look up at the stairs. "You look incredible, as per usual," he said, smiling now as his sister twirled a bit in her dress. Kierra had always dressed well, finding and wearing colors and styles that fit with her bright hair and strong body perfectly. And tonight was no different. Her gown was a deep red, like Liam's uniform, that hugged her until the waist before cascading down into ribbons.

Kierra gave him a tight smile as she pretended to adjust his tie, leaning in to whisper, "She's coming in a minute, Nuva is helping with her hair."

"Nuva?" he asked, confusion wrinkling his features.

But Kierra only winked as the doors to the upper level opened again and the air was sucked from his lungs.

At the top of the stairs stood Nuva in her traditional dress uniform. But behind her, peeking through like the sun on a cloudy day, was Lora. She was in the dress he'd bought her, which fit her like a glove, and had makeup on her face—courtesy of Kierra, no doubt. But his attention snagged on her hair. Her beautiful wine-red hair that was now cut to her shoulders.

By the time she had made it down the stairs he realized he'd been staring and cleared his throat. "You clean up good, princess," he observed, trying to calm his beating heart.

"You don't look half bad yourself, prince," Lora smiled, inclining her head to him in a small bow.

Liam took her hand and kissed it while Garrison tugged on one of the short curls, giving her a wink before making his way to the door with the others. Nuva rolled her eyes as she passed them, making her way to Kierra's side and kissing her on the cheek. He couldn't help himself as he began to stare again.

"I, uh—" She stammered nervously, pulling at her loosely curled hair.

"You cut your hair," he finished for her, tucking one of the curls behind her ear.

"Nuva did, actually," she corrected, looking up at him, her eyes sparkling with an emotion he couldn't quite place.

"I love it," he said quietly, his eyes meeting hers.

"You do?" Her brows pinched a bit before she shook her head, causing her hair to twirl around her. "Not that I care what you think," she added quickly, a small smile working its way across her face.

"Of course not," he said, smiling in earnest now. "Do *you* like it?" He tracked every movement she took.

"I do." She smiled up at him.

"Then that's all that really matters." He smiled back and his heart ached at the sight of her.

She beamed, and he thought his heart might explode. "Thank you for the dress," she noted, looking down at the gown.

"Well, the only other time I've seen you in nice clothes, Nuva picked them out... So I figured it was time you got to *feel* like a princess," he said with a soft smile.

"So your note said," she replied, smiling up at him again. They looked at each other nervously for a moment before he worked up the nerve to extend his arm.

"Shall we?" he asked.

She looked at him in a way that had his heart squeezing before nodding slightly. Holding her head high, she took his arm, looping hers through his. "We shall."

***

The party was exactly how Kalon had remembered it being. The large greenhouse at the back of the Damaris estate had been decorated in autumn colors, the plants mostly moved to create a space for dancing. Tables lined the walls and plant covered alcoves, and food and drinks were scattered along different surfaces throughout the wide room.

The musicians started off with slower songs for the older people to enjoy then they would eventually speed the music up, calling out dances that were more complicated and fun. He had watched as Garrison's parents led the first several dances, Garrison stepping in to dance with his mother halfway through.

Kalon circled the room in a faster waltz with Gamma, though his attention was scanning the alcoves during each turn.

"If you want to dance with her that badly, child, just go ask her," Gamma's voice was full of mischief as she twirled to the rhythm of the song.

He drew his attention back to his grandmother. "There is no other dance partner I would rather have," he said sweetly, making sure to keep his focus on the steps as they twirled again around the room.

His grandmother harrumphed, and he realized his gaze had wandered again.

As the song ended and another started, Gamma dropped his hands. "I think I need a refreshment, perhaps you could get one for me child?" she asked, fanning herself slightly.

He whipped his attention back to his grandmother, worry bracketing his face. "Of course, yes." And then he was off, moving across the room toward the refreshment table.

A flash of red and pale orange drew his attention and his gaze found Lora, who was standing next to one of Garrison's cousins, both looking extremely uncomfortable.

"Erik," he called out, turning their direction. "I think your brother was looking for you over by the musicians," he explained, nodding toward where the music emanated from.

Erik nodded his thanks as he walked away, leaving an open spot next to Lora.

"Thank you," she whispered, smiling and taking a sip of her wine.

"Anytime," he replied, picking up a tart and taking a bite. "So, no dancing?" he asked between chews.

"I haven't exactly been asked," Lora drawled, smiling over her cup and glancing sidelong at him.

He swallowed his tart quickly, discarding the rest on a tray. He wiped his hands loosely on his trousers as he turned to Lora. "Well, we must remedy that." He opened his hand to her. "May I—"

Kierra suddenly took his hand, grabbing Lora, too, as the next song, a faster tune, required groups of six to dance together. Liam and Nuva had paired off, leaving Garrison to grab hold of Lora's hand and Kierra to grab his.

"This is one of my favorite dances!" Kiera shouted to Lora over the buzz of music and festivities. And then they were off, twirling and rotating, holding hands and moving in circles. The dance was a series of partner and group moves, repeated while the whole room moved counterclockwise.

Kalon twirled Kierra, moving in time with the music, but his gaze never left Lora, who, after the first turn, was smiling brightly in Garrison's grasp.

At the end of the song he immediately stepped toward Lora, but the next song started and she and Garrison were off in a twirling jig. From then on she was passed between his friends, even dancing once with Gamma and Mr. Damaris.

With each pass her smile grew and his heart warmed. As a particularly rowdy song ended he looked for Lora, whom he'd only lost sight of as he'd spun Nuva, but she was nowhere to be seen. The crowd dispersed and came back together for the next dance, but still no Lora. There was a flash of red to his right and Kalon smiled as he made his way onto the terrace.

CHAPTER 42

A DANCE

Lora

"Having too much fun in there?" Kalon asked by way of greeting, striding onto the terrace where Lora was perched, overlooking the gardens below.

"I just needed a moment to breathe," Lora admitted, straightening as he approached. He had discarded his jacket when the dancing began, and his shirt sleeves were rolled up to his elbows, revealing his muscular arms, and his hands in his pockets in a casual stance. A burst of desire panged through her, and she almost reached up to smooth out his shirt. *Almost.*

"It can be a little overwhelming," Kalon agreed, coming to lean on the ledge of the terrace balcony next to her.

"We don't have anything like this in Attica," she said, distracting herself so she didn't reach over and touch him.

What is going on with her? "Not that I participated in shit anyways," she added, leaning next to him despite herself.

"My mom used to tell Ki and me about a time when our holidays, the Drakes and the Shades, were very similar." He looked out over the gardens, his smile bracketed with sadness at the mention of his mother.

"Really?" she asked, looking for anything to chase away those shadows in his amber eyes.

"Yeah," he said with a deep breath, his attention coming back to her and settling on her eyes. "After all, we both worship the same sleeping gods," he added, a smile now playing on his lips.

She let out a small chuckle. "That's true. I guess I just can't imagine this kind of party in the Shadowlands," she admitted.

"They weren't big party throwers?" Kalon asked, the question sarcastic but laced with a hint of genuine curiosity.

"Not in Attica." Her mood soured at the thought. "And I wouldn't know about anywhere else," she added before he could ask.

"I see. So, you are overwhelmed?" There was no hint of amusement or condescension in his tone, only genuine concern.

She looked up at him, a flurry of emotions swelling in her stomach. "I guess you could say that. It's fun, don't get me wrong, more fun than I've really ever had, but I'm still a little worried I'll mess up a dance or step on someone's toes," she said with a chuckle, looking over her shoulder toward the party still raging inside, revelers' laughs reaching them all the way outside. "I'm much better at fighting than twirling," she added, a smirk now playing on her lips. "As you know."

Kalon broke out into a smile accompanied by a soft chuckle. "I'd say you do a lot of twirling whilst you fight, princess," he said with a wink, facing her fully. "And dancing is no different."

"I know," she admitted. "Kierra walked me through all the dances earlier so that no one lost their toes if they asked me to dance, but—"

Kalon stepped toward her, his hand outstretched.

"What are you doing?"

"Risking my toes apparently," he said with a smile, inching a step closer to her, hand still outstretched.

"You want to dance out here?" she asked, looking around. *With me?*

Yes princess, with you, his eyes seemed to say, the words filling her head as if he'd said them aloud. "Kierra isn't the best teacher, and if you're as terrible as you say you are, you need a proper lesson. Lucky for you, I am an excellent teacher. And I have an extra toe, so nothing to fear," he said, grabbing her hand and pulling her in close.

"Really?" she asked, shocked, looking down at Kalon's feet.

"No. But it sounded good," he said with a smile. "And," he added, his smile turning into a smirk, "you were temporarily intrigued by me."

"Ha," she let out a soft laugh. "I guess so... in a weird way of course," she joked. "What will we dance to?" The music inside was loud, but it couldn't really be heard from on the terrace.

"Whatever we want." Kalon looked at her in earnest now, and somehow, she had migrated so close to him that they shared breath.

She took a breath that went nowhere. "Can I be honest?" she asked, heat creeping into her cheeks.

"Always," Kalon answered, his gaze never leaving hers, the fire in his eyes she had seen the night before seeming to rekindle.

Heat spread in her core and she made to move away, but Kalon closed the space between them, taking the air out of her lungs. "Fighting with you is far less daunting than this," she admitted, making a point to hold up their joined hands. He squeezed her hand once, and the breath she didn't know she'd been holding gushed out of her.

"So let's fight then," he said, his smile broadening as her face set into a look of confusion.

"While holding hands?" She made a point to wiggle their joined hands in the air in front of him.

"That's basically what dancing is. Here I'll show you. Do you trust me?" he asked, his grip tightening gently as another smile played on his lips.

"Enough I suppose," she retorted, parroting what they had said to each other many times before. Meeting his amber gaze, the heat in her core seemed to spread as their eyes locked.

"Enough will do," Kalon all but whispered, his smile spreading, and then they were moving.

The dance had been quick at first, a series of twirls and steps that she caught onto surprisingly fast. Kalon was right, Kierra had been a shit teacher. With him leading the way she had learned the basic steps within minutes of practicing, and she managed to step on his toes only twice within the whole first sequence.

Kalon shifted then, pulling her in tight after an exciting series of twirls. She laughed in earnest as he spun himself, twirling around her like a professional dancer before returning his hand to hers. He spun her once more, his eyes nearly glowing gold by the time she returned to him. The music inside slowed, and so too did their steps.

"This place isn't what I expected," she admitted, looking around as Kalon spun her slowly in time with the music. "At all," she added, looking over the grounds to where revelers danced and couples snuck into bushes down in the gardens below.

"What were you expecting?" he asked, pulling her in from her twirl and holding her so close to his body she could feel his heart beating. It echoed her own.

She looked out again over the garden, the warmth she had felt before cooling. "It doesn't matter," she said, pulling away.

After a second, Kalon let her go, his hands falling slack beside him. "Are you mad?" he asked, concern lacing his words as he watched her make her way back to the terrace balcony.

"Mad? No. Surprised? Maybe. A not-so-small piece of me is glad you aren't all bloodthirsty, warmongering, cave people," she admitted, returning to her leaned position on the balcony edge.

"Only a small part?" Kalon inquired, his eyebrows raising as he joined her, his muscles flexing as he too leaned on the balcony.

A smile worked its way onto her face "At least if you were, it would make everything I've done feel less awful. Like we could all be monsters together." The admission caught her by surprise. She stiffened as she realized what she had said, what she had basically admitted to.

Kalon didn't recoil from her. There was no fear or anguish in his eyes, only shining...hope? *What is he hopeful for?*

You're not a monster, his eyes seemed to say, dancing with that fire from before. She looked away, heat creeping back into her cheeks.

He cleared his throat. "You know," he said, turning his gaze toward the gardens below, "Garrison and I used to basically run this place."

"So you've told me," she said halfheartedly, thankful for the change in topic.

"Oh so now you listen?" he teased. "Well if you remember correctly, we used to run wild in the woods and then we'd sneak into Gamma's kitchen and steal about a dozen cookies and come out here and hide in Mr. Damaris's garden maze." He beamed at the memory, and his renewed happiness sent a wave of warmth through her.

"Mr. Damaris's garden maze?" she asked, turning to lean her back on the banister so she could see him better.

"Oh yeah," Kalon said, joy lacing every word. "Garrison's dad is mad into flowers—any you see around their house, and especially out here, are all tended to by him. Honestly, he'd live out here if he could."

Lora could feel the happiness the memories brought in every word.

"It is lovely," she agreed, "but what's a garden maze?"

Kalon's eyes sparkled even more with amusement. "You see those hedges down there, how they weave and interlock in places?" He pointed over toward the right side of the gardens.

She nodded. "Yeah?"

"Well, there is a path in between them."

"No way." She squinted her eyes toward the hedges. They were huge, but a path *within* them, she'd never heard of such a thing.

"Yes way," he teased. "The path is small and twists and turns a bunch, but it's there. When we were kids, we used to race to see who could finish the maze faster. I always won." He beamed with confidence and bravado.

Lora's eyebrows shot up in disbelief.

"Okay fine, Garrison won sometimes but don't tell him I admitted that, I'll swear I didn't and call you a liar." His smile was genuine and broad, and Lora could help but laugh in earnest now, Kalon's eyes seeming to hone in on her smile.

"Beautiful," he muttered under his breath.

"What?" She cocked her head, wondering if she'd heard him right.

"The maze," he said, clearing his throat, "is beautiful. Especially in the daylight."

"I can imagine," Lora conceded, a strange sense of disappointment filling her. "I bet in the dark it's impossible to see anything in there," she added, trying to shake away the misplaced feeling. *What is going on with me tonight?*

***

Kalon

"You know," Kalon said, trying to bring that beautiful smile back to Lora's face. "During parties, couples use it to sneak off since they couldn't be seen and then—*you know*." He raised his eyebrows up and down quickly, and then winked. "Before they got caught."

Lora tilted her head, an eyebrow raising in question. "I actually don't know...but based on, whatever the hell that was, I can make an assumption."

He laughed, nudging her lightly in the side for the jab. She rocked sideways with the force, laughing slightly, and then rocked back into him, her body resting on his. She didn't pull away. He swallowed, and his heart pounded in his ears.

"Did you ever—" Lora started.

"Oh, loads of times," he cut her off, clenching and unclenching his fists.

"I see." Her smile fell a bit.

He blinked at her before explaining, "Garrison and I made a game out of that, too."

"Oh..." Disappointment radiated from her as she pulled away from him, righting herself as she settled back onto her elbows. Her body felt freezing, despite the warm fall breeze.

He scrambled for something to say to bring her back to him, to chase away the shadows dancing in her eyes. "One time," he stammered, "we caught so many that Gamma had us cleaning dishes for a week as punishment." He chuckled, but she remained stoic, stiffening more somehow. *Play with me*, he pleaded to her mind. *Just look at me, please.*

"Caught?" She sounded angry and confused all at the same time.

"Yeah, we used to sneak into the maze during parties and douse couples with buckets of water. It was a hoot. Garrison always won that one, though, but only because he could lift heavier buckets than I could." He was word vomiting now, saying any and everything to get her to look at him. Apparently something in his monologue had gotten her attention, because she whipped her head back to him, mouth slightly open. She definitely looked pissed.

"What?" *Oh shit, what did I say?* She whacked him on the arm. "Ow! What was that for?"

"I thought you meant..." She trailed off, looking back over the edge toward the darkened maze. *Are her cheeks a bit redder than before?*

"What did you think I meant?" he asked, a smirk spreading across his features.

Her eyes widened as she nodded toward the maze again.

Oh yeah, her cheeks are definitely red. That's when it hit him... "You thought I meant *people*? That I took a bunch of *people* into the maze?" He let out a laugh that made his stomach cramp. Lora's face was reddening, either from embarrassment or anger, which made him laugh harder.

"How am I supposed to know what you meant! You seem to have had several lovers. It wouldn't surprise me..." She trailed off as he laughed even harder, earning him another whack on the arm and a serious look.

He finally stopped laughing, rubbing at his arm. "It may not *surprise* you, princess, but it *would* make you jealous," he purred, watching her cheeks somehow deepen in shade.

"What? No it wouldn't," she protested, a bit too quickly.

"Yes it would, princess. That's why your cheeks are so red," he pointed out, loving every minute of this conversation.

"They are not!" she said, rubbing at her cheeks in indignation.

"Oh yes they are. Redder than your beautiful hair." He moved a strand of hair that had blown across her face. *I love this hair. Even cut, it's somehow more stunning.*

She froze under his gentle touch, glancing up at him. "That's the second time you've said that."

"Said what?" he asked, mildly confused. He was barely listening, watching a strand of hair dance in the soft breeze. It was mesmerizing.

"That my hair is beautiful." She faced him fully, her eyes swimming with an emotion he couldn't quite place.

"It's actually the third," he corrected.

"What?" It was her turn to look confused.

"I mean, I told Ki weeks ago I liked your hair," he explained, feeling heat creeping into his own cheeks.

"Really?" she asked, clearly not believing him.

"Really," he admitted, eyes settling on hers. Her eyes never failed to captivate him. They were a soft brown, like coffee with creamer. He was lost in them.

"Hmm," she murmured sadly, shadows filling her eyes.

"Why does that surprise you?" he asked, searching her eyes for understanding but only finding tense discomfort.

"It's just, my hair has always been a point of contention for my—for the Shades." She let loose a shuddering breath and rubbed at her wrists. Kalon tracked the movement.

"Is that why you cut it?" The pain in her face was threatening to send him to his knees.

Lora sighed through her nose. "I just wanted…" Her words trailed off as her gaze fell onto her hands, the smell of salt mixed with her jasmine scent.

"Hey." He gently took her chin between his fingers. "I understand."

He did understand, in a way. It's why he had gotten the cottage in Avalon. She needed to do something for herself, to take away the bad that had been associated with her hair for so long and do something *she* wanted. He could completely relate. She wouldn't look at him, but he could see some silver lining her eyes. He tucked another stand behind her ear, marveling at the silky curl.

Another pause, then Lora looked up at him, a small, hesitant smile on her lips. She cleared her throat before saying under her breath, "I am jealous, by the way."

That snatched his attention back, causing him to lower his hand. "I knew it," he said jokingly, though he was sure his heart was beating out of his chest. *How can she not hear how loud it is?*

"But not of people going into the maze with you," she amended with a smirk.

"No?" he said coyly, trying to sound unbothered by her admission. *Is that true?* He held his breath, disappointment lingering in his stomach where butterflies had just been.

"Nope," she said casually, again turning to where she was leaning on the banister next to him. "I'm jealous that you had a fun childhood." The admission seemed to shock her as much as him because she frowned, her gaze lingering on her wrists where he knew scars from canthite chains would always be.

The air was sucked from his lungs in an instant. He felt like he'd just received a blow to his gut. *Oh.* "Well I can tell you some stories that weren't so fun if that would help…" He was scrambling again, he had to find a way to take the frown off her face, to bring back that smile, that laugh that made him dizzy.

"I'm also jealous that I never got to race you through the maze," she confessed, a small smile playing on her lips. "I'm sure I would have won," she added, now looking up at him, amusement chasing away the last of the shadows in her eyes.

He let out the breath he hadn't realized he was holding. "Oh ho! Someone feels very confident in their abilities, must I remind you of our first challenge where I won…" He trailed off as she whacked his arm again.

"You mean where I let you win," she smirked then winked, but the smirk faded as he dodged her blow, and began striding away. "Wait, where are you going?" she called after him, straightening from her leaned position to track his movements toward the stairs.

"To the maze," he called over his shoulder. "Unless you are all talk?"

"Oh I'm more than just talk," she objected, and he could hear her footsteps racing to catch up with him.

They ran down the grand stairs together, jumping onto the soft grass below.

"Come on, I know the entrance—" He took her hand and pulled her toward the maze.

Lora didn't budge. "Um...cheating much?" she said, eyebrows lifted so high they almost disappeared into her hairline.

"Me? Cheating? You wound me, princess," he exclaimed, making a dramatic movement like she'd wounded him gravely. She rolled her eyes, but a small smile spread across her face. "No cheating. I only know the entrance, not the exit, I promise." He flicked her on the nose and she batted his hand away. "Try your best not to be too disappointed when you lose," he added, taking her hand again and walking them toward the entrance.

"Seeing as you're used to it, at least it won't be a new sensation for you," she retorted, and he could feel the smile in her words. He let out a low sigh of relief and jabbed her with his elbow at the dig.

"Ready?" he asked, eyeing her sideways.

"Born ready," she replied, hunkering down into a starting position.

Another smile bloomed on his face as he, too, dug his heels into the sodden earth. "On your mark," he took a deep breath. "Get set." He glanced at her but she was all eyes ahead, focus centered on the maze in front of her.

"Go!" she shouted, launching herself into the dark maze, her dress streaming behind her as her legs broke through the slits.

A heartbeat later he took off after her, dodging the lower hanging branches and passing pathways he was pretty sure were dead ends. He had flown over the maze earlier and had seen the pattern - not that he had cheated or anything, but he at least knew the general direction. And by the sound of panting, Lora could sense the dead ends too.

He hurtled past a path, seeing her bright hair flash in the moonlight. He took a sharp turn, meaning to cut her off, but instead slammed headfirst into the hedge. Her laughter rang out—she'd led him that way on purpose.

Kalon shook off the leaves as he began running again. He couldn't hear her, but he followed her scent as he rounded corners. At full speed, they were both laughing as they crashed into each other. His head spun as he rose to his feet, putting out a hand to help Lora up. Her dress had opened where the slits were and his attention snagged on the tan, strong leg that was now fully visible.

"You did that on purpose," she said, ignoring his hand and clambering to her feet next to him.

"Oh, like you leading me into that bush?" he said accusingly, dusting himself off.

She cut her eyes at him as she, too, removed leaves caught in her hair and gown. She looked back up at him, and taking two small steps, was now very close to his face. He wasn't sure why but he held his breath as she stood on her tiptoes and, reaching up to his face, gently pulled a small twig out of his hair.

She smiled, and in the moonlight he saw a bit of a blush grace her cheeks—*or maybe she's just winded*, he told himself.

He opened his mouth to say—well, he wasn't sure what—but the sound of footsteps and muffled voices had him grabbing her by the waist and pulling her into an alcove in the hedge, throwing his body over hers so her bright dress wouldn't be seen. Moments passed, and they stayed in that position until the couple they'd heard rushed passed, giggling to themselves.

He stepped away but didn't go far. They still shared breath.

"Well this feels familiar," Lora snorted, pushing some of her hair out of her face.

"At least no one's threatened to kill us yet," he added, tracking the ruby strands.

"Or assumed I was a prostitute," Lora laughed, her breath going nowhere.

"The night is still young." He smiled down at her.

"True," she added, meeting his gaze. "Especially since we aren't making out in public." The smile that played on her lips made his knees wobble. *Get yourself together, man*, he thought as she looked down at her hands, her hair falling loosely to the side.

"I hate that that was our first kiss," he admitted, his forehead leaning on the top of her head.

Lora stiffened under him. "What do you mean?" It was barely louder than a whisper.

"I mean, it should have been different."

"Different how? How should it have been?"

He wasn't sure she was breathing, and he wasn't sure he was, either. He took her chin in his fingers and tilted her head up so that their gazes met. Her eyes were practically shining, and it took every ounce of willpower not to fall over.

"Kalon," she started, emotion dancing in her eyes. His gaze dropped to her mouth, and she trembled as he held her there.

He could see it all play out in his mind:

He leaned in, his lips grazing hers ever so lightly, and a rush of lighting spread through him. His stomach nearly took flight as a hoard of butterflies fluttered about rapidly within. It was featherlight, gentle, and had sparks of fire spreading through his body. He needed more.

He dipped his head lower and placed his lips fully on hers. At first, she didn't move. But as he swept his lips over hers again she opened her mouth to him, sliding her fingers into his hair and around his neck. With the third pass of his lips, it was like they were starved animals, and the only thing that would satiate them was this kiss, this moment together.

He slid his tongue into her mouth and nearly moaned at the wonder of it all. She tasted perfect and he knew every part of her would be this perfect. Her jasmine and ember scent wrapped around him and he wished he could suffocate on it.

He nipped at her lip and the little gasp she let out had him nearly coming on the spot. More*, he heard her whisper in his mind. She wanted more. And he wanted to give it to her.*

He hoisted her up and she instinctively wrapped her legs around his waist, pressing herself against his hardness. Holy shit, he might die from this. "You're going to be the death of me"*, he breathed, or maybe thought. Either way, she ground against him harder as their kiss deepened, their pace quickening with their heartbeats.*

"Lora." He said her name like a prayer as she ground against him, teasing him with her tongue and teeth as he kept her

pinned against him. The heat inside him was building, and he knew if he kept this up, he may just embarrass himself, but he couldn't stop. He didn't want to stop. She was perfect. She was perfect and beautiful and clever and cunning and his.

As if she heard his thoughts, their kiss slowed and she deepened it, running her hands through his hair and cupping his face.

He pulled out of their kiss, breathing heavily and, tilting her head back gently, trailed kisses down her neck as he eased her to her feet. Her breathing was equally as heavy as he made his way back up to her face. One look at her eyes and he was willing to risk it all right then, he opened his mouth, his arm burning—

***

Lora

Kalon held Lora's chin, and the look in his eyes had her insides melting. Then all the heat was doused out of her, literally, as a bucket of cold water was dumped on them from above.

"Shit!" The water soaked through Kalon's clothes instantly, but luckily Lora was relatively dry save for her hair and the side of her dress. Unluckily, a wet Kalon was much hotter. She had been moments away from telling him everything, from giving him any and everything he wanted. That *she* had wanted.

She heard Garrison and Liam's laughs ring out moments later as they rounded the corner of the maze, both laughing hysterically. Kalon, dripping and now shivering from the cold, faced the laughing idiots. When they realized just who they had poured water on they roared louder, their laughter carried well beyond that corner of the maze.

"Found him!" called Garrison as he approached Kalon, bucket still in hand, "We've been looking every—" He paused upon seeing Lora, mostly dry and still hidden in the alcove. Liam bumped into him from the abrupt stop.

"Found *them*," Garrison amended, a knowing smirk spreading across his face. Lora made to move but Kalon was still blocking the only way out of the alcove, radiating with a predatory ire.

"We've been looking for both of you," Liam said, bypassing Garrison and coming to Kalon's side. "We didn't want Lora to miss the fire show!" He was beaming, happy as ever, and not at all concerned about how pissed Kalon looked.

"I was showing Lora the maze," Kalon said, straightening to his full height and running his hands through his wet hair. *Holy shit, that's hot.* Garrison gave him another knowing look and opened his mouth, but Kierra cut him off.

"There you two are!" Kierra's voice rang out with excitement as she bounded into the alcove, past Kalon and pulled Lora out with her. "We saved you both a seat on the hill but we have to hurry to get there in time!" She pulled her along so quickly, Lora was almost tripping over her dress. Lora chanced a glance back at Kalon, who snatched a towel from Garrison's arms as they walked after them.

Somehow Kierra knew the route to take through the maze, and within three turns, she was pulling Lora up a grassy hill and onto a blanket. Nuva and Ortega were already sitting there, drinks in hand. Nuva, upon seeing Lora's wet hair and dress, smirked. She chose to ignore it as Liam, Garrison, and Kalon sat with them. Garrison sat eagerly on one side of her while Kierra sank into Nuva's lap. Kalon looked momentarily at the area next to her before plopping down next to Garrison on the edge of the blanket. Liam was the last to settle, sitting on Lora's other side.

"For you my lady," he said, handing her a plate with a huge piece of cake on it.

"For me?" She took the plate and the fork he offered.

"Of course! I noticed you missed the cake portion of the evening and I know how much you like chocolate." He was prattling but was stopped mid-sentence by her kiss to his cheek.

"This, Liam, is why you are my favorite."

The medic beamed, his ebony cheeks darkening a shade as he ate his own slice.

"What? No cake for us?" Nuva asked, feigning offense, as Kierra drank deeply from the wine bottle Nuva had been holding.

"He doesn't like you as much as he likes her," Garrison said over the cheer of the people below them, sneaking a hunk of cake while Liam was distracted. Kierra stuck out her tongue as Nuva flipped him off, the pair's eyes both filled with amusement.

Lora chanced a glance at Kalon, who all but stared at her. A smile played on her lips as she bit into the cake and *moaned*. It was the best cake she had ever had, tasting of everything good and holy in the world. She went to tell Liam just as the night sky erupted in colors. Dragons of every shape and size were darting about the sky, illuminating it with their fire in a dazzling display. She was transfixed by the intertwining shades of reds, oranges, and even blues. She had never seen anything so beautiful.

Beautiful, the word rang in her head. And while she told herself it was only her thoughts, a little voice told her that if she glanced over to her left, a prince would be looking at her and not the illuminated sky. A prince she had almost kissed. A prince she had *wanted* to kiss. She had all but seen it play out—how he would have kissed her softly at first, and then she would have wrapped her legs around him...

This time, when the bright colors blazed in the sky, it wasn't just the fire that burned her cheeks, but a new kind of heat that left her both excited and terrified.

CHAPTER 43

NO MORE DELAYS

Lora

After the fire show, the group gathered around another big bonfire, singing songs, dancing, and laughing. Lora watched as they all danced around the fire—these brave, wonderful souls—and felt something she hadn't felt in a very long time.

Safe.

She and Kalon had danced too, and by the end of the night, when everyone else was drunk and singing bawdy tunes, she found herself sitting snuggled between Kalon's legs, watching their friends.

Liam, who was considerably more sober than most of the others, sat next to her and Kalon, deep in conversation about where they should travel next. Apparently there was a specific route that would take them right past a town with good herbs Liam wanted.

"Liam, brother, this can wait until the morning I'm sure," Kalon said, patting the medic on the back.

Liam let out an exasperated sigh. "It's not like other herbs, not like the ones from the South. But these could really help in healing tonics, think of it Emir."

Emir—the name snagged her attention. She turned to ask Liam what he meant about the dragon, but the medic had already wandered off into the crowd.

Kalon noted her straighten and looked at her quizzically. She could almost hear him asking, *And what has you perking up?*

Her brow was still furrowed as she tried to think through what Liam had been saying before he mentioned the dragon. "Why does Liam want to get more herbs?" she asked while her mind turned over the conversation. No one had mentioned the dragons in several days, which felt odd to her.

An unrecognizable emotion passed over Kalon's features, but it was gone before she could identify it. "He thinks that there could be an herb that helps heal non-riders," Kalon explained, tugging on her braid slightly.

Her brow furrowed further. "But then why would he need Emir?" His jaw clenched. "Kalon?"

He smiled down at her, but it didn't fully reach his eyes, and she felt his walls slowly building in his mind. "Honestly, he's a bit drunk, princess. I'm not even sure what it all means myself." He tried to laugh, but it sounded hollow in her ears.

Her shoulders sagged a bit as she realized she was still not a part of this group—not fully. And why should she be trusted? She was an outsider. A no one. A traitor—

"Hey," Kalon said, interrupting her thoughts. He smiled down at her then, a true smile. "When we get home everything will make sense. All this—it'll be clearer. I promise." She leaned into his warmth then, letting it fill her fractured soul.

Home. He had said it as if Castle Pridama belonged to her too, now, as if she belonged. But she knew it was all a lie, a lie that, when exposed, would ruin everything.

So one thing already *was* clearer to Lora—she needed to leave, before it was too late.

***

The next morning Lora found herself sneaking from her room in the guest wing, the door clicking softly behind her. They had all stayed up drinking and singing for what felt like an eternity, finally falling asleep only an hour or so before dawn, with Kalon depositing her at her door with a featherlight kiss on her cheek before striding after Garrison.

"Good morning, Lora."

Gamma's voice startled her, causing her to nearly drop one of the canteens of water she was screwing the top on. "Gamma! You scared me!"

The woman pinned her with a knowing stare, her eyes catching on the pack Lora had on her shoulder. "Going somewhere?"

"I..." she started. "It's time for me to go." She wasn't sure why, but she felt like the old woman already knew her reasoning.

Gamma cocked her head to the side, her white hair spilling over her shoulder, so like Kierra's. "Just you?" she asked, though it felt more like an accusation than a question.

"Ah...yes. Just me," she admitted, stuffing the canteen into the bag.

"Alone?" she clarified, still hedging on an accusatory tone and drifting closer to Lora.

Heat flooded her cheeks. "I am more than capable—"

"Forgive me child, I am not questioning your capabilities, rather your desires," she amended, making her way to where Lora awkwardly stood. "You *want* to be alone?" The glint to her eyes caused a different kind of heat to creep into Lora's cheeks.

Gamma's eyes softened and her face fell into a knowing, inviting look, making Lora *want* to tell the truth—to her, and to Kalon. But instead she explained, "Kalon and I made a deal, and I fulfilled my end of the bargain. It's time I go."

"I see...and you must go alone?" she pressed again, emphasizing the last word while glancing behind Lora, to the hallway that led to the other rooms, where her friends slept. *To Kalon*, her little voice seemed to whisper.

She tracked the woman's gaze and looked over her own shoulder. She could still hear their laughter from the night before. The pit in her stomach hardened. She had wanted so badly to be a part of it. To laugh and dance with them, to be loved. But it couldn't be, not after everything she'd done. They would never forgive her, and even if they did they would always be in danger. She took a shaky breath, all but whispering, "I have no one else to go with."

"You sure about that?" Gamma asked, still looking beyond Lora. "I have a feeling both of my grandchildren would be rather sad at your departure. Especially without a goodbye." Lora remained looking down the hall, but she knew the woman now looked at her—she felt her gaze like a brand on her head.

She took another less-shaky breath. "It is better this way." She squared her shoulders, the orange sweater of Kierra's hanging loosely over her leggings. She had contemplated not taking it, but Kierra wouldn't miss it, and, well…it smelled like Kalon.

"For who, exactly?" Gamma's tone had hardened enough that Lora stiffened in surprise. The woman was staring at her through knowing eyes, most of the softness now gone.

"Gamma, I…" she sighed. The woman had to know, she felt it in her bones that the woman knew. "I don't belong here."

Gamma let out a short, loud laugh. "None of us belong here child, that's why we are all here—so we can not belong together." She glanced out the hallway window, a bit of softness returning to her eyes.

"No, it's not that. I'm not like them," Lora struggled to explain, but Gamma needed to know, to understand. "I don't… I'm not…*good*."

Another harsher laugh. "*Good*? No one around that fire last night is *good*." Gamma's eyes narrowed as Lora sagged. So, *she doesn't fully understand.*

"Gamma, I've done things… If they knew the things I've done they'd never forgive me." Lora felt the burning in her throat and the stinging in her eyes. She needed to go before this got too far, before she blurted the truth and lost everything. At least if she left this way, her last memories would be happy ones.

"Lora, child." Gamma's voice was honey now as she made her way to Lora's side. "Let me walk with you."

Lora wasn't sure what that would do, but didn't object as Gamma looped her arm through hers and they began walking toward the front of the house.

Gamma was silent for a while before she quietly said, "Not one person out there hasn't done something they aren't proud of, either on their own accord or under orders from someone else." She shot the woman a sideways glance, her eyes stinging with those unshed tears. "So trust me when I say, they would understand. My *Kalon* would understand."

She looked out the window as they passed, the morning sun beginning to make an appearance, painting everything in vibrant pinks and blues, making her think of mornings on the road with her friends. That's what they had become—her friends. Her mind wandered to Kierra and Kalon, on how they had danced together around the fire. A single tear escaped as she remembered the siblings—both having suffered so much, yet still laughing and dancing.

"You know," Gamma drawled, not looking at Lora, "when Kierra came back, she did not speak often of her time away, but when she did, it wasn't always nightmares."

Lora stiffened. No one, except Gamma, had mentioned Lora and Kierra's time together this whole trip.

"But I will say this," Gamma continued, either unaware of Lora's discomfort or not caring. "The thing that haunted her the most from her time was leaving you behind."

Lora drew her gaze back to the old woman then. She seemed to glow from within, with an inner peace Lora knew she would never know. She didn't know what to say. How to explain to the kind woman that none of what she said mattered. She was not like Kierra, forced to do things because she was enslaved by the enemy. She was not a soldier fighting for a cause. She was simply a weapon, a monster.

She opened her mouth—to say what, she didn't know—when Gamma spoke again, this time with that harder, more serious tone. "Kierra's story is one you know well. But my Kalon—he shares many of the same scars you do."

Lora looked down at her wrists, thinking back to what Liam had said all those nights ago about Kalon's scars.

Gamma noted her attention and smiled sadly. "Not just those kind, I'm afraid."

Lora's attention snapped back to Gamma as the old lady peered into her eyes, into her very soul. "Lora, my child." Gamma pulled her close, holding her to her chest. "You are strong and brave and you fight hard for what you believe in. Do not be afraid to let them see that. Do not be afraid to let him in." Gamma moved her hands gently up and down on Lora's back and Lora felt a warmth spreading in her, rivaling the empty cold.

"But what if…" A sniffle, and tears fell freely from Lora's eyes. "What if what I believe in is gone?"

Gamma didn't miss a beat. "Then fight for something—*someone*—else." Gamma's knowing eyes bore into hers, and she found herself full of so much love for the woman and her kindness, she couldn't help as more tears fell freely down her cheeks.

The old woman held Lora tight as she cried, stroking her back lovingly.

After several heartbeats Lora unfolded herself from the old woman and took a shaky breath.

Gamma merely looked up at her, love still shining in her eyes, with a new sparkle of something akin to childhood mischief.

"I must admit," she said, releasing Lora and patting her arm as they continued walking, "that I had more than one motive in hugging you just then."

Lora looked around warily, and Gamma merely slowed her steps a fraction. "If you still wish to leave I understand," she said, straightening to her full height. "But I will not let you sneak away, not when it would hurt my grandchildren."

And with a wink, Lora and the old woman rounded the corner—walking straight into Kalon.

"Princess?" Kalon's eyes were alight with confusion as they settled on Lora. She felt the heat blaze in them as their gazes met. Despite the topics that had just been discussed, Kalon's gaze made Lora's toes curl in her boots.

"Hello child," Gamma said by way of greeting, patting Kalon on the cheek.

Kalon, who hadn't seemed to realize his grandmother was even in the hall, let alone standing next to him, nearly jumped out of his skin. "Gamma! I didn't see you there." He bowed slightly to the older woman.

She waved a hand dismissively. *Clearly,* the smirk on her face seemed to say. Lora let out a soft chuckle and Kalon's attention whipped back to her, his gaze snagging on the bag on her shoulder. His eyes darkened. "What's going o—"

"Lora here was just about to head out and train," Gamma interrupted, nodding to Lora, that knowing look returning to her eyes. "And I was offering to take her laundry down to the kitchens since I am heading that way." Even though she was speaking to her grandson, her gaze had lingered on Lora.

Kalon looked between the two women, obviously confused.

Gamma smiled, patted Kalon on the cheek, then nodded to Lora. "I'll be seeing you two outside shortly," she said, giving Kalon a pointed look.

"And remember what I said girl," she added to Lora. When Lora shook her head in confusion the woman continued, "Find something else."

Then she strode toward the kitchen with Lora's packed bag in hand. She glanced over her shoulder at Lora, a smirk and a wink her only farewell.

When Lora looked back at Kalon, he had a quizzical look on his face, with one eyebrow raised and a smirk on his lips. "What was that all about?" he asked, looking between Lora and where his grandmother had disappeared down the hallway.

She wasn't even sure she could form words due to the lump in her throat, but in fear of making this whole moment even more awkward, she tried to explain. "I was on my way out and she was just there, in the hall. So she walked me to the door."

"You could have woken me," Kalon said, motioning for them to also start walking down the hall.

"Why would I do that?" she asked apprehensively.

"So you wouldn't have to train alone. Plus," he added with a sly grin, "I do believe there was a time when you *wanted* to train with me."

Lora rolled her eyes—of course he'd bring up the pirates. "That was different—"

"I guess it seems now *you're* the one afraid." Kalon's grin was pure wickedness, and her toes curled again as the pair made their way to the doors.

"So you were scared?" she teased, following after Kalon through the arched doorway.

"Scared of you?" Kalon asked, and she held her breath. "Never. Scared of getting my ass whooped in front of a shit ton of pirates, oh yeah."

Lora loosed a shuddering breath as a smile spread across her face. Something in her warmed like the first sparks of a fire. "So how do you feel about getting your ass whooped in front of an entire estate?" she asked, prancing into the sparring ring they'd walked into.

"It would be my pleasure." Kalon's smile was full of delicious promise as he rolled his shoulders and sank into a fighting stance.

***

The pair sparred for several hours, taking breaks only to drink water or re-wrap their hands. The sun was high in the sky, causing fresh beads of sweat to slide down Lora's back and forehead.

"You know," Kalon breathed, after a sloppy left hook that she easily dodged, "my aunt has been trying to secure a trade agreement with several kingdoms on the Southern Continent for years now."

She ducked to avoid a kick before throwing her own. "Is that so?" Another swing, another dodge.

"And I've volunteered to go after the war." Kalon spun twice, once to dodge her, the other to land a well-placed blow to her side.

Lora spun, throwing three consecutive punches and landing two. "Is *that* so? Maybe you can look me up when you get there." All the spinning and sweating was making Lora a bit lightheaded, but still she continued.

"It's a fairly expensive trip," Kalon said, noting her discomfort and seizing the opportunity to sweep her feet out from under her. He missed, but barely. "But," he added, retreating several steps, "it's cheaper for two."

She took his momentary retreat as a victory and made to advance. "Is that so—"

This time when Kalon struck out she landed on her back, feet in the air. "It is so," he confirmed, smirking down at her and offering her his hand.

She ignored his offer and hopped to her feet, sinking back into her fighting stance. "And what," she breathed through a sloppy punch, "would I be doing until the war ended?"

Kalon's eyebrows shot up as he caught her next punch, spinning her until her back was pinned against his chest. "Who said anything about you?" he purred in her ear.

She twisted, jabbing with her loose elbow before twirling back out of his arms. "Asshole."

They collided in a swarm of kicks and hits, only to separate again when they were both gasping.

"I will say though," Kalon started, his eyes sparkling like liquid gold, "that war camp food is very dull in taste. It could use some spicing."

She gaped at him, righting herself. "Did you just offer for me to be a war camp *cook*?"

Kalon chuckled and started to speak, but she threw herself on him in a barrage of swings and hit until she had managed to get him to the floor, her body holding his torso to the ground.

"I'm asking you to stay." There was no joking anymore. Kalon's eyes were clear and full of promise. Warmth spread through Lora and she felt the fractures of her heart starting to mend. Kalon was searching her eyes, his own shining bright. "Will you Lora? Will you stay?"

Lora took a deep breath, her heart beating so fast she was surprised she couldn't hear it. Kalon was searching her face, his expression falling every moment that passed. She opened her mouth but he continued talking.

"Kierra could always use more help, and I know Liam wanted to keep an eye on your wounds. Garrison seems to like you, and Nuva wanted to learn that knife trick…"

"And you?" She asked, moving off of him, "Do you want me to stay?" She held her breath as he sat up, dusting off his shirt.

"You are invaluable to me, Lora."

The admission hit her in the heart and she felt light and heavy all at once.

He stood, offering his hand to her. "As a soldier, of course. Your knowledge of the battlefield..."

"Asshole." She cut him off with a jab to the stomach that had her off balance enough to where she fell into him. He caught her and held her to his chest.

"Stay, Lora. For me," he said, his eyes darkening to liquid honey.

She felt her heart in her chest. "I..."

Kierra burst through the doors leading from the terrace, carrying a tray of wonderful smelling pies and sandwiches. "Courtesy of Gamma!" she exclaimed, plopping on one of the chairs that sat around the edge of the ring. Her hair was in a tight bun today. When she beheld Lora and Kalon, a sly smile worked its way onto her face, her eyebrows raising. "Am I interrupting something?"

Lora pushed off of Kalon, her face turning a dark shade of crimson as heat crept into it. Kalon looked at her a moment longer before muttering something under his breath as he made his way over to his sister.

Kierra giggled as she added, pulling an envelope from her pocket, "Also, we got a missive from Aunt Tura."

Lora's blood froze in her body, but she kept her face calm as she ate one of the toasties from the tray.

Kalon had expressed his mild concern about his aunt's reaction to Lora being alive, and well—involved. But at the time, he had said they had more than enough time to worry about it. Apparently, that time had run out.

Kalon shot a sideways glance at her, a tight smile playing on his lips, before opening the letter.

"Well that was short," Kierra noted from behind him, standing on the chair to read over his shoulder.

"Tura keeps things short and simple," Kalon replied, folding the paper and putting it in his pocket.

"No more delays," Kierra said in a mock commanding voice. "Return at once." "What a bore." she added, picking through the sandwiches until she found one that was jelly-filled.

"I guess that decided that, then," came Garrison's voice from behind them. He and Liam were dressed for sparring with Nuva trudging in behind them looking more green than her usual tan.

"Settles what?" she asked anxiously, looking between the Drakes, her gaze landing on Kalon's.

"We're all going home princess," Kalon said with a smile. "Tomorrow."

***

Lora had barely slept at all the night before, too excited to be riding the dragons. Everyone had looked at her at the dinner table when she'd all but jumped with excitement when Kalon had announced they'd be flying back to Castle Pridama.

Despite not knowing what awaited her in Pridama, Lora couldn't help her excitement about flying. She still dreamt about how it felt last time, to be in the clouds, the wind whipping her face. She had asked Kalon jokingly before they went to bed if Emir was still holding a grudge.

He had paled a bit before smiling tightly. "Don't you trust me?"

She had rolled her eyes but let out a small laugh. "Enough, I guess"

"Enough will do." He had smiled, adding, "Plus, no one can hold a grudge against you that long."

Lora wasn't too confident in his response as she waited for the dragons to land. She had been on the large grassy knoll outside the estate for the since sunrise, having slipped out of her bed to hug Theo goodbye before coming out here to wait for the dragons. Garrison had come out with a warm tea for her to drink fifteen minutes after she'd arrived, seeming to have the same idea.

She had looked behind him, hoping to see Kierra or Kalon, but to no avail. Garrison tracked her gaze. "They already left," he explained, sipping on his own apple cider.

She looked at him dumbfounded. "What do you mean? Kalon said we'd all be traveling together?" Everything had been a whirlwind yesterday trying to get ready to leave, so she hadn't seen much of any of her friends besides dinner. And after dinner Kalon had spent most of the night with Theo, saying his goodbyes. She pretended she was disappointed that Kierra hadn't said goodbye this morning. That that was the only reason for the sinking feeling in her chest.

Garrison shot her a knowing look from the corner of his eye before continuing. "They were called away to a meeting, and will meet us halfway once we ditch the dragons."

She wasn't sure what to make of that, so the pair sat in silence until two dragons had landed not twenty minutes later, each rocking the earth as they settled on their haunches, ready for riders.

"Just the two?" she asked, making her way toward the larger, black dragon who was tracking her every movement.

"Liam won't be joining so there is no need for a third," Emir's voice rumbled through her.

"So who is the second dragon for then?" she asked, looking at the smaller, albeit still scary, brown one before bringing her gaze to Emir.

"Garrison."

She blanched slightly. Before she could say anything, Garrison made his way over to Emir, pack in hand. "An escort today," he said, nodding toward the brown dragon. "How fancy." But as he made to toss his pack on Emir's back, Emir lowered his head, becoming eye level with Garrison and blocking the path, causing the bag to fall to the ground.

"Just Lora today." There was only primal command in his voice, and it left no room for questions.

"You sure?" Garrison asked, looking nervously between the two of them. "Last time she flew she got a little—"

"Last time she flew, she was not one of us." Emir rumbled so loudly in her mind, Lora was sure her eardrums would rupture from the inside out. *"This time is different."*

Garrison glared at the dragon, a bold move as its teeth were inches from his throat, but the dragon seemed only slightly annoyed. A silent conversation passed between the two and Garrison seemed inclined to argue verbally, but the brown dragon clicked its jaws a couple of times. Garrison finally let out a long sigh.

Holy shit. Am I about to ride a dragon, alone?

"I hope you know what you're doing," he said to Emir. "Stay close," he added as he began to walk away. "And don't fall off," he said to Lora as he continued to march over to the brown dragon.

Once Garrison mounted the brown dragon, Lora returned her attention to Emir. "I don't know what I'm doing," she admitted, looking around a bit apprehensively.

"*I will guide you,*" Emir chuffed.

"Don't let me fall," she whispered as she climbed up his large front leg and seated herself where Garrison usually sat.

"*Never.*"

And with absolutely no warning whatsoever, Emir launched them into the bright morning sky.

CHAPTER 44

TRUTH REVEALED

Lora

Emir had flown them right above the clouds, giving her a spectacular view of the morning sun, still just breaking over the horizon. The clouds around and below her were washed in pinks and purples, and she felt a sensation of pure joy jolt through her that wasn't all her own. *This must be why Kalon loves sunrise so much*, she thought, letting her hair flow around her.

They banked sideways, Emir's wing gliding through a cloud, causing swirls of mist and water droplets to twirl around Lora's fingers. "Incredible," she whispered, letting her fingers trail through the mist as Emir leveled out.

There was a low rumbling in his chest, as if he too, agreed with her assessment. They flew in silence above the clouds until the sun sat high above her in a brilliantly vibrant blue sky. She saw glimpses of Garrison and the brown dragon every now and then, but Emir kept them cloistered high above the world, far from anyone and anything else.

I wish Kalon was here, she thought, watching a flock of birds fly far below them. She'd been thinking of him most of the ride, wondering what he looked like, carefree and flying. Garrison had always had such a freeing glow about him after they flew. She assumed Kalon would look even more resplendent.

"*You haven't spoken since we took off.*" Emir's words rattled through her.

"I'm just enjoying the view," she admitted out loud, leaning back and letting the suntan her face. "I also wasn't sure you'd want to talk to me after I nearly shot you last time." A breathy laugh left her at the admission.

The dragon beneath her chuffed and she assumed it was a laugh. "*Who could hold a grudge against you that long?*" he asked, his voice cool and calm, familiar even.

Lora laughed out loud, "That's exactly what Kalon said last night."

Emir tensed under her momentarily before relaxing again.

She suddenly had a thought. "Can you do any tricks?" she asked over the wind. "I know you aren't a show pony, but—"

"*What kind of tricks?*" came Emir's voice, almost playfully.

"I actually don't know..." she admitted. "*Have any in mind?*"

"*We could roll?*" he offered, amusement lacing his voice.

She let out a short laugh. "A roll? Are you crazy? I barely stayed on during takeoff!" *Although it would be cool to be able to show Kalon that she could do a roll on a dragon...*

"*Don't you trust me?*" Emir's voice rumbled through her.

"*Enough I guess,*" she thought, smiling at her and Kalon's little joke.

"*Enough will do.*" Emir's voice sounded different than before... more like...

She stiffened slightly, her head snapping to the back of the dragon's. "What did you just say?" she stammered, her heart rate speeding up.

Emir's head swung around, his amber eyes locking with Lora's and for a brief moment she felt a wave of fear coated anticipation that was purely *his*.

"Emir," she started, her body going numb. "What did you just say?" It wasn't a question.

Emir blinked slowly, the amber of his eyes dancing in the sunlight, like pools of liquid gold—just like...

"*Princess.*" The familiarity with which he said her nickname had her skin prickling.

"Kalon calls me that."

The dragon stiffened beneath her. "*Perhaps I have learned it from him,*" he suggested, eyes now bracketed with concern.

Lora's heart raced in her chest. "How is it that I have never seen the two of you together?" she asked, praying he had a good answer.

"*I do not know the whims of humans,*" Emir responded, dismissing her question and swinging his head back to the front.

"Emir," she started again, her voice raspy. "Where is Kalon?" Still, the dragon merely looked ahead. "Why haven't I ever seen him fly with you? Why haven't I seen the two of you together, ever? Why is it always Garrison who rides you, but you are Kalon's dragon?" She bombarded him with questions, but still, the dragon's focus remained forward.

A small gust of wind and Garrison and the brown dragon appeared beside them, far enough away to not hear but close enough in case they were needed – because she was freaking the fuck out. She couldn't get a full breath down. "Emir, what's going on? Where is Kalon? Emir!" She screamed, forgetting that he could hear her torrent of thoughts.

"Emir!" she shouted again, but the dragon had gone silent, blocking their pathway to each other.

"*Kalon.*" She thought his name the way he'd said hers – like a prayer. The dragon's body froze beneath her as his head jerked, their eyes meeting, and she saw it then, the truth that had been in front of her the whole time.

"*Kalon,*" she thought again, and the dragon blinked, the only confirmation she needed. "*Kalon.*" The thought had the betrayal shredding her heart as angry tears welled in her eyes. "Put. Me. The fuck. Down."

Did you like *Out of Embers and Shadows*?

Did you know that reader reviews are very important to an indie author's success? They validate our work and help others find our stories. If you enjoyed *Out of Embers and Shadows*, please leave a review filled with stars on Goodreads or Amazon.

***

Don't forget your free gift! Click here
to tell me where to send it.

ABOUT THE AUTHOR

Have you ever gone on a hike that was really, really, really, long? Well, the conception of *Out of Embers and Shadows* was on said type of hike when Shelby Oval's partner dragged her 20 miles into the mountains of Slovenia. The only way she could push through the grueling hike - dragons. She imagined having her own and soaring above the clouds, and once she made it to the top, she imagined riding it back down to the ground. From the hike Oval began to play with the idea of dragons and war, building a world that would quickly become the baseline for *Out of Embers and Shadows*.

While Oval is a teacher by day, she is fighting wars, falling in love, and building worlds by night as she furthers her Shadowfire adventures. She loves to read fantasy and explore the different worlds other authors have created which is why she got a master's in literature from the University of Glasgow - it was all for the books! If you can't find her reading or teaching or writing, then her partner has probably dragged her on another hike up another mountain - which means another book is sure to come soon!

The *Shadowfire* series is just one of many projects she is working on so there are plenty more opportunities to read her works. So whether you enjoy hiking or not - let's all hope Shelby Oval's partner keeps dragging her on outdoor adventures!

ACKNOWLEDGMENTS

It's crazy to me that I have actually written a book! A whole book! I have always loved imagining and creating worlds and characters so it's absolutely wild to me that others are now getting to see my "head movies" (as my partner calls them) played out on the page.

I would be remiss if I did not thank a couple of people, starting with said partner. Goob, you've already gotten a mention in the dedication but I must thank you again for listening to my crazy rants at all hours of the day. I am inspired to be a better writer and a better person through loving you.

To my mom – I know you also got a shoutout in the dedication but how do I not thank you again for sparking a love for reading in me at an early age. Thank you for requiring me to read the books before the movies and encouraging me to imagine constantly.

To Carter, my second sounding board after Goob, thank you for reading every draft and edit, regardless of the spelling and grammar mistakes. Thank you for your honest feedback and willingness to let me rant about my ideas. Without you I would not have made it to this point! I hope you're ok with reading the next 5 books!

And lastly, to my amazing editor, your commentary throughout the editing process gave me such hope and excitement through the grueling editing process. I hope you too are ready for the next adventure Kalon and Lora are going to take!

To those of you who have read this far, I'd like to thank you as well! It has long been a dream of mine for you to see the magic that lives in my head and I still have so much left to share. So, with that being said, do you trust me?

Printed in Great Britain
by Amazon